GLOBAL INDIGENOUS HORROR

BERNADETTE MARIE CALAFELL, MARINA LEVINA,
AND KENDALL R. PHILLIPS, GENERAL EDITORS

GLOBAL INDIGENOUS HORROR

EDITED BY NAOMI SIMONE BORWEIN

UNIVERSITY PRESS OF MISSISSIPPI / JACKSON

The University Press of Mississippi is the scholarly publishing agency of the Mississippi Institutions of Higher Learning: Alcorn State University, Delta State University, Jackson State University, Mississippi State University, Mississippi University for Women, Mississippi Valley State University, University of Mississippi, and University of Southern Mississippi.

Interior art: *Raven's New Purse* by Jon Thunder.

www.upress.state.ms.us

The University Press of Mississippi is a member of the Association of University Presses.

Any discriminatory or derogatory language or hate speech regarding race, ethnicity, religion, sex, gender, class, national origin, age, or disability that has been retained or appears in elided form is in no way an endorsement of the use of such language outside a scholarly context.

Copyright 2025 by University Press of Mississippi
All rights reserved
Manufactured in the United States of America

∞

Publisher: University Press of Mississippi, Jackson, USA
Authorised GPSR Safety Representative: Easy Access System Europe -
Mustamäe tee 50, 10621 Tallinn, Estonia, gpsr.requests@easproject.com

Library of Congress Cataloging-in-Publication Data

Names: Borwein, Naomi Simone, editor.
Title: Global indigenous horror / edited by Naomi Simone Borwein.
Description: Jackson : University Press of Mississippi, 2025. |
Series: Horror and monstrosity studies series |
Includes bibliographical references and index.
Identifiers: LCCN 2024041384 (print) | LCCN 2024041385 (ebook) |
ISBN 9781496856173 (hardback) | ISBN 9781496856180 (trade paperback) |
ISBN 9781496856197 (epub) | ISBN 9781496856203 (epub) |
ISBN 9781496856210 (pdf) | ISBN 9781496856227 (pdf)
Subjects: LCSH: Horror tales—History and criticism. | Horror in literature. |
Indigenous authors—Interviews. | LCGFT: Essays. | Literary criticism.
Classification: LCC PN56.H6 G56 2025 (print) | LCC PN56.H6 (ebook) |
DDC 809/.9164—dc23/eng/20241120
LC record available at https://lccn.loc.gov/2024041384
LC ebook record available at https://lccn.loc.gov/2024041385

British Library Cataloging-in-Publication Data available

CONTENTS

Preface by Shane Hawk ix
Acknowledgments xi
Introduction: Global Indigenous Horror 3
    NAOMI SIMONE BORWEIN

PART 1. INDIGENOUS WAYS OF THEORIZING

Chapter 1. "It Runs in the Family": The *Rougarou* as Relative in
Contemporary Métis Stories 33
    JUNE SCUDELER

Chapter 2. Oka-Nada: Historical Contagion and Haunting Back in
Jeff Barnaby's *Blood Quantum* 50
    KRISTA COLLIER-JARVIS

Chapter 3. Ways of Theorizing and Transient Phenomena
(Section I). 76
    NAOMI SIMONE BORWEIN

Chapter 4. Ways of Theorizing in Practice (Section II) 107
    NAOMI SIMONE BORWEIN

PART 2. INTERROGATING DISCOURSE AND VARIATIONS OF INDIGENOUS HORROR

Chapter 5. Blak Horror, Blak Narratology, and Lisa Fuller's
Ghost Bird. 125
    KATRIN ALTHANS

Chapter 6. Indigenous Horror in Latin America 140
PERSEPHONE BRAHAM

PART 3. INDIGENIZING GOTHIC-HORROR AESTHETICS?

Chapter 7. From Silence to Excess: Indigenous Educational Gothic . . 163
JADE JENKINSON

Chapter 8. Indigenizing Gothic Comics: Unsettling the
Colonial Specter 186
SABRINA ZACHARIAS

Chapter 9. The Bayonet Scar: Judy Watson's Aboriginal
Gothic Arts Practice 206
JAYSON ALTHOFER

PART 4. ACTUALIZATION-CONCEPTUALIZATION: H/HORROR INTERVIEWS WITH DARK SPECULATIVE WRITERS SELF-IDENTIFYING AS INDIGENOUS

Interview A: Shane Hawk 241
NAOMI SIMONE BORWEIN

Interview B: Dan Rabarts 246
NAOMI SIMONE BORWEIN

Interview C: Stephen Graham Jones 254
NAOMI SIMONE BORWEIN

Interview D: Gregory C. Loui. 256
NAOMI SIMONE BORWEIN

Interview E: Gina Cole 261
NAOMI SIMONE BORWEIN

Epilogue: Dis/insp/secting *Global Indigenous Horror* 264
    NAOMI SIMONE BORWEIN, JUNE SCUDELER,
    KRISTA COLLIER-JARVIS, AND KATRIN ALTHANS

About the Contributors 279
Index 283

Preface

As we step into the eerie, haunting, yet enthralling domain of Indigenous Horror, we are confronted by an uncanny amalgamation of fear, folklore, and social commentary. This literary genre, though only recently gaining momentum, bears the profound and indelible imprint of centuries-old narratives, recasting ancient traditions and mythologies into a space that is at once disconcerting and empowering.

Naomi Simone Borwein, the respected scholar behind this edited volume, has conducted rigorous research into the genre of Horror, borne out of the rich oral traditions and lived experiences of Indigenous communities worldwide. Her work spotlights the power of Horror as a medium to voice pressing issues such as land dispossession, cultural erasure, systemic racism, and more. These narratives, far from being mere ghost stories, serve as profound critiques of postcolonial power structures and the ongoing trials of Indigenous populations.

Contributors' explorations reveal the genre's capacity to disrupt conventional narratives, centering Indigenous voices as active agents in their own stories while privileging Indigenous knowledges in scholarship. This volume is a departure from a Eurocentric literary gaze, providing a platform for Indigenous voices, both academic and creative, to express their unique experiences, histories, and worldviews. Despite the inherent fear associated with Horror, this genre becomes a tool for empowerment, enabling Indigenous communities to assert their narratives and reclaim their spaces in literature.

This volume, carefully curated by Borwein, invites you to engage with a diverse selection of Indigenous Horror literature and mixed-media narratives from around the globe, including works by writers such as Gina Cole, Dan Rabarts, Lisa Fuller, Stephen Graham Jones, Owl Goingback, Cherie Dimaline, Alex Soop, and many others. The incisive essays within offer a comprehensive exploration of this genre, delving into the intricate dynamics between the local and the global, the traditional and the contemporary, the human and the monstrous.

Global Indigenous Horror allows one to approach Indigenous Horror not merely as a genre but as a potent narrative space where the spectral and social merge, where the uncanny becomes a critique, and where the monstrous mirrors the human. Let this exploration unsettle, challenge, and engage you, opening up new horizons of understanding and appreciation for this emerging genre's power and potential. The cumulative analysis, building over the next several hundred pages, serves not only as a testament to Indigenous Horror's promise but also as a catalyst for conversations and the production of further volumes. The continued evolution of this genre underscores the need for an ongoing commitment to the study and amplification of Indigenous narratives within the global literary landscape.

—SHANE HAWK

Acknowledgments

Many thanks to Deanna Reder, Lee Murray, Nicholas Diak and Michele Brittany, Simon Bacon, Brooke Collins-Gearing, and Judith Borwein. The complexity of seeing this volume to completion is a feature of both the subject matter and the event-based context in which the project developed: through the COVID-19 pandemic, across various "dystopic" ecological disasters, on different continents, and in the midst of rising geopolitical tensions that directly impacted certain contributors—some of whom were silenced by such circumstances.

GLOBAL INDIGENOUS HORROR

INTRODUCTION

GLOBAL INDIGENOUS HORROR

NAOMI SIMONE BORWEIN

The title of this volume, *Global Indigenous Horror*, is meant to elicit debate. While contentions swirl around the emergent genre category, this book is exploratory and starts with one overarching premise, to contextualize and apprehend ways of theorizing modern Indigenous Horror fiction, as produced by self-identifying practitioners, drawing insight from the spectrum of Indigenous and non-Indigenous scholarship and investigating various critical and creative approaches. This epistemological process is exemplified by exploratory and experiential Indigenous literary critiques like those of Douglas First Nation scholar Peter Cole in *Coyote and Raven Go Canoeing*, where reader and writer are welcomed to a conversation, a "journey shaped out of words" (2006, 26). In *Global Indigenous Horror*, this exploratory "journey" is guided by the four-part structure of discourse created by the form of the book: criticism, author interviews, an epilogue that explores settler and Indigenous viewpoints, and editorial commentary. This introduction offers the synoptic overview required to understand the structure of the book. It gives the reader the tools necessary to unpack the theorizing taking place in this volume. By the end of the volume, discourse and analysis become literal—are enacted, embodied, or actualized. Through this process or journey, the volume itself asks readers to think about what constitutes Global Indigenous Horror and the potential benefits and limitations of cross-cultural and intertribal analysis.

Global Indigenous Horror does not seek to be a tokenizing, essentialist perspective drawn from various national myths and discourses, but a process of inquiry about what Global Indigenous Horror actually *is* and how it exists inside, outside, and beyond the literary canon. There is an active process of "redefining and expanding upon what" Indigenous scholars "have considered thus far as 'literature,'" and theory (Henzi 2016, 488–89). The same is true of Indigenous Horror literature (Jones 2023, xiii). Concomitantly, contemporary trends in literary theory and cultural practice manifest themselves in popular debates and academic turf wars, which often focus on the appropriation of common themes and glossaries (or categorizations) associated with non-Indigenous and Indigenous discourse on Horror. Such contentions feed current critical trends.

Many Indigenous Horror writers and filmmakers engage with these trends and debates, even within the pages of their writing or the metacritiques in the stories told by the camera, for instance, tied up in terms like lensing, unsettling, otherizing, and gaze. As part of privileging the Indigenous gaze in Horror fiction, Cheyenne and Arapaho Horror writer Shane Hawk explores such themes in his short story "Behind Colin's Eyes" (2023). He does so through overt reimagining of American stereotypes around "the Indian way?" and "Hollywood Indians" (2023, 162). These are reinscribed through the actualization of being lensed: "[O]utside-me turns away observing itself in the passenger mirror. I grow crooked grin" as a representation of "the white man's Indian" seen through a reflection, and, being lensed, "my own eyes invert back onto me" (173). But he also does so on the visual and conceptual level. These debates are widespread, expansive, varied, intertribal, tribe specific, and cross-cultural; to give a sense of the scale and diversity of these debates, consider the following examples, elements of which exist in every chapter in this volume. The implied binary of "de-Westernizing" and decolonizing is visible in rhetoric that surfaces around academic debates in the afterlife of postcolonial politics. "De-Westernizing" and decolonizing are two global or universalizing responses to colonial projects, as is, for example, decolonial aesthetics (King, Navarro, and Smith 2020). There are heated debates around appropriation of Indigenous writing, image, agency, and identity both textual and literal by "white academics" (or settler scholars) as an extension of ethnography and colonial power structures (P. Cole 2006, 29). Equally, there are Indigenous discourses around glossaries and categorizations (Tuck and Ree 2013) as projections or constructions of Indigenous alterity (otherness), identity, and community—community being one focal point of Indigenous Horror. But giving a single definition at this point is counterintuitive to the exploratory approach of the volume. Transepistemological contentions arise and are caused by different knowledge systems intersecting that surround the notion of genre, and specifically the Horror genre. Settler scholar Sarah Henzi notes of Indigeneity and alternative genre in her contribution to Cree-Métis scholar Deanna Reder and Linda M. Morra's edited volume on approaches to Indigenous literary practice that "[t]he question of genre is a slippery notion in the field of Indigenous Studies: the line between literary and non-literary" is sometimes blurred, and the remixing and unsettling of genres and literary "devices is a common practice for many [Indigenous] artists" (2016, 488). Genre is a western categorization system, or construct, that can be in juxtaposition to conceptual models popularized by modern Indigenous scholars, where dominant "conventional theories of cultural studies and popular culture do not account for the historical and political specificities of Indigenous productions" (Henzi 2016, 488–89). Other "Indigenous theories" that have yet to reach the Horror genre privilege the use of relationalities, the Indigenous relational orders of land-sky-water-based knowledges (Yazzie and Baldy 2018; Smith 2021) using visualization and actualization over western theory-based conceptualization alongside oral storytelling practices.[1]

Other debates surround community and Indigenous modernity, and tribal elders' reactions to modern Indigenous Horror. For instance, they react against the use of horror subjects by Indigenous Horror authors and filmmakers that are taboo, potentially drawing on sacred Creation myths, privileged knowledges, and more (Browning 2014; Marin 2021). Some Native writers address this contention through respectful engagement with h/Horror in consultation with community and tribal systems (Scudeler and Rabarts in this volume). (h/Horror denotes both Horror as a genre form and horror as an aesthetic or sensory response or experience.) Additionally, there are lively debates about capitalization of the term Indigenous (Indigenous/indigenous or Aboriginal/aboriginal), as an aftereffect or reappraisal of western semiotic systems, the implicit power structure undergirding linguistics and the literary canon. For instance, Coeur d'Alene/Spokane (Salish) writer Sherman Alexie (2023) and Māori and Pākehā (New Zealand settler) filmmaker Barry Barclay (2003) have engaged with the "I" in BIPOC.[2] Alexie connects identity and politics before moving to theoretical and philosophical notions such as the "reservation of the mind" and its "Indigenous Kaleidoscope" (2023). Barclay's metaphoric explorations of Greek tombstones helps him define Māori ways of knowing in Fourth Cinema as a philosophical concept that is actualized on screen and page (2003, 7–11). In line with such debates, labels are often "reduced to a single dichotomy; Indigenous and non-Indigenous" (Davis 2023), a binary as flawed as the distinction between primitive and civilized. (Many Indigenous practitioners are intertribal or mixed race, like Barry Barclay or Pasifika/Pākehā writer Gina Cole.) Interestingly, "primitive and civilized" is one of the foundational dichotomies of the Gothic. Yet, by giving primacy to the word "Indigenous" (displacing "western" by labeling it "non-Indigenous") in a reallocation or reappropriation of western power structures, contentions about capitalization quite naturally extend to debates in Indigenous communities surrounding the process of Indigenizing versus being "Indigenized." Debates about Black versus "Blackfella" (an Aboriginal Australian) is an offshoot of this particular argument around syntax and capitalization (Latimore 2021). It is a blurring and homogenization of Aboriginal Australia through global minority voices transcribed into the Global South movement. Building on a hemispheric essentializing vision of minority identity, scholarship is evolving into areas of the planetary through neocolonial discourse (Keetley 2020; Latimore 2021; Bhattacharjee and Ghosh 2021; Spivak 2003, 101) that is picked up by Indigenous Futurism and apocalyptic discourse. A popular vein of fiction and scholarship, Indigenous Futurism was first defined as a movement of future present and past Indigenous perspectives, and of discovery and recovery in postapocalyptic reality, after colonization and often utilizing speculative genres, with planetary, science fiction, eco themes undergirded by Indigenous ways of knowing (Vowel 2022; Dillon 2003, 2012). As part of Indigenous Futurism that is often tied to postapocalyptic horror visible in the mainstream today, representations of the anthropomorphism of sacred land (Berkes 2012) are linked with living fossil motifs (of vanishing Indigenous cultures) and other apocalyptic discourse(s) (Nixon 2020; Edwards, Graulund, and Höglund 2022). This trend is connected to the "new," seemingly organic representation of modern western genre systems that extend through decolonial aesthetics popularized by Walter Mignolo—to classifications of water, land, sea, and sky epistemologies—considering "ontologies as epistemic inventions" (Mignolo 2018, 177). As a corollary, scholars are developing Noël Carroll's "cross-art, cross-media" Horror (2003, 13) and "fantastic biologies" of "recurrent structures of horrific imagery" (Carroll 2020, 147) for reading Indigenous Horror (see, for example, chapter 7). The debates continue to transform and evolve.

With the increased production of both Indigenous Horror fiction and its critique, including in prefaces to anthologies, various forms of "Indigenous Horror" scholarship on narrative are beginning to engage with some of the aforementioned issues or contentions both as part of the politics of genre and as a way of developing this new field of literary studies. There are myriad, diverse Indigenous cultures across the globe (hoʻomanawanui 2018, 123),[3] and this book can only attempt to offer a noncomprehensive cross section of examples. But what is "Indigenous Horror" and how do scholars and practitioners theorize (or conceptualize aesthetics) in relation to the heterogeneous global trends of non-Indigenous and Indigenous cultures? How do horror tropes and themes function (Wisker 2005; Cardin 2017; Nevins 2020; Moreland 2018)—as "Horror Theory Now" (Corstorphine 2023)—in situ with integrant elements of Indigenous Horror "literature" and "fiction"? . . . against popular syncretic, somatic, holistic, or synchronic approaches? . . . and why?

AN INITIAL DEFINITION

To unsettle the lensing effect of *definition* itself, and before offering an initial definition, it is important to understand how such a definition is produced. "Global Indigenous Horror" is an umbrella term not widely visible in scholarship. In this volume, it is qualified with the designation of "literature," which is originally a western construct. Like any genre term, it is a categorization system. Within the pages of *Global Indigenous Horror*, the "journey" incorporates the process of definition and encompasses experimental engagements with aesthetics and ways of theorizing as well as conceptualizing, actualizing, and visualizing. A hybrid mode, "Global Indigenous Horror" is unavoidably both non-Indigenous and Indigenous in its constituent and originary parts.[4] In the hands of self-identifying Indigenous fiction writers who unsettle genre and create new Horror, various culturally specific horrors and other ways of conceptualizing are visible. Note that Indigenous writers self-identify for a variety of reasons, much like any other category used for grouping and essentializing people. Another important factor is the diversity of ways that myriad writers on the speculative spectrum of literary production (that "blurry line") define or reject, "shun," the Horror "label" as a genre, as an aesthetic, as an appellation or qualifier; some of those railing against "horror writing . . . pushed back into the niche" from whence it came (Nahrung 2004). While such a reaction is sometimes visible in the interviews in Part 4 of this volume, a burgeoning style of, or approach to, Indigenous h/Horror also becomes visible, which offers some foundations for ways of theorizing this genre.[5]

When defining Global Indigenous Horror literature, it is necessary to make space for some additional Indigenous concepts of "literature." In *Coyote and Raven Go Canoeing*, Peter Cole rebukes the idea of literature and genre forms from the western world, with the neologism "i/teriture" as a rejection of the "exoticized," "demonized," "contained other," which challenges "everything [that] has become academized anthropologized even indigenousness / the cult of white-expertise permeates who validates whom? // . . . filled with saccharine clichés [. . . and] metaphor" (2006, 152–53; spacing is intentional and meaningful in the original text) by, for example, innovative use of white space as hybrid orality transformed onto the page. From an Oceanic perspective, Witi Ihimaera and Tina Makereti comment in their introduction to *Black Marks on the White Page* (2017): "Perhaps the division between different forms . . . doesn't necessarily make sense" from the standpoint of diverse Indigenous worldviews. By inverting the mainstream Horror lens for Indigenous horror(s): "Word | stories | art | songs | dance | mythologies | ancestors | film | contemporary life | poetry" as categories or units "may all exist in the same moment, in the same space, and none of it is untrue" or "invalid" (Ihimaera and Makereti 2017, 12). Thus, Indigenous Horror fictions and their critical exploration in this volume result in theoretical and generic conventions being innovatively reorientated or remixed—as a part of the fabric of actualizing ways of knowing in which, for instance, Indigenous Horror practitioners may be "borrowing legends and lore from [other] tribes" (Shane Hawk interview in this volume). There are global Indigenous networks of scholars and writers with diverse cultural-tribal origins (Borwein, Glanfield, and Jungic 2022). Certain Indigenous scholars radically subvert linguistic-semiotic structures that feed western theorizing about the Horror lens. They subvert linguistic and semiotic approaches with different epistemological and ontological structures in which, for example, h/Horror can be a language coded in land, water, the sky-stars-cosmos, and planetary-based orientation systems. These systems or structures collide, on impact, in new media frameworks—for instance, emphasized in Indigenous "Fourth VR" theorizing (Wallis and Ross 2021, 313) through the immersive quality of epistemologies experimentally actualized, as "experiential realities" visible in Indigenous speculative fiction (Justice 2018, 141). Such horror(s) of cultural and aesthetic lenses intersect with what in western discourse would be read as horror realism and the fantastic, myth and metaphysics, but also non-Indigenous *Ways of Being* (Bridle 2022), and traverse various non-Indigenous media and platforms that are increasingly interwoven with Indigenous creative forms and narrations—slipping between Virtual Reality and, for example, music, performance, orality, visual arts and storytelling, film, literature, and social media.

Ways of Theorizing Horror

What are some "ways of theorizing" Indigenous horror experience? How do we conceive of such a thing? Think of ways of theorizing as a modern approach to knowing actualization, visualization, and conceptualization as alternatives to "theory" in Indigenous stories. The following examples from Navajo, Inuit, Aboriginal Australian, and Māori sources showcase the difference between ecological or apocalyptic horror in an Indigenous way of theorizing and popular horror representations of indigeneity within various media. Therefore, various culturally specific Indigenous frameworks[6] offer insight into innovative approaches for ways of knowing the Horror genre. Navajo scholar Henry H. Fowler's description of the hogan in "[i]nscribing a regular hexagon" (2021) across its eight vertices (A–H) highlights the potential function of Navajo geometry as a lens for reading Indigenous horrors, and Indigenous Horror as a genre. The Navajo hogan, as a building and a conceptual model, integrates states of being and becoming, and experiencing, with ways of knowing that bind body, mind, and spirit to the construction of the hogan, which is at the center of Navajo culture and identity, while amplifying connections to constellations (e.g., Corvus, Orion, and Scorpius) across the summer and winter solstices, and the equinox. The hogan is constructed with the movement of a Navajo person walking around its circumference, guided by the sunlight, by framing the light entering the hogan itself through an aperture, whereby, for example, a deviation of the angles of the building's construction caused by a shift in the orbital cycle of the planet (which effects the angle of light) intimates an ecological "apocalypse" in Navajo tradition (Fowler 2021). As a way of theorizing Horror, the hogan suggests a moving integrated system of angles and light read through body, culture, land, and spirit. This is akin to an Indigenous practical-theoretical model made literal.

Other examples offer further insight into different "ways of theorizing" Indigenous Horror. Inuktitut (language) and Inuit (people) conceptualizations can be read through the aurora borealis, light, and the cosmos. It can be argued that the experimental visualization and acoustic techniques used to produce the light effects alongside transformative layering of images of real and lived horror can be tied to Indigenous reconceptualizations of being "off the grid" encoded in a given visual story. The broader notion of "off the grid" is used by Mohawk scholar Edward Doolittle to describe the nature of *being* (Indigenous) outside a non-Indigenous society and epistemological system (2018, 101) as one site of horror or rupture. This notion is connected to orientations and logic systems of *being* and *becoming* that suggest representations of Indigenous identity. In a culturally specific conceptual vision, this being and becoming off-grid is experimentally represented in, for instance, manifestations of the past-present-future in the Inuit short film *Three Thousand* (2017) by Asinnajaq (Isabella Weetaluktuk). The aesthetic is also tied experimentally to Creation, orality, sacred narration, biology, earth, heredity, and the hybrid medium itself. In the film, the network of ice floes or icebergs mirror a matrix of "ghostly" spirits of Creation—oral stories, relational orders, identity, and more. The imagery reflected between elements of the filmic universe equally connect to innovative reorientations of Indigenous land-water-based epistemologies, often linked to land- or place-based Horror. This is reminiscent of the circular movement of light and dark around the villain, Mandrake, and use of the off/on grid in the Māori Horror film *Coming Home in the Dark* (Ashcroft 2021), building from Māori mythology (oral origins transcribed through witness testimony) and philosophical extensions of Barry Barclay's Fourth Cinema (2003) as one way of comprehending an inherently hybrid, Global Indigenous Horror lens. "Fourth Cinema" is "an umbrella term that he [Barclay] feels can contain the multiple forms of Indigenous cinema as it operates on an international level, yet one that can still reflect the specifics of individual cultural formations and iterations" (Murray 2008, 2). *Coming Home in the Dark* exudes place-based Indigenous Horror motifs framed in a hybrid aesthetic. (The aesthetic can be understood through the Creation framework of the Māori, the Whakapapa, which maps relationships or relational orders between all things.) Ashcroft's Māori auteur lens helps construct an Indigenous Horror epistemology that reappropriates and unsettles settler narratives.

Redressing ways of theorizing, consider processes by which "horror and monstrosity are actualized" (Borwein 2020, 155) as one conceptualization of an Aboriginal Australian Horror lens—itself drawing from many Aboriginal mobs with certain epistemological similarities yet orthogonal, tribe-specific elements, examined in "Synchronic Horror and the Dreaming" (Borwein 2020, 155)—a piece that is addressed by Katrin Althans in chapter 5. But as culturally specific Horror, what does that mean? A tribe-specific Horror can resonate with global Indigenous variations on ways of knowing and other Indigenous conceptual frameworks, together forming a body of knowledges.

Note the similarity to the global conceptualizations of Mi'kmaw Elder Dr. Albert Marshall's Two-Eyed Seeing (or *Etuaptmumk* in Mi'kmaw), which embraces "learning to see from one eye with the strengths of Indigenous knowledges and ways of knowing, and from the other eye with the strengths of mainstream knowledges and ways of knowing, and to use both these eyes together, for the benefit of all" (Reid et al. 2021, 243)—emphasized through intriguing ways of theorizing the "i/" of "i/teriture," an Indigenous breaking down of the designation of western literature and the eye/lens (P. Cole 2006, 152–53). Andrea Reid and colleagues extend Two-Eyed Seeing to build a conceptual-visual model (as a pictogram circle in four complex parts) that incorporates forms of heterogeneous (global) Indigenous ways of knowing (2021, 243). The motion implied in the Two-Eyed Seeing model can be considered, alongside the Gay'wu Group of Women's Songspiral model of "ongoing co-becoming and interweaving through song" (2019, 274), as a form of oral storytelling, a "more-than-human" "relational creativity"

(Gay'wu Group of Women 2022, 435), in which spirals are a "line within a cycle" going on continuously (Gay'wu Group of Women 2019, xvi). Songspiral in lieu of Aboriginal Dreaming metaphysics can be used to explain the motion and states implicated in my theoretical model of Aboriginal Horror (Borwein 2018, 2020), a model that Althans debates through Blak narratology in chapter 5. (Jayson Althofer explores Aboriginal Dreaming and Anglo-Australian colonialism in chapter 9.) In the reality of postcontact Indigenous identities, ways of being and becoming in literary production create moments of rupture, which punctuate moments of horror. The above specific examples suggest the multiplicity of approaches to ways of theorizing.

As already stated, this volume does not seek to be a tokenizing perspective in which analysis and fiction are essentialized, drawn from various national myths and discourses, but a process of inquiry about what Global Indigenous Horror *actually is*, for the purposes of theorizing and ways of knowing, and why it matters. In "Notes for the Long Rebellion," his preface to *Why Indigenous Literatures Matter* (2018), Daniel Heath Justice states that "diverse literatures of Indigenous peoples" are "important to Indigenous and non-Indigenous readers alike, although perhaps for different reasons" (xviii).[7] He notes that "[c]ontext is vital to understanding" stories "in all their functions and forms . . . whether vocalized, embodied, or inscribed" (xix). Indeed, speculative fiction in "its most transformative modes" offer diverse "interpretive strategies" (Justice 2018, 142). For many Indigenous writers, the Horror genre, more so than realistic fiction, is a good tool for examining decolonization, self-determination, and ethical considerations (148) and "to reflect" tribe-specific fantasies and nightmares beyond the "oppressive worldview" or stereotype that constructs Indigenous peoples as "walking anachronisms" (151). On a deeper level, elements of their stories offer "the mature, experiential realities" extant "in most traditional Indigenous systems" (Justice 2018, 141). Like Stephen Graham Jones, Justice's critical analysis addresses Indigenous Horror and storytelling, engaging with fiction and genre.[8]

There are ways of theorizing horror embedded in Indigenous fiction—reminiscent of metacritiques by Hawk and Jones. The influential Indigenous Horror writer Owl Goingback, metafictively and as part of orality, incorporates Creation tales, shapeshifters, zombies, hauntings, horrors, "and creatures of Cherokee legend and lore" into his various works (2018b, 4); for instance, in the short story "Animal Sounds," "[t]he Earth is a great island floating in a sea of water," using the Indigenous symbolism of "four cords" (2018a, 37) tied to various ways of knowing. Here, Goingback questions and reimagines with carefully placed absurdity the skeleton motif of classic Horror: "He watched in horror as the skeleton pulled itself out of the ground" (2018a, 45). In the Horror Writers Association (HWA) interview series "Indigenous Heritage in Horror," Goingback acknowledges that he employs a Choctaw-Cherokee weaving metaphor, "creating the same tingles of terror as the movies," and uses Indigenous characters who offer "a different way of looking at things," emulating oral storytellers who weave "teaching [elements] into the narrative" (Goingback 2021). Weaving metaphors as nodal associations between being and meaning sutured into the woven fabric are visible across many Indigenous epistemologies and form one well-known conceptualization model (Smith 2021; Kovach 2021). HWA interviews in the series by Shane Hawk and Theodore C. Van Alst Jr. conducted in November 2023 reflect a practice of unsettling traditional genre to redefine Indigenous horror. *Green Fuse Burning* (2023), by L'nu'skw (Mi'kmaw) writer Tiffany Morris, is itself an actualization of both Indigenous horror and its lenses and discourses. Interestingly, Raymond Gates uses Aboriginal (Australian) Horror metaphysics in his narrative landscape to intersect Indigenous epistemologies and ways of knowing (Browning 2014; Future Fire 2018). Other unique ways of theorizing can be seen in, for instance, Aviaq Johnston's story "The Haunted Blizzard" in the collection *Taaqtumi: An Anthology of Arctic Horror Tales* (Johnston 2019). *Taaqtumi*, an Inuktitut word meaning "in the dark," foregrounds Indigenous horror with "the storm," which is "full of bad things" (Johnston 2019, 4) and is connected to the knowledges held by "the elders" who "never tell us what it brings"—"shadow" (4). Another powerful example is Gina Cole's Pasifika metaphor of the "whirlpool" in *Na Viro* (2022). "[S]piraling, whorls, and branching (netting) of nodes in braiding and weaving as theoretical constructs or ways of knowing have many permutations seemingly ubiquitous across groups" (Borwein, chapter 3 of this volume), which has led to Indigenous uneasiness with theorizing "about indigenous weaving metaphors and textual interpenetration linguistic multifurcation" of "spindle whorls" read through primitivism (P. Cole 2006, 28). In speculative fiction of certain Kānaka Maoli (Native Hawaiians), such whirlpools partly form the conceptual core of mana (Loui 2017; see also Gregory C. Loui interview in this volume). Interestingly, Pacific Oceania Indigenous worldviews span from Polynesian, "Māori cosmogony" to beyond (Pomare and Cowan 1977, 3, 7). Contributions to *Global Indigenous Horror*, specifically through authors' engagements with their craft(s), consider ways of knowing the Horror lens, lived horror, and notions of being "lensed" as cultural appropriation and objectification, as described for instance by award-winning Māori (Ngāti Porou) author Dan Rabarts (in his interview in this volume) through his use of Horror's dark speculative forms and his related conceptual models.

Developing an "Unlensed"[9] Lens?

In his foreword to *Never Whistle at Night*, Blackfoot Horror legend Stephen Graham Jones begins with an allegory or story by Native historian Joseph M. Marshall III (2023, xi). Jones situates long-standing "wild Indian" stereotypes—which still proliferate in mass media today and resurface in Indigenous Horror in America (xi–xii). He does so to invert that colonial "white man's Indian" lens and expose what Indigenous Horror is from a Native perspective. More than theorizing, it's an actualization, as advocated by Blaire Topash-Caldwell (2020, 81, 86) through story, metaphor, and image. As if in response to Justice's claims about real and realist fiction (2018, 139, 148), Jones notes: "We now have to expand the borders of the real, to allow for, say, two timelines to simultaneously exist" in the post-1492 reality (Jones 2023, xii). Jones captures and describes an image of highway horror in which "one of those riders needs to look back at the driver in that car, which would mean this is going a touch further than 'intersection.' There's recognition, now" (xiii). He makes the driver Native. Unsettling the lived horror of Marshall's story and colonialism, the Indigenous Horror version or metaphor would be enacted when, through "the rearview mirror," they see "the paint on their own face that they can't account for" (xiii). This description is a powerful rewriting or unsettling of the images of Native horror that becomes one way of actualizing theory.

Integral to ways of theorizing in Indigenous Horror literature, there exists experimentation with time-space, orientation and direction, relational orders, and land-based horror embedded (and emended) in narrative landscapes and the interaction of Horror's constituent parts. Astronomical and physical phenomena often captured in legends and myths (sometimes macabre from non-Indigenous perspectives, like dead souls and dead children) are trussed to complex Indigenous logic systems and ways of being. Global Indigenous Horror Literature sits beyond axiomatic logic schema and ontological fields, through to redefined spatial logic, urban spaces, Creation and cosmology, and theories of alterity and conceptual modeling from water-, sky-/star-, and land-based knowledges, contained in the white spaces and ink of the pages of Horror fiction by self-identifying Indigenous practitioners. The nominally "theoretical" lens on Indigenous h/Horror negotiates (a) transstructural variations of local and regional Horror; (b) global generalizations from heterogeneous Indigenous perspectives, and ways of knowing in global Indigenous cultures versus local Indigenous cultures; (c) actualizations and conceptualizations of horror—through lived experience; and, (d) functions in varying proportionality with/in, off-grid in conjunction with the ever-changing site of Global Indigenous Horror, which moves relationally with "Global Horror." Such an approach requires redressing the western theory-practice paradigm with actualization and conceptualization through visual-conceptual models and frameworks, fortified by the tensions that exist between Indigenous and non-Indigenous knowledge systems as they navigate Indigenous modernity and hybrid H/horror within the Global Horror context and without.

REVIEWING VEINS OF LITERATURE

If one does a search for "Global Indigenous Horror literature" or "Global Aboriginal Horror literature," one gets no exact results at major databases such as MLA Bibliography International, JSTOR, ProQuest, WorldCat.org, Google Scholar, and various other library search engines and catalogs.[10] The same can be said for the term "Global Indigenous Horror."[11] This absence is a feature of its newness as a genre. Also, it reflects the contentions that impact and shape those labels and categorization structures at the foundation of said genre, including a divide between Gothic and Horror, where Gothic is an inherently binary genre defined by relations between psyche/landscape good/evil and modern/archaic,[12] and Horror is an affect or sensory genre of shock fear and terror. Equally there is a perceived divide between Gothic and Indigenous, which Krista Collier-Jarvis addresses in chapter 2 of this volume. The division between global and local as manifested in the Gothic Horror variant of glocal is a non-Indigenous alternative to Two-Eyed Seeing. Xavier Aldana Reyes defines glocal within the Gothic canon to include "texts that have international status in their global spread" but at the same time "express local identities" (Aldana Reyes 2018, 98). As much as the Gothic is a colonial project, global can be seen as a derivation of hegemonic globalization. There is also a clear divide between genre aesthetics (as western forms) versus visualization-actualization-conceptualization models alongside ways of knowing, and more. This is compounded by the critical trajectory of Horror scholarship and what sort of themes—many of which are valid and important—are allowed into the discourse, such as intergenerational trauma, literary survivance and resistance, "de-Westernization," and decoloniality. It is imperative to cast a wide net and harvest from various veins of scholarship to see Global Indigenous Horror developing across disciplines and cultural spaces.

This volume offers a timely and innovative reimagining. Threads of Global Indigenous Horror are contained in Global Horror and often are projected through a global dominant lens under which eminent non-Indigenous scholars place Aboriginality/Indigeneity within Horror's neoliberal internationalism, or mythification (e.g., Punter 2018). This placement is similar to the movement or genre of Global Gothic, seen in the essays in Glennis Byron's *Globalgothic* (2013), especially Fred Botting and Justin D. Edwards's "Theorising Globalgothic" (2013). Sometimes this merely amounts to a redressing of (cannibalist) monsterization and the (horror-ethnographic) anthropologic Other in relation to the tropes of nature and preternatural fear (Tamsil 2023, 369). Conversely, Ritwick Bhattacharjee and Saikat Ghosh's 2021 edited volume *Horror Fiction in the Global South* dissects h/Horror at the intersection of cultures, narratives, and their representations through the popularized theoretical lens known as the Global South, which is trussed to neo/decolonialism, comparative world literature, and global literature, sometimes derogatorily labeled "World Lite" (*n+1* 2013). Research on "de-Westernization" partly follows such a vein of scholarship.

While there is a paucity of critical volumes on Global Indigenous Horror, new works on Global Horror are starting to surface. Many editions are situated in the cinematic or celluloid tradition, such as *Global TV Horror* (Abbott and Jowett 2021) or *Global Horror Cinema Today* (Towlson 2021), the latter including analyses of Indigenous Horror films like *Slash/Back* (Innuksuk 2022), *Blood Quantum* (Barnaby 2019), and fragments of tradition in various nation-state films informed by "Indigenous myths" (Towlson 2021, 186, 13, 104). Jon Towlson's afterword gestures toward the coming "rise of Indigenous Horror" cinema (185)—riding a new wave of global Indigenous cinema that is expanding "organically," as a visual "storytelling revolution" (Towlson, quoted in Bergstrom 2015; Wente 2019, 42). Scholarly literary focus on Indigenous Horror is slowly following suit, with literary theorizing and ways of knowing straggling behind. Within genre criticism, Indigeneity is still subsidiary to Global Horror and often read through ecological themes and horror realism, or Cosmic and Folkloric Horror, yet still under that lens—where, through genre hybridization, Global Horror intersects various local structures, spiritualisms, and cultures (Ritzer and Schulze 2016, 17). These elements are part of the consideration when trying to understand ways of knowing what Global Indigenous Horror is and is not. Cree scholar Jacob Floyd (2023) describes "Indigenous Horror in the Twenty-First Century" through visual media; his analysis is contained in Simon Bacon's global text, *The Evolution of Horror in the Twenty-First Century* (2023a). Elsewhere, Indigenous Horror fiction is "elevated" to the appellation of Horror literature often without extensive exploration of the disjunct in what literature is itself (Nevins 2020; Cardin 2017; Corstorphine and Kremmel 2018). Such trends suggest "[t]he [recent] rise of indigenous horror" (Elliott 2019) as a hybrid genre and form that is heralded within popular media, as well as within the Gothic and Horror community. However, a parallel trend in the genre is also developing in certain Indigenous fiction spaces.

Part of the newness of the genre is implied by Mohawk scholar Gage Karahkwí:io Diabo in the journal *Transmotion* (2022),[13] referencing the story collection *Taaqtumi*. "While the stories are rich enough to speak for themselves," on a conceptual level "the lack of a critical introduction or accompanying essay is unfortunate, not just because Indigenous horror is an increasingly" visible, viable field (Diabo 2022, 164–71)—emphasizing the critical literary importance of prefaces, forewords, or introductions like that of Jones (2023). The use of prefaces and critical introductions is a standard path for nascent genres to develop scholarship before canonicity. But what does entering the canon mean for authentic self-representation? As a barometer, interviews and essays on Horror studies and Gothic studies are starting to be published (Álvarez Trigo and Heise-von der Lippe 2022, 31–43), and through the HWA's Indigenous Heritage in Horror interview series (HWA interview series 2021, 2023; Goingback 2021) and Asian Pacific Islander/Asian Native Hawaiian Pacific Islander (API/ANHPI) Heritage Month (HWA interview series 2023), sometimes building on, or reacting against, "white academic" discourse and appropriated fictions. As previously noted, there are currently no critical volumes dedicated solely to the topic of "Global Indigenous Horror" or "Global Indigenous Horror Literature." Broader volumes that have been produced engage with elements of Indigenous Horror and its literary politics ranging through a spectrum of other debate topics and themes, for instance *Troubling Tricksters: Revisioning Critical Conversations*, edited by Deanna Reder and Linda M. Morra (2010), which is antithetical to scholarship on Tricksterology and the "political sociology and anthropology of evil" (Horvath and Szakolczai 2020)—situating the trickster figure that recurs variously in Indigenous and Folkloric Horror (e.g., Keetley and Heholt 2023; Bacon 2023b).[14]

Reactions against "Global Indigenous Horror" engage with genre discourses and delve into applications of orality and contentions around "literature" as a non-Indigenous form, utilizing scholarship by Indigenous academics about new conceptual models, alterity, horror realism, and more. The application of this experimental hybridity helps create a genre in which global Indigenous perspective(s) are a foundation of many approaches. Some settler and Indigenous scholars are starting to offer a way of reinscribing a conceptual Horror model that situates, privileges, or makes space for Indigenous knowledges. What follows are active examples of horror elements, Indigenous and non-Indigenous, that move fluidly. Indigenous Horror Futurism, as one contemporary trend, is sometimes tied to readings in Black and Native contexts through "anti-blackness" in "otherwise worlds" (King, Navarro, and Smith 2020), which Peter Cole refers to in the following manner:

> every/where other/wise pervasive the past and future are not trapped outside the eternal now elsewhere   elsewhence wise and whither
>
> when our stories are stolen brokered borrowed if you will   held hostage in academia trans/fixed onto alien media. (2006, 49; original spacing)

Cole's experimental reconceptualization of written language opens up an avenue to rethinking supposed constants. The cover of Tiffany Lethabo King, Jenell Navarro, and Andrea Smith's *Otherwise Worlds* (2020) has implied Creation stories that are etched in the cosmos, as in time-space, and resonate with the apocalyptic Anthropocene, where Indigeneity and Indigenous epistemology are reabsorbed—as further examined in chapters 3 and 4. There is a trend to read Indigeneity through the Anthropocene as eco-racial, whereas on a planetary scale, the Anthropocene (Hamilton 2016, 93–106) is "an irreversible rupture of the Earth system itself, the overshoot of the planetary boundaries that had provided a 'safe operating space for humanity'" (Thomas et al. 2016, 932). This undergirds the apocalyptic horror inflection of the speculative. For instance, such themes are incorporated into analysis in Simon Bacon's *The Anthropocene and the Undead* (2022), utilizing the Symbiocene, a newly invented era, and term, coined in 2011 and developed with Aboriginal Australian land-based knowledges. More generally this mirrors a parallel approach, like Donna Haraway's sympoiesis (2016b). Krista Collier-Jarvis explores Haraway's work in her analysis in chapter 2 of this volume, and also notes in the epilogue to this volume that sympoiesis, a "multispecies approach," is reminiscent of the Mi'kmaw concept of *Netukulimk*. Haraway's theorizing (2016a) is used to structurally undergird Justin Edwards, Rune Graulund, and Johan Höglund's 2022 volume on the Gothic Anthropocene, which inadvertently highlights the complex relationship between Indigenous Horror epistemology, the environment, and the Gothic.

Indigenous Horror anthologies are actively writing back to popular trends seen in scholarship, such as Blackfoot storyteller Alex Soop's series of short story collections, including *Whistle at Night and They Will Come: Indigenous Horror Stories*, volume 2 (2023) and *Midnight Storm Moonless Sky: Indigenous Horror Stories*, volume 1 (2022)—described by the publisher on the book's jacket as "a wicked glimpse into the genre of Indigenous Horror" on Turtle Island.[15] Other examples include *Taaqtumi*

(Christopher 2019), Shane Hawk's self-published short story collection *Anoka* (2020), and the international best-selling Penguin anthology *Never Whistle at Night* (2023), coedited by Hawk and Theodore C. Van Alst Jr. Elsewhere, traces can be found embedded in *Other Terrors* (Liaguno and Mason 2022), *The Valancourt Book of World Horror Stories* (Jenkins and Cagle 2020), and *Classic Monsters Unleashed* (Aquilone 2022); the latter contains Indigenous Horror icon Owl Goingback's short story "Blood Hunt." It is clear from "The Future(s) of Indigenous Horror" that this is an "exciting new field" (McCormack 2022) in which "the broader mode of Indigenous Horror" as a genre (Gil'Adí and Mann 2021, 250–51) is visible in the work of its fiction practitioners (see the interviews in Part 4 of this volume). With the increasing prevalence of Aboriginal or Indigenous Horror in global mass media, in tandem with coverage of the horrors of disinterred atrocities of Indigenous genocides, a careful examination of literary theory, ways of theorizing, and reception beyond the domain of dominant (post/de) coloniality or minority designations is necessary and provides a unique understanding of the "constituent parts" of this movement and its powerful praxis or off-grid ways of knowing horror in literature.

Overlapping Vogues in "Aesthetics"

This volume is guided by an experimental exploratory approach that asks the reader to look at the cross-cultural and intertribal production of contemporary Indigenous Horror and ways of theorizing literature, but also to consider mixed-media examples—because Indigenous narratives do not traditionally sit in any given non-Indigenous literary form or genre. This edition examines recent developments related to vogues in Global Horror that impact theoretical approaches and ways of theorizing to Aboriginal/ Indigenous Horror, including reception and context. In contrast with critical and popular debates, aesthetics and ways of theorizing are also drawn from global vogues in research, many of which are addressed or tribe-specifically remixed, unsettled, or undone in this volume.[16] Such vogues include Global Horror and Global Fear; Native Fear; and Apocalyptic Futurism and the cross-fertilization of Afro-Futurisms, Pasifika Futurisms, and Indigenous Futurisms. Horror is relational, connected to Indigenous Futurism through, for example, expressions of lived horror and narrative elements that use Horror aesthetics. Decolonial Gothic Horror trends are unsettled, haunted back, and reinscribed (in chapters 2, 8, and 9). Cosmic Horror and (Global) Folk Horror can sometimes expand mythic and cosmogenic dimensions of Indigenous identity (partly unsettled in chapters 1 and 4). Other trends include Global Black Horror[17] and Monster Anthropology, connected to monstrosity and different ontological realities (explored in chapter 5); country, land, place, space (chapter 9), topographies, and constellations (chapter 3); and posthumanism, "deep logic," and various Aboriginal/Indigenous metaphysical constructs (chapters 3 and 4). Additionally, broad vogues include Indigenizing Horror iconography in theory versus Indigenizing cultural production (in the mainstream and academia); these vogues in theorizing are often impacted at the aesthetic and epistemological level by the politics of time and synchronisms and the politics of Horror. These threads (or vogues) intersect, collide, and exist simultaneously in theoretical explorations of Indigenous Horror.

In investigating both western universalist and Indigenous transnational, national, and regional theories, texts, and approaches, this volume as a whole examines how such epistemologies and ways of knowing as ways of theorizing are constituted and what movements, disciplinary nomenclature, cultural caches, knowledge systems, or trends they reflect and refract. The approach of the volume helps differentiate Global Horror, which explicates Indigenous experience through a classic Horror lens, from Global Indigenous Horror, which is both an umbrella term and representative of a conceptualization-actualization-visualization framework (Reid et al. 2021), a different epistemology of h/Horror. A careful analysis of concepts embedded in, for example, the metaphor of aurorae (chapters 3 and 4) allows the reader to move past a posthuman reading of Horror and provides more depth and diversity to the hybrid theoretical matrix of Global Horror. This sort of application of theory and critical trajectories in "Global" Indigenous Horror has not been undertaken and as such requires careful treatment and assessment.

Contents of the Volume

This book explores Global Indigenous Horror as a uniquely hybrid genre that creates a platform for Indigenous creators. The structure of the book is defined by ways of knowing and various theoretical approaches—avoiding the binary, poststructural failing of modern theory applied to Indigenous production. This introductory chapter is an overview of Global Aboriginal/ Indigenous Horror trends, aesthetics, and approaches as much as a methodological or conceptual baseline. It functions as a synoptic rupture of non-Indigenous ways of thinking necessary for understanding and engaging with this "intertextual journeying" (P. Cole 2006, 307) through the parts of the volume. Individual contributor chapters are captured moments of Indigenous Horror analysis and offer a reappraisal or unsettling of theoretical lenses often applied to the subject matter. Implementing Indigenous methodology, somewhat akin to a yarning circle, contributors have been given the space they need to articulate their perspectives—thus, the varying lengths of chapters. Chapters are divided into four parts, four being an important number for many Indigenous knowledge systems. The structure evolved organically to address the diversity of voices and approaches to Global Indigenous Horror, and in doing so it naturally mirrors Two-Eyed Seeing approaches described in the volume. Indeed, contributor chapters are grouped not by geographical or cultural variation but along a spectrum from a strong emphasis on "ways of knowing" to a critical inspection of the Horror genre through tribe-specific Indigenous Gothic aesthetics across non-Indigenous cartographic boundaries and against and beyond nation-states.

The "journey" (or exploration) of Global Indigenous Horror begins with Part 1: Indigenous Ways of Theorizing, which focuses on ways of knowing in relation to analyzing set examples of Indigenous Horror from the Métis and *rougarou* to the Mi'kmaw and zombie fish to a Two-Eyed Seeing approach used to investigate the metaphor of the aurora, which has a long colonial history. June Scudeler's contribution, "'It Runs in the Family': The *Rougarou* as Relative in Contemporary Métis Stories" (chapter 1), proffers an active employment of Métis (hybrid) epistemologies and storytelling approaches, applying a Métis worldview to the figure and inspecting "hybrid" speculative fiction produced by Métis author Cherie Dimaline. In "Oka-Nada" (chapter 2), Krista Collier-Jarvis extends Mi'kmaw ways of knowing, and lived horror, to the Indigenous cod zombieverse through a haunted/haunting dynamic—haunting being one popular vein of anticolonial criticism. The use of the fishery system as one way understanding ways of theorizing is addressed in chapters 2 and 3. My "Ways of Theorizing and Transient Phenomena (Section I)" (chapter 3), through an experiential journey, explains the application of both Indigenous methodologies and high theory used as an exploratory examination of a western metaphor. I develop an Indigenous Horror lens while interrogating the structure and meaning of popular aurora metaphors, and examine associated Indigenous (e.g., Māori, Cheyenne and Arapaho, Oceania Pasifika, Blackfoot, Inuit, and Kānaka Maoli) and non-Indigenous (settler) knowledges that undergird them. In "Ways of Theorizing in Practice (Section II)" (chapter 4), I extend these knowledges to textual analysis informed by author interviews to showcase a conceptualization-actualization framework.

The analyses in Part 2: Interrogating Discourse and Variations of Indigenous Horror move from ways of knowing and theorizing (in Part 1) to an active exploration of discourses in variations of Indigenous Horror, to expand the lens of genre and the discourse in the book to the literal level. Katrin Althans's discussion piece (chapter 5) on Blak Horror and Blak Narratology is articulated partly through Wuilli Wuilli author Lisa Fuller's 2019 novel *Ghost Bird*. Persephone Braham (chapter 6) critiques forms of Indigenous Horror in Latin America, analyzing associated contexts like Andean Horror, the "horrors of exploitation," and genocide through the transmediation of "the crying woman myth," La Llorona, and serpent films and by proxy representations of diverse Indigenous identities. Braham implicitly questions where the Horror industry, culture, and scholarship sit in an extraction/extractivist process.

After exploring some ways of knowing and literalizing debates in the earlier pages of this volume, in Part 3: Indigenizing Gothic-Horror Aesthetics?, the exploratory approach or "journey" continues with examples of Indigenizing the genre from very different perspectives. Jade Jenkinson (chapter 7) theorizes "Indigenous Educational Gothic" through a comparative analysis of novels by various Indigenous authors, moving from the Anishinaabe of the conglomerate of Native North Americans across Canada and the United States (including the West Coast Salish and the East Coast Mi'kmaq), to the Unangax̂ of the Aleutian Islands and the Waanyi of Australia. Sabrina Zacharias (chapter 8) evinces the visual and textual basis of "Indigenizing Gothic Comics" through Cherokee and Cree women and the MMIWGT2S crisis—an abbreviation for Missing and Murdered Indigenous Women, Girls, and Trans and Two-Spirit Folks. Jayson Althofer (chapter 9) excogitates on Waanyi woman Judy Watson's "Aboriginal Gothic Arts Practice" in relation to the blood-stained Anglo-Australian museum system. He examines the phantasmogenetic, cultural, and colonial dimensions of Aboriginal textual and visual arts.

The contributions in Parts 1, 2, and 3 explore myriad conceptual and theoretical approaches in scholarship, while Part 4: h/Horror Interviews with Dark Speculative Writers Self-Identifying as Indigenous offers actualization of these hypothetical concepts in the pages of horror and speculative fiction. Part 4 grounds the analysis in practical terms through Indigenous writers' own assessments and voices as expressed in interviews with Shane Hawk (Cheyenne and Arapaho), Dan Rabarts (Ngāti Porou), Stephen Graham Jones (Blackfoot), Gregory C. Loui (Kānaka Maoli), and Gina Cole (Pasifika). Interviewees are asked pointed questions that relate to the discourse on theorizing and Indigenous epistemology. The structure of these semiopen qualitative interviews, collected through email correspondence, are based partly on Indigenous storywork methods advocated by Jo-Ann Archibald and colleagues (2019), Margaret Kovach (2021, 166, 176), and others, along-side contemporary models that center Indigenous knowledges in (hybrid) speculative genres. The author interviews are critical contributions; indeed, articulation of actualized aesthetics and styles are integral (a) to exploring h/Horror through multisensory transactions, (b) to interrogating representative stereotypes of, for instance, nature and eco-fictions extracted from Indigenous stories, and (c) to discussing reception, craft, and the label of "genre." Rather than a traditional conclusion drawing on the initial overview offered in the introduction, Part 4 is followed by an epilogue: "Dis/insp/secting *Global Indigenous Horror*" by Naomi Simone Borwein, June Scudeler, Krista Collier-Jarvis, and Katrin Althans. The epilogue functions as a conversation between set settler and Indigenous scholars in *Global Indigenous Horror* about genre and practice that furthers the synoptic praxis of the volume.

What appears across contributions is a simple, reproducible method or approach for ways of theorizing or knowing Indigenous Horror in practice that can be understood as a toolbox for meaningful engagement with Indigenous Horror literature, outlined below:

1) **introduce** an Indigenous elder, author, or scholar and/or a way of knowing,
2) **position** the contributor doing the analysis,
3) **juxtapose** (or **reconcile**) settler and Indigenous traditions, practices, or conceptualization-visualization-actualization models,*
4) **inspect** or **question** frames of reference,
5) **center** Indigenous methodologies or knowledges, and
6) **offer** an Indigenous h/Horror "lens" or vision.

*active respectful engagement with source material and authors or creators

The book structure is part of the methodological approach used in this volume, which seeks to inspect the contentions, turf wars, and debates around the meaning and constraints of the phrase used as the book's title, *Global Indigenous Horror*, as well as the nature of practice, theory, context, and trends without the limitations of any set, culturally loaded classifications or systems of thought—like the horror realism paradigm governing much neoliberal international interpretations of the offal of vogues and movements associated with Indigenous Horror. The analyses in this volume address and also reach beyond standard explorations of ontological, epistemological, materialist metaphysics, decolonial (or anticolonial) aesthetics, and spiritual-ecological nexuses, hyperrealities, and futures that feed most mainstream Horror theory and production. As Global Horror continues to supersede and incorporate regional forms of Indigenous myth and identity, it catalyzes popular vogues in the rise of "Global Indigenous Horror" that threaten to universalize how viewers read Horror literature, understand orality, or consume other media narratives. Investigating Indigenous Horror through ways of knowing allows a global readership to engage with new conceptualizing-visualizing-actualizing methods that apply to diverse Indigenous Horror fictions, offering scholars a toolbox of unique "ways of theorizing" as alternatives to classic Horror theory. Ultimately, this volume is the beginning of a necessary discussion about a new field of genre studies.

NOTES

1. Also visible in scholarship is how horror as metaphor translates within and between culture (Kövecses 2005), and how metaphor as a concept can or cannot be a "methodological-ontological-epistemological" "lens" for cross-cultural, hybrid "genre" analysis, which is the space of Global Indigenous Horror and is addressed in chapters 3 and 4 of this volume. Broader debates about horror tropes can also be seen as recentering Indigenous aesthetics and can be understood as reconceptualizing colonial binaries. Examples include through aesthetics/(not)aesthetics, genre/(not)genre, metaphor/(not)metaphor, as an extension of Mohawk scholar Edward Doolittle's math/(not)math analogy that suggests another relational order for reconstructions of horror themes, elements, and motifs (personal communication, September 4, 2020). Dan Rabarts, in his interview in Part 4 of this volume, suggests there is a similarity between mathematical structures and Indigenous (Māori) horror metaphysics.

2. The acronym BIPOC refers to Black, Indigenous, and other people of color.

3. This edited volume focuses on Aboriginal/Indigenous Horror largely produced by Indigenous creators and writers, and spans heterogenized forms and cultures across the globe, situated in various national imaginaries and a plethora of Indigenous spaces. This vision includes Indigenous groups whose migration and diaspora within other countries offer new perspectives.

4. Careful approaches as "complex, hybridized projects" (Pulitano 2003, 3) can redress the risk of perpetuating "an us/them universe, keeping apart two worlds and two worldviews that could and should talk to one another" (2).

5. In the context of a literary definition, Global Indigenous Horror becomes a balancing act: an "act of survivance," resistance, exuberance, and reappropriation (Vizenor 2008) between Indigenous systems, epistemologies, and world (literary) views, all intersecting and overlapping with non-Indigenous forms of Horror.

6. As Peter Cole says, "a framework is a journey/ing" (2006, 27).

7. See also Jace Weaver, Craig S. Womack, and Robert Warrior's *American Indian Literary Nationalism* (2006).

8. Jones's foreword to *Never Whistle at Night* (2023) and Justice's analysis offer popular and critical perspectives on Indigenous Horror stories.

9. For instance, globalizing Elder Marshall's Two-Eyed Seeing into heterogeneous Indigenous models through experiment reconfigures what the literary Horror genre

looks like and can, through land-, water-, and star-celestial-based methodologies and epistemologies, also showcase the horror of lived experience, "emphasizing the importance of ancestral reconnection to Indigenous futurities" (Yazzie and Baldy 2018, 20), which is in tension with Walter Mignolo's 2018 decolonial aesthetics and theorizing of land-water biological ontologies.

10. This observation is as of January 1, 2024.

11. A large body of Horror scholarship is driven by and envisioned through anglophone critique.

12. Analysis of "Gothic metaphysics" as a post-Kantian, posthumanist understanding of the Gothic is one response to the binary being tied to colonial projects.

13. While calling attention to the need for more theorizing in Indigenous horror, Hogan Schaak defines "transmotion" as a theory of horror defined by "visionary resistance" and a rejection of "regenerative violence" through metatextual "generative violence" (2023, 95, 118–19).

14. However, elsewhere, "Indigenous Horror" is placed within "World Literature Today" (Hall 2023, 26), and how it is placed offers insight into accepted theoretical approaches: metaphorically steeped in weaving descriptors like "throwing away" the "two-dimensional Polaroid picture" (as a metaphor for World Literature) to "observe the tapestry" of Indigenous Horror literature (Hall 2023). In world literary studies, Anders Pettersson examines the applications of "Western Genre terms to (other literary cultures') genres around the world" (2006, 281, 302–5) via non-Indigenous forms. Following the prevalence of terms in comparative literature like global, world, and planetary, such ideas sit on the doorstep of contentions about Indigenous epistemology and metaphysics. Within genre studies, scholars like John Frow (2007, 2015), Wai Chee Dimock (2007), and Franco Moretti (1988) have postulated genres as living, moving, and multivalent—and genres as part invention, the cyborg-like classifications of organic systems. This hybrid representation of genres that are living, taxonomic, and organic systems is explicated by Walter Mignolo (2018) in relation to "decoloniality," and, alternatively, expanded into notions of genre planetarity by Dimock and others; Dimock describes the concept of genre planetarity through nested sets of meaning and function, understood as "Set and Subset" (2007, 1–2). Conceptually, she moves genre theory from the "global" to (western) models of the universe. Such ideas are also connected to the work of Gayatri Chakravorty Spivak and Donna Haraway. I contend that movements like the "de-Westernization" of Horror are partly an extension of decolonial aesthetics (Mignolo 2018) and non-Indigenous (but not necessarily dominant white) epistemologies.

15. The phrase "wicked glimpse" also implies a non-Indigenous audience and commodification.

16. Chapters are a mixture of regionally specific and synoptic, comparative critiques.

17. Taking into account that "Indigenous Gothic could be something of a misnomer" for "Indigenous Horror" (Schoonover 2022, 295–303), pieces in the volume also explore oral traditions, objects and artifacts, and the visual fields as transcendental negative space that is often used for the extension of theory between genres and forms—for instance, in the western canon, Roland Barthes applies "neutral" Zero Degree Theory (1953) to his paintings at the Barthes/Burgin exhibition (Barthes and Manghani 2020, 35), while Homi K. Bhabha (1988) redresses the location of culture in transcendental negative space through Anish Kapoor's sculpture.

BIBLIOGRAPHY

Abbott, Stacey, and Lorna Jowett, eds. 2021. *Global TV Horror*. Cardiff: University of Wales Press.

Aldana Reyes, Xavier. 2018. "Fantaterror: Gothic Monsters in the Golden Age of Spanish B-Movie Horror, 1968–80." In *B-Movie Gothic: International Perspectives*, edited by Justin Edwards and Johan Höglund, 95–107. Edinburgh: Edinburgh University Press.

Alexie, Sherman. 2023. "The 'I' in BIPOC: Not All Native Americans Are Leftist Political Activists." May 15. https://shermanalexie.substack.com/p/the-i-in-bipoc.

Althans, Katrin. 2019. "Aboriginal Gothic." In *Twenty-First-Century Gothic: An Edinburgh Companion*, edited by Maisha Wester and Xavier Aldana Reyes, 276–88. Edinburgh Companions to the Gothic. Edinburgh: Edinburgh University Press.

Álvarez Trigo, Laura, and Anya Heise-von der Lippe. 2022. "Posthuman/Cyber-Gothic: An Interview with Anya Heise-von der Lippe." *REDEN: Revista Española de Estudios Norteamericanos* 3, no. 2: 31–43.

Aquilone, James, ed. 2022. *Classic Monsters Unleashed*. Anchorage: Black Spot Books.

Archibald, Jo-Ann [Q'um Q'um Xiiem], Jenny Bol Jun Lee-Morgan, and Jason De Santolo, eds. 2019. *Decolonizing Research: Indigenous Storywork as Methodology*. London: Zed Books.

Ashcroft, James, dir. 2021. *Coming Home in the Dark*. Light in the Dark Productions / MPI Media Group. https://www.imdb.com/title/tt6874762/.

Asinnajaq [Isabella Weetaluktuk], dir. 2017. *Three Thousand*. National Film Board. https://www.nfb.ca/film/three_thousand_inuktitut_version/.

Bacon, Simon, ed. 2022. *The Anthropocene and the Undead: Cultural Anxieties in the Contemporary Popular Imagination*. Lanham, MD: Lexington Books.

Bacon, Simon, ed. 2023a. *The Evolution of Horror in the Twenty-First Century*. Lanham, MD: Lexington Books.

Bacon, Simon, ed. 2023b. *Future Folk Horror: Contemporary Anxieties and Possible Futures*. Lanham, MD: Lexington Books.

Barclay, Barry. 2003. "Celebrating Fourth Cinema." *Illusions: A New Zealand Magazine of Film, Television and Theater Criticism* 35 (Winter): 7–11.

Barnaby, Jeff, dir. 2019. *Blood Quantum*. Prospector Films.

Barthes, Roland. 1953. *Le degré zéro de l'écriture*. Paris: Éditions du Seuil.

Barthes, Roland, and Sunil Manghani. 2020. "Colouring, Degree Zero." *Theory, Culture & Society* 37, no. 4: 35–42.

Bergstrom, Aren. 2015. "An Indigenous New Wave of Film." *3 Brothers Film*, October 30. https://3brothersfilm.com/blog/2015/10/30/an-indigenous-new-wave-of-film.

Berkes, Fikret. 2012. *Sacred Ecology*. 3rd ed. New York: Routledge.

Bhabha, Homi K. 1988. *Anish Kapoor*. Berkeley: University of California Press.

Bhattacharjee, Ritwick, and Saikat Ghosh, eds. 2021. *Horror Fiction in the Global South: Cultures, Narratives and Representations*. New Delhi: Bloomsbury India.

Borwein, Naomi Simone. 2018. "Mistranslating Australian Aboriginal Horror in Theory and Literary Practice." In *The Palgrave Handbook to Horror Literature*, edited by Kevin Corstorphine and Laura R. Kremmel, 61–75. Cham, Switzerland: Palgrave Macmillan.

Borwein, Naomi Simone. 2020. "Synchronic Horror and the Dreaming." In *Horror Literature from Gothic to Post-Modern: Critical Essays*, edited by Michele Brittany and Nicholas Diak, 141–63. Jefferson, NC: McFarland.

Borwein, Naomi Simone, Florence Glanfield, and Veselin Jungic. 2022. "Indigenizing University Mathematics." *CMS Notes* 54, no. 2 (March). https://notes.math.ca/wp-content/uploads/2022/02/Indigenizing-Mathematics-2.pdf.

Botting, Fred, and Justin D. Edwards. 2013. "Theorising Globalgothic." In *Globalgothic*, edited by Glennis Byron, 11–24. Manchester: Manchester University Press.

Bridle, James. 2022. *Ways of Being: Animals, Plants, Machines; The Search for a Planetary Intelligence*. New York: Farrar, Straus and Giroux.

Browning, Daniel. 2014. "Beyond Unaipon: Part 1." Australia Broadcasting Company, June 21. https://www.abc.net.au/radionational/programs/awaye/beyond-unaipon3a-part-1/5527076.

Byron, Glennis, ed. 2013. *Globalgothic*. Manchester: Manchester University Press.

Cardin, Matt, ed. 2017. *Horror Literature through History: An Encyclopedia of the Stories that Speak to Our Deepest Fears*. 2 vols. Santa Barbara, CA: Greenwood.

Carroll, Noël. 2003. *The Philosophy of Horror; or, Paradoxes of the Heart*. New York: Routledge.

Carroll, Noël. 2020. "Fantastic Biologies and the Structures of Horrific Imagery." In *The Monster Theory Reader*, edited by Jeffrey Andrew Weinstock, 136–47. Minneapolis: University of Minnesota Press.

Christopher, Neil, ed. 2019. *Taaqtumi: An Anthology of Arctic Horror Tales*. Iqaluit, NU: Inhabit Media.

Cole, Gina. 2022. *Na Viro*. Wellington, New Zealand: Huia Publishers.

Cole, Peter. 2006. *Coyote and Raven Go Canoeing: Coming Home to the Village*. McGill-Queen's Native and Northern Series, no. 42. Montreal: McGill–Queen's University Press.

Corstorphine, Kevin. 2023. "Horror Theory Now: Thinking about Horror." In *The Evolution of Horror in the Twenty-First Century*, edited by Simon Bacon, 13–26. Lanham, MD: Lexington Books.

Corstorphine, Kevin, and Laura R. Kremmel, eds. 2018. *The Palgrave Handbook to Horror Literature*. Cham, Switzerland: Palgrave Macmillan.

Davis, Wade. 2023. "The Term 'Indigenous,' in Its Current Use, Might Be Doing Us All a Disservice." *Globe and Mail* (Toronto), March 27. https://www.theglobeandmail.com/opinion/article-the-term-indigenous-in-its-current-use-might-be-doing-us-all-a/.

Diabo, Gage Karahkwí:io. 2022. "Review Essay: Little Books, Big Horror." *Transmotion* 8, no. 2: 164–71.

Dillon, Grace L., ed. 2003. *Hive of Dreams: Contemporary Science Fiction from the Pacific Northwest*. Corvallis: Oregon State University Press.

Dillon, Grace L., ed. 2012. *Walking the Clouds: An Anthology of Indigenous Science Fiction*. Tucson: University of Arizona Press.

Dimock, Wai Chee. 2007. "Introduction: Planet and America, Set and Subset." In *Shades of the Planet: American Literature as World Literature*, edited by Wai Chee Dimock and Lawrence Buell, 1–16. Princeton, NJ: Princeton University Press.

Doolittle, Edward. 2018. "Off the Grid." In *Contemporary Environmental and Mathematics Education Modelling Using New Geometric Approaches: Geometries of Liberation*, edited by Susan Gerofsky, 101–21. Cham, Switzerland: Springer.

Edwards, Justin D., Rune Graulund, and Johan Höglund, eds. 2022. *Dark Scenes from Damaged Earth: The Gothic Anthropocene*. Minneapolis: University of Minnesota Press.

Elliott, Alicia. 2019. "The Rise of Indigenous Horror: How a Fiction Genre Is Confronting a Monstrous Reality." CBC Arts, October 17. https://www.cbc.ca/arts/the-rise-of-indigenous-horror-how-a-fiction-genre-is-confronting-a-monstrous-reality-1.5323428.

Floyd, Jacob. 2023. "Indigenous Horror in the Twenty-First Century." In *The Evolution of Horror in the Twenty-First Century*, edited by Simon Bacon, 185–98. Lanham, MD: Lexington Books.

Fowler, Henry H. 2021. "Indigenous Ways of Knowing." Paper presented at the Indigenizing University Mathematics session, Canadian Mathematical Society Winter Meeting, December 7, Simon Fraser University, Burnaby, British Columbia.

Frow, John. 2007. "'Reproducibles, Rubrics, and Everything You Need': Genre Theory Today." *PMLA* 122, no. 5: 1626–34.

Frow, John. 2015. *Genre*. 2nd ed. Abingdon, Oxon., England: Routledge.

Fuller, Lisa. 2019. *Ghost Bird*. St. Lucia, Australia: University of Queensland Press.

Future Fire. 2018. "Interview with Raymond Gates." February 19. http://press.futurefire.net/2018/02/interview-with-raymond-gates.html.

Gay'wu Group of Women. 2019. *Songspirals: Sharing Women's Wisdom of Country through Songlines*. Crows Nest, Australia: Allen and Unwin.

Gay'wu Group of Women. 2022. "Songspirals Bring Country into Existence: Singing More-Than-Human and Relational Creativity." *Qualitative Inquiry* 28, no. 5: 435–47.

Gil'Adí, Maia, and Justin L. Mann. 2021. "New Suns." *ASAP/Journal* 6, no. 2: 241–55.

Goingback, Owl. 2018a. "Animal Sounds." In *Tribal Screams*, 39–56. Trieste, Italy: Independent Legions Publishing.

Goingback, Owl. 2018b. Introduction to *Tribal Screams*, 4. Trieste, Italy: Independent Legions Publishing.

Goingback, Owl. 2021. "Indigenous Heritage in Horror: Interview with Owl Goingback." Horror Writers Association, October 11. https://horror.org/indigenous-heritage-in-horror-interview-with-owl-goingback/.

Hall, Heather. 2023. "What to Read Now: Indigenous Horror." *World Literature Today* 97, no. 2 (March): 26–27.

Hamilton, Clive. 2016. "The Anthropocene as Rupture." *Anthropocene Review* 3, no. 2: 93–106.

Haraway, Donna J. 2016a. *Staying with the Trouble: Making Kin in the Chthulucene*. Durham, NC: Duke University Press.

Haraway, Donna J. 2016b. "Tentacular Thinking: Anthropocene, Capitalocene, Chthulucene." In *Staying with the Trouble: Making Kin in the Chthulucene*, 30–57. Durham, NC: Duke University Press.

Hawk, Shane. 2020. *Anoka: A Collection of Indigenous Horror*. N.p.: Black Hills Press.

Hawk, Shane. 2023. "Behind Colin's Eyes." In *Never Whistle at Night: An Indigenous Dark Fiction Anthology*, edited by Shane Hawk and Theodore C. Van Alst Jr., 158–74. New York: Vintage Books.

Hawk, Shane, and Theodore C. Van Alst Jr., eds. 2023. *Never Whistle at Night: An Indigenous Dark Fiction Anthology*. New York: Vintage Books.

Henzi, Sarah. 2016. "Betwixt and Between: Alternative Genres, Languages, and Indigeneity." In *Learn, Teach, Challenge: Approaching Indigenous Literatures*, edited by Deanna Reder and Linda M. Morra, 487–92. Waterloo, ON: Wilfrid Laurier University Press.

hoʻomanawanui, kuʻualoha. 2018. "Indigeneity." In *The Routledge Companion to Media and Fairy-Tale Cultures*, edited by Pauline Greenhill, Jill Terry Rudy, Naomi Hamer, and Lauren Bosc, 122–32. New York: Routledge.

Horror Writers Association (HWA) Interview Series. 2021. "The HWA Honors Indigenous Peoples Day." October 10. https://horror.org/the-hwa-honors-indigenous-peoples-day-2/.

Horror Writers Association (HWA) Interview Series. 2023. "Asian Pacific Islander/ Asian Native Hawaiian Pacific Islander (API/ANHPI) Heritage Month." May. https://horror.org/.

Horvath, Agnes, and Arpad Szakolczai. 2020. *The Political Sociology and Anthropology of Evil: Tricksterology*. Abingdon, Oxon., England: Routledge.

Ihimaera, Witi, and Tina Makereti. 2017. Introduction to *Black Marks on the White Page*, edited by Witi Ihimaera and Tina Makereti, 8–13. Auckland: Penguin Random House New Zealand.

Innuksuk, Nyla, dir. 2022. *Slash/Back*. Sierra/Affinity.

Jenkins, James D., and Ryan Cagle, eds. 2020. *The Valancourt Book of World Horror Stories*, vol. 1. Richmond, VA: Valancourt Books.

Johnston, Aviaq. 2019. "Iqsinaqtutalik Piqtuq: The Haunted Blizzard." In *Taaqtumi: An Anthology of Arctic Horror Tales*, edited by Neil Christopher, 1–10. Iqaluit, NU: Inhabit Media.

Jones, Stephen Graham. 2023. Foreword to *Never Whistle at Night: An Indigenous Dark Fiction Anthology*, edited by Shane Hawk and Theodore C. Van Alst Jr., xi–xvi. New York: Vintage Books.

Justice, Daniel Heath. 2018. *Why Indigenous Literatures Matter*. Waterloo, ON: Wilfrid Laurier University Press.

Keetley, Dawn, ed. 2020. *Jordan Peele's "Get Out": Political Horror*. Columbus: Ohio State University Press.

Keetley, Dawn, and Ruth Heholt, eds. 2023. *Folk Horror: New Global Pathways*. Cardiff: University of Wales Press.

King, Tiffany Lethabo, Jenell Navarro, and Andrea Smith, eds. 2020. *Otherwise Worlds: Against Settler Colonialism and Anti-Blackness*. Durham, NC: Duke University Press.

Kovach, Margaret. 2021. *Indigenous Methodologies: Characteristics, Conversations, and Contexts*. 2nd ed. Toronto: University of Toronto Press.

Kövecses, Zoltán. 2005. *Metaphor in Culture: Universality and Variation*. Cambridge: Cambridge University Press.

Latimore, Jack. 2021. "Blak, Black, Blackfulla—Language Is Important, But It Can Be Tricky." Reconciliation Australia, November 5. https://www.reconciliation.org.au/jack-latimore -blak-black-blackfulla-language-is-important-but-it-can-be-tricky/.

Liaguno, Vince A., and Rena Mason, eds. 2022. *Other Terrors: An Inclusive Anthology*. New York: William Morrow.

Loui, Gregory C. 2017. *21st Century Orc*. Kindle.

Marin, Mike J. 2021. "Cinema Red: Natives and Horror." Vision Maker Media. https://visionmakermedia.org/cinema-red/.

McCormack, Brendan. 2022. "Announcing New *CanLit Guides* Chapter: 'The Future(s) of Indigenous Horror: *Moon of the Crusted Snow*,' by Gage Karahkwí:io Diabo." *Canadian Literature* 250: 131–34.

Mignolo, Walter D. 2018. "Colonial/Imperial Differences: Classifying and Inventing Global Orders of Lands, Seas, and Living Organisms." In *On Decoloniality: Concepts, Analytics, Praxis*, by Walter D. Mignolo and Catherine E. Walsh, 177–93. Durham, NC: Duke University Press.

Moreland, Sean. 2018. "Introduction: The Critical (After) Life of *Supernatural Horror in Literature*." In *New Directions in Supernatural Horror Literature: The Critical Influence of H. P. Lovecraft*, edited by Sean Moreland, 1–9. Cham, Switzerland: Palgrave Macmillan.

Moretti, Franco. 1988. *Signs Taken for Wonders: Essays in the Sociology of Literary Forms*. Translated by Susan Fischer, David Forgacs, and David Miller. London: Verso.

Morris, Tiffany. 2023. *Green Fuse Burning*. Hamilton, ON: Stelliform Press.

Murray, Stuart. 2008. *Images of Dignity: Barry Barclay and Fourth Cinema*. Wellington, New Zealand: Huia Publishers.

n+1. 2013. "World Lite: What Is Global Literature?" no. 17 (Fall). https://www.nplusonemag.com/issue-17/the-intellectual-situation/world-lite/.

Nahrung, Jason. 2004. "Why Are Publishers Afraid of Horror?" *Courier-Mail* (Brisbane, Australia), March 20.

Nevins, Jess. 2020. *Horror Fiction in the 20th Century: Exploring Literature's Most Chilling Genre*. Santa Barbara, CA: Praeger.

Nixon, Lindsay. 2020. "Visual Cultures of Indigenous Futurism." In *Otherwise Worlds: Against Settler Colonialism and Anti-Blackness*, edited by Tiffany Lethabo King, Jenell Navarro, and Andrea Smith, 332–42. Durham, NC: Duke University Press.

Pettersson, Anders. 2006. "Conclusion: A Pragmatic Perspective on Genres and Theories of Genre." In *Literary History: Towards a Global Perspective*, edited by Anders Pettersson, Gunilla Lindberg-Wada, Margareta Petersson, and Stefan Helgesson, 278–306. New York: De Gruyter.

Pomare, Sir Maui, and James Cowan. 1977. *Legends of the Maori*. New York: AMS Press.

Pulitano, Elvira. 2003. *Toward a Native American Critical Theory*. Lincoln: University of Nebraska Press.

Punter, David. 2018. "Global Horror: Pale Horse, Pale Rider." In *The Palgrave Handbook to Horror Literature*, edited by Kevin Corstorphine and Laura R. Kremmel, 191–201. Cham, Switzerland: Palgrave Macmillan.

Reder, Deanna, and Linda M. Morra, eds. 2010. *Troubling Tricksters: Revisioning Critical Conversations*. Waterloo, ON: Wilfrid Laurier University Press.

Reid, Andrea J., Lauren E. Eckert, John-Francis Lane, Nathan Young, Scott G. Hinch, Chris T. Darimont, Steven J. Cooke, Natalie C. Ban, and Albert Marshall. 2021. "'Two-Eyed Seeing': An Indigenous Framework to Transform Fisheries Research and Management." *Fish and Fisheries* 22, no. 2 (March): 243–61.

Ritzer, Ivo, and Peter W. Schulze, eds. 2016. *Genre Hybridisation: Global Cinematic Flows*. Marburg, Germany: Schüren Verlag.

Schaak, Hogan D. 2023. "Bleeding All Over the Shelves and Tracking It Out into the World: Theorizing Horror in the Indigenous North American Novels *The Only Good Indians* and *Empire of Wild*." *Studies in the Fantastic*, no. 15 (Summer–Fall): 94–126.

Schoonover, Madelyn Marie. 2022. "Indigenous Futurisms and Decolonial Horror: An Interview with Rebecca Roanhorse." *Gothic Studies* 24, no. 3: 295–303.

Smith, Linda Tuhiwai. 2021. *Decolonizing Methodologies: Research and Indigenous Peoples*. 3rd ed. London: Bloomsbury Academic.

Soop, Alex. 2022. *Midnight Storm Moonless Sky: Indigenous Horror Stories*, vol. 1. Calgary: Durvile and UpRoute Books.

Soop, Alex. 2023. *Whistle at Night and They Will Come: Indigenous Horror Stories*, vol. 2. Calgary: Durvile and UpRoute Books.

Spivak, Gayatri Chakravorty. 2003. *Death of a Discipline*. New York: Columbia University Press.

Tamsil, Ilma Saakinah. 2023. "Java in Indonesian Horror Films." *PERSPEKTIF* 12, no. 2 (April): 367–76.

Thomas, Julia Adeney, Prasannan Parthasarathi, Rob Linrothe, Fa-ti Fan, Kenneth Pomeranz, and Amitav Ghosh. 2016. "*JAS* Round Table on Amitav Ghosh, *The Great Derangement: Climate Change and the Unthinkable*." *Journal of Asian Studies* 75, no. 4 (November): 929–55.

Topash-Caldwell, Blaire. 2020. "'Beam Us Up, Bgwëthnënë!' Indigenizing Science (Fiction)." *AlterNative* 16, no. 2: 81–89.

Towlson, Jon. 2021. *Global Horror Cinema Today: 28 Representative Films from 17 Countries*. Jefferson, NC: McFarland.

Tuck, Eve, and C. Ree. 2013. "A Glossary of Haunting." In *Handbook of Autoethnography*, edited by Stacy Holman Jones, Tony E. Adams, and Carolyn Ellis, 639–58. Walnut Creek, CA: Left Coast Press.

Vizenor, Gerald, ed. 2008. *Survivance: Narratives of Native Presence*. Lincoln: University of Nebraska Press.

Vowel, Chelsea. 2022. "Writing toward a Definition of Indigenous Futurism." Literary Hub, June 10. https://lithub.com/writing-toward-a-definition-of-indigenous-futurism/.

Walkiewicz, Kathryn. 2021. "The Generative Refusal of Mixtape Narratives and Hybrid Monsters in Stephen Graham Jones's *Mongrels*." *ASAP/Journal* 6, no. 2 (May): 403–30.

Wallis, Keziah, and Miriam Ross. 2021. "Fourth VR: Indigenous Virtual Reality Practice." *Convergence* 27, no. 2: 313–29.

Weaver, Jace, Craig S. Womack, and Robert Warrior. 2006. *American Indian Literary Nationalism*. Albuquerque: University of New Mexico Press.

Wente, Jesse. 2019. "Doing All Things Differently." *Film Quarterly* 72, no. 3 (Spring): 42–43.

Wisker, Gina. 2005. *Horror Fiction: An Introduction*. London: Bloomsbury Academic.

Yazzie, Melanie, and Cutcha Risling Baldy. 2018. "Introduction: Indigenous Peoples and the Politics of Water." *Decolonization: Indigeneity, Education & Society* 7, no. 1: 1–18.

Part 1

Indigenous Ways of Theorizing

CHAPTER 1

"It Runs in the Family"

The *Rougarou* as Relative in Contemporary Métis Stories

June Scudeler

In Métis writer Cherie Dimaline's 2019 novel *Empire of Wild*,[1] Elder Ajean states: "You think all we have around here is good men and handsome women like me? There's just as many bad. We gotta keep it in balance. . . . Someone has to" (2019a, 146). Using healthy doses of humor and sarcasm, Ajean doesn't position people as good or evil but sees balance as the ultimate responsibility, especially for her family and her community. This nonbinary way of thinking extends to the *rougarou* (there are variant spellings), a Métis werewolf-like creature, a syncretic mixture of a French werewolf or *loup garou* and Cree and Anishinaabe shapeshifters. A powerful and scary figure sometimes believed to be in league with the *li jyhaab* or the devil, the rougarou serves as a warning not to offend the Creator. The rougarou is terrifying not simply because it is a werewolf-like creature who can attack and even kill people but because a community member can become a rougarou due to its destructive impulses and appetites. In cultures like the Cree and Anishinaabe, where it is not polite to tell people what to do, figures like the *wihtikow*, the Cree cannibal monster, are the basis of cautionary tales against greed. Also tied to christian strictures, the rougarou serves the same function in Métis communities.

According to settler scholar Amy J. Ransom, the loup garou was brought to so-called Canada by the French as a figure of colonization, and the caricature was spread and extended by narratives, "interacting with what Old

World discourse termed 'savage' peoples and their lore" in a "supposed new territory" (2015, 251). The rougarou shares similarities with the loup garou, especially the taboo against failing to observe religious practices. Similarly, French scholar Adrienne Durand-Tullou observes, the loup garou can "break taboos and risk, by their non-conformist attitudes, disturbing the social life of the group to which they belong" (cited in Ransom 2015, 255). Ransom translates Pamphile Lemay's Quebec-based 1896 loup garou story in which the loup garou's "eyes are like burning coals . . . its ears sand up like horns. . . . They prowl looking for someone to deliver them." The loup garou can be destroyed by drawing blood, but "[y]ou'd kill the Christian" (Ransom 2015, 258). What is different in many Métis stories is that the rougarou can be brought back into the community instead of being killed.

The rougarou, according to the aunt in Métis scholar Warren Cariou's story "Dances with Rigoureau," can change "their luck, change their voice, change their face. Their bodies too, I hear" (Cariou 2010, 157). This ability to change differentiates the rougarou from their progenitors, the French loup garou. People must decide to become a rougarou, which ties into Cree and Anishinaabe shapeshifter stories, and this can be important for healing and ceremony. Personal choice is paramount in rougarou stories; people are out of balance, harming their community rather than being bitten by another werewolf and turning into one at a full moon.

The rougarou is a form of social control that induces people to act for the greater good of the community. Men who hit women will become a rougarou, or hunters who have "shot so many deer, [their] freezer is overflowing but the herd is thin" (Dimaline 2019a, 4) are urged to stay indoors at night. Dimaline also explicitly links the rougarou to missing and murdered Indigenous women, girls, and two-spirit people, whom the Elders warn: "I wouldn't go out tonight. Someone saw the rougarou just this Wednesday . . . sharpening his claws with the jawbone of a child" (4). Although the rougarou reminds us not to harm the community, Métis writers also use the rougarou to challenge colonized ways of thinking by exploring issues that are often interwoven such as themes of christianity, violence against Indigenous women, girls, and two-spirit people, and resource extraction.

Using films and texts by Maria Campbell, Warren Cariou, Marjorie Beaucage, and Cherie Dimaline, and a story translated by Sherry Farrell Racette from *Stories of Our People / Lii zistwayr di la nassyon di Michif: A Métis Graphic Novel Anthology*,[2] I will situate the rougarou as a creature that affirms the importance of Métis ways of knowing in the past and in contemporary times. The rougarou is also a fluid creature who can be a figure of pity, because it has been a bad relative. Do "all our relatives" include the rougarou?

How do you be kin with a terrifying creature that has "eyes red like embers and saliva [coming] out of each side of its open mouth, showing enormous pointed teeth?" (Letourneau 2006, 14).

In *Monster Theory: Reading Culture*, settler scholar Jeffrey Jerome Cohen situates monsters as culture bodies because the "monster's body quite literally incorporates fear, desire, anxiety, and fantasy . . . giving them life and an uncanny independence" (Cohen 1996, 4). The word "uncanny" comes from the German *unheimlich*, which translates as unhomely, something that is simultaneously familiar but also invokes fear. But is the rougarou, a creature steeped in Métis traditions, uncanny? Based on Sigmund Freud's notion that fear is based "in something previously known and in which the repressed is made suddenly recognizable" (Cohen 1996, 3), the uncanny can be a useful way to examine horror because it brings to the fore what has been hidden. The uncanny is a "feeling of existential uncertainty," because "horror often arises out of a blurring or transgressing of clear category distinctions" (Jones 2018, 17–18). The werewolf is a good example of the uncanny because of the blurring between human and beast, a reflection of, as I will discuss, how the Métis are misread as liminal people by colonizers.

However, the rougarou is not a "folkloric" figure fixed in the past but a creature who still has lessons for Métis people; the rougarou is a teaching that makes us think of how our actions impact our larger community. Carol Warrior (Koniag Sugpiat/Dena'ina Athabascan/A'aninin) stresses that "temporal blurring in Indigenous narratives, from an Indigenous worldview (in which time is always relative or relational), is more often a source of strength for Indigenous protagonists—a strength that is often viewed as a threat, or even monstrous, from western characters' perspectives" (Warrior 2015, 19). Again, binaries are not an adequate framework in which to discuss the rougarou. Although the rougarou is a fearsome creature, it attacks people for violating social contracts. Cariou affirms that in "Métis stories, the rigoureau is often a heroic figure, or, if it is a villain, this villainy is positioned in such a way that it might still be seen as heroic" (Cariou 2010, 161), while Métis writer Darren Préfontaine notes that "[s]upernatural elements are always present in traditional Métis stories. Stories about black dogs appearing out of nowhere and doing things out of the ordinary are quite common in the Métis Oral Tradition" (2003, 2–3), a tradition that Métis people continue today in contemporary forms like graphic novels.

In the graphic novel collection *Stories of Our People*, Métis Elder Joe Welsh emphasizes: "You know, we talk about differences in communities. There's a family difference of course. . . . There were different versions" (Racette 2016, 156). Not only are there regional differences in rougarou stories, but there are differences within families, exemplified by the versions of these stories described in Racette's interview with the Elders. They swap stories about men who may have been rougarous, adding to the stories and even changing them. But they agree that "those people had the presence of those bad spirits . . . because they weren't following a good way of life. They weren't following their religion. They were being bad people. And they were the ones that were victims. They were victimized by the Roogaroo. The Roogaroo came to get them" (Racette 2016, 155). The rougarou seeks out people who are out of balance, not living in a good way and thus harming the larger community. While the rougarou is a terrifying being who can attack people, sometimes a person turns into a rougarou by seeing another rougarou or by not being a good community member, unlike werewolves, who must first be bitten by another werewolf. In other words, the rougarou has agency over the decision to change into a horrifying creature; they are victims because they put their individual needs over the community. However, in Maria Campbell's story, a female rougarou is seen as an outsider because she has lived in the city and refuses to be constricted by gender roles and catholicism.

For Elder Gilbert Pelletier, the rougarou is not simply a scary beast but also a figure of pity, someone who has lost their way. Pelletier doesn't say that the rougarou isn't following a particular religion, but that they were being bad by breaking community standards. Joe Welsh builds on his wife Norma's story about a guy who was magically "supposed to be in Fort Qu'Appelle one minute and Lebret the next," which are four miles apart. Joe also heard a similar story "from an old guy in Duck Lake" (Racette 2016, 158). For Joe Welsh, a community can have "three different versions of a legend, and they all have to do with morality and being decent. . . . The Catholic Church's version naturally was the meanest. You didn't have a hope in hell, but the other two you had a way of redemption" (Racette 2016, 158), a key difference between catholicism and stories rooted in Cree and Anishinaabe teachings.

A key difference between werewolves and rougarous is that the latter can change form at will, instead of waiting for a full moon, although not all rougarou stories follow this principle because stories differ in each community. The rougarou is a syncretic creature, also intimately tied to christianity, for example, as a warning not to break lent.[3] Settler scholar Darryl Jones hypothesizes that the werewolf is a creature of polytheistic religions rather than monotheistic ones because it reflects "the unity of humanity and nature" in contrast to the lack of beast transformations in monotheistic religions, "most of which emerged from the necessities of desert survival, and thus [stress] an essential separation of humanity and nature, which is a force to be mastered and controlled" (Jones 2018, 84). This tension is echoed in the rougarou punishing those who disobey christian strictures but also, as in *Empire of Wild*, selling Indigenous lands to settlers. Jones also notes that the lycanthrope or werewolf is "both a punishment and metaphor for savagery" (2018, 86), an idea that Cariou also raises.

"Dances with Rigoureau"

Cariou's story "Dances with Rigoureau" involves multiple ironies, particularly the nod to the film *Dances with Wolves* directed by and starring Kevin Costner as a white savior. Cariou's aunt tells him "I know it runs in our family" when they discuss his Uncle Eli's shenanigans with gambling or with women (Cariou 2010, 157); Uncle Eli is a trickster-like figure who is sometimes a bad albeit charming relative. She explains: "[A] rigoureau was not a werewolf . . . but someone who could change himself at will" (157). Cariou contends that "any recognition that humans are part animal would short-circuit the colonial paradigm of maximizing profit through the utilization of land and animals. . . . [T]he rougarou also represents a fear of an unstable humanity . . . a humanity that is hybrid" (160). The word "hybrid" always makes Métis people wary as we're seen as mixed, rather than as a people and a Nation. Unfortunately, hybridity and being of mixed blood are convenient descriptors used by non-Métis people, misnomers that have racist origins. The werewolf is a monstrous warning against hybridity because "the erotic depravity of the lycanthrope is represented as the possibility of miscegenation or bestiality" (Cariou 2010, 160), preconceptions that are still applied to Métis people.

Métis artist Sherry Farrell Racette traces the vexed history of Métis leader Louis Riel (1844–1885), who is a prime example of these so-called traitorous tendencies. A community leader of two resistances in 1869 and 1885 against the Canadian government for ignoring Métis rights, the catholic Riel was hanged in 1885 after a trial by an all-white, protestant jury. The colonial fear of miscegenation, "the perceived horror towards the perceived polluting properties of First Nations' blood and the assumed illegitimacy of biracial children," stained the colonizers' perception of Métis peoples (Racette 2001, 47). In this view, the Métis, like the rougarou, are monstrous creatures, an absurd characterization by the colonizers.

Cariou's weaving together of the political implications of seeing Métis as untrustworthy with the rougarou is perceptive. When Riel was on trial for "treason" by the Canadian government, the prosecution made much of the "lurking presence" of Indian heritage in him (quoted in Racette 2001, 47). "What do we see?" the prosecutor asked. "In the changing light of his dark Indian eye we see the civilized man struggling with the Indian" (quoted in Racette 2001, 47; my emphasis). . . . This mercurial quality was what most terrified the prosecutor. In this colonial mindset, it appeared that Riel could take on the appearance of a civilized man, but he was also liable to transform into a savage without warning. (Cariou 2010, 161)

Métis people were to the colonizers inhuman and monstrous. While Métis people are slightly above "Indians" in terms of "civilization" because of our syncretic culture, we are still untrustworthy, ready to unleash our savagery against the Canadian state. My own ancestors helped and fought alongside Métis war chief Gabriel Dumont in 1885, an act of monstrosity in the Canadian government's eyes. But by using Métis ways of knowing about "transformational power . . . the rigoureau's hybridity can be seen not as a curse but as a source of strength: the power to shift one's own identity, the power of bodily self-determination" (Cariou 2010, 161), a strength that runs through Cariou's family and the larger Métis community. Cariou situates the rougarou as a form of Métis bodily sovereignty, a creature in charge of their destiny. However, as tragically exemplified by Riel, while the rougarou may be able to shift between human and other-than-human, outside forces can misread the creature.

"ROU GAROUS"

Elder and writer Maria Campbell uses a gendered lens in her story "Rou Garous" to show that a woman's bodily sovereignty is threatening to catholic-imposed patriarchy in a Métis community. "Rou Garous," a story told to her by a male Métis Elder in the Michif language, undercuts the village priest's admonishment that an independent woman should be feared. In Campbell's story, it is the community, not the rougarou, that is the bad relation. Campbell made offerings to the Elders to translate "Rou Garous" and other stories with "gifts of blankets, tobacco, and even a prize Arab stallion" (Campbell 2010, 4). The title of the resulting collection, *Stories of the Road Allowance People*, refers to the term used by "white government and landowners to describe the dispossessed Métis who, having nowhere to go after the Resistance of 1885, built their homes on unoccupied crown lands" usually used for railroads or roads (Campbell 2010, 4). Homes were burned and the Métis chased out as railways and roads expanded; these liminal spaces are reminiscent of the shapeshifting space of the rougarou, underlining that the Métis people had no area to call home.

"Rou Garous" may seem like a cautionary tale about the creature, but the nameless "narrator's mother, in fact, provides a commentary on the Rou Garou story in which she suggests that this demonization of the Rou Garou is an insidious method of colonial coercion" (Cariou 2010, 163). The rougarou in question is a woman and, as Cariou points out, because she is a "former urbanite, a loner, a disbeliever, and a strikingly beautiful woman, she is marked in the community as an outsider" (163). She is called "Josephine Jug of Wine" because she lived "in dah big city for a long time" (Campbell 2010, 30), not because of drinking. This nickname highlights her outsider status and her being female; "Jug of Wine" evokes decadence and immorality because she is a woman who lived in the corrupt city. Her lack of faith is also a marker of difference because, as the narrator reminds us, "My mudder he[4] say / jus cause Josephine he don believe in dah Virgin Mary / dat don give us dah right to call him a name like dat" (Campbell 2010, 30).

The narrator begins his story of the rougarou with an animated "You ever heerd about dah Rou Garous?" He continues:

> Well dere humans you know
>> Jus like you an me
> But something happen to dem and dey turn to dogs in dah night
>> Dats right!
> Some of them dey even turn into wolfs.
>> Dats shore funny issn it?
> How tings like dat dey can happen on dis eart. (Campbell 2010, 34)

The narrator shares our astonishment that such creatures exist in the world. Notice that the narrator sees Cree people as relatives even as he relegates the stories firmly in the past, illustrating why Josephine's lack of catholicism makes her seem suspicious. The narrator believes that the rougarou are something from "dah dark side of dah eart." But he is ambivalent about this dark view of the creature: "lees I think dey was from dah dark side. / Maybe I think dat cause dats what dah Prees he tells us. / He claims dere use to be lots of dem in dah ole days / dat was before all of us become good Catlics" (Campbell 2010, 35). The narrator uses a significant number of qualifiers; he thinks that rougarous are from the dark side of the earth and is somewhat aware of the power the catholic priest has over the community. The priest claims there were lots of rougarous before they were "saved" by civilizing colonizers and catholicism. But the old ways still survive in spite of colonization, especially for women.

Josephine must feel out of place in a small community after living in the city. She is viewed with suspicion by some people as she keeps to herself, only visiting people with her husband. The narrator's mom is also an outsider, as we discover that she follows the old ways in secret.[5] When the brakes in George L'Hirondelle's fancy car fail, Josephine is blamed for being hit by the car while in her rougarou form. George later spies on Josephine, her body black and blue, while she packs her suitcase, leaving her husband Chi Kaw Chee[6] bereft, wandering outside looking for her. George fought in "dah war," which "was jus plain hell," so he didn't believe in "Rou Garous Cheepies and dah Jesus Chrise" (Campbell 2010, 41). But the hairs on the back of George's neck stand up when Josephine "look him right in dah eyes an / George he can move" (Campbell 2010, 48). George makes the sign of the cross because he believes that Josephine was as evil as World War I, where he saw bodies in trenches. He turns to catholicism rather than to the old ways when confronted by a rougarou.

The narrator's mother is outraged at her son's account of Josephine because Josephine is an independent woman. He tells us, "My ole granfawder he could turn hisself into a bear / An I knowed dis ole woman when I was a boy / dat one he turn hisself into a kiyute" (Campbell 2010, 34). Cariou notes that the narrator reveres stories when they happen in the past but is afraid of these stories in the present: "He has unwittingly adopted a colonized mindset in relation to the old ways. The mother's comments suggest that he should perhaps think of Josephine as something more like a hero than a pariah" (Cariou 2010, 165). The narrator shows a gender bias in his thinking because he mostly accepts what men (Tommy, the priest) tell him about Josephine even though "my Mudder he was real mad when I tell him what Tommy he tell me. He say dah Prees he win again an he give anudder woman a bad name" (Campbell 2010, 48–49). We learn that his mother "have dah seeing" and looks after Chi Kaw Chee. We feel her frustration when she tells the narrator, "Josephine was a good woman an George he was jus a stupid man. An me too" (50), making us wonder if the narrator is aware that Josephine is the heroine of the story because he is, after all, a stupid man who listens to colonized stories about Josephine.

EMPIRE OF WILD

Cherie Dimaline's *Empire of Wild* tells the story of Joan Beausoleil's frantic struggle to rescue her Anishinaabe husband Victor, who has turned into the evangelical christian minister Eugene Wolff, from being a rougarou. In contrast to the uncertain narrator in "Rou Garous," Dimaline makes the

THE *ROUGAROU* AS RELATIVE IN CONTEMPORARY MÉTIS STORIES   41

rougarou unambiguously a force complicit with gendered violence, colonization, and resource extraction. Settler journalist Marsha Lederman states that *Empire of Wild*

> was inspired in part by an article Dimaline read . . . about a controversial evangelical Christian movement targeting Indigenous people—and fronted by Indigenous leaders. "Who in the hell are these [awful people] leading these missionaries? . . . Who are these Indigenous people that are leading their people to this vulnerable state? And I immediately thought: That's something the Rogarou would do." (Lederman 2019)

"A New Hunt," the prologue to the novel, situates the reader in Métis worldviews: "Old medicine has a way of being remembered, of haunting the land where it was laid. People are forgetful. Medicine is not" (Dimaline 2019a, 1). Dimaline goes on to tell the story of the Métis people of Drummond Island, Ontario, Dimaline's own community, which was moved in 1828 when the United States was handed the land (1). They were displaced again from Lake Huron by white cottagers. Land is of the utmost importance to Joan's community and is the reason why Victor has vanished; he urges Joan to sell her father's land and angrily leaves after she tells him she will not do it. Victor is punished for acting like a colonizer by being turned into a rougarou.

Although the Reverend Wolff looks identical to Victor, he spouts christian anti-Indigenous rhetoric during his sermons: "A drum is not a heartbeat—only the heart God gave you can beat the right way" (Dimaline 2019a, 121). It is extremely painful for Joan to see her husband in this way even as it echoes his disregard for her land. And, as we learn later in the novel, Victor as the Reverend Wolff is also deadly. As a newly formed rougarou unable to control his impulses, he kills Joan's beloved Mére (grandmother) because she is against mining and has discouraged her family from working in an extractive industry. Even though Joan saves Victor, it will take a long time for her to forget his actions as a man and as a rougarou.

Dimaline uses rougarou stories from her community, where she "was instructed to stay behind with her beloved grandmother, Mere—whose voice guides all of Dimaline's writing—and her aunts at her great-auntie Flora's house" to hear and learn stories (Carter 2019). Stories about the rougarou inspired *Empire of Wild*; as Dimaline says: "I know I'm a 44-year-old woman, but I still believe in the rougarou. It was something quite spooky, beautiful and brutal, and that's why I want to write it. I had the best time" (quoted in Carter 2019). The rougarou is both metaphor and a real creature that is part of the contemporary world, as it "roamed the roads that connected Arcand [where Joan and her family lives] to the larger town across the Bay where Native people were still unwelcome two centuries on" (Dimaline 2019a, 3), a liminal creature who moves in colonized and colonizer spaces.

Empire of Wild, in Dimaline's words, asks the question, "what happens when colonization looks away from our land and our children and what happens when it comes for our gods? And what are the ways in which they will resist?" (Dimaline 2019b). With residential schools closed (although Indigenous children are still grossly overrepresented in the child welfare system) and Indigenous peoples like the Wet'suwet'en fighting against pipelines in their territory,[7] I'm not sure if land, children, and "gods" can be separated. Joan's family debates working for the mining industry, with some vehemently opposed and some seeing the work as a way to pay bills. Christianity is integral to wrenching Indigenous peoples from their lands to make way for resource extraction. When a bereft Joan mistakenly enters an evangelical christian revival tent (fittingly set up in a Walmart parking lot), she is struck by how weird the scene is, "the white walls and carpeted runner leading up to the stage, even the folding chairs . . . like weapons from a dead civilization displayed in a museum" (Dimaline 2019a, 27). Dimaline neatly subverts the rhetoric of the vanishing "Indian" preserved in museums even with the realization that these colonizing discourses still have power to erase Indigenous ways of knowing. Thomas Heiser, the mastermind behind the traveling church, is the connection between christianity and resource extraction. He is undertaking "relentless PR for the new pipeline consultations" even as he curses the Métis, who now had to be consulted instead of being ignored (Dimaline 2019a, 46). He can control dogs and wolves, viewing christians as "house cats" (48) who can be easily controlled. A *Wolfssegner*, whose Bavarian ancestors controlled wolves and their kin, Heiser has learned "that if you can control the darkest part of a community, you held the key to the entire thing" (278). For Heiser, controlling rougarous means using Victor to attack and kill Joan's Mére.

Victor becomes a rougarou because he disrespects the land. Joan's plot of land makes her happy because "the place reminded her who she was" (Dimaline 2019a, 72). So, it comes as a shock when Victor wants to sell the land. Victor becomes monstrous because he is so greedy with Joan's land, imagining it to also be his land. He becomes horrific in his disregard, but he is also someone to be pitied because he misunderstands the significance of Joan's land. Not only does Victor betray the land by going to developers for an estimate, but he also tells Joan that "it's not your dad's land anymore; it's yours. And I thought it was ours" (73). Victor is buying into the patriarchal idea that he would also own the land because he married Joan, a notion she refutes with a look: "It's not *yours* to sell." She then says the words that will cause Victor to leave: "I can't believe you would even ask. It's like you don't know me at all. That makes me feel really lonely, Victor" (73). Ironically, Victor heads to his trapline, showing that he knows the importance of land, even as he wants to sell Joan's.

Joan saves Victor by using Ajean's traditional knowledge; she needs to remind Victor "that he is a man under it all. You can do it by making the thing bleed" (Dimaline 2019a, 272). But there is also a psychological aspect to being a rougarou that carries responsibility. Victor tells Guillaume Robitaille, another rougarou under Heiser's sway: "'You're being hunted by another rougarou,' Victor tapped his own temple with his forefinger, then tapped his heart. 'In here'" (Dimaline 2019a, 285). Being a rougarou is a form of cultural and spiritual assimilation into Euro-Canadian values that make Victor disrespect Joan's connection (and his own connection) to her family's land.

Joan does get Victor back, but only by sacrificing one of the people closest to Joan, her twelve-year-old nephew Zeus, named "after the god responsible for werewolves" (Dimaline 2019a, 50). Ajean's admonishment about keeping things in balance means that Joan must trade her beloved Johnny Cash–loving nephew, who has helped her in her quest, for Victor. Zeus believes that he was "taken" because of his hatred for his mother (Dimaline 2019a, 292). Zeus then goes in his rougarou form to Ajean's, who hopes she can hold him off with bone salt until Joan arrives.[8]

It is the women using Métis ways of knowing who will (hopefully) defeat the rougarou. Dimaline makes it clear that violating standards of respect for land, women, and kinship upsets the precarious balance of community, meaning the rougarou will get you. But the rougarou also helps Joan. Dimaline explains: "There is a part of the Rogarou that is trying to reach Joan. She is in love and she is genuinely in love and it is a good love. So that is the point where he can dance a bit closer to her. But he can't take her. But he can remind her who she is by reminding her that *she* exists" (Michal 2020). The love not only for Victor but for Zeus, Ajean, and her family jars her out of her fog of grief, inspiring her to rebecome a woman of action and independence. Ajean tells Joan that she needs to remind the rougarou that he is a man "by making the thing bleed. Make him remember" (Dimaline 2019a, 78). The rougarou reminds her that she is a strong woman.

"ATTACK OF THE ROOGAROOS!"

As in *Empire of Wild*, "Attack of the Roogaroos!," from *Stories of Our People*, shows the continuing relevance of the rougarou for contemporary Métis people. The decision for the anthology to have both written texts of the

Elders' stories and illustrations balances respect for the stories with attracting youth and graphic novel readers to oral stories using a popular format (Préfontaine 2016). Influenced by Maria Campbell's *Stories of the Road Allowance People*, also published by the Gabriel Dumont Institute, "Attack" is written by Janice DePeel (Métis) from stories by Métis Elders Gilbert Pelletier, Norman Fleury, and Joe and Norma Welsh, and interviews by Sherry Farrell Racette. In "Attack," Virginia Lavallée is out berry picking, musing about how well she knows the land and her community. She knows that "the respect and affection she felt for them was reciprocated. If she took care of them, they'd take care of her, her family, and her community," reminiscent of Ajean's exhortation to live a balanced life. She runs into a rougarou, different from "any other animals that she'd ever seen," with disturbingly human eyes (DePeel 2016, 144). Virginia hits the rougarou on the head with a stick, causing it to run away. Métis constable Jack Pelletier drives her home, where she discovers that her husband Earl has an ugly purple goose egg and bruises. Virginia realizes her husband is a rougarou, so she knicks his ear because that is a way to cure a rougarou, but unfortunately he moves, losing his ear in the process.

As in Cariou's story, being a rougarou runs in the family. Earl and Virginia's pregnant daughter Isabella sees her disfigured father, causing her son to kick violently in her belly. There is peace in the family for thirteen years until carcasses of small animals are found in the community. Constable Pelletier goes to visit Isabella and her husband Harold, after doing research on the rougarou. He discovers "that the legend of the roogaroo is that pregnant women should avoid anything that looked ugly or frightening or their baby would be born that way," sharing that Isabella's *kokum* (Cree for grandmother) "saw a woman in the community attacked by a wild black dog. A few weeks later she found out she was pregnant with [Isabella's] father" (DePeel 2016, 151). Harold is adamant that their new baby can't be a rougarou, even as Pelletier points out the headless rabbit carcass near their front door. Then, "a thin wail could be heard coming from inside the house. Then the sound changed and became something different. The sound came from the house and from the forest, from the heavens and from the ground" (152), an all-encompassing horror that makes Isabella and Harold realize that their thirteen-year-old son Drew is a rougarou.

Harold and Isabella have very different reactions to the news, perhaps reflecting that women tend to be the carriers of stories. "Attack of the Roogaroos!" is told both by men and by women, but it is written by a woman.[9] Harold is outraged at the idea that his son is a rougarou. Instead, he believes that Drew is acting like a normal teenager, accusing Isabella of not supporting their son "for months now—as far as you're concerned he can't do anything right! This is superstitious thinking! . . . You just can't relate to our boy. Drew's acting like any other boy. If I told you some of the things I did when I was his age" (DePeel 2016, 152). He laughs at his memories, while Isabella has a very different idea of Drew's behavior:

> I've been asking for your help, but you refuse to see what I'm telling you. Harold, there is something wrong with our son. He's withdrawn. He's distant, and he's even stopped going to church. He told mom that he doesn't believe in God! And the boys that he calls friends are a gang as far as I'm concerned. Two of them have already been charged with petty crimes—how long before it's our son? (DePeel 2016, 152–53)

Pelletier then points out the carcass, prompting Harold to say to him in Michif: "Dimaen ka itistahan Drew chi kikwayakoohk il vyeu" (Tomorrow, we will take Drew to the Old People) (153), showing that Harold finally accepts the dire situation his son is in.

"Attack of the Roogaroos!" is a cautionary tale about the importance of respecting the power of traditional stories in contemporary times. In the end, both Harold and Isabella know, as Isabella emphasizes, that by reconnecting "to our traditions, we'll help Drew. . . . We'll help ourselves, and our community will benefit since we are keeping the traditions of our people alive" (DePeel 2016, 153). While Harold initially takes the individualistic and patriarchal "boys will be boys" approach, Isabella, like Virginia Lavellée, outlines the rougarou and how to defeat it in communal terms. The women know that the best approach to helping Drew is to take him to the old people. Isabella and Harold go to church, but as with the narrator in "Rou Garous," the old ways are the best way to help Drew, not just to cure him of being a rougarou but to help him find a sense of purpose in his life. Connecting with his Métis culture will help him find his path. Some of the stories about rougarous say that people must want to be a rougarou, so Drew has to decide to be a part of his community, with all the responsibilities of kinship that that requires. He must be a good relation to be cured of being a rougarou.

ROUGAROU

Filmmaker, cultural worker, two-spirit Elder, and community-based video activist Marjorie Beaucage produced a delightful 2014 short film *Rougarou* with third- and fourth-grade students at Stobart School in Duck Lake, Saskatchewan, near Beardy's and Okemasis's First Nations. She is a profoundly community-based filmmaker; "her goal has been to pass on the stories, knowledge and skills that will make a difference for the future" (Santa Fe Art Institute n.d.). The story that she tells the children is an old Métis story that has been passed down in her family. She asks the children, "Did you ever hear about rougarous?," reminiscent of the question the Métis Elder in "Rou Garous" asks listeners at the beginning of his story.

Beaucage tells the story by involving the children in her simple but effective film, which begins with a dark blue background and images of black trees and hills as in a children's book. She tells them: "People change for different reasons. In the old days, the old people, they used those animal spirits to make people better, they wanted to make them well, like heal the sick. Did you ever hear about people who are healers? And their animals are healers too" (Beaucage 2014). She tells the story of an old man, Calbert, who lived in her family's village but had gotten lost when he lived in the city because of "drinking and doing bad things." He comes home to the village but acts differently, walking alone at night, especially during the full moon. He is a loner who has lived in the city, like Josephine in Maria Campbell's story.

After a round dance (the children sing and drum the song), Beaucage's grandpa hits something with glowing green eyes while driving his truck, the same fate as Josephine Jug of Wine. Grandfather sees the glowing eyes in the bush, which belong to Old Man Calbert, a sight that "made his hair stand up and gave him the chills." The next night, Old Man Calbert shows up at her grandpa's house to play cards, but he is "all black and blue, like somebody beat him up pretty bad," which is also how Josephine in "Rou Garous" is found. Old Man Calbert stops drinking and wins at cards all night. The children ask what happened to Old Man Calbert: "After that, my grandmother told me, old man Calbert stayed sober for a long time and then he just disappeared one day. Maybe that rougarou just let him because he was a changed man after that." Like Josephine, Old Man Calbert is an outsider because he went to the city, although Calbert is also an alcoholic.[10] He wanders alone at night, separate from his community and those who might support him. Grandpa knows that Old Man Calbert is a rougarou, but he invites him into his house to play cards and serves him coffee. For Old Man Calbert, alcohol is the rougarou, and kindness from the community is what puts him on a good path.

Beaucage not only tells the children the story but enacts community by involving the students in her film. They eagerly answer Beaucage's questions, howling like coyotes and quacking like ducks, awed by the rougarou's glowing green eyes. The children are clearly having a good time acting in the film, appearing as grandpa, Old Man Calbert, and the other card players. They are learning the rougarou story as part of Métis tradition: "storytellers would have a young person participate in an activity where they acted out the principle of the story. In this way, through experiential learning, the story's lesson was made real and could be more easily remembered" (Préfontaine 2003). Cariou, Campbell, Dimaline, Racette and colleagues, and Beaucage use storytelling in contemporary media to both preserve and contemporize rougarou stories, as reflected in the ending of Beaucage's film. The children ask Beaucage what the teaching of the story is. She answers: "The rougarou comes to give you a chance to change your ways. He comes from the dark to bring you to the light. Once you can find somebody to be your friend, even when he knows you are a rougarou, you will be changed." Rather than people seeing the rougarou as simply evil or bad, the rougarou reminds us that balance is the key to healthy communities. The rougarou is our relative.

The rougarou can symbolize many things—straying from a good path, disrespecting women, girls, and two-spirit people, extracting resources, alcoholism, colonization—but all these stories show that the rougarou is vital in the lives of Métis people.

NOTES

1. Dimaline also includes a rougarou story in her 2017 best-selling young adult novel *The Marrow Thieves*.

2. I would also like to acknowledge *A Howl: An Indigenous Anthology of Wolves, Werewolves, and Rougarou*, a graphic novel collection edited by Elizabeth LaPensée (Anishinaabe and Métis), which was released after this chapter was written.

3. Lent is a special time of prayer, penance, sacrifice, and good works in preparation of the celebration of Easter (Saunders n.d.).

4. Michif, one of the Métis languages, is a syncretic language, using Cree verbs and grammar with French nouns. Cree doesn't have gendered pronouns, which explains the shifts from he to she that are not connected to the sex or gender of the person being spoken about.

5. We are hearing a filtered version of the story through the narrator's Uncle Tommy and then through the narrator, who is telling us what his mother said. The narrator admits, "we all talk about him like he was somebody we all / knowed real good. / Like me. / I never knowed him but I soun like I do" (Campbell 2010, 40).

6. Chi Kaw Chee's name is actually Harry T'staymow, which means tobacco.

7. For more information on issues involving the Wet'suwet'en people, see https://unistoten.camp/.

8. Ajean explains that salt bone comes from a special extra bone that "[p]eople from Red River, on your mere's side, had been growing . . . for generations" (Dimaline 2019a, 144). Putting ground-up salt bone around your house ensures that "no spirit, no rougarou can come in" (146).

9. However, I don't want to replicate colonial gender binaries by stating that all women are story carriers and that men don't carry stories. Two-spirit and Indigiqueer people also carry knowledge and stories.

10. We never learn what bad things he was doing in the city, but simply being in the city is seen as suspicious.

BIBLIOGRAPHY

Beaucage, Marjorie [RainbowWarrior]. 2014. *Rougarou*. Vimeo. https://vimeo.com/109408088.

Campbell, Maria. 2010. "Rou Garous." In *Stories of the Road Allowance People*, rev. ed., translated and put on paper by Maria Campbell. Saskatoon, SK: Gabriel Dumont Institute of Native Studies and Applied Research.

Cariou, Warren. 2010. "Dances with Rigoureau." In *Troubling Tricksters: Revisioning Critical Conversations*, edited by Deanna Reder and Linda M. Morra, 157–67. Waterloo, ON: Wilfrid Laurier University Press.

Carter, Sue. 2019. "How *The Marrow Thieves*' Author Cherie Dimaline's Stint as a Magician's Assistant Helped Her Write about a Werewolf." *Toronto Star*, September 12. https://www.thestar.com/entertainment/books/2019/09/12/authors-foray-into-adult-fiction-rooted-in-magical-mtis-childhood.html.

Cohen, Jeffrey Jerome. 1996. *Monster Theory: Reading Culture*. Minneapolis: University of Minnesota Press.

DePeel, Janice. 2016. "Attack of the Roogaroos! Prose Story." Gabriel Dumont Institute of Native Studies and Applied Research. Virtual Museum of Métis History and Culture, March 17. https://www.metismuseum.ca/resource.php/148354.

Dimaline, Cherie. 2019a. *Empire of Wild*. Toronto: Random House Canada.

Dimaline, Cherie. 2019b. "Survival: Cherie Dimaline; Turning to Indigenous Knowledge." *The Walrus*, December 6. https://thewalrus.ca/survival-cherie-dimaline/.

Jones, Darryl. 2018. *Sleeping with the Lights On: The Unsettling Story of Horror*. Don Mills, ON: Oxford University Press.

Lederman, Marsha. 2019. "Cherie Dimaline Grew Up in a Culture Where Stories Were Crucial. Now, She's Publishing *Empire of Wild*, the First in a Four-Book Deal." *Globe and Mail* (Toronto), September 23. https://www.theglobeandmail.com/arts/books/article-cherie-dimaline-started-out-writing-pornography-and-now-has-a-four/.

Letourneau, Henri. 2006. "A Rougarou Story." In *Metis Legacy II: Michif Culture, Heritage, and Folkways*, edited by Lawrence J. Barkwell, Leah M. Dorion, and Audreen Hourie, 12–14. Saskatoon, SK: Gabriel Dumont Institute of Native Studies and Applied Research.

Michal, Melissa. 2020. "A Native Woman Battles Neocolonialism and Werewolves in 'Empire of Wild.'" *Electric Literature*, November 25. https://electricliterature.com/cherie-dimaline-empire-of-wild/.

Préfontaine, Darren R. 2003. "Métis Storytellers." Gabriel Dumont Institute of Native Studies and Applied Research. Virtual Museum of Métis History and Culture, May 30. http://www.metismuseum.ca/resource.php/00747.

Préfontaine, Darren R. 2016. "Introduction to Métis Stories." Gabriel Dumont Institute of Native Studies and Applied Research. Virtual Museum of Métis History and Culture, March 17. https://www.metismuseum.ca/resource.php/148343.

THE *ROUGAROU* AS RELATIVE IN CONTEMPORARY MÉTIS STORIES 49

Racette, Sherry Farrell et al. 2001. *Metis Man or Canadian Icon: Who Owns Louis Riel?* Exhibition catalog. Winnipeg: Winnipeg Art Gallery.

Racette, Sherry Farrell et al. 2016. "Attack of the Roogaroos! Oral History Transcript." Gabriel Dumont Institute of Native Studies and Applied Research. Virtual Museum of Métis History and Culture, March 15. https://www.metismuseum.ca/resource.php/148353.

Ransom, Amy J. 2015. "The Changing Shape of a Shape-Shifter: The French-Canadian Loup-Garou." *Journal of the Fantastic in the Arts* 26, no. 2: 251–75.

Santa Fe Art Institute. N.d. "Alumni: Marjorie Beaucage." https://sfai.org/alumni/marjorie -beaucage/.

Saunders, William. N.d. "History of Lent." Catholic Education Resource Center. https://www.catholiceducation.org/en/culture/catholic-contributions/history-of-lent.html.

Warrior, Carol Edelman. 2015. "Baring the Windigo's Teeth: Fearsome Figures in Native American Narratives." PhD thesis, University of Washington. https://digital.lib .washington.edu:443/researchworks/handle/1773/33820.

CHAPTER 2

OKA-NADA

HISTORICAL CONTAGION AND HAUNTING BACK IN JEFF BARNABY'S *BLOOD QUANTUM*

KRISTA COLLIER-JARVIS

In the 2022 Inuit-made horror/science fiction film *Slash/Back*, a group of Inuit teens navigating life in Pangnirtung, Nunavut, a remote arctic community, find themselves faced with the task of saving their friends and families from an alien invasion. Like many alien invasion narratives,[1] the aliens in *Slash/Back* not only invade the land but also invade the bodies of the animals and Indigenous people inhabiting the land. While *Slash/Back* is not a zombie film, the aliens function similarly to zombies, and the film addresses issues comparable to those that inform narratives in the subgenre. For example, the first zombies who shuffled onto the screen—the dark-skinned, enslaved creatures from Victor Halperin's 1932 film *White Zombie*, were embodiments of the "trope of losing one's independence to a greater power" (Bishop 2015, 8). While the "greater power" in *White Zombie* is largely representative of the Depression-era imagery of long food lines, "a tedious job, a bleak economy, or a help-less government" (Bishop 2015, 8), *Slash/Back* is a colonial narrative whose "greater power" is the threat of forced assimilation. The aliens—a not so thinly veiled metaphor for colonizers—take over Indigenous bodies and force them to attack one another in a manner quite reminiscent of a zombie pathogen. In the end, the young protagonists in *Slash/Back* only succeed in destroying the aliens with the use of traditional Inuit teachings that they learned from their parents and their Elders. *Slash/Back* embodies the blending of traditional

Indigenous knowledge with the themes and tropes that define contemporary genres and subgenres such as horror and science fiction, alien and zombie narratives. Many Indigenous authors and filmmakers are taking up this blending with the goal of disrupting national narratives that are predicated on reinscribing colonialism again and again upon the bodies, lands, and cultures of Indigenous peoples. In "Is There an Indigenous Gothic?," Michelle Burnham (2014) argues that Indigenous Gothic narratives "represent Native American contributions to—but also Native American interventions in—American Gothic" (228), and I might add, Canadian Gothic.

This chapter focuses on Indigenous-made zombie narratives that use a technique Teresa A. Goddu has termed "haunting back" (1997, 132), which allows these narratives to interrupt Canadianism and its role in ongoing colonization, disrupting historical contagion and reclaiming bits of the histories that have been silenced by, damaged by, or misrepresented within Canada's national narratives. While there are still only a handful of Indigenous-made zombie narratives in existence, including Lisa Jackson's short film *Savage* (2009), Rodrick Pocowatchit's film *The Dead Can't Dance* (2010), Richard Van Camp's short story "On the Wings of This Prayer" (2012), Stephen Graham Jones's works *Zombie Bake-Off* (2012) and *Chapter Six* (2014), and Jacques L. Condor/Maka Tai Meh's short story "Those Beneath the Bog" (2013),[2] I focus on Jeff Barnaby's *Blood Quantum* (2019), a film in which Indigenous peoples are immune to a zombie infection. *Blood Quantum* haunts back against many Indigenous-centered conflicts, but I look primarily at how the film responds to the Cabot foundation myth, the 1981 raids at Restigouche, the 1990 Oka Crisis, and the Settler practice of identification known as blood quantum. Ultimately, Indigenous-made zombie narratives blend traditional Indigenous knowledge with contemporary monsters to unveil how the history of the ideology informing the national narratives of Turtle Island (North America) is predicated on Indigenous oppression. Furthermore, these narratives are represented as contagion. By haunting back, Indigenous storytellers unsettle these national narratives and respond to Billy-Ray Belcourt's approach to decolonization: "dreaming up worlds that can bear all of us, worlds that slip-slide into others without disavowing their hybrid alterities" (2016, 22), worlds populated by zombies.

THIS WILL JUST TAKE A MINUTE . . .

Blood Quantum begins with a scene that haunts back against the stories of John Cabot, such as the first *Canadian Heritage Minute*, which was released when the docuseries first hit cable television in 1991. This *Minute* considers the 1497 voyage of John Cabot, sailing from Bristol, England, to Canada aboard the *Matthew*. According to the *Minute*, Cabot and his crew were stopped by cod so dense that, as the Cabot character states at the end of the video, it would "be enough to feed our kingdom . . . until the end of time" (*Heritage Minutes* 1991). The discourse with which this *Heritage Minute* constructs the narrative of "discovery" suggests that Canada sees itself as a land of plenty that provides "enough" for all its inhabitants. In fact, the use of the term "Kingdom" suggests that food will be plentiful not just for England but for all parts of its dominion, including its colonies. However, this narrative is what Joanne Wright would call a foundation myth:

> Foundation myths are the primary organizing myths of nations: they establish a common history, a common origin, and a national identity. Their significance stems from the idea that "[t]he sense of 'whence we came' is central to the definition of 'who we are.'" . . . They mythologize and sanctify an imaginary beginning to the nation, or take the historical "facts" of the nation's origins and legitimate them from a particular political perspective. (2004, 20)

Cabot's claim to discovery had already been legitimized prior to the release of the *Heritage Minute*; however, its appearance within the *Minutes* solidifies his claim as part of Canadian heritage. As a result, it becomes a primary organizing narrative of Canadian nation building. Therefore, arguably, the Cabot character's statement summarizes a central element in the national narrative of Canada, but in laying claim to its foundation and positing itself as a common history via the collective pronoun "our," it erases, perhaps as part of the promise of consumption, the Indigenous peoples and nations across Turtle Island.

The *Heritage Minutes* generally play a significant ideological role in shaping the popular narrative of Canada due to their content and the frequency with which they air. The *Minutes* originally appeared on major cable television networks and prior to films at Cineplex theaters (Reid 2013). By the late 1990s, the *Minutes* were also included in home video releases of Universal Studios films (Reid 2013), so they were initially undeniably designed to reach a large portion of the Canadian viewing population. Because of their status as "history," the CRB Foundation (see below) "offer[ed] them free to TV stations, and since they confer valuable Canadian content points, their total exposure nationwide now runs at more than thirteen hours of air-time every month" (Moore 1995),[3] which equated to approximately 780 *Minutes* per month at the height of their viewing. While they no longer seem to air on cable television or at the theater, Historica Canada still produces a few new ones each year (under the label "Heritage Minutes—#partofourheritage"). The *Minutes* appear so often that many Canadians can quote their taglines (Graham 2012), and because the length of the *Minutes* is similar to that of a commercial, we cannot deny the fact that audiences consume them within a commercial framework. The *Minutes* therefore sell a part of Canada and Canadian identity. For instance, Emily West argues that the *Heritage Minutes* are designed to "fill the gaps in Canadian collective memory" to buttress the nation by constructing a national pride that functions as an ideological defense mechanism protecting Canada from "threats" (2002, 213–14). The producers seek to achieve this by presenting the illusion that the *Heritage Minutes* are "unmediated" and "multicultural," thus encouraging a more authentic relationship between Canadian viewers and their "history," as well as to avoid appearing as if they further a particular political agenda (West 2002, 214). However, as Wright points out, foundation myths are always already rooted in a political perspective (2004, 20). Therefore, we can turn to Glen Norcliffe, who argues that the central questions we need to ask when approaching histories such as those outlined in the *Canadian Heritage Minutes* are "whose history?" and "which history?" (1999, 97).

When it comes to whose history is represented by the *Heritage Minutes*, the histories of Indigenous peoples are often excluded or misrepresented. For example, in the Cabot *Minute*, Cabot speaks directly to King Henry VII of England and his royal court; therefore, the "our" is not necessarily inclusive of those outside the royal court. In fact, because "our" possesses the "Kingdom" in the tagline, it can only include the colonizers—those who possess the kingdom—and this excludes the colonized. When it comes to Indigenous representation, of the ninety-six *Minutes* currently in existence,[4] only ten intersect with Indigenous peoples, and many of these misrepresent them and reinforce negative stereotypes. The 2005 *Minute* relaying the story of the Ojibwe military hero Tommy Prince, for example, dedicates more screen time to depictions of Canadian military signifiers (his medals), and the dialogue presents a list of his personal issues, including alcoholism, poverty, and "family troubles," than it does to Prince himself (*Heritage Minutes* 2005b). While it can be argued that such "troubles" plague many veterans upon returning from war, another *Heritage Minute*, "Home from the Wars," which aired the same year as "Tommy Prince" and represents the return of veterans (all of whom appear to be white), focuses solely on the benefits afforded them by the Canadian government (*Heritage Minutes* 2005a). While this latter *Minute* does not explicitly state that Indigenous veterans are excluded from government assistance after a war, the dearth of visible minorities in the *Minute* suggests otherwise.

Ultimately, the exclusion or misrepresentation of oppressed groups from the national narrative stems, in part, from the fact that Canada is considered to be "multicultural." Erin Peters notes how "Canadian national identity has long been fraught with plurality, leading to a noticeable lack of any unifying national culture or distinctiveness" (2013, 250); therefore, for Canada's plurality and diversity to flourish, a national identity cannot exist. Peters goes on to note how "[i]n a country of so much cultural plurality, the concept of a universal Canadian cultural identity is controversial to say the least, and most certainly contested by Canada's many social groups" (255). This is because national identity in Canada either already excludes certain groups or is inherently contradictory. I argue that both are true. To have a national identity requires the erasure, homogenization, or subsuming of Canada's many subgroups into one Canadian identity, yet Canadian identity is posited as a plurality and, as such, already requires diversity and resists said erasure, homogenization, and subsuming, leading to an inherently contradictory national identity.[5] Therefore, the history represented by the *Heritage Minutes* is the contradictory history of whiteness that perceives itself as multicultural, infecting the Canadian imaginary with this narrative, and yet still requires the misrepresentation or erasure of Indigenous peoples to exist.

We can address the cultural inception of the *Heritage Minutes* to gain a more thorough understanding of whose history is represented by the *Minutes*. The *Minutes* were originally sponsored by the Charles R. Bronfman (CRB) Foundation Heritage Project, which was established in 1986 to "enhance Canadianism" (Rukszto 2005), but what is Canadianism? This question immediately arose with Confederation in 1867 and has been an ongoing challenge to answer. Therefore, it is connected with the search for a *foundation* myth, one that is set in opposition to anything and everything that threatens its ideals. Canada uses the *Heritage Minutes* to rationalize the need for Canadianism and mobilize its mythologized identity against possible "threats," primarily Indigenous sovereignty. For instance, Canada reportedly experienced an identity crisis in the 1980s and early 1990s because, prior to 1971, it was considered to be a bilingual and bicultural country. When Prime Minister Pierre Trudeau introduced a multicultural policy in 1971, Canada spent the next few decades trying to reconcile multiculturalism as its new national identity (Peters 2013, 255). Due to Canada's status as a "young country struggling to find an identity independent of Britain and the United States" (Metcalfe 1987, 177), it looks to its media "to define a national identity in crisis by relating the fate of particular individuals to wider political, economic, and cultural issues" (Jackson and Ponic 2001, 43), which becomes a kind of collective memory or the establishment of a Canadian imaginary.

According to Erin Peters, the need for a "collective memory" rises in response to "heightened national disunity" (2013, 251); therefore, there is a correlation whereby the *Minutes* as a perceived representation of "collective memory" emerged just when Canada reached its "heightened national disunity" within an apex of tension regarding its multicultural identity. Clearly, in the *Heritage Minutes*, "the new memories being presented are seeking to define the Canadian past [biculturalism] through present-day issues [multiculturalism]. This act silences the actuality of the past in order to portray an idealized version for the purpose of constructing a desired collective memory for the sake of present and future" (Peters 2013, 261). Silencing becomes a rationalized by-product of creating Canadian identity, one that is naturalized via hegemony in the manner of one of its so-called parent nations—Britain.

Ultimately, the *Heritage Minutes* as a vessel of Canadianism function within a colonial program and are designed to construct and uphold an ideology exclusive of, misrepresentative of, and damaging to Indigenous nations. Returning to the Cabot *Minute*, Canadianism manifests in, first, the myth of abundance, and second, the myth of exceptionalism for Europeans coming to Turtle Island. These two myths are significantly challenged in *Blood Quantum*, but to understand the film's role in responding to the myths, we must first explore the myths themselves. The first myth, that of abundance, is evident in the representation of the cod, which are portrayed as "so thick, they stayed our ship" (*Heritage Minutes* 1991), so the resources were fished as if they would never disappear. According to Sarah Praskievicz, when the focus is placed on "supply in the natural environment" as opposed to other potential stressors, such as a sudden increase in the population that consumes said supply, the myth of abundance emerges (2019, 1068). A myth of abundance mistakes a lack of resource scarcity as resource security (Praskievicz 2019, 1077–78). Essentially, a lot of cod (a lack of resource scarcity) does not constitute cod forever or cod for all (resource security), but the manner in which Cabot posits the cod as "enough" collapses this distinction and leads to the myth of abundance.

As a result of the myth, the cod—like many resources extracted from Turtle Island—were treated like a "nonrenewable resource," meaning sustainability was never taken into consideration as they were being fished (Norcliffe 1999, 101). One such reason, of course, is that the Settler concept of sustainability was not present at the end of the fifteenth century; however, the myth of abundance precedes the rise of sustainability in a way that ensures any attempt to regulate cod fishing was, is, and will continue to be ineffective. Additionally, the cod are posited only as a source of food. In no way does the Cabot character suggest that the cod have additional uses;

therefore, they function solely within the narrative of consumption, and any narrative of consumption—especially one lacking in sustainable discourse—I argue, falls into the trappings of overconsumption. The intersection between consumption and a lacking discourse on sustainability is where zombies emerge within the narratives that I discuss here.

Like most colonial resources, the cod are not left on the shores of Turtle Island but are shipped back to England to ensure that the "Kingdom" is fed. By the end of the sixteenth century, the English were bringing thousands of tons of cod back to England (Pringle 1997, 37). The colonial narrative is therefore linked to both the export as well as the overconsumption and inevitable extinction of resources. As a result, the moment Cabot saw the cod, the cod were destined to extinction. While impossible to accurately determine the cod statistics around Newfoundland during Cabot's voyage, Cabot paved the way for the decline of the cod population. In Canada, cod fishing peaked in 1968 at 810,000 tons (Pringle 1997, 37), and then the industry began to collapse. In 1992, a moratorium was put in place (Norcliffe 1999, 107), but it was too late. The moratorium came a year after the Cabot *Heritage Minute*, when Canadians were ensured that there would be "enough" cod "until the end of time." By the end of the twentieth century, the cod population had not recovered, and numbers continue to decline (Norcliffe 1999, 107). While the cod are not yet extinct, they are considered critical and classified as "endangered" by the Committee on the Status of Endangered Wildlife in Canada (Thorne 2020). Essentially, even though "[f]oreign fishing had shattered the ecology of the Northwest Atlantic fisheries[, t]he Canadian government proceeded to finish off the survivors" (May 2001). The declining numbers combined with a 30 percent increase in the fishing quota in 2019 (Munro 2020) means that population recovery looks bleak, and we have Cabot as well as the *Heritage Minutes* to thank for the inevitable extinction of the cod.

The second myth speaks to Canadian exceptionalism by claiming initial discovery, highlighting that the cod "stayed" the ship and ensuring that the "kingdom" is fed. According to Rachel Bryant (2017a), "[e]xceptionalism is the code system Settler peoples have used across centuries to signify their cultural preeminence"; specifically, it refers to "the compulsive logic through which Settlers from multiple states and across centuries have come to imagine themselves as deserving of the great material bounties that were supposedly bequeathed to them as they aggressively seized control of Indigenous lands." Bryant goes on to note how "Canada invokes its exceptionalism when it wants to fracture and endanger lands and waterways with another oil pipeline, or when it wants to build another hydroelectric dam in Labrador that will flood and distort Innu or Inuit hunting grounds." Therefore, Canadian exceptionalism emerges as a way to rectify the imperialistic tendencies I previously mentioned; it is simultaneously tied to land, the exploitation of resources and collapse of sustainability, and ongoing conflict with Indigenous peoples. This entanglement manifests in the material monster of the zombie in Indigenous-made zombie narratives. As such, Indigenous peoples become the antithesis of Canadian exceptionalism; they function both as a threat to Canadian exceptionalism but also a required Other for it to exist.

The *Heritage Minutes* repeat Canadianism and its myths of abundance and exceptionalism, even today. Consistent exposure to the ideology that cod will "be enough to feed our kingdom . . . until the end of time" precedes, and makes silent, the narrative of resource depletion as well as its effects on Indigenous nations. I call this "historical contagion," which is an epidemic that has infected Canada. While it may be impossible to cure our national narratives of historical contagion, the inclusion of previously silenced voices in the form of counternarratives can slow the rate of infection. Katarzyna Rukszto argues that the "very visibility [of the *Heritage Minutes*] as mass-circulated products invites other cultural spaces to make them a site for critique, appropriation and/or humour" (2005, 75); therefore, from the moment the *Heritage Minutes* emerged, they were destined to invite counternarratives. While Rukszto points out that "[t]he Minutes attempt to reproduce the dominant discourse of Canadian identity, focusing on a multiculturalist idea of national unity out of difference" or a "core myth of Canadian history," the multitude of counternarratives produced "speaks to the incongruity between the dominant language of national identity promoted by the Heritage Project, and the actuality of social relations of difference and inequality that historicize and politicize counter-narratives of the nation" (74–75). Nowhere is this more evident than in horror counternarratives produced by Indigenous peoples.

1497: SOMETHING FISHY IS GOING ON

The burgeoning of Indigenous Gothic in the twenty-first century represents D. Bruno Starrs's (2014) "literary retaliation" whereby previously silenced Indigenous authors and filmmakers have "wrestl[ed] the keyboard away" and are finally "writing back," or in this case, haunting back. According to Teresa A. Goddu, who coined the term, "haunting back" occurs when oppressed groups who have been haunted by a nation's narratives co-opt those narratives and reposition themselves and their oppressors in a different haunting/haunted dynamic (1997, 132). Despite Goddu's original use of "haunting back" being in reference to American slavery narratives, such as the novels of Toni Morrison, it can also be applied to narratives by other oppressed groups, including Indigenous peoples. The term "haunting" does not necessarily connote the presence of ghosts or specters. Etymologically, "haunting" has its origins in the thirteenth century, referring to the action of practicing something habitually or frequenting a place (*Oxford English Dictionary*). Avery Gordon (2020) uses "the term 'haunting' to describe those singular and yet repetitive instances when home becomes unfamiliar, when your bearings on the world lose direction, when the over-and-done-with comes alive, when what's been in your blind field comes into view"; essentially, when what has been silenced or repressed returns à la Freud. It is we, the Indigenous, who have been silenced and repressed, primed to return and haunt, and for Belcourt, "[h]aunting speaks us into existence" (2016, 30). Therefore, while ghosts and specters become the usual embodiments of haunting, they are just the typical vessels through which oppression manifests; they are not the sole purveyors of it.

Many Indigenous horror narratives make persistent references to conflicts between Indigenous nations and the Canadian government because these narratives expose how the repetition of national narratives becomes historical contagion, a kind of haunting for oppressed groups who have been excluded from, misrepresented within, or damaged by them. Newer nations, such as Canada and the United States, are invariably vulnerable spaces for haunting back to emerge because their search for identity "signals a fear of contagion" (Goddu 2000, 267), and while haunting back can take many forms, unsurprisingly, and keeping in line with Goddu's argument, Indigenous-made narratives exploit the fear of contagion, manifesting not necessarily as ghosts or specters but as contagion: zombies. Therefore, Jeff Barnaby's 2019 Indigenous made, "anti-colonial" (Carleton 2020) zombie film *Blood Quantum* is a prime example of haunting back.

Blood Quantum is set in 1981 and follows a group of Indigenous survivors of a zombie viral plague. Specifically, the film follows a Mi'kmaw family who establish a safe zone on the fictional Red Crow Indian Reservation, where they protect both Indigenous and Settler survivors, although the inclusion of the latter is a point of contention for some characters. Like most zombie narratives, the infection eventually makes its way into the safe zone, leading to the downfall of the reservation. The film ultimately ends with two Indigenous survivors, Joss and Joseph, and Joseph's white, pregnant girlfriend, Charlie, floating away on a fishing boat. Despite her infection, Charlie gives birth to a human baby before she succumbs to the zombie virus—thereby revealing how the baby passes blood quantum, because in the film, Indigenous survivors, and only Indigenous survivors, are immune to the zombie virus.

Blood Quantum opens with a scene that haunts back against Cabot's foundation myth, emphasizing conflicts regarding fishing rights and access to consumption. In this scene, Gisigu, the Elder figure, returns from a fishing trip and finds himself surrounded by zombie fish—essentially, "stayed" in a very Cabot-like manner. While he stands ashore and guts his catch of the day, the gutted fish begin to move. Gisigu looks troubled as the camera pans out, ending with an extreme long shot of him standing alone, looking small, framed on the left by concrete ruins and on the right by a small, wooden fishing cabin. The zooming out from Gisigu suggests that whatever has infected the fish is not relegated to this single time and space; while it may have started with the fish (as with Cabot), it is a much larger issue. Extreme long shots show "the relative insignificance of the character struggling against their environment" (Heiderich n.d., 7); thus, Gisigu is posited as relatively insignificant within this newly zombie-infested landscape. However, throughout the film, Gisigu proves to be a strong character whose actions ensure the continuation of Mi'kmaq culture.

Gisigu's scene embodies two of the main qualities of haunting back. The first quality is when the narrative "expose[s] the cultural contradictions of national myth" (Goddu 1997, 10). The second is when the Indigenous characters are centered or come out as the victors in the end (Dyer 2020, 364–65). For the first quality, the zombie fish expose the cultural contradictions of Cabot's foundation myth—and its myths of abundance and exceptionalism. As we determined, the myth of abundance mistakes a lack of resource scarcity as resource security, so the fish in *Blood Quantum*, unlike the cod in 1497, represent a source of food that might be abundant (lack of resource scarcity) but is also inedible (rejecting resource security). As such, *Blood Quantum* haunts back during the opening scene by exposing the contradictions in the myth of abundance, because the fish resist the two primary aspects of Settler resource positioning—consumption and extinction. The reduction of fish in 1497 to a single role—food—for Settlers is overhauled in *Blood Quantum* as the zombie fish become the consumers. The fish thus refuse to become "disposable models to humans," as Donna Haraway would call it (2010, 54). As a result, the humans (Indigenous and Settler alike) in *Blood Quantum* must rethink their relationship to the fish, and by extension, the other species in the film, in a kind of way that destabilizes signifiers and species hierarchies. When a food resource such as cod is "mined more like a nonrenewable resource" as previously discussed, then "the resource cycle [is] being taken to its limits" in what Norcliffe identifies as the point of extinction (1999, 101). *Blood Quantum* reveals the potential to shift resource positioning in a way that disrupts the Settler consumption and extinction imperatives.

For example, not only do the fish shift away from being a signifier of food, but they also become monsters and purveyors of contagion—embodying a similar signification to the Settler zombies in the film. The suggestion, then, is that the Settlers are not superior species-wise to the fish; the two have much in common, occupying a similar position within the food chain. The myth of abundance solidifies the eventual extinction of the resource; however, the fish in *Blood Quantum* haunt back by resisting extinction. In contrast to the cod, which are near extinction, it is impossible to elicit the extinction of the zombie fish. The fish can no longer be consumed, but if they were, they would not nourish; they would destroy their consumers with the zombie pathogen. Therefore, consumption in the film is an inherent contradiction—the fish are a food source that is inedible. It is this inherent destruction from something meant to nourish that elicits haunting back.

However, to fully understand the relationship between resource positioning and extinction, we must first address the idea of extinction more broadly. "Extinction" is an anthropocentric term. This is apparent when we consider how the "sixth great extinction" is largely defined as resulting from "engulfing wars, extractions, and immiserations of billions of people and other critters for something called 'profit' or 'power'" (Haraway 2018, 4), all of which are human-centered determinants. Therefore, while our understandings of "extinction" involve the loss of a species, the "great mass" modifier, at least in this sixth iteration, refers to the human species and other species serving human means. Due to its anthropocentric roots, the reality is that the sixth great extinction is about the loss of humans and/or the species we see as serving human means.

Selina R. Cole and Melanie J. Hopkins argue that "mass extinctions change the trajectory of evolution by restructuring ecosystems, altering the dominant types of functional ecological groups, and affecting patterns of morphological evolution" (2021, 1). During the zombie outbreak in *Blood Quantum*, we learn that Indigenous peoples are immune—whether that immunity arises in tandem with the zombie infestation or has always been a part of Indigenous being is unclear. Essentially, in a haunting back against exceptionalism, Indigenous peoples in Barnaby's world are naturally selected to survive the zombie apocalypse.

But this reversal also leads me to the second quality of haunting back in which Indigenous peoples are centered. In *Blood Quantum*, Indigenous actors make up the majority of characters: Indigenous characters occupy the positions of both protagonist and antagonist, and in the end, Indigenous characters are the only remaining survivors as a result of extinction selectivity. Indigenous bodies, through their immunity and on-screen dominance, are restructured within a new postcolonial or decolonial ecosystem. While narratives of first contact usually contradict themselves by representing the Indigenous populations of Turtle Island as both absent (terra nullius) and "savage," the extreme long shot in Gisigu's scene suggests that he—the Indigenous man—is the one who is alone upon a deserted landscape where everything is in ruin, is both present and the last signifier of civilization. Indigenous peoples are therefore the antithesis of savagery, and the film haunts back against this outdated stereotype. Even though inserting more Indigenous characters in the narrative is one of the central tenets of haunting back, as Kester Dyer (2020) argues, it does not necessarily constitute haunting back on its own, so it needs to work in tandem with exposing contradictions within the national narratives. Haunting back and Indigenous-made zombie narratives are not merely rewriting history from the point of view of previous, silenced Indigenous groups, nor are they simply remaking the zombie narrative with Indigenous characters. The inclusion of non-Indigenous characters is crucial because, in these narratives, "[w]hite survivors have to confront one of the deepest fears of a racist society: What would happen if the shoe were on the other foot and the racial power balance upended?" (S. Gordon 2020). For this to occur, both Indigenous and non-Indigenous characters are required. In contrast, Indigenous characters are largely absent in the referent narratives, such as the Cabot *Heritage Minute* (1991). Additionally, narratives that haunt back are not making claims to the truth of historical conflicts but rather function as an alternative but synchronous history or what Raul Cârstocea has called "synchronous nationalisms"[6]—those "numerous competing nationalisms . . . varying across both the spatial and temporal axes" (2022, 482). Cârstocea argues that when two histories or nationalisms are restructured, "binary understandings of nationalism [as well as] the essentialist reification that can contemplate a single ideal type as a dominant or even exclusive manifestation of nationalism in a given territory" are also challenged (481–82).

Even though Rukszto argues that "the imitation of a text necessarily legitimates the original text" (2005, 76), meaning that to rewrite the history risks reinforcing the ideology of the original narrative, which would be counter to the purpose of haunting back, *Blood Quantum*'s dismantling of Settler binarism by representing synchronous nationalisms resists reification. If we borrow Rukszto's ideas, the haunting back is "both transgressive and conservative" (76). The question remains, though, what is the purpose of haunting back if it does not claim truth and it does not rewrite history? To answer this, we can turn to Kiowa Gordon, the actor who plays Lysol in *Blood Quantum*. Gordon points out how "ever since natives were in cinema, it's always been somebody else's voice, and somebody else's face, and somebody else's makeup on them. Now we can actually take that back" (quoted in Yamato 2020).

Indigenous-made narratives are "ushering in a new age for the next generation to say, 'OK, let's go out there and take our lives back'" (Kiowa Gordon, quoted in Yamato 2020). In Gisigu's scene, for example, the Indigenous survivor may seem insignificant standing alone upon a land of contagion, but this is just the beginning of a narrative in which he and his community can finally take back the land.

No Rest(igouche) for the Salmon

While I argue that the opening scene of *Blood Quantum* with Gisigu and the zombie fish is a haunting back against the 1497 "discovery" of Newfoundland, it is also a haunting back against the 1981 raids at Restigouche, which Barnaby witnessed firsthand (Bramesco 2020). Not only is the film set in the same year as Restigouche, but Barnaby had his cast and crew watch Abenaki filmmaker Alanis Obomsawin's 1984 documentary *Incident at Restigouche* in preparation for filming, so they would have a better idea of the conflicts informing *Blood Quantum* (Yamato 2020). Barnaby admits that Obomsawin "was the only Native film-maker that I had to look up to and build my ideas around" (Bramesco 2020). Inspired by her work, Barnaby went into filmmaking, believing that it was both a "form of social protest" and an effective means through which to educate Indigenous peoples and Settlers alike about Indigenous culture and history (Bramesco 2020). Barnaby admits that he also filmed scenes in the same locations where the raids took place and that appear in Obomsawin's coverage of the incidents (Carleton 2020). These scenes and their connections to Restigouche are not explicitly explained to the audience—one must be familiar with the events themselves and/or the media coverage of said events to understand the references—and the way Barnaby presents them draws on a long history of horror's ability to unsettle.

In June 1981, the Quebec Provincial Police (QPP) raided the Listuguj community (which is part of the Restigouche region) to restrict the Atlantic salmon fishing rights of the Mi'kmaq—what Gabriel Béland (2021) calls part of the ongoing "salmon wars." After initially asking the Mi'kmaq to withdraw their fishing nets and the Mi'kmaq refusing, asserting their treaty rights (CBC News 2021), the QPP confiscated the nets, violently beat several protesters, and arrested nine members of the Listuguj community (Béland 2021). A few days later, the police returned to confiscate any additional nets, firing rubber bullets and tear gas (CBC News 2021). The initial reason given by the Quebec government for the raids was sustainability (CBC News 2021), but the motivations are much more complex than this. For instance, the salmon fishing yields of the Atlantic provinces, Greenland, and Iceland in 1981 totaled 3,285 metric tons, as described in Obomsawin's *Incident at Restigouche* (1984). Obomsawin does not provide the exact numbers of salmon fished by the Quebec fisheries, but she does explain that the New Brunswick fisheries only took in 109 metric tons. As one travels farther inland, the salmon yields drop in number. Because Quebec is so far inland, it experienced a significant decline in Atlantic salmon (Béland 2021). To recover some of these loses, the government targeted the fishing rights of the Mi'kmaq (Béland 2021). However, the Mi'kmaq of Restigouche only yielded six metric tons of salmon in 1981, considerably less than any other region (Obomsawin 1984). A few weeks after the raids, Lucien Lessard, former minister of recreation, hunting, and fishing with the Parti Québécois at the time, claimed that "somewhat peace" [*sic*] (as quoted in Béland 2021) had been reached. In March 1982, a deal was signed that limited the quotas of Mi'kmaq fishermen; however, the deal did not take hold, so the following year the Mi'kmaw Band Council developed their own fishing law (CBC News 2021).

Mike Isaac, who witnessed the Restigouche raids firsthand, highlights how the events were "traumatic," but they also created "opportunities to overcome" that trauma (as quoted in CBC News 2021). This is exactly how Barnaby seems to have approached the conflict. In an interview with the *Globe and Mail*, Barnaby reveals that one of his earliest memories of contact with people from off Listuguj was a rifle butt to the head during the 1981 raids (Black 2020). Therefore, Restigouche marks Barnaby's "first contact"—literally—which was clearly a colonial encounter that inspired much of his film.

After Gisigu's contact with the zombie fish, there is a series of Dutch angles that are employed to unsettle the history of Restigouche. A Dutch angle occurs "when horizontal and vertical lines go askew" (Bowen and Thompson 2013). Essentially, the camera is tilted, throwing those lines off. The result is that "it causes a sense of uneasiness . . . [and is often used to convey] when a character is sick or drugged or a situation is 'not quite right.' . . . [T]he imbalance will make the viewer feel how unstable the character or environment really is" (Bowen and Thompson 2013, 119). As such, they are common in horror films. The Dutch angles in *Blood Quantum* include various points of view of a city, the water, a bridge that looks suspiciously like the Honoré Mercier Bridge in Montreal, and a cemetery; the first two perspectives are representative of Restigouche, while the latter two are representative of the 1990 Oka Crisis. These Dutch angles are used for the scenes that happen to be eerily similar to the media images of both Oka and Restigouche, but as askew, unbalanced versions of these images. The suggestion here is that something is "not quite right" with those images and the way they construct our histories and national narratives. Barnaby is signaling to us that we need to decenter Canadian history—literally turning it over and looking at it from different perspectives.

OKA-NADA: OUR HOME AND *NATIVE* LAND

In an early scene in *Blood Quantum*, Indigenous survivor Lysol is depicted antagonizing a zombie soldier who is strapped to the side of a shipping container at the entrance to Red Crow. Lysol is standing face to face with the zombie, and the scene is filmed in profile, which makes it potentially familiar to both Indigenous and non-Indigenous peoples growing up in Canada during the 1990s. It is a reference to Shaney Komulainen's iconic photograph called *Face to Face* from the 1990 Oka Crisis, which was a well-publicized dispute between Indigenous peoples and the Quebec and Canadian governments (Lazowski 2015). The Oka Crisis lasted seventy-eight days in Kanehsatà:ke and Kahnawà:ke—a Mohawk village and reserve, respectively, located in Quebec. The dispute began with government approval for the expansion of a private golf course into the Pines, which is part of the Mohawk Nation, including a Mohawk burial ground. What started as a small protest on a dirt road resulted in the deployment of the QPP and eventually the Canadian Armed Forces. The Mohawk were teargassed and bombarded with concussion grenades; a gun battle ensued; the Mercier Bridge, a major bridge between Montreal and its south-shore suburbs, was blocked; and two people, one Canadian corporal and one Mohawk Elder, were killed. Ultimately, the land was never developed. Instead, the Interim Land Base Governance Act formally designated the land as belonging to the Mohawk, but in reality, it's "no-man's-land—neither native reserve nor municipal park" (*National Post* 2019). However, in 2019, the year that *Blood Quantum* came out, developer Grégoire Gollin turned the land over to the Kanehsatà:ke Mohawk Council in what he claimed to be a "spirit of reconciliation" (*National Post* 2019). In spite of that, some Mohawks in Kanehsatà:ke point out that Gollin has spearheaded projects over the years that have infringed on Mohawk territory, and they view his "reconciliatory" efforts merely as a bid for a tax break (*National Post* 2019). As such, *Face to Face* represents not just the incident at Oka but the ongoing narrative of Indigenous-Canadian conflicts.

Face to Face, and what it signifies, spread like historical contagion across the nation, infecting Canada with a narrative that is damaging to Indigenous nations. For example, the caption for the photograph reads, "Canadian soldier Patrick Cloutier and Brad Laro[c]que alias 'Freddy Krueger' come face to face in a tense standoff at Kanehsatake in Oka." Larocque is an Anishinaabe warrior, so there is an irony rooted in the fact that the single visual representation of Oka doesn't even contain a member of the Mohawk Nation, exposing the media's hand in constructing pan-Indianist narratives that flatten the diversity of Indigenous peoples. The moniker, Freddy Krueger, refers to the knife-fingered serial killer from the *A Nightmare on Elm Street* films (1984–2010); he kills his victims in their dreams, which effectively also kills them in the waking world. Therefore, Larocque is posited only as monster in the caption to the photograph, whereas Cloutier is marked with his Canadian identity and his contributions as a soldier, suggesting that the monster (the Indigenous Other) is not Canadian but is rather the antithesis of Canadian identity—one that threatens Canadianism. While "Freddy Krueger" is one of many aliases voluntarily adopted by the Indigenous warriors to protect their identities, the caption for Komulainen's image also functions as a kind of interpellation creating a human/monster dialectic whereby we view the Canadian soldier as human and the Anishinaabe warrior as monster. For instance, after *Face to Face*, Cloutier was often described as "stoic" and "heroic" (Wells 2022). The *Globe and Mail* even compared him to "the man who stared down a Red Army tank in Beijing's Tiananmen Square" (as quoted in Wilkes and Kehl 2014, 491). He was even fast-tracked up the ranks to master corporal before being demoted in 1992 due to cocaine use and alcohol-induced violence (Wells 2022). However, Larocque's use of "Freddy Krueger" demonstrates how monstrosity can haunt back. Krueger's real power lies in destroying dreams—both literally, as he infects dreams and turns them into nightmares, as well as figuratively, because he forces his potential victims to stop dreaming altogether. Krueger functions as a disruption of and warning against the pursuit of the American Dream—not unlike Larocque's disruption of and warning against the Canadian Dream, wrapped up in the symbolic nature of the golf course, a signifier of affluence and capitalistic pursuits. Because Larocque voluntarily adopts this alias, he is haunting back by using horror as a form of resistance.

The contradictory nature of national narratives on Turtle Island manifests most prominently within the imaginary of the human/monster binary. *Blood Quantum* haunts back against Oka by flipping and interrogating this binary. In the scene in which Lysol is depicted face to face with the zombie soldier, the positions of the soldier and the Indigenous warrior have been inverted—both physically, as Lysol occupies the physical space inhabited by Cloutier in Komulainen's photograph, but also regarding who is human and who is monster. In the scene from *Blood Quantum*, the soldier is the zombie, so Barnaby takes monstrosity off the body of the Indigenous warrior and places it on the white

Canadian soldier instead. Because the human/monster binary is "integral for the creation and maintenance of dominant/imperial national identities" (Wilkes and Kehl 2014, 482), Barnaby's flipping of the human and monster calls into question exactly who or what the dominant national identity is.

This questioning is also apparent in the fact that in *Blood Quantum*, the Indigenous survivors are immune to the zombie pathogen. Donna Haraway argues: "Immune systems are not a minor part of naturecultures; they determine where organisms, including people, can live and with whom" (2003, 31). Therefore, immunity suggests that Indigenous peoples can live on Turtle Island. Haraway's multispecies work is designed to destabilize binaries; thus, the second part of her argument—"with whom"—also suggests that Indigenous peoples can live alongside the zombies because their immunity exists in response to this relationship. As such, Indigenous people require the presence of Settler zombies for their immunity to exist and have meaning, and Settler zombies require the presence of Indigenous survivors for food. This becomes a somewhat symbiotic, interconnected web of species relationships rather than a mere binary. Indigenous-made zombie narratives respond to the imaginary human/monster binary in three steps: first, they take up the national narrative; second, they flip the positions of the human/monster; and, finally, they expose the differences between the two as false or constructed. The way Barnaby draws on haunting back to respond to the first two steps is clear, but the third can only be understood by looking closely at the Settler practice called blood quantum.

JUST ONE DROP OF BLOOD

The twist that sets *Blood Quantum* apart from other zombie narratives is that immunity is linked to race. Immunity means it is only Settlers who become zombies, which is an inversion to what Eric Savoy calls "'the face of the tenant'—[or] the specter of Otherness that haunts the house of national narrative" (1998, 13–14), because it is Settler survivors who must now seek refuge within the reservation. According to Michelle Burnham, this Gothic inversion reveals that "it is the settler colonist whose face has taken up an unwelcome tenancy in the Native American home, and whose threatening presence haunts [the] American Indian narrative" (2014, 227). The Settler therefore becomes the monster—the Other—that has taken up residence on Indigenous land again. When Settler survivors seek refuge within Red Crow, it becomes "colonial whiplash," when "white people who haven't turned into zombies are at the mercy of the oppressed" (S. Gordon 2020). Indigenous-centered immunity means that Settlers must turn to Indigenous survivors for help, but specifically, the Settlers must find safety on the reservation.

In one scene, a pregnant Charlie leads three Settler survivors to Red Crow. The group consists of a young girl, infected and wrapped in a blanket, her father, and a youth named Lilith who is later revealed to also be infected. After the young girl is shot, her distraught father is pushed, stumbling into the safe zone, still carrying the blanket that had been wrapped around his daughter. Indigenous survivor James turns to him, yelling "are you fucking crazy" as she rips the blanket, saturated in infected blood, from his arms and throws it into a fire. Jason Asenap (2020) argues: "This time . . . the small-pox blankets are infectious to the 'other side,'" suggesting that the infected blanket haunts back against the diseases brought over by Europeans. While the use of smallpox blankets as a weapon against Indigenous peoples during colonization has never been confirmed, the effects of diseases transferred from Settlers to Indigenous populations cannot be debated; for example, in 1862, smallpox decimated approximately half of the Indigenous peoples in what is now British Columbia (Elliott 2019). Asenap (2020) therefore calls Barnaby's use of the infected blanket "sweet revenge upon those who brought disease to Indigenous lands." By ripping the blanket from the father's hands and throwing it into the fire, James is highlighting how the bodies of Settlers are infectious, and when James follows this by stating, "Don't forget; ain't nobody immune here but us," she reveals how the infected blanket presents a higher risk to Settlers than it does to Indigenous peoples.

The film's title, *Blood Quantum*, refers to the laws in the United States that determine Indigenous identity and access to reservations. While Canada does not have blood quantum in the sense that the United States does, it does have a similar system in the Indian Act, which determines Indigenous status as well as access to reserves. The blood quantum system has been criticized as a mode of Indigenous erasure, and Charles Bramesco (2020) precisely refers to the practice as "genocidal." While it can be argued that Barnaby is supporting blood quantum laws because immunity and Indigeneity seems to be blood centered in the film, what he is actually doing is calling into question its reliability. For example, as previously noted, the film ends with an infected Charlie giving birth on a fishing boat. Even though Charlie is infected, the baby turns out to be human; the implication is that the baby is Indigenous *enough* to be immune. However, what resists blood quantum is that blood quantum and the Indian Act are presumably no longer officially being upheld by the infrastructure that constructed them. They are, after all, legal designations requiring a legal and governmental institution to enforce them. The zombie narrative is about collapsing structures, such as legal and governmental systems, that construct and maintain difference—collapsing the national narratives and asserting Indigeneity via immunity to haunt back against Canadian infrastructure. Because Indigenous peoples are considered to be immune in *Blood Quantum*, immunity becomes synonymous with Indigeneity, and this means that within the human species, only the Settlers become zombies. While other races may be susceptible to the zombie virus, they seem largely absent from the film. Thus, destroying the zombie becomes a form of resistance, and immunity as haunting back is represented by it being rooted in the body, by it being natural, and by its existing only within a multispecies framework. When these three qualities are considered in tandem, immunity becomes a form of haunting back against the binary dialectic and reveals the potential to interrupt Canadianism.

First, the simultaneous potential and danger of Barnaby's zombieverse is that it emphasizes difference at the bodily level. Indigenous immunity suggests that, at the most basic, biological level, Indigenous bodies are different from other human bodies. In one respect, this difference emphasizes Indigeneity—a resistance to assimilation—as Indigenous survivors cannot become zombies; however, in another, it reinforces the existence of an essentialist, biological, racial difference. Kester Dyer (2020) argues that "Indigenous characters have developed a physical immunity to the contagion, presumably due to their prior exposure to colonialism and its ongoing iterations." For Dyer's argument to function, colonialism must be posited as a kind of virus because prior exposure to the "colonialism virus" means that the immune systems of Indigenous people have had hundreds of years of constant exposure for immunity to develop. If we are to take Dyer's ideas as a launching point for thinking about immunity, the suggestion here is that the zombie also signifies everything that whiteness (the Settler) signifies, such as "patriarchy, and, most of all, the destruction of our natural world" (Newell 2020). If Indigenous bodies are indeed biologically different due to centuries of exposure to colonization as Dyer argues, then Indigenous bodies resist everything signified by whiteness and are therefore primed to also protect the natural world, but they can only do so, I argue, by "making-with" whiteness in complex entanglements.

Second, immunity is natural. One theory in *Blood Quantum* is that the land brought forth this virus as a way to eliminate invasive species and establish a kind of land-back movement, suggesting that the virus and thus immunity come from the land itself. Scientifically, this makes sense; for example, when humans travel into areas that they have not previously explored, they make contact with microbes that they haven't yet encountered (Wald 2021, xiv). If the zombie virus in *Blood Quantum* is native (so to speak) to Turtle

Island, then contact with the virus becomes deadly for those who are newer to the area. Regardless, the zombie infestation allows for a restructuring of dominant groups and reveals "extinction selectivity," which is when some species are more likely than others to go extinct due to aspects of their ecology (Cole and Hopkins 2021, 1). Essentially, Indigenous peoples in Barnaby's world are naturally selected to survive the zombie apocalypse.

Third, according to Haraway, "[i]mmune systems are not a minor part of naturecultures; they determine where organisms, including people, can live and with whom" (2003, 31). In ecological terms, we can consider immunity as a kind of symbiogenesis (Haraway 2003), which suggests that the species involved require one another for stasis. Essentially, the immunity of Indigenous peoples requires the monstrous presence of Settlers. *Blood Quantum* takes this idea a little further by creating a zoonotic virus that spreads across species and collapses distinctions between certain species such as fish, dogs, and humans. Because zombie narratives posit a set number of species in what Haraway would call "holobionts—that is, symphonic or fugal assemblages of living and nonliving entities that are necessary to each other's being" (2019, 567), *Blood Quantum* suggests that fish, dogs, and humans (Indigenous and Settler alike) are necessary to each other's "being." The lack of overt discussions of other species within the narrative does not suggest that they are not also crucial to holobionts' being but rather that more thorough research might reveal these species as the most affected by the complex history of North American colonization.

While the ending to *Blood Quantum* seems to fall into the trappings of the zombie subgenre, Barnaby's ending is actually more hopeful in terms of haunting back against reserves and reservations. *Blood Quantum* ends with Gisigu making a last stand at the edge of the reservation, fighting the zombie horde to give Joss, Joseph, and a pregnant, infected Charlie the time they need to escape. In the only scene accompanied by traditional drumming, Gisigu stands on a concrete ruin and cuts down hordes of zombies; he goes down fighting. However, the scene switches from live action to animation whereby Gisigu emerges from beneath the mass of zombies and proclaims, "None of you are getting past this line." Gisigu's refusal to let the Settler zombies leave the reservation suggests that they are now relegated to it. The Indigenous survivors end up having to vacate their reservation and in the end setting out on a bleak journey, but what this really says is, they are no longer confined to the reservations that they were relegated to for so long. This is a land-back movement—a haunting back—whereby the Settler zombies are left at the edge of the reservation while the Indigenous survivors sail off to reclaim any and all parts of their land.

Conclusion: Enough to Feed the Kingdom . . .

In 1997, the same year that Ottawa lifted some of its cod fishing regulations, a replica of Cabot's ship—the *Matthew*—set sail to commemorate the five-hundred-year anniversary of the famous voyage (Pringle 1997). The simultaneity of the lifting of the regulations as the *Matthew* set sail suggests that for the *Matthew* to be as authentic as possible, the cod must be readily available. More than this, though, is the suggestion that the cod are doomed to be refished into eradication and the colonial story retold. *Environmental Magazine* (2001) points out that "[i]t's not certain that Canada has learned from its mistakes with the cod. The fishery has simply turned to alternative species further down the food chain and, in at least some instances, may be pushing their populations towards collapse." Similar to the blood quantum laws, moving down the food chain becomes a kind of assimilation by slowly eliminating species, resulting in the destruction of biodiversity.

Indigenous-made horror haunts back, but it unfortunately also reaffirms national narratives; in fact, any response or reproduction risks reaffirmation. Therefore, reaffirmation is the peril that Indigenous-made narratives risk when they haunt back. Zombie narratives are multitudinous in their ability to produce meaning, so what are Indigenous-made zombie narratives doing differently beyond risking reaffirmation? Scott Gordon (2020) argues that *Blood Quantum* transforms "the close-range, torso-clawing violence of zombie films [into] a vehicle for a larger story about genocide." I have argued that history itself and the stories we tell are a kind of contagion; therefore, narrative vehicles such as the *Heritage Minutes* begin as epidemics that infect the population. We can turn to Indigenous-made narratives in general but not necessarily to cure ourselves of these national narratives; instead, because history is a constructed narrative, the addition of Indigenous-made counternarratives provides a broader and more complete story. Just as immunity itself is not a "cure" and does not eliminate the zombie infection, so too are narratives that haunt back not something that eliminates or replaces national narratives; they are just a parallel and tandem approach to history.

However, what *Blood Quantum* also reveals is that conflicts such as Cabot's role in colonial settlement, as well as Restigouche and Oka, are not self-contained. Many Indigenous political and social conflicts are transhistorical and trans-Indigenous, crossing time as well as tribal and community affiliations. Conflicts are intertwined with and therefore become representations of a larger colonial history. However, this also means that Indigenous counternarratives have the potential to reach beyond the confines of the reservation.

These narratives suggest that when the end of the food chain is reached, the systems of oppression can be unsettled in a way that shifts the direction of the food chain. However, this is only possible by adopting a multispecies approach ensuring that humans function within the food chain, not solely as consumers but also as possible consumables. In this manner, Indigenous-made zombie narratives ensure that there will be enough to feed the kingdom . . . until the end of time.

NOTES

1. *The Thing* (1982), *Puppet Masters* (1994), *The Faculty* (1998), *Starship Troopers 2: Hero of the Federation* (2004), and *The Host* (2013), just to name a few.

2. There are a number of narratives about zombie-like figures, such as the windigo/wendigo/wheetago, in addition to those listed here. Additionally, many of these narratives draw on the language and allude to these Indigenous zombie-like figures. However, only the narratives listed here use the term "zombie," and it could be problematic to assume Indigenous figures as zombies without the authors or filmmakers deliberately drawing attention to them.

3. Christopher Moore's article was originally published in 1995 at the height of viewership.

4. At the time of writing in 2022, ninety-six *Minutes* had been produced.

5. Critics such as Marjorie Johnstone, Ian Angus, Phil Ryan, and Minelle Mahtani have noted that paradox is an inherent part of Canadian identity.

6. Cârstocea's synchronous nationalisms are initially in reference to southeastern Europe.

BIBLIOGRAPHY

Asenap, Jason. 2020. "Indigenous People Face Down Zombies and Win in 'Blood Quantum.'" *High Country News*, April 30. https://www.hcn.org/articles/indigenous -affairs-indigenous-people-face-down-zombies-and-win-in-blood-quantum.

Barnaby, Jeff, dir. 2019. *Blood Quantum*. Prospector Films.

Béland, Gabriel. 2021. "'Salmon War' 40 Years Ago: 'The Reaction May Have Been Too Harsh.'" *Toronto Star*, June 11. https://www.thestar.com/news/canada/2021/06/11/salmon -war-40-years-ago-the-reaction-may-have-been-too-harsh.html.

Belcourt, Billy-Ray. 2016. "A Poltergeist Manifesto." *Feral Feminisms*, no. 6: 22–32. https:// feralfeminisms.com/a-poltergeist-manifesto/.

Bishop, Kyle William. 2015. *How Zombies Conquered Popular Culture: The Multifarious Walking Dead in the 21st Century*. Jefferson, NC: McFarland.

Black, Sarah-Tai. 2020. "Blood Quantum's Jeff Barnaby on the History and Horror of His Indigenous Zombie Movie: 'I Feel Like I Barely Got Out of This One Alive.'" *Globe and Mail* (Toronto), April 27. https://www.theglobeandmail.com/arts/film/article-blood -quantums-jeff-barnaby-on-the-history-and-horror-of-his/.

Bowen, Christopher J., and Roy Thompson. 2013. *Grammar of the Shot*. New York: Focal Press.

Bramesco, Charles. 2020. "'I'm Indigenizing Zombies': Behind Gory First Nation Horror *Blood Quantum*." *Guardian*, April 28. https://www.theguardian.com/film/2020/apr/28/blood-quantum-horror-film.

Bryant, Rachel. 2017a. "Canadian Exceptionalism Is about Land and Resources." Early Canadian History, April 10. https://earlycanadianhistory.ca/2017/04/10/canadian-exceptionalism-is-about-land-and-resources/.

Bryant, Rachel. 2017b. *The Homing Place: Indigenous and Settler Literary Legacies of the Atlantic*. Waterloo, ON: Wilfred Laurier University Press.

Burnham, Michelle. 2014. "Is There an Indigenous Gothic?" In *A Companion to American Gothic*, edited by Charles L. Crow, 223–37. Chichester, W. Susx., England: John Wiley and Sons.

Carleton, Sean. 2020. "Decolonizing the Zombie Apocalypse: An Interview with Jeff Barnaby about His New Film 'Blood Quantum.'" Canadian Dimension, April 26. https://canadiandimension.com/articles/view/decolonizing-the-zombie-apocalypse-an-interview-with-jeff-barnaby-about-his-new-film-blood-quantum.

Cârstocea, Raul. 2022. "Synchronous Nationalisms: Reading the History of Nationalism in South-Eastern Europe between and beyond the Binaries." *National Identities* 24, no. 5: 481–503.

CBC News. 2021. "40 Years after Listuguj Salmon Raids, Mi'kmaw Community Is Asserting Control over Ancestral Fishing Rights." June 11. https://www.cbc.ca/news/canada/montreal/40-years-listuguj-salmon-raids-leads-to-fishing-agreements-1.6062729.

Cole, Selina R., and Melanie J. Hopkins. 2021. "Selectivity and the Effect of Mass Extinctions on Disparity and Functional Ecology." *Science Advances* 7, no. 19: 1–11.

Condor, Jacques L. [Maka Tai Meh]. 2013. "Those Beneath the Bog." In *Dead North: Canadian Zombie Fiction*, edited by Silvia Moreno-Garcia, 132–63. Holstein, ON: Exile Editions.

Dyer, Kester. 2020. "Anticipating the Colonial Apocalypse: Jeff Barnaby's *Blood Quantum*." In *Pandemic Media: Preliminary Notes toward an Inventory*, edited by Philipp Dominik Keidl, Laliv Melamed, Vinzenz Hediger, and Antonio Somaini, 363–73. Lüneburg, Germany: Meson Press.

Elliott, Alicia. 2019. "The Rise of Indigenous Horror: How a Fiction Genre Is Confronting a Monstrous Reality." CBC Arts, October 17. https://www.cbc.ca/arts/the-rise-of-indigenous-horror-how-a-fiction-genre-is-confronting-a-monstrous-reality-1.5323428.

Environmental Magazine. 2001. "A Run on the Banks: How 'Factory Fishing' Decimated Newfoundland Cod." February 28. https://web.archive.org/web/20110520115335/http://www.emagazine.com/archive/507.

Goddu, Teresa A. 1997. *Gothic America: Narrative, History, and Nation*. New York: Columbia University Press.

Goddu, Teresa A. 2000. "Introduction to *American Gothic*." In *The Horror Reader*, edited by Ken Gelder, 265–70. London: Routledge.

Gordon, Avery F. 2020. "Revolutionary Feminisms: Avery F. Gordon." Interview by Brenna Bhandar and Rafeef Ziadah. Verso Books, September 2. https://www.versobooks.com/blogs/news/4842-revolutionary-feminisms-avery-f-gordon.

Gordon, Scott. 2020. "The Colonial Zombie Whiplash of 'Blood Quantum.'" Tone Madison, October 20. https://www.tonemadison.com/articles/the-colonial-zombie-whiplash-of-blood-quantum.

Gore, Amy. 2018. "Gothic Silence: S. Alice Callahan's *Wynema*, the Battle of the Little Bighorn, and the Indigenous Unspeakable." *Studies in American Indian Literatures* 30, no. 1 (Spring): 24–49.

Graham, David. 2012. "Sixty More Seconds of Canadian History." *Toronto Star*, October 15.

Halperin, Victor, dir. 1932. *White Zombie*. United Artists.

Haraway, Donna. 2003. *The Companion Species Manifesto: Dogs, People, and Significant Otherness*. Chicago: Prickly Paradigm Press.

Haraway, Donna. 2010. "*When Species Meet*: Staying with the Trouble." *Environment and Planning D: Society and Space* 28, no. 1: 53–55.

Haraway, Donna. 2018. "Staying with the Trouble for Multispecies Environmental Justice." *Dialogues in Human Geography* 8, no. 1: 102–5.

Haraway, Donna. 2019. "It Matters What Stories Tell Stories; It Matters Whose Stories Tell Stories." *Auto/Biography Studies* 34, no. 3: 565–75.

Heiderich, Timothy. N.d. "Cinematography Techniques: The Different Types of Shots in Film." Videomaker. https://oma.on.ca/en/contestpages/resources/free-report-cinematography.pdf.

Heritage Minutes. 1991. "John Cabot." Historica Canada. https://www.historicacanada.ca/content/heritage-minutes/john-cabot.

Heritage Minutes. 2005a. "Home from the Wars." Historica Canada. https://www.historicacanada.ca/content/heritage-minutes/home-wars.

Heritage Minutes. 2005b. "Tommy Prince." Historica Canada. https://www.historicacanada.ca/content/heritage-minutes/tommy-prince.

Innuksuk, Nyla, dir. 2022. *Slash/Back*. Sierra/Affinity.

Jackson, Lisa, dir. 2009. *Savage*. Lisa Jackson: Filmmaker. https://lisajackson.ca/filter/fiction/Savage.

Jackson, Steven J., and Pam Ponic. 2001. "Pride and Prejudice: Reflecting on Sport Heroes, National Identity, and Crisis in Canada." In *Sport and Memory in North America*, edited by Stephen G. Wieting, 43–62. London: Frank Cass.

Jones, Stephen Graham. 2012. *Zombie Bake-Off*. Portland, OR: Lazy Fascist Press.

Jones, Stephen Graham. 2014. *Chapter Six*. N.p.: Tor Books.

Lazowski, Anna. 2015. "One Photograph Shaped How Everyone Saw the Oka Crisis." CBC Radio, September 18. https://www.cbc.ca/radio/unreserved/reflections-of-oka-stories-of-the-mohawk-standoff-25-years-later-1.3232368/one-photograph-shaped-how-everyone-saw-the-oka-crisis-1.3232786.

Leggatt, Judith. 2019. "Reconciliation, Resistance, and *Biskaabiiyang*: Re-Imagining Canadian Residential Schools in Indigenous Speculative Fictions." In *Canadian Science Fiction, Fantasy, and Horror: Bridging the Solitudes*, edited by Amy J. Ransom and Dominick Grace, 135–49. Cham, Switzerland: Palgrave Macmillan.

Metcalfe, Alan. 1987. *Canada Learns to Play: The Emergence of Organized Sport, 1807–1914*. Toronto: McClelland and Stewart.

Miller, Liz, and Kester Dyer. 2020. "Critical Transportability and Indigenous VR." Presentation to the Immersivity and Technological Innovations Virtual Conference, October 28, Montreal. https://www.youtube.com/watch?v=ME6koD4HT7U.

Moore, Christopher. 1995. "Our History, Minute by Minute." *The Beaver* 75, no. 3 (June): 53–55.

Munro, Kathleen. 2020. "Northern Cod Failure Continues as Fisheries and Oceans Canada Rolls Over Last Year's Harmful Decision to Hike Up Quota." Globe Newswire, July 9. https://www.globenewswire.com/news-release/2020/07/09/2059898/0/en/Northern -Cod-Failure-Continues-as-Fisheries-and-Oceans-Canada-Rolls-Over-Last-Year-s -Harmful-Decision-to-Hike-Up-Quota.html.

National Post. 2019. "Land at Centre of Oka Crisis Surrendered by Quebec Developer, 29 Years Later." July 11. https://nationalpost.com/news/developer-offers-disputed-oka-land -to-kanesatake-mohawks-as-ecological-gift#:~:text=On%20Thursday%2C%20the%20 29th%20anniversary,in%20a%20phone%20interview%20Thursday.

Newell, C. H. 2020. "*Blood Quantum* Takes a Nasty Bite Out of Colonialism and Whiteness." Father Son Holy Gore, May 9. https://fathersonholygore.com/2020/05/09/ blood-quantum-takes-a-nasty-bite-out-of-colonialism-whiteness/.

Norcliffe, Glen. 1999. "John Cabot's Legacy in Newfoundland: Resource Depletion and the Resource Cycle." *Geography* 84, no. 2 (April): 97–109.

Obomsawin, Alanis, dir. 1984. *Incident at Restigouche.* National Film Board of Canada.

Peters, Erin. 2013. "The *Heritage Minutes*: Nostalgia, Nationalism, and Canadian Collective Memory." In *The Memory Effect: The Remediation of Memory in Literature and Film,* edited by Russell J. A. Kilbourn and Eleanor Ty, 249–66. Waterloo, ON: Wilfrid Laurier University Press.

Pocowatchit, Rodrick, dir. 2010. *The Dead Can't Dance.* Vision Maker Media.

Praskievicz, Sarah. 2019. "The Myth of Abundance: Water Resources in Humid Regions." *Water Policy* 21, no. 5 (September): 1065–80.

Pringle, Heather. 1997. "Cabot, Cod and the Colonists." *Canadian Geographic* 117, no. 4 (July–August): 31–39.

Reid, Emily. 2013. "Heritage Minutes." *The Canadian Encyclopedia*, July 14. Updated by Nicki Thomas and Andrew McIntosh, April 11, 2024. https://thecanadianencyclopedia .ca/en/article/heritage-minutes.

Rukszto, Katarzyna. 2005. "The Other Heritage Minutes: Satirical Reactions to Canadian Nationalism." *Topia: Canadian Journal of Cultural Studies* 14 (Fall): 73–91.

Savoy, Eric. 1998. "The Face of the Tenant: A Theory of American Gothic." In *American Gothic: New Interventions in a National Narrative,* edited by Robert K. Martin and Eric Savoy, 3–19. Iowa City: University of Iowa Press.

Simonpillai, Radheyan. 2019. "TIFF 2019: Indigenous Artists Are Using Horror to Unpack Colonial Trauma." *Now Toronto,* September 4. https://nowtoronto.com/movies/news -features/indigenous-horror-blood-quantum-tiff-2019.

Starrs, D. Bruno. 2014. "Writing Indigenous Vampires: Aboriginal Gothic or Aboriginal Fantastic?" *M/C Journal* 17, no. 4. https://www.journal.media-culture.org.au/index.php/ mcjournal/article/view/834.

Thorne, Tammy. 2020. "Plan to Put Critically Depleted Northern Cod on a Healthy Path Long Overdue, Says Oceana Canada." Oceana, April 28. https://oceana.ca/en/press-center/press-releases/plan-put-critically-depleted-northern-cod-healthy-path-long-overdue-says#:~:text=Although%20northern%20cod%20continues%20to,and%2010%2C559%20tonnes%20in%202019.

Van Camp, Richard. 2013. "On the Wings of This Prayer." In *Dead North: Canadian Zombie Fiction*, edited by Silvia Moreno-Garcia, 164–73. Holstein, ON: Exile Editions.

Wald, Priscilla. 2021. Preface to *Embodying Contagion: The Viropolitics of Horror and Desire in Contemporary Discourse*, edited by Sandra Becker, Megen de Bruin-Molé, and Sara Polak, xiii–xviii. Cardiff: University of Wales Press.

Wells, Jennifer. 2022. "A Warrior, a Soldier and a Photographer: Remembering the Oka Crisis." *Toronto Star*, August 22. https://www.thestar.com/news/insight/2015/08/22/a-warrior-a-soldier-and-a-photographer-remembering-the-oka-crisis.html.

West, Emily. 2002. "Selling Canada to Canadians: Collective Memory, National Identity, and Popular Culture." *Critical Studies in Media Communication* 19, no. 2: 212–29.

Wilkes, Rima, and Michael Kehl. 2014. "One Image, Multiple Nationalisms: *Face to Face* and the Siege at Kanehsatà:ke." *Nations and Nationalism* 20, no. 3 (April): 481–502.

Wright, Joanne H. 2004. *Origin Stories in Political Thought: Discourses on Gender, Power, and Citizenship*. Toronto: University of Toronto Press.

Yamato, Jen. 2020. "How Indigenous Zombie Horror Film 'Blood Quantum' Became Prescient in the Pandemic." *Los Angeles Times*, May 8. https://www.latimes.com/entertainment-arts/movies/story/2020-05-08/blood-quantum-indigenous-horror-zombie-pandemic-jeff-barnaby

CHAPTER 3

WAYS OF THEORIZING AND TRANSIENT PHENOMENA (SECTION I)

NAOMI SIMONE BORWEIN

In mainstream Canadian news, Dene Elder Jonas Antoine describes his "awed" engagement with the aurora borealis: "[W]histle to the northern lights. And whistling makes them dance. But if they're down too low, . . . [t]hey'll come down and chop your head off. . . . We truly believed it, because you know when you whistle, they really do come down" (interviewed in Barton 2019). Elsewhere (Cheyenne and Arapaho) Shane Hawk and (Mackinac Bands of Chippewa and Ottawa Indians) Theodore C. Van Alst Jr.'s coedited volume *Never Whistle at Night: An Indigenous Dark Fiction Anthology* (2023) is marketed as "sublimely sinister," as per the publisher's back-cover copy, and Blackfoot storyteller Alex Soop's collection *Whistle at Night and They Will Come: Indigenous Horror Stories*, volume 2 (2023), is placed as part of a "wicked glimpse" of the genre of Indigenous Horror, likewise as per the publisher's blurb. They are both Horror titles that reference Indigenous oral myths of the northern lights. Elsewhere, Indigiqueer thriller *Kwêskosîw: She Whistles* (2021), a short film directed by Plains Cree Thirza Cuthand, is another overt example of the use of the oral myth. It is "almost universal," changing from "nation to nation, but basically the same thing: don't whistle at the northern lights" or don't whistle at night, "and don't disturb the ancestors" (Simpson 2021). Within popular speculative genre criticism, the unseen, dispersive, and misapprehended horror of transient phenomena, like the aurora borealis or aurora australis, are trussed to Indigeneity. The Indigenous methodological framework applied to this chapter on the aurora, its various aspects and related audio/visual transfers onto the land and into the sky, extends the experiential journey approach of the volume. Indigenous ways of knowing are used to enact an exploratory examination of a western metaphor (e.g., a transient or transformative metaphor like the aurora). Such a metaphor is widely visible in diverse Indigenous oral myths and gets used to stereotype and sell Indigenous Horror in the mainstream, but is also sometimes utilized in Indigenous fiction. Thus, the journey/ing process is used to examine a mixture of high theory and Indigenous ways of knowing to delineate "ways of theorizing" (theorizing that privileges ways of knowing) Indigenous Horror.

In a variety of Indigenous Horror volumes and visual pieces, the northern/southern lights, or painted sky, transform from a cosmogonic myth of heterogeneous traditions (hoʻomanawanui 2018, 123; Noori 2013; Wilson 2014). Such celestial spectacles transform into abstract functionality in Horror theorizing. Here, non-Indigenous cosmic subjectivity (Deleuze and Guattari [1987] 2004) and traditionally uneasy relations with metaphysics collide, creating incommensurate understandings of being in/of materialities and objective becoming (Hart 2021, 81–85; de Freitas and Sinclair 2013, 454; Skow 2015, 44). The reimagining of perceptual-conceptual systems through Indigenous ways of knowing, iteratively and situationally, realign theoretical frameworks, or frames of references. In mainstream culture, "dark possibilities" of the northern lights are genrefied and anthropomorphized into solar "flare[s] fatale" (Slade 2013, 20) through exoticizing, romanticizing, or fetishizing lenses. For instance, they are embodied paratextually in the ambient and atmospheric resonance of preternatural (Anthropocene) light, often "Indigenized" in Horror discourses (Bacon 2022; Edwards, Graulund, and Höglund 2022). In criticism and popular fiction, a global diaspora projecting "Indigenous" images and knowledges transforms ways of knowing, which are then tinctured with non-Indigenous metaphors. These hybrid metaphors, in turn, inadvertently transform ways of apprehending the symbolic schema of the metaphor of the aurora itself. Such a fusion of Indigenous and non-Indigenous origins induces a rejection by Indigenous scholars, and a disruption of the "haunting glossaries" or categorization systems of Horror metaphors (Walkiewicz 2021; Garba and Sorentino 2020; Tuck and Yang 2012; Tuck and Ree 2013; P. Cole 2006). Processes of visual/oral codification moving into and out of contemporary speculative genres imply the use of a generative and hybrid form of co-becoming extant in Indigenous Horror fiction. To develop an understanding of horror elements as part of a distinct theoretical construct (or way of theorizing) in Indigenous speculative fiction relies on integrating or bringing together analyses of texts and self-identifying authors' perceptions of their own craft-practice (see chapter 4). For example, Gina Cole's (Pasifika) Pasifikafuturist "whirlpool" in *Na Viro* (2022) in juxtaposition to the paradigm of the dark matter vortex (G. Cole 2020) is used to reimagine the movement and meaning of celestial systems that "paint the sky." Dan Rabarts's (Ngāti Porou) spiritual ethical temporal-spatial experimentations with dark fantasy settings textualize the aurora australis as "impending planetary apocalypse" (see his interview in this volume). Conversely, Stephen Graham Jones (Blackfoot) indicates an abstract conceptualization of a theoretical horror moment or cascade of moments (interview in this volume)—within an Indigenous frame of reference, and alongside questioning of what constitutes authentic ("valid") and often essentialist Indigenous tropes or stereotypes in Horror fiction. While the analysis in this chapter builds partly on Indigenous and non-Indigenous metaphor, it is not an application of metaphor but instead an interrogation of its form, and its associated genre taxonomy. Thus, the argument in this chapter traces the often clichéd and ultimately diffuse lens of aurorae to inspect the hybrid, exploratory, and generative ("theoretic") space of new global heterogeneous Indigenous Horror.

Defining the aurora (the northern, southern, or arctic lights) through ways of theorizing means asking integratory or interpretive questions—How? Why? Where? When?—about the expression and life of the aurora as a visualization and a transient interactive alternative to western Horror praxis, which helps articulate a conceptual Horror model. What follows is an experiential rupture of linear western thought processes. The aurora has a long colonial history of capturing the colonial imagination. The phenomenological and celestial states of aurorae are also embedded in Indigenous oral tradition and are variously seen as representative of the following: spirits, Creation, and fragments of oral memory; extensions of cosmological, cosmogonical, and cultural knowledge systems; and associated super-supra-terrestrial and astronomical phenomena like blazing stars, comets, meteors, rainbows, and clouds. The western (scientific) perspective on this light display of varying color and intensity is often heavily romanticized. However, the spirals and ripples, waves, and curtains of light are seen in western science as the result of "disturbances in the magnetosphere caused by solar" winds and storms (Khare 2019, 261), which alter the trajectories of charged particles in its plasma. Pushed down into the atmosphere or siphoned off in an interaction-exchange, they manifest, for example, in ecological and Sci-Fi or Cli-Fi Horror as transitional moments and ruptures of the logic of epistemological systems (visible for instance in Chickasaw author Linda Hogan's 1994 *Solar Storms* or Gina Cole's 2022 *Na Viro*). To a western gaze, comets host aurorae because they cause disturbances in electrons. Consider one Anishinaabe concept: "Comets of Knowledge" or "networks of understanding" between "humans, animals, and forces not seen" and "the space and sparks around them" (Noori 2013, 35, 37) are symbolic of an Indigenous alternative to metaphor that encompasses untranslatable elements of, for instance, Anishinaabe language and visual-oral associations, through the "sounds, morphemes, and transitive animate constructions that do not even exist in English" (55). These elements are the nonlinear connections of "nature" and the "universe" such as that visible in an "Anishinaabe view of the constellations Orion and the Pleiades" (54). This sort of transmaterial relational order has similarities in heterogeneous Indigenous cultures. (That is to say that relational orders may have different frames of reference or relationality.) For instance, through a completely different tribe-specific knowledge system, in *Legendary Tales of the Australian Aborigines*, arguably the first "Aboriginal Australian" Horror author, David Unaipon (Ngarrandjeri), describes how "[a]ll the stars and constellations in the heavens, the Milky Way, the Southern Cross, Orion's Belt, the Magellan's Cloud, have a meaning . . . [and] legends connected with them all" ([1930] 2006, 7). Suggestive of a topographical or even a topological patterning, where "[t]he oval line may represent the sun on its course, or to be more exact, my race has the knowledge of the earth's motion. There are old men in each tribe who study the stars and their positions in the Heavens at night, at certain times of the year" (10). The embedded connectivity of meaning in the aforementioned examples can be understood as disruptions of metaphor theory and "applicable" categories of horror through relation, orientation, and interaction with said "transient phenomena."

If metaphors can be thought of as non-Indigenous symbolic concept systems, while "comets of knowledge" reflect a nonlinear, layered Indigenous and animate matrix, then, for instance, meteors within Aboriginal Australian Dreamings similarly reflect another interrelated transformative scaffolding. But western scientific knowledge systems observe that comets host aurorae. Drawing on oral testimony and other data as a form of cultural astronomy or cultural ethnography, Duane W. Hamacher and Ray P. Norris note that meteors represent the impact of "meteoritic phenomena and material (including comets, meteors, meteorites, tektites, and cosmic impacts) on society" (2010, 88). A subset of "[Aboriginal] groups believed that a deceased person's flesh could transform into a star or vice-versa" or even "fireballs" or entities, "spirits of the deceased" (90). Indeed, "[t]he Yir-Yoront of Cape York Peninsula believed that when a man died, his spirit became a star, with the transformation accompanied by a meteor" (Lauriston Sharp, quoted in Hamacher and Norris 2010, 90). This description implicitly binds material levels of transformation and generative *being* with the cosmos—manifested through the aurora. (Note that careful navigation of ethnographic, oral, and translated Indigenous knowledge is essential for understanding how this image and metaphor gets read in the mainstream.)

As an alternative logic system, the mathematical lens'—indicated by, for instance, Unaipon's "oval line"—is used to evince Indigenous star mapping and celestial objects. Various distinct Indigenous understandings bolster interchanges of "making" and "unmaking" between oral tradition and Creation(s) in/through/with/of the northern/southern lights. For instance, conceptually this can be understood through the projection of the northern lights onto what Robin Wall Kimmerer of the Potawatomi Nation describes as the living snow—"for the death of rivers and the memory of snow" (2013, 383)—mapped onto the "knowledge garden" (Peterson 2023), where snow, as one multifarious way of knowing, refracts the knowledge in the sky and is made substantive and material. Elsewhere, in Aboriginal Australian cultures, the southern lights project onto the sculptured configurations and pictograms of constellations that are carved in the rocks and rivulets of New South Wales, exposing the connection between sky and land. Examples of such space, time, and being "conceptualized" through "tracking the movements of the stars and planets" are also visible among the Skidi Pawnee and Native Pueblo (Ezeife 2011, 4). Consider star mapping as a representation of (more than) the material, spiritual, and theoretical world. It is an example of (not)metaphor (extending Mohawk scholar Edward Doolittle's notion of not/math), a simultaneous, dynamic conceptualization for apprehending a vision of the constituent relational working parts of the "universe" through a star map as described by Ojibwe elders. In particular, in William Wilson's map included in *Ojibwe Sky Star Map*, he employs

> traditional Ojibwe x-ray style to paint the Ojibwe constellations. This style is symbolic of seeing the unseen. It is an allegory for the material world and spirit world. The brightly colored internal organs and anatomical shapes are a glimpse into the inner layers of our bodies. . . . We are seeing the picture as the spirits see us. They see right through. (Lee et al. 2014, 2)

These anatomical shapes and brightly colored internal organs shifting in the cosmos imply celestial phenomena of Creation stories and are mirrored in the dramatic visual displays of the aurora as part of Creation myth. Additionally, as described through the *Ojibwe Sky Star Map*, this un/seen being and (what a non-Indigenous scholar would conceive of as) materiality offers a capture of a conceptual moment, or unit, that is helpful for understanding ways of theorizing Indigenous horror aesthetics and narrative structures/patterns. If aurorae are representationally the "river of light" or "river of stars" through various interpretations and traditions, and "everything" "is in the stars" (Lee et al. 2014, 36), as told by an anonymous Ojibwe Elder, then "[w]hen a person dies, it is said 'shiikawasegaa,' which means, 'no more light, the light moves on,'" and the elder refers to the spirit as "starlight" (28). The movement of light becomes one multifoliate scaffolding or pathway for understanding various matrices of knowledge under the umbrella of the aurora.

In examining adaptations of media, forms of auditory and visual story-ing, and sensory data to explore ways of theorizing, consider first Matthew Lyon Hazzard (2019), who uses Ēriks Ešenvalds's six-movement score *River of Light* (2014), itself a "sonic analog" to the northern lights: an "analog for the otherwise silent wonder of the aurorae" (Hazzard 2019, 1). This is, in fact, a misinterpretation of the audible crackles and whistles of the northern lights described by Dene Elder Jonas Antoine (Barton 2019). Hazzard views this as an attempt "to capture the oscillations, changes in color, and atmo-spheric qualities of the lights through sound" (Hazzard 2019, 1). Sound is an important counternarrative in visual storytelling. However, from a western scientific perspective, simulating the dynamics of auroral phenomena through a visualization framework that explores virtual astronomy on a large scale (e.g., Fu 2003, 228) is a counter to the conceptual model of Gina Cole's Pasifi-kafuturist holographic three-dimensional whirlpool—an anti- or not/- meta-phor—where "lights sparked inside the holographic maelstrom" (2022, 49) and "lights flashed and exploded along the meteor's edges. A series of sonic booms . . . vibrating" (45), experienced and embodied textually in virtual reality simulation. From a western perspective, this framework unpacks the dynamic constructs of visuospatial reasoning and astrological community, through panoramic images and knowledges' spatial reasoning recognition (Fu 2003, 228). It may seem similar but is at a perpendicular to Gina Cole's anticolonial inspection of celestial phenomena (which are communal, spiri-tual, and individual) through Indigenous Oceanic meaning systems. The multilayered actualization-conceptualization approach in Gina Cole's *Na Viro* (2022) resembles Keziah Wallis and Miriam Ross's (2021) exploration of "Fourth" Virtual Reality Indigeneity, transmediating Barry Barclay's Te Ao Māori—or the Māori world's—Fourth Cinema. Cole's celestially coded holo-graphic whirlpool, reflected and refracted from the cosmos onto the water, thus allows one to read slippery "genre" elements with a critical awareness of visual-abstract-conceptual meanings, drawing on, for instance, Pasifika knowledges. Having experientially unsettled the standard western lens or thought process through the above examples, now consider the construction and "definition" of Indigenous Horror through the labels of literature, genre, and metaphor through the co-becoming of theory and practice.

THE CO-BECOMING OF THEORY AND PRACTICE

A key contention in debates about the genrefication of Indigenous horror, be it lived or mythic, is the appropriation of cultural knowledge and caricature of meaning itself through stock Horror tropes and metaphors. Their praxis is often cast as the liminality of genre elements that have shifting (global, often cosmogonic-anthropologic) meanings: for instance, the supernatural in *From Animus to Zombi* (Gibson and VanderVeen 2022) as speculative erasure of cultural specificity, which forms a transformative metaphor and lens. What is metaphor and how can it be cross-culturally understood?

(NOT)METAPHOR: ON METHODS AND APPROACHES

Armand Garnet Ruffo notes in "Inside Looking Out: Reading Tracks from a Native Perspective" that there is a long literature on "the problem of cross-cultural interpretation" (1993, 163). It is exacerbated by what is universal to whom (Boscov-Ellen 2020, 70; Borwein, Glanfield, and Jungic 2022), and by the global and local rendering of Indigeneity from the perspective of both Indigenous nation(s) and dominant nation-state(s)—impacted by the range and scope of Indigenous cultures worldwide (hoʻomanawanui 2018, 123). In reading metaphor, the critic once had to "rely on ethnological information to interpret the metaphorical structures and their thematic import," coding, decoding, and recoding with a loss of context (Ruffo 1993, 163). It is a phenomena of symbolic meaning expounded on by George Steiner in *After Babel* through a poststructural, semiotic grid that is incommensurate with Indigenous knowledge (1998, xiv). Chippewa scholar Gerald Vizenor explores such concepts, interrogating Steiner's theorizing about semiotics and translation (Vizenor 2008, 1). In *The Sacred Hoop*, Paula Gunn Allen states that critics "must clarify symbols and allusions . . . must define or describe whole perceptual-interpretive systems" (1986, 2)—representations of the aurora can be thought of as a metaphor system. Influential studies on Indigenous methodologies have relied on ideas around metaphor and conceptual framing to provide a process for centering Indigenous knowledges (Kovach 2021, 81). (Not)metaphor can be understood as a variable for a logical alternative to western metaphor, espoused by Paul Ricoeur and Ferdinand de Saussure, with disrupted hierarchies of parataxis and para-hypotaxis for metaphor and its related metonymy—which acknowledges the inability to articulate a one-to-one translation of meaning from non-Indigenous to Indigenous forms. (Not)metaphor can be extended to an interrogation of the system(s) of meaning.

Genre is another system or taxonomy of meaning. In the introduction to *Black Marks on the White Page*, Witi Ihimaera and Tina Makereti frame their edited volume with the following Indigenous Oceanic understanding of genre: "Perhaps the division between different forms—fiction, creative nonfiction and poetry—doesn't necessarily make sense to an Indigenous Oceanic world view. Word | stories | art | songs | dance | mythologies | ancestors | film | contemporary life | poetry" as categories or units "may all exist in the same moment, in the same space, and none of it is untrue" or invalid (2017, 12). A contributor to Ihimaera's volume, Gina Cole elsewhere notes: "Oceanic writers do not see genre divisions in the same way as the white literary establishment" (2020, 47), further stating that such writers exist "behind a shroud of invisible and shifting definitions of genre" (47), as a transient or motile phenomenon like representations of the aurora. "[S]tylistic innovation . . . comes from the border crossings that many of our writers are making between literature" and other forms, "various genres of literature," and platforms and visual arts (Ihimaera and Makereti 2017, 12). It is in this space-time that constructs of theorizing are born, and these reflect the kinds of experimentation that can take place when "worlds intersect" (12). Here, practice "exemplifies the kaupapa," principles or ideas as foundational for action, set in relation to Whakapapa, a Māori concept (13). Kaupapa is reconceived within *Black Marks on the White Page* as "complex, diverse, and rich histories and cultures" (13). A similar stance on discourse and genre in relation to Aboriginal Literature (and ways of knowing) in Australia can be found within Adam Shoemaker's 1989 *Black Words White Page*. Peter Cole of the Douglas First Nation (Xa'xtsa Nation)—in what is known as British Columbia—enacts an intertextual journey in and through his volume *Coyote and Raven Go Canoeing* (2006, 27). Cole explores the dichotomy between black words and the white page through a conversation between Indigenous peoples from around the globe.

In written passages, syntax, and the schemas of knowledge association (or relations), metaphor and the meaning of languages are in stark juxtaposition to "semiotics." The aurora system is a constellation of meanings and levels of materiality. The following example showcases one way of reading relationality in such a model. For instance, the story of the Blackfoot bee is a warning to respect the natural world, illustrated as motion, arc, the sound the bee makes as it glides, and the relation, distance, and abstraction to environmental positioning of its meaning (Czuy 2021) in writing and how this presents in textual, seemingly descriptive and metaphoric (mesh of radial), languages. It is a feature of the reassociation of meaning and knowledges. What happens in this conceptual-actualization description when the Blackfoot bee turns around and stings you, as it might in a Horror fiction?

Building an approach with a heterogeneous (Global) Indigenous community network, and using the neologism "i/teriture" in the place of western "literature" designations, as utilized by Peter Cole (2006, 153), orality is made the foundation of the epistemological approach to "writing sp a ces" (3)[2] as a rejection of the "exoticized" other, demonized other, "contained" other; the work challenges "everything [that] has become academized anthropologized even indigenousness the cult of white-expertise permeates   who validates whom?" "filled with saccharine clichés" (153). The text actively employs "metaphor" (152), syntactic, sequentially and visually emphasized by the distilled (intentionally disrupted semiotic) relations between white/black space and black/white ink, and the process as a "canoe journey shaped out of words" (26). Some of the experimental white space represents the voices and understandings of the First Peoples of Canada as white ink, "ineffable silence" (26, 27). From the section "Shaping the Canoe" (21) to "In Creating a Framework" (24), to develop this approach using microvariations of language and meaning reconceptualized experimentally, Cole continues "with the transfer of these words from computer screen pencil   pen / thought feeling spirit sound to paper," extended to "the canoe comes [*sic*] from   the forest and from place of mind spirit memory ancestor . . . it might seem the canoe and tree are from a conceptual space they are from spirit   and heart" (24). Herein "meanings beyond western rationality" of "the supernatural of myth of reading nature," the ways of knowing before "iconography" highlight "the value of powerful teaching of the supernatural domain of the interconnection of all things" through "what and who is   *reflection refraction diffusion diffraction*" (157, 3). Popular use of the aurora in Indigenous Horror representations follow a tendency in mainstream culture to read indigeneity through "the supernatural / of myth of reading nature" (24, 157). In the context of Indigenous Horror, this method draws on conceptual-visual frameworks, centers Indigenous Knowledges (Kovach 2021, 45–46, 81; P. Cole 2006, 24), and makes space for the inherent hybridity of the form. Even the idea of place-based horror has to be reevaluated through, for example, what in Cree epistemology can be understood as "tools to help us enter a place, a sacred, beyond physical place," where "place does not capture what I want to say, since place is too often limited to physicality or, the more postmodern/poststructural conceptualization of location, and these tools are aspects of our means to access knowledge" (Michael Hart, interviewed in Kovach 2021, 85). (It is the same articulated issue: metaphor held captive by and fortified through a semiotic space.) Place is complicated by ideas around the sacred, Creation, and "cosmology" within Indigenous communities, where "[t]here are strict cultural protocols that must be respected" (Lee et al. 2014, 35) such as when and how some "stories are to be told" (36). In the context of horror, this is exponentially more problematic—entering into taboo (Dan Rabarts interview in this volume). Conceptual methodologies and theorizing work in tandem.

In exploring the genre label of Horror for/of/from Indigenous cultures, scaffolding outside standard classifications often draw on the production of oral aesthetics. In "Writing Voices Speaking," Kimberly M. Blaeser notes that some "[c]ontemporary Native authors work to translate" "language," "form, culture, and perspective. And within their written words, many attempt to continue the life of the oral reality," which presents a structure of "supra-literary intent" (1999, 53). This overtly presents in prefaces and fictions by Indigenous Horror authors such as Shane Hawk. Chippewa scholar Gerald Vizenor advocates bridging philological theories and practices in fiction as an "aesthetics of survivance," through the continuance of storytelling (1999, 1). His analysis is a rebuke of the metaphysical and poststructural constructs of Jacques Derrida and George Steiner—their intertextual universes, drawing implications for Indigenous languages and structures—emphasized by Vizenor's epigraph: "When a language dies, a possible world dies with it" (Steiner 1998, xiv, quoted in Vizenor 2008, 1). On the "symbolic practices of language" (Steiner 1998, 138), Steiner describes languages "making and remaking" (230), as disparate from being and becoming

> at the level of human psychic resources and survivance. . . . There even when it is spoken by a handful, by the harried remnants of destroyed communities, a language contains within itself the boundless potential of discovery, of re-compositions of reality, of articulate dreams, which are known to us as myths, as poetry, as metaphysical conjecture. (1998, xiv)

Vizenor's assessment ruptures these western hyperrealities that frame Indigenous identity (2008, 20). As part of an understanding of metaphor, the transmission of meaning, the categorization and relation of meaning, not only coconstructs but allocates horror and the rupture of domains, or spheres, outside or beyond the syntactic level (Vizenor 2008, 4). The "decolonial potential of horror and haunting" (Walkiewicz 2021, 403), drawing on the "haunting" lexicon of Eve Tuck and C. Ree (2013), further "disrupts the standard form and genre of the 'glossary' to problematize how a typical glossary *visually and discursively taxonomizes knowledge production*" (Walkiewicz 2021, 403, my emphasis). Conventionally, modern western genre can be thought of as the virtual transmission of data (meaning) through evolving, abstract constructs, systems, or units of knowledge. In a sense, the motility of concrete and abstract forms mimics aspects of how interactive transient phenomena, like aurorae, respond and effect other boundaries: (serpiginous) liminalities, geneses, narratives, images, symbols, and intersections. In narrative, the breaking down of systems and taxonomies creates junctures for horror events and Horror plot points. These constituent elements of structure(s) connote a prolix (not)metaphor, which is non-Western and can be reevaluated with Indigenous water-land-sky-based knowledges. These knowledges as ways of theorizing are a part of narrative landscapes in Indigenous Horror, through layers of sensory evocations and atmospheric and spectral associations.

HETEROGENEOUS AURORA MYTHS

The northern and southern lights have a long and bloody colonial history. In 1868, British artist and explorer Frederick Whymper wrote experientially of the aurora borealis in *Travel and Adventure in the Territory of Alaska*: "a graceful, undulating, ever-changing 'snake' of electric light; evanescent colours, pale as those of a lunar rainbow, ever and again flitting through it and long streamers and scintillations moving upward to the bright stars, which distinctly shone through its hazy, ethereal form" (178). Whymper's passage is part of a phantasmagoric engagement with scientific and natural phenomena in the Victorian era, mythologizing and romanticizing the beauty and mystery of the aurora in descriptive prose. Such images have become ubiquitous in the west, and in popular culture. There are similar observations of the Arctic and southern lights by Captain James Cook: arches and curtains of luminosity, of "spiral rays, and in a circular form" (1777, quoted in Akasofu 2009, 47), and yet Cook is a "purveyor" and "figure of horror for us [Indigenous peoples]" (Gina Cole interview in this volume).[3] In her back-cover endorsement of Robin Wall Kimmerer's *Braiding Sweetgrass* (2013), Elizabeth Gilbert writes that the author weaves "two lenses of knowledge together" as a "journey every bit as mythic as it is scientific, as sacred as it is historical," much like the intersectional imagery of the aurora as a metaphor. Such myths transcend heterogeneous Indigenous groups from around the world. Dene Elder Jonas Antoine describes his "awed" engagement with the "crackling" of the northern lights:

WAYS OF THEORIZING AND TRANSIENT PHENOMENA (SECTION I)   87

[W]histle to the northern lights. And whistling makes them dance. But if they're down too low, . . . [t]hey'll come down and chop your head off. . . . We truly believed it, because you know when you whistle, they really do come down. This is something your parents and your grandparents told you, so of course you believed them. Other parts of the North, they believed that you could inhale the northern lights and they would kill you. Some people say it's the spirits of children who were stillborn. (Interviewed in Barton 2019)

Variations on translated oral myths of aurorae are extant, as in the following:

a. "The Maoris thus believe that the southern lights (aurora austra-lis) are reflections in the sky of huge fires kindled by descendants of those ancient voyagers, who are signalling to their distant kinsmen in the Polynesian Isles" (Brekke and Egeland 1983, 2);

b. "The Mandan of North Dakota saw the aurora as fires over which the great medicine men and warriors of northern lands simmered their dead enemies in enormous pots" (Eather 1980, 111);

c. Point Barrow Inuit "dislike to go out on a dark night, but if obliged to, they generally carry a bone or ivory snow-knife or a long-bladed steel knife, to keep off Tuña and Kiolya (Aurora), which they believe to be equally evil; but Tuña especially is concerned in producing all the evils of life" (Ray et al. 1885, 42).[4]

As with (c) above, Ernest W. Hawkes's (1916) translation of Inuit aurora myths can be coded as a macabre inflection of oral tradition, when elements are read out of the Indigenous context from which the apprehension of horror arises:

The place to which the spirit finally takes its departure depends more on the mode of death of the deceased than the manner of his life. Those who have been murdered or have committed voluntary suicide and women who die in childbirth are recompensed with the highest heaven, located in the Aurora Borealis . . . playing football with a wal-rus head. . . . Deformed children who exhibit some monstrosity which aroused the supernatural fears of the Eskimo are strangled at birth. Those who die a violent death are compensated by *being translated* . . . [to the] Aurora Borealis. (Hawkes 1916, 137, 109, my emphasis)

Non-Indigenous and Indigenous theorizing about Indigenous Horror some-times draws on these ethnographic accounts of "monstrosity." The diaspora of oral tales in boundary tribes like the "Labrador Eskimos" underscores the "fragmentary or abbreviated form" (Hawkes 1916, 141) of many myths at their origin. Taking the portrayal of the aurora in "The Heavenly Regions" recorded by Hawkes in 1916, the first section of the passage reflects the scale and ratio of the epistemological space: "The ends of the land and sea are bounded by an immense abyss, over which a narrow and dangerous pathway leads to the heavenly regions. The sky is a great dome of hard material arched over the Earth. There is a hole in it through which the spirits pass to the true heavens" (153). There is an implicit horror in the unknown, outside the bounds of the known. The second section of the passage focuses on pathways of multisensory celestial phenomena: "The spirits who live there light torches to guide the feet of new arrivals. This is the light of the aurora" (153). Hawkes further describes how "[t]he whistling crackling noise which sometimes accompanies the aurora is the voices of these spirits trying to communicate with the people of the earth. They should always be answered in a whispering voice," and he concludes: "The heavenly spirits are called selamiut, 'sky-dwellers'" (153). Modern Indigenous Horror inspects the taboo of whistling at the northern lights or at night, disrupting the ancestors and Creation stories. Hawkes's translation or retelling accentuates how we (past-present-future) read and code the star-keepers' (or elders') tales of sky-dwellers. Such recoded interpretations, often superficially macabre, are skewed into dystopic hyperrealisms of myth and misarticulated metaphors from oral telling, translated into descriptive passages in Horror fictions in a "hyperpresent now" (Fricke 2019, 107). Yet, they implicitly pinpoint the motility of Indigenous ways of knowing as theorizing, like the stars rushing (crackling) through/with the sky in directional, shifting orientations, and the reallocation of material being/is/of "every/where other/wise" (P. Cole 2006, 49).

For Hawkes, the aurora metaphor, embedded in myth, is understood through multisensory pathways of spectral effects in parallel with a layered scale, ratio, and spatial temporalities, as an experiential, composite lens partly created by translation—which also punctuates moments of translation of the horrific. The afterlife of these myths, as oral knowledge transcribed into text, is a hybrid (altered) construct. Recapitulation and paraphrasing changes meaning. Such myths, and the structures of metaphors constituted in the passages (the interconnections and relationalities) should be read as a whole, in context, and understood that way—to avoid excessive loss of original meaning. Otherwise, from the perspective of ways of theorizing, the by-product of translation is potentially *horrific*. Contemporary Indigenous metaphor is undergirded by the orientational import of Hawkes's "immense abyss" (1916, 153), recalling Michael Fortescue's early research on

WAYS OF THEORIZING AND TRANSIENT PHENOMENA (SECTION I)   89

Inuit orientational systems and the relationality of the abyss waiting outside the cultural universe(s) of the Inuit (1988, 24). Suggestive of water- and land-based knowledge tinctured by a western vision, in Hawkes, "[t]he ends of the land and sea are bounded by an immense abyss, over which a narrow and dangerous pathway leads to the heavenly regions" (1916, 153), latently connecting the pathways, currents, structures, or trajectories of knowledge to the multisensory immersion/dispersion in/of aurora borealis, where the "sky is a great dome of hard material arched," a convex lens, "over the earth" (1916, 153), with a hole (an aperture) for transference of states of being. Through the action of knowledge systems, the transformation of flesh into stars chronicled in Indigenous witness testimony proffer a way of theorizing such transformations beyond the one-four+ (or Z) dimensional spaces of standard Global Horror theorizing.

HETEROGENEOUS (GLOBAL) INDIGENOUS LENSES

How does one understand ways of theorizing Horror, its symbolic-conceptual-metaphoric relational structures and patterning? What follows is a brief summary of select heterogeneous Indigenous lenses, which connect ways of knowing, and the structures and relationalities of light, color, water-fire-land-sky, celestial and transient phenomena, and more.

A parallel generalization of the concept framework of Mi'kmaq Two-Eyed Seeing is visible in the Yolngu, Haudenosaunee, and Māori traditions (Reid et al. 2021, 248). The structure of the Double Canoe of the Māori, with each canoe hull representing a worldview, implicitly extends to Aotearoa (the Māori name for New Zealand), translating into "the long white cloud" or "long bright land" (Pomare and Cowan 1907, 1:3) encircled by water and striated epistemologically by interactive foundations or actions of being, darkness, and light. The spiraling, whorls, and branching (netting) of nodes in braiding and weaving as theoretical constructs or ways of knowing have many permutations, seemingly ubiquitous across groups, which has led to a rejection by Indigenous scholars of theorizing "about indigenous weaving metaphors and textual interpenetration linguistic multifurcation" of "spindle whorls," and noils, read through primitivism (P. Cole 2006, 28). These motions and formations mirror the visual arrays and particulate relations of the aurora.

Consider two examples of objects that function as embodied ways of theorizing. In both the hogan (a geometrical, hexagonal domicile) and the Navajo circle inscribed within it, angles are in relation to ceremony, and song is in relation to artwork, as described by Navajo scholar Henry H. Fowler in his 2021 talk "Indigenous Ways of Knowing." Scale, ratios, and proportions in relation to a person's body give the hogan and the person a sense of "uniqueness"—as a theoretical notion divergent from the western stance on "mapping alternative ontology" (singular) through mathematical bodies and materiality (de Freitas and Sinclair 2013, 454) or objective becoming of moving spotlight theory in a block universe (Skow 2015, 44). With the movement inside the hogan (a hexagon with points A to H), a "slight change of 2 degrees in the observation of the sun's position" is understood as "[t]he shift of the earth, the axis that's causing climate change" (Fowler 2021). Circular movement around the outer wall of the hogan associated with an unmoving watcher in the center creates an invisible hexagon using the position of the "walker" (a notion that is tied to sky walkers and speculative Indigenous horror fictions). Positions at vertices such as F and G are "synchronized with their thought," corresponding to states of being, underlying the "beauty to envision and imagine the space. . . . Similarly to points B and H" (Fowler 2021). Winter solstice, "when the light comes in . . . is a representation of Orion," while "summer solstice is the Scorpius," "the changer the transformation" that "relate" to "how they travel" through the cosmos. Recall that Creation stories about the aurora also map such travel through the sky through spirit beings and the ancestors. The "Navajo practice of creating a hexagon" offers an encapsulated theoretical universe that presents *being* as physically concomitant with other states, in which the universe is guided partly by the movement and refraction of light presenting "nature as art" (Fowler 2021). (This is in contrast to western theorizing, such as James Bridle's 2022 *Ways of Being*, which inspects human-nonhuman planetary sentience and transformation in the cosmos.) The construction through the hogan is both a nexus and multifoliate space where theory forms, through light, shadow, movement, concentric layers of being, and integration between states, the cosmos, culture, and nature as defined by the Navajo; these are also cognitive structure(s) (Fowler 2010, 70). The hogan and Navajo circle have (intertribal) similarities to circles of the Niitsitapi (Blackfoot people)—due to common antecedents. Blackfoot medicine wheel circles use four colors: yellow east, red south, black west, and white north, with a cross in the center of the circle. The circle represents life, eternity, the universe or creator, and many other interconnected symbolic meanings. Stone circles are sacred sources of healing that connect Indigenous people to their internal selves and the world through ceremonies or as decoration (Friesen 1997, 137).

Indigenous scholar of Mayan ancestry Vivian M. Jiménez Estrada (2005) offers an example of a generalizable Indigenous conceptual framework for research methodology (44) that resonates with knowledges held in the hogan. Communicated through the metaphor of the Ceiba or Tree of Life: "Maya cosmology [cosmovision and understandings], as the Popol Vuh narrates, identifies reality not as linear and unidimensional but as circular and multidimensional. The Ceiba is the axis through which the world goes through, which also comprises Maya epistemology or the study of systems of thinking and knowing" (45). The aurora is similarly a system of thinking and knowing and the place of ancestral stories. Furthermore, consider "the symbolism of alder posts in a Nêhiýaw [Cree] ceremonial teepee" (Kovach 2021, 58), where "[t]he posts (or poles) offer a structural foundation for the hides or branches that enfold them. The ceremonial teepee gives shelter and holds ancient knowledges inside. There are many examples for conceptual frameworks expressed through metaphor found in Indigenous methodological research" (58). Such conceptual-metaphor frameworks have many variations but suggest that the aurora, which has been romanticized and westernized in the white imaginary, is such a framework. In Aboriginal Australia, the Dreaming, as an English term for words like the Jukurrpa (in Warlpiri), which host a network of concept-meanings (Nicholls 2014; Spencer and Gillen [1899] 1968), and Songspirals (transcendental and importantly invisible in a western construct), represent ways of knowing. They imply a metaphysical lens for apprehending the multiplicative universe and relational knowledge connected to the song lines. Song lines are threads of oral memory as rivers of stars that open "the way to the promised land, to the River of Stars [the Milniyawuy River and the Milky Way], the land that lies beyond the universe" (Gay'wu Group of Women 2019, 121–22). This image of the stars is easily mistranslated into non-Indigenous Horror (and speculative) tropes manifested, for instance, in Country, the sky and heavens, and ceremonial tradition.

Such concept-icons like the Tree of Life or "mysterious" stone circles are altered to create both non-Indigenous and Indigenous horror metaphors and symbols—as seen in Indigenous Horror fiction. If objects-ideas and ways of knowing become a unifying Indigenous metaphor to conceptualize a given knowledge system, the "metaphoric possibilities to conceptually frame" an "overarching" design or way of theorizing (Kovach 2021, 58) suggest hybrid "symbolism" that "holds ancient" and modern "knowledges inside" (58). Investigating transient phenomena offers a way of rupturing old semiotic understandings and western codifications of Indigenous horror "metaphor" that differentiate concrete and abstract systems of knowledge—like aurorae in Indigenous oral, visual, and written stories.

WATER-BASED KNOWLEDGE (LENS-FOUNDATION APPROACH)

While water is life endowing, and part of the makeup of living beings, some inherently horrific qualities to water are toyed with in contemporary Indigenous speculative fiction. These horrific aspects include asphyxiation, drowning, and body decay—the culling of the individual by the communal through water; the play of darkness and sunlight, refraction and absorption through the viscosity and depth of water itself as it interacts with and filters out rays of light and limits the color spectrum; distorted starlight (as constellations of celestial objects) on water's rippled expanse; and the objects hidden in the lower ranges of seabeds or riverbeds and the currents that draw bodies away. These are water-based, potentially horrific motifs of many Indigenous Horror fictions. Recall that the northern and southern lights are mapped onto the land and the stars, and simultaneously are a part of Creation stories.

Consider a creative understanding and actualization through water knowledge(s) in tandem with land- and solar-celestial-based knowledge(s) for theorizing (horror) and ways of knowing reflected in, and constituent of, narrative landscapes and spaces. From a western scientific perspective, water is unique in that it has four states of being (vapor, liquid, ice-solid, and plasma)—and four is an important number for Indigenous knowledges. "In the Tlingit language, water is *héen*. The Tlingit are Indigenous peoples of the Pacific Northwest Coast of North America. *Héen* is a fundamental tenet in Tlingit cosmology and a highly resilient counterstory to" "narrow," essentialist "readings of 'modern' water"—engaging with Indigenous Futurism, "future rivers," melting glaciers, and decolonial rhetoric of the Anthropocene while exploring "an alternative ontological awareness of glaciers" (Hayman, James, and Wedge 2018, 80, 77).[5] Melanie Yazzie and Cutcha Risling Baldy note: "The waters that run through Indigenous lands are the arteries that feed us— humans and more-than-humans" (2018, 1). Like wind or the solar expanse, which are animated, water has complementary, multifoliate meaning and agency, for instance water memory and bodies of water. Michael Fortescue writes of the relationality of Inuit orientational systems (across Inuit nations) guided or demarcated by water-land-direction through linguistic analysis (1988, 6, 20). "The highly localized senses of the demonstrative system . . . may refer to diametrically opposed directions on either side of a deep fjord. . . . [W]hen one examines the orientational terms" between local and larger regions, they have certain "common demonstrative terms, supplemented by specific wind direction terms" that "are held more or less constant, independent of the local vagaries of the coast line" (3). As one example of another way of understanding local-global theorizing, Fortescue's observations connect subdivided regions/spaces/wind/coast/sky to relational pockets of Inuit (sub) culture and meaning—still connected to the great Inuit nation. Orientations of theory structures based on land-water-linguistic modeling (across heterogeneous Inuit communities) "need to be mentally swiveled around—perhaps by 45 degrees" (Fortescue 1988, 3). This angle of rotation mirrors the swirl or whirl, but a radial conceptual alteration or transformation of lenses of aurorae (as transient phenomena) is insufficient. Through water-based knowledge, Yazzie and Baldy (2018, 2) "conceive of radical relationality," meaning, and shape from the rheology, or transformation of states, of water "as a term that brings together the multiple strands of materiality, kinship, corporeality, affect, land/body connection, and multidimensional connectivity coming primarily from Indigenous [scholars]" like Kim TallBear. They create a "multidirectional, multispatial, multitemporal, and multispecies theory of relationships and connections [that] forms the terrain of decolonized knowledge production" (Yazzie and Baldy 2018, 2). This space fortifies decolonial trends in Indigenous h/Horror analysis—where horror is lived experience and Horror is genre. As part of land-solar-celestial-based knowledge, fluidity in theorizing for materialities offers another way of reconceptualizing the "cosmic subjectivities" of western theorizing.[6]

In concert with the notion of a water-land-sky-based knowledge complex, consider a horror nexus as the actualized ways of theorizing that intersects with place—place-based horror is often found in Indigenous Horror. For instance, an early Bronze Age place-based manifestation is a visualization of these ideas. It is a moment of conceptual integration orthogonal to the Ojibwe sky star map (Wilson 2014, 2, 3). The rediscovering of a sacred Bronze Age pool, once believed to be just a rectangular pool, is now understood to be a massive religious sanctuary aligned with the stars. It is a star pool, or Bronze Age infinity pool (1436–1428 BCE), rivaling Stonehenge, England, as a site that feeds narratives of pagan myth-horror and the celestial (Nigro 2022; Metcalfe 2021). (Here, the argument in this chapter is actively drawing on popular news media representations of such phenomena and ideas.) In proximity, the structure appears to be "the [reflected and refracted] sky"—at the point when the observer enters "another world," as described by Cornell University archaeologist and dendrochronologist Sturt Manning (Metcalfe 2021). The horror of moving between states is equally mirrored in stories of the Greco-Roman underworld and mistranslation of non-Indigenous, pantheistic Creation myths. The physical movement toward the star pool exposes or reveals the "the surface, effectively [visualized as] the edge of the land around the sky," as Manning describes, and the folding together of the horizon on a vitreous surface is seen as a conjunction of the land and sky. In order to actualize a more than "4D ways of theorizing" model, now consider the star pool in relation to examples of material being of theory/lenses/perspectives through Aboriginal Australian aqueducts and ancient Indigenous (British Columbian) water systems. They are two different ways of knowing and represent a theoretical abstraction of a system, and the praxis of water coaction-ing, where scarcity as horror can be understood outside western paradigms of, for instance, eco-Horror, anthropological monster discourse, or Folk Horror.

Caught up in present-day media representations of Indigenous h/Horror, two ancient structures disinterred by natural disasters expose the holistic logic of Creation tales embedded in culture and Indigenous Horror and tied to ecology (as a non-Indigenous notion). Thus, the following examples offer a way of theorizing Indigenous horror that would not be initially coded as horrific to a western audience, instead being swept up in common trends to Indigenize eco-Horror. Earthquakes and fire reveal "mysterious" and "ancient" coastal and inland water systems that function as more than ontological lenses. These structures (as concepts) capture an alternative theory-practice paradigm that replicates the striated complexity of Wilson's sky star map—as a way of theorizing. In Victoria, Australia, an area of dormant volcanos, the arid land peppered with obsidian and old lava tracts, "[a]n ancient aquatic system older than the pyramids has been revealed by the [recent massive apocalyptic] Australian bushfires" (Cheung 2020). The newly visible Aboriginal aqueducts within the Budj Bim Cultural Landscape were used by the Gunditjmara people to harvest eels (UNESCO 2019). Equally, on the Forbidden Plateau in British Columbia, lands of the Kómoks First Nation, "speakers of the extinct Pentlatch language" unearthed "[a]n underwater mystery on Canada's coast" with "Ancient Indigenous Technology": "After an earthquake [7.3 magnitude] exposed thousands of mysterious wooden stakes off Vancouver Island, researchers spent over a decade figuring out what they mean" (Payton 2022). From the structure that was uncovered, "the stakes formed patterns." What it "represented" was a "puzzle" of assemblages, scale, and complexity, with one heart shaped and one chevron shaped at high tide, where "individual nubs of Douglas fir and western red cedar became 900 little black points on a field of white—like a photographic negative of stars in the nighttime sky," with astronomical allusions. "Patterns began to emerge and repeat," representing "remains of an immense, highly coordinated, sophisticated fish trap system" for harvesting salmon (Payton 2022). The system forms an integrated assemblage of parts—knowledge, practice, tradition, and innovation to stave off the real horror of starvation. Read through "aboriginal technological frameworks" (P. Cole 2006, 29) as the suprafunction of water and land, its (back)eddying movements, set lines, and relational orders: "[W]e used what the newcomers called frameworks / to gather our relations the salmon nations / these   were our installations and properties and sets / molding us to the places of the river which named us / through our naming of them the land languaged us / with the breath it gave us we spoke to identify (actually to relate) our connecting / our fishing platforms and scaffolds" (P. Cole 2006, 29, original spacing).[7] The nodal connections between ideas and images suggest actualized, adaptive theorizing of "condition/al/s" from "laconic geographies," the "frameworks and workings" of the "clarity (or not) / of the water": "ready to enact the prayer / which adapted us," and "a few weeks of good fishing meant survival rather than starvation" as part of lived horror (and colonization):

> "[I]f" was not an overly used morpheme in our vocabulary // our frameworks and workings took into account the clarity (or not) / of the water its speed its dervish it placidity its negotiativity . . . rather than prepositionally related ad/hered to it / we were and are not speci/fic/ally different from salmon / steelhead rainbow silver trout. (P. Cole 2006, 29, original spacing)

There is an implicit suggestion of the perception of (non-Indigenous) horror of the individual being indistinguishable from the trapped fish (P. Cole 2006, 29). Here, "its dervish" as metaphor is an antimorpheme anodyne in the form of a conceptualization, in reaction to the real (taxonomic) horror of "becoming reductively subsumed into rationalist scientist discourses / substrates of linnaean classification strategies" (29). These examples offer a way of theorizing the would-be abstraction and concrete in the transmission of working "aesthetics" through "physical" objects with sacred, spiritual, and communal being: modern hybrid Indigenous metaphors of land, the relationality and fluidity (and movement) of water- (ice-vapor-liquid-plasma), sky- (stratospheric-astronomical-astral), and land-based knowledge. They have many permutations and connections that offer insight into how such (not)metaphors (being; stories; objects; etc.) are told, circulated, understood, and impacted by gravitation (of the moon and sun), earthquakes, and tidal motion as much as by their cosmological/cosmogonic meaning. For instance, as Julie Cruikshank writes in *Do Glaciers Listen?*, "[g]laciers, like stories told about them, are enigmatic" (2005, 69). Connecting non-Indigenous water knowledge to a transitional form of glaciers is used to highlight a retelling of an Indigenous ("onto-phenomenological knowledge" system and) perspective:

Surging glaciers, in particular, are sometimes solid, sometimes liquid, and always flowing. They are shapeshifters of magnificent power. Like tidal zones, they signify transitional spaces. Aboriginal elders who speak knowledgably about such glaciers refer to observing, listening and participating in ritualised respect relations with glaciers and go to great lengths not to disturb them. In northern Athabaskan and Tlingit traditions, the line between human and non-human beings is less distinct than some might imagine. (Cruikshank 2005, 69)

This passage about the ontology and agency of the glacier in conjunction with its transformative states is an example of a horror lens (in scale and ratio) and underscores the way, more generally, that horrors "signify transitional spaces" (69), like transient phenomena as (not)metaphors do, subsumed in fiction by dark entities, often borrowed from myth. Through a way of theorizing, the melting glacier provides insight into the constants and the transformation of states of being, and materiality swept away in global allegories and allusions, with similarity to interactive parts of the aurorae, spectral and transient phenomena as elements of horror tales—transferring conceptual and abstract to the formal, not just the actualized to the articulated.

Simultaneously read, the myths, lenses, and physical structures that bind and girder states of being and co-becoming have come to represent apocalyptic and climatic (eco)horror. Disinterred by the impact of global warming, the aqueduct and "ancient" fishery (water) structures bridge epistemological scaffoldings of the water-land and heavens; they represent an embodied way of theorizing. In and of themselves, they are not horrific but instead as knowledges in situ become-reflect tools or lenses for Indigenous theorizing and engage with the filter of contemporary Horror. A global media reading of these "apocalyptic" events through the lurid appeal of horror emphasizes how culture(s) code, recode, apprehend, and produce meaning (fear, terror, shock, aberration), in parallel to ways of knowing (land, water, sky, culture).

Unmoderated Indigenous Horror is taboo to the strict protocol of sacred, spiritual, and communal (ethics), and social order, where individualism is communalism in a traditional sense and horror narratives in the contemporary hybrid form are a breakdown of relations between self/tribal groupings through rubrics of elders (star keepers) and narrators. Narrative is embedded in the land, sky, water, and language. Aurorae are a manifestation of that interactive experiential mesh: transient, constant, and elusive. In modern Horror, these are often used by Indigenous scholars to represent apocalyptic events through elemental, atmospheric, and (in western nomenclature) multisensory a/effects in their own writing.

A Note on Global Eco-Horror and Aurorae

In *Prismatic Ecology*, edited by Jeffrey Jerome Cohen, Lowell Duckert's "Maroon" is a translation of the aurora myth that is tied to global eco-theory and eco-cyborg Horror as an extension of eco-bio-theory's infiltration of ideas that color Indigenous ways of knowing: "allochronic and allotropic" "reflecting (ratio)nality" "in/appropriate/d others," the "humans beneath the monstrous skin" (Cohen 1996, 24n36, repurposing Haraway; see Haraway 1999, 299), status, reservation, and connection beyond colonial power that equally feed Cohen's theorizing through Donna Haraway, Karen Barad, Bruno Latour, and others. Duckert theorizes the aurora through the patterning and subsectioning of the phrase "The sky is firing" (2013, 44) and through Samuel Hearne's observations on the "Northern Indians," whom Hearne states "call the Aurora Borealis, Ed-Thin; that is, Deer" (Hearne [1795] 2006, 227; Duckert 2013, 44). To describe "the practical reasons behind the mythology of 'Ed-Thin,'" Hearne "provides two theories" that "are founded on [an arcane] . . . principle one would not imagine" (Duckert 2013, 45) and illuminated through depictions of sensory experience:

> [W]hen a hairy deer-skin is briskly stroked with the hand in a dark night, it will emit many sparks of electrical fire. . . . The idea which the Southern Indians have of this meteor is equally romantic, though more pleasing, as they believe it to be the spirits of their departed friends dancing in the clouds; and when the Aurora Borealis is remarkably bright, at which time they vary most in colour, form, and situation. (Hearne [1795] 2006, 243)

Characterized by others as "aesthetics of the ecorhapsodic," buried in aurorae myth, as beyond the western sublime, "[e]corhapsody operates through parataxis and metonymy," producing a "sparkle" (Morton 2009, 54–63, 45, 61) that is as well tied to "ambient poetics" (Abba, Dovey, and Pullinger 2020, 150), parts of which, the ambient environment, the gem-like sparking, are drawn into eco-horror critique. Indigenous ways of knowing such transient phenomena break down western lexicons and glossaries. These ideas extend to the anthropogenic/anthropomorphic tendencies of global theory in Horror studies, in which:

> [i]f nature exists, it needs eyes, and "I"s, and hands, and minds, and eyeglasses, to look at itself. Beyond the color green there is an ecology that hosts zombies, bioluminescence, aurora borealis, and gamma

rays. In the disanthropocentric horizon of this ecology, turning our prismatic "eye/I" into a tool of reciprocity is the only way we have to see the world. (Iovino and Oppermann 2013, 336)

This statement is highly suggestive of current trends in eco-Horror, not just "I" but "eye" in many creolized and multiplied lenses. Here, their "tool of reciprocity" (Iovino and Oppermann 2013, 336) is a simulacrum of Two-Eyed Seeing approaches gilded by a multicultural prismatic vision. But many such approaches are built on and apply dynamic systems and fuzzy logic (Bruin-Molé and Polak 2021, 6)—and these, too, sometimes burgeon from discourses and theories of (natural, virtual, and artificial) contagion narratives (e.g., Priscilla Wald).[8]

What has been presented thus far is an exploration of both Indigenous and non-Indigenous manifestations of (narrative and literary) theory and myth from heterogeneous groupings with implications for a disruption of "h/Horror" ways of theorizing. The aurora, its interactions and relationality, offers a conceptual framework to move from old ethno-meteorological and anthropological lenses that romanticize oral myths to authentic visual-conceptual models. Theorizing "materiality," and co-being and becoming of Horror motifs means understanding their transformation, actualization, and existence, from the structure and function of glacier ice (now melting) to the fluidity (ebb and flow) of water, to the trajectories of light, vapor, plasma, and the movement of the solar system[9] projected onto and through the land. Such a vision implies the connectivity and motility of constituent parts, as an integrated and relational moving whole, that exposes a differently "sequential," "nonlinear," horizontal-lateral-off-grid spread of meaning and denotation, where horror is still the rupture of knowledge (or logic) systems created by a breakdown in the epistemological function of a given system or systems. The interactions of transient phenomena in such a (not)metaphoric space punctuate textual moments of horror. These moments become one part of the narrative landscapes of an Indigenous Horror genre.

The analysis in this chapter emphasizes that it is inherently elusive, trying to capture what in Global ways of theorizing are "transient phenomena"—as the interactive catalytic(s) of horror fortified by Indigenous and non-Indigenous epistemologies. Shapeshifting "tropes" of theorizing in fiction have their own vitality and diaspora, independent of the western genre critique and canon. Unfurling the trajectory of Horror theory, as read through transient phenomena in this chapter, entails tracing the threads or foundations of ways of theorizing within physical and literary structures. Tracing spectral and celestial features through trends in theorizing Indigenous horror, or horror Indigeneity related to the cosmogonic and cosmological (as one global theory vogue), this chapter takes the example of transient phenomena. As part of myth, Creation, culture, and narrative practice, the aurora or "transient phenomena" disrupts standard metaphors that function like "comets of knowledge" within other systems/lenses. The analysis in this chapter reevaluates how one reads or recodes a theoretical lens with ways of knowing (Lee et al. 2014, 2–3) from virtual reality to X-ray style and mana, to abstraction, borrowing from literary, artistic, performative, and oral-filmic forms. The unraveling of horror into a visual codex of "aesthetics" and ways of theorizing suggests the complexity underlying literary-theory criticism of Indigenous h/Horror.

Notes

1. To a western reader, this would refer to mathematical optimization, spatial concept knowledge, and the like.

2. Note the use of experimental white space in quotations from Peter Cole.

3. I actively cite author interviews from Part 4 of this volume in an attempt to include their voices and agencies in this analysis/discussion.

4. The Point Barrow Inuit beliefs have some nominally superficial similarity to the Quinkins (the Imjim and Timara) of Aboriginal Australian myth.

5. There is a trend to read Indigeneity through the Anthropocene as eco-racial, where on a planetary scale, the "Anthropocene" (Hamilton 2016, 93–106) is "an irreversible rupture of the Earth system itself, the overshoot of the planetary boundaries that had provided a 'safe operating space for humanity'" (Thomas et al. 2016, 932). This undergirds the apocalyptic horror inflection of the speculative.

6. For example, consider Gilles Deleuze and Félix Guattari's oft-cited non-Indigenous metaphysical models (like concrete-abstract machine assemblages), and the movement and metaphorical states of their rhizome (network concept) theory. In the context of an "invisible" cultural knowledge or reservoir, the rhizome is constituted by lines (or vectors). While "experimental" rhizome theory may be "an antigenealogy," it geospatially-metacognitively "pertains to a map that must be produced constructed . . . detachable, connectable, reversible, modifiable," with "multiple entryways" and an "acentered, nonhierarchical, non-signifying system . . . defined solely by a circulation of states" (Deleuze and Guattari [1987] 2004, 23). The "becomings," those "made of plateaus," are, as Deleuze and Guattari envision, "any multiplicity connected to other multiplicities by superficial underground stems" that "form or extend a rhizome"; "writing a book is a rhizome" (24)—decentered, mechanistic, yet relying on "organic" crystalline formations. Such an approach to reorientation must be gilded to cultural-specific knowledge systems in theorizing—for instance, the land/body connection. Glenn A. Albrecht's eco-philosophy of the "Symbiocene" (coined in 2011), as an integration of human-nature through "sumbiosic praxis" (through the term itself also drawing on Greek origins), is a post-Anthropocene lens confronting the potentially cosmic, universal futures of apocalyptic devastation (Albrecht 2017), as a way of knowing "ghedeist," a neologism defined as "the awareness of the spirit or force that holds things together, a secular feeling of interconnectedness in life between the self and other beings (human and

non-human)" (Albrecht 2019, 151), which incorporates old and new Aboriginal Australian epistemology and spirituality, synchronisms, and time-place associations (151). The operational state of Deleuze and Guattari's plateaus are not conceived through compound, multifarious states of being-co-becoming that stem from Indigenous otherwise-being-knowing-connectivity and what constitutes "organic" through orientating systems (e.g., water-land-sky).

7. In quotations from Peter Cole, a slash mark indicates a line break in the original text; a double slash indicates a line break and extra line space.

8. Through global lenses and global media, "[i]mages shape international events and our understanding of them," "[m]apping [complex] visual global politics" (Bleiker 2018, 1, 16, 41). Ideas around fear and Indigeneity and the "marginalizing [of I]ndigenous spiritualities and cosmologies" (Conway 2013, 60, 153; Sullivan 2005, 104, quoted in Bleiker 2018) are trussed to capitalism—in titular eco-theory of "tentacular thinking" and Lovecraftian mythos with the "Anthropocene, Capitalocene, Chthulucene" (Haraway 2016, 52–53)—often neoliberal, essentialist, and hyperrealist Horror-Gothic readings of Indigeneity (e.g., Edwards, Graulund, and Höglund 2022). On "apocalyptic chic" and ideology, Justin McBrien notes that "[f]ocusing on a dystopic future allows the privileged to ignore the dystopic horror that already exists today for a great many people on this planet" (2019). In "Our Ancestors' Dystopia Now: Indigenous Conservation and the Anthropocene," Kyle Powys Whyte describes how "some [I]ndigenous peoples already inhabit what our ancestors would have likely characterized as a dystopian [Anthropocene] future" (2017, 2), manifested in Gerald Vizenor's 2016 *Treaty Shirts: October 2034—A Familiar Treatise on the White Earth Nation* as a transgressing of, for instance, Margaret Atwood's dystopic futurism. This engagement with mainstream horror stories of the Anthropocene is a rejection of or rebellion against metamythic, hyperrealist national discourse(s), which is therein embodied visually and politically coded. It also implicitly reflects the dispersive, insidious "nature" of certain vogues in global Horror. Highlighting a culturally topical trend in "Black Indigeneity," in "Decolonial (Re)Visions," Lou Cornum and Maureen Moynagh posit, within speculative aesthetics, that a "Black or Indigenous novum," defined as a scientifically viable narrative innovation, is "about reclaiming those embodied histories for an alternative reading of the current moment" (2020). Reconstituting this Black/Native novum blurs ontogenies in the "rise of fictionality" (Cornum and Moynagh 2020), potentially complicating uniquely dystopian horrors (and reimaginings) of future-past-present in different Indigenous peoples, and their divergent apparatus (and systems) of horror ways of theorizing. Other vogues and diasporas of "Black Indigeneity" have been tied to the iconography of Jordan Peele and his Horror. The influential Horror writer Stephen Graham Jones is marketed as the "Jordan Peele of Indigenous horror literature" in the paratext to his 2021 novel *My Heart Is a Chainsaw*—a Horror subgenre built on antecedent writers like Owl Goingback. It is suggestive of a burgeoning global, heterogeneous field of Indigenous Horror fiction in need of the development or articulation of processes and ways of knowing as ways of theorizing (elements of working horror "aesthetics").

9. It is an alternative to seminal western theorizing that moves, for example, from two-dimensional painting to three- and four plus–dimensional sculpture, to mixed media forms, and that invokes transcendental negative space (Crowther 2001, 86; Barthes and Manghani 2020, 35).

BIBLIOGRAPHY

Abba, Tom, Jonathan Dovey, and Kate Pullinger, eds. 2020. *Ambient Literature: Towards a New Poetics of Situated Writing and Reading Practices*. Cham, Switzerland: Palgrave Macmillan.

Akasofu, Syun-Ichi. 2009. *The Northern Lights: Secrets of the Aurora Borealis*. Anchorage: Alaska Northwest Books.

Albrecht, Glenn A. 2017. "Solastalgia in the Anthropocene and the Ghedeist in the Symbiocene." Psychoterratica, July 22. https://glennaalbrecht.wordpress.com/2017/07/22/solastalgia-in-the-anthropocene-and-the-ghedeist-in-the-symbiocene/.

Albrecht, Glenn A. 2019. *Earth Emotions: New Words for a New World*. Ithaca, NY: Cornell University Press.

Allen, Paula Gunn. 1986. *The Sacred Hoop: Recovering the Feminine in American Indian Traditions*. Boston: Beacon Press.

Bacon, Simon, ed. 2022. *The Anthropocene and the Undead: Cultural Anxieties in the Contemporary Popular Imagination*. Lanham, MD: Lexington Books.

Barad, Karen. 2007. *Meeting the Universe Halfway: Quantum Physics and the Entanglement of Matter and Meaning*. 2nd ed. Durham, NC: Duke University Press.

Barclay, Barry. 2003. "Celebrating Fourth Cinema." *Illusions: A New Zealand Magazine of Film, Television and Theater Criticism* 35 (Winter): 7–11.

Barthes, Roland, and Sunil Manghani. 2020. "Colouring, Degree Zero." *Theory, Culture & Society* 37, no. 4: 35–42.

Barton, Katherine. 2019. "Legends of the Northern Lights." Interview of Dene Elder Jonas Antoine. CBC News, December 10. https://newsinteractives.cbc.ca/longform/legends-of-the-northern-lights/.

Blaeser, Kimberly M. 1999. "Writing Voices Speaking: Native Authors and an Oral Aesthetic." In *Talking on the Page: Editing Aboriginal Oral Texts*, edited by Laura J. Murray and Keren Rice, 53–68. Toronto: University of Toronto Press.

Bleiker, Roland, ed. 2018. *Visual Global Politics*. Abingdon, Oxon., England: Routledge.

Borwein, Naomi Simone, Florence Glanfield, and Veselin Jungic. 2022. "Indigenizing University Mathematics." *CMS Notes* 54, no. 2 (March). https://notes.math.ca/wp-content/uploads/2022/02/Indigenizing-Mathematics-2.pdf.

Boscov-Ellen, Dan. 2020. "Whose Universalism? Dipesh Chakrabarty and the Anthropocene." *Capitalism Nature Socialism* 31, no. 1: 70–83.

Brekke, Asgeir, and Alv Egeland. 1983. "The Northern Light in Folklore and Mythology." In *The Northern Light: From Mythology to Space Research*, 1–9. Berlin: Springer Verlag.

Bridle, James. 2022. *Ways of Being: Animals, Plants, Machines; The Search for a Planetary Intelligence*. New York: Farrar, Straus and Giroux.

Bruin-Molé, Megen de, and Sara Polak. 2021. "Embodying the Fantasies and Realities of Contagion." In *Embodying Contagion: The Viropolitics of Horror and Desire in Contemporary Discourse*, edited by Sandra Becker, Megen de Bruin-Molé, and Sara Polak, 1–14. Cardiff: University of Wales Press.

Cheung, Eric. 2020. "An Ancient Aquatic System Older than the Pyramids Has Been Revealed by the Australian Bushfires." CNN, January 22. https://www.cnn.com/2020/01/21/asia/budj-bim-australia-bushfire-intl-hnk-scli/index.html.

Cohen, Jeffrey Jerome. 1996. "Monster Culture (Seven Theses)." In *Monster Theory: Reading Culture*, edited by Jeffrey Jerome Cohen, 3–25. Minneapolis: University of Minnesota Press.

Cohen, Jeffrey Jerome, ed. 2013. *Prismatic Ecology: Ecotheory beyond Green*. Minneapolis: University of Minnesota Press.

Cole, Gina. 2016. *Black Ice Matter*. Wellington, New Zealand: Huia Publishers.

Cole, Gina. 2020. "Wayfinding Pasifikafuturism: An Indigenous Science Fiction Vision of the Ocean in Space." PhD diss., Massey University, Manawatu, New Zealand.

Cole, Gina. 2022. *Na Viro*. Wellington, New Zealand: Huia Publishers.

Cole, Peter. 2006. *Coyote and Raven Go Canoeing: Coming Home to the Village*. McGill-Queen's Native and Northern Series, no. 42. Montreal: McGill–Queen's University Press.

Conway, Janet M. 2013. *Edges of Global Justice: The World Social Forum and Its "Others."* Abingdon, Oxon., England: Routledge.

Cook, Captain James. 1777. *A Voyage towards the South Pole and Round the World*, vol. 1. London: W. Strahan and T. Cadell. https://gutenberg.net.au/ebooks/e00044.html.

Cornum, Lou, and Maureen Moynagh. 2020. "Introduction: Decolonial (Re)Visions of Science Fiction, Fantasy, and Horror." *Canadian Literature* 240: 8–18.

Crowther, Paul. 2001. *Art and Embodiment: From Aesthetics to Self-Consciousness*. Oxford: Oxford University Press.

Cruikshank, Julie. 2005. *Do Glaciers Listen? Local Knowledge, Colonial Encounters, and Social Imagination*. Vancouver: University of British Columbia Press.

Cuthand, Thirza, dir. 2021. *Kwêskosiw: She Whistles*. Fanning Feathers Productions.

Czuy, Kori. 2021. "Protocols of Indigenous Mathematics." Paper presented at the Indigenizing University Mathematics session, Canadian Mathematical Society Winter Meeting, December 2–7, Simon Fraser University, Burnaby, British Columbia. https://www2.cms.math.ca/Events/winter21/abs/ium.

De Freitas, Elizabeth, and Nathalie Sinclair. 2013. "New Materialist Ontologies in Mathematics Education: The Body in/of Mathematics." *Educational Studies in Mathematics* 83, no. 3 (July): 453–70.

Deleuze, Gilles, and Félix Guattari. (1987) 2004. *A Thousand Plateaus: Capitalism and Schizophrenia*. Translated by Brian Massumi. London: Continuum.

Derrida, Jacques. 1994. *Specters of Marx: The State of the Debt, the Work of Mourning and the New International*. Translated by Peggy Kamuf. Abingdon, Oxon., England: Routledge.

Duckert, Lowell. 2013. "Maroon." In *Prismatic Ecology: Ecotheory beyond Green*, edited by Jeffrey Jerome Cohen, 42–62. Minneapolis: University of Minnesota Press.

Eather, Robert H. 1980. *Majestic Lights: The Aurora in Science, History, and the Arts*. Washington, DC: American Geophysical Union.

Edwards, Justin D., Rune Graulund, and Johan Höglund, eds. 2022. *Dark Scenes from Damaged Earth: The Gothic Anthropocene*. Minneapolis: University of Minnesota Press.

Ešenvalds, Ēriks. 2014. *River of Light*. Soundtrack by Swedbank Choir and Artūrs Ancāns, conductor. https://www.eriksesenvalds.com/works/rivers-of-light.

Ezeife, Anthony N. 2011. "The Schema-Based Mathematics Study: Enriching Mathematics Teaching and Learning Using a Culture-Sensitive Curriculum." *Canadian and International Education* 40, no. 1: 41–56.

Fortescue, Michael. 1988. *Eskimo Orientation Systems*. Meddelelser om Grønland, Man and Society 11. Copenhagen: Commission for Scientific Research in Greenland.

Fowler, Henry H. 2010. "Collapsing the Fear of Mathematics: A Study of the Effects of Navajo Culture on Navajo Student Performance in Mathematics." PhD diss., Fielding Graduate University. https://eric.ed.gov/?q=%22no+child+left+behind%22&ff1=souPr oQuest+LLC&ff2=locArizona&ff3=subMathematics+Achievement&id=ED522184.

Fowler, Henry H. 2021. "Indigenous Ways of Knowing." Paper presented at the Indigenizing University Mathematics session, Canadian Mathematical Society Winter Meeting, December 7, Simon Fraser University, Burnaby, British Columbia.

Fricke, Suzanne Newman. 2019. "Introduction: Indigenous Futurisms in the Hyperpresent Now." *World Art* 9, no. 2: 107–21.

Friesen, John W. 1997. *Rediscovering the First Nations of Canada*. Toronto: Brush Education.

Fu, Chi-Wing. 2003. "A Visualization Framework for Large-Scale Virtual Astronomy." PhD diss., Indiana University.

Garba, Tapji, and Sara-Maria Sorentino. 2020. "Slavery Is a Metaphor: A Critical Commentary on Eve Tuck and K. Wayne Yang's 'Decolonization Is Not a Metaphor.'" *Antipode* 52, no. 3 (May): 764–82.

Gay'wu Group of Women. 2019. *Songspirals: Sharing Women's Wisdom of Country through Songlines*. Crows Nest, Australia: Allen and Unwin.

Gibson, Rebecca, and James M. VanderVeen. 2022. "Afterword: Then and Now and After." In *Global Perspectives on the Liminality of the Supernatural: From Animus to Zombi*, edited by Rebecca Gibson and James M. VanderVeen, 185–89. Lanham, MD: Lexington Books.

Hamacher, Duane W., and Ray P. Norris. 2010. "Meteors in Australian Aboriginal Dreamings." *WGN, Journal of the International Meteor Organization* 38, no. 3: 87–98.

Hamilton, Clive. 2016. "The Anthropocene as Rupture." *Anthropocene Review* 3, no. 2: 93–106.

Haraway, Donna J. 1999. "The Promises of Monsters: A Regenerative Politics for Inappropriate/d Others." In *Cybersexualities: A Reader on Feminist Theory, Cyborgs and Cyberspace*, edited by Jenny Wolmark, 314–66. Edinburgh: Edinburgh University Press.

Haraway, Donna J. 2016. *Staying with the Trouble: Making Kin in the Chthulucene*. Durham, NC: Duke University Press.

Hart, Michael. 2021. "After Tea (Interview)." In *Indigenous Methodologies: Characteristics, Conversations, and Contexts*, 2nd ed, by Margaret Kovach, 81–85. Toronto: University of Toronto Press.

Hawk, Shane. 2020. *Anoka: A Collection of Indigenous Horror*. N.p.: Black Hills Press.

Hawk, Shane, and Theodore C. Van Alst Jr., eds. 2023. *Never Whistle at Night: An Indigenous Dark Fiction Anthology*. Toronto: Penguin Random House Canada.

Hawkes, Ernest W. 1916. *The Labrador Eskimo*. Geological Survey Memoir 91. Ottawa: Government Printing Bureau.

Hayman, Eleanor, Colleen James, and Mark Wedge. 2018. "Future Rivers of the Anthropocene or Whose Anthropocene Is It? Decolonising the Anthropocene!" In *Decolonization: Indigeneity, Education & Society* 7, no. 1: 77–92.

Hazzard, Matthew Lyon. 2019. "From Light into Sound: Recreating Aurora Borealis in Ēriks Ešenvalds's *Rivers of Light*." Project report, California State University, Long Beach.

Hearne, Samuel. (1795) 2006. *A Journey to the Northern Ocean: The Adventures of Samuel Hearne*. Surrey, BC: TouchWood Editions.

Hogan, Linda. 1994. *Solar Storms*. New York: Simon and Schuster.

hoʻomanawanui, kuʻualoha. 2018. "Indigeneity." In *The Routledge Companion to Media and Fairy-Tale Cultures*, edited by Pauline Greenhill, Jill Terry Rudy, Naomi Hamer, and Lauren Bosc, 122–32. New York: Routledge.

Ihimaera, Witi, and Tina Makereti. 2017. Introduction to *Black Marks on the White Page*, edited by Witi Ihimaera and Tina Makereti, 8–13. Auckland: Penguin Random House New Zealand.

Iovino, Serenella, and Serpil Oppermann. 2013. "After Green Ecologies: Prismatic Visions." In *Prismatic Ecology: Ecotheory beyond Green*, edited by Jeffrey Jerome Cohen, 328–36. Minneapolis: University of Minnesota Press.

Jiménez Estrada, Vivian M. 2005. "The Tree of Life as a Research Methodology." *Australian Journal of Indigenous Education* 34, no. 1: 44–52.

Jones, Stephen Graham. 2021. *My Heart Is a Chainsaw*. New York: Simon and Schuster.

Khare, Neloy. 2019. *Atmospheric Research in Antarctica: Present Status and Thrust Areas in Climate Change*. Boca Raton, FL: CRC Press.

Kimmerer, Robin Wall. 2013. *Braiding Sweetgrass: Indigenous Wisdom, Scientific Knowledge, and the Teachings of Plants*. Minneapolis: Milkweed Editions.

Kovach, Margaret. 2021. *Indigenous Methodologies: Characteristics, Conversations, and Contexts*. 2nd ed. Toronto: University of Toronto Press.

Lee, Annette S., William Wilson, Jeffrey Tibbetts, and Carl Gawboy. 2014. *Ojibwe Sky Star Map: Constellation Guidebook; An Introduction to Ojibwe Star Knowledge*. St. Cloud, MN: Native Skywatchers.

Loui, Gregory C. 2017. *21st Century Orc*. Kindle.

McBrien, Justin. 2019. "This Is Not the Sixth Extinction. It's the First Extermination Event." Truthout, September 14. https://truthout.org/articles/this-is-not-the-sixth-extinction-its-the-first-extermination-event/.

Metcalfe, Tom. 2021. "Bronze Age 'Infinity Pool' Hosted Supernatural Water Rituals, Archaeologists Say." Live Science, June 30. https://www.livescience.com/bronze-age-infinity-pool-supernatural-rituals.html.

Morton, Timothy. 2009. *Ecology without Nature: Rethinking Environmental Aesthetics*. Cambridge, MA: Harvard University Press.

Nicholls, Christine Judith. 2014. "'Dreamings' and Place: Aboriginal Monsters and Their Meanings." The Conversation, April 29. https://theconversation.com/dreamings-and-place-aboriginal-monsters-and-their-meanings-25606.

Nigro, Lorenzo. 2022. "The Sacred Pool of Baʻal: A Reinterpretation of the 'Kothon' at Motya." *Antiquity* 96, no. 386 (April): 354–71.

Noori, Margaret. 2013. "*Beshaabiiag Gʻgikenmaaigowag*: Comets of Knowledge." In *Centering Anishinaabeg Studies: Understanding the World through Stories*, edited by Jill Doerfler, Niigaanwewidam James Sinclair, and Heidi Kiiwetinepinesiik Stark, 35–57. East Lansing: Michigan State University Press; Winnipeg: University of Manitoba Press.

Payton, Brian. 2022. "Can Ancient Indigenous Technology Help Save BC's Salmon?" *The Walrus*, updated April 5. https://thewalrus.ca/can-ancient-indigenous-technology-help-save-bcs-salmon/.

Peterson, Tim. 2023. "Robin Wall Kimmerer Explains Indigenous Traditional Knowledge." Grand Canyon Trust, April 18. https://www.grandcanyontrust.org/blog/robin-wall-kimmerer-explains-indigenous-traditional-knowledge.

Pomare, Sir Maui, and James Cowan. 1907. *Legends of the Maori.* 2 vols. Wellington, New Zealand: Harry H. Tombs.

Ray, Patrick Henry, John Murdoch, Charles Valentine Riley, Asa Gray, William Healey Dall, and Charles Anthony Schott. 1885. *Report of the International Polar Expedition to Point Barrow, Alaska, in Response to the Resolution of the [US] House of Representatives of December 11, 1884*, vol. 1. Washington, DC: Government Printing Office.

Reid, Andrea J., Lauren E. Eckert, John-Francis Lane, Nathan Young, Scott G. Hinch, Chris T. Darimont, Steven J. Cooke, Natalie C. Ban, and Albert Marshall. 2021. "'Two-Eyed Seeing': An Indigenous Framework to Transform Fisheries Research and Management." *Fish and Fisheries* 22, no. 2 (March): 243–61.

Ricoeur, Paul. 1981. *The Rule of Metaphor.* Translated by Robert Czerny. Toronto: University of Toronto Press.

Ruffo, Armand Garnet. 1993. "Inside Looking Out: Reading Tracks from a Native Perspective." In *Looking at the Words of Our People: First Nations Analysis of Literature*, edited by Jeannette C. Armstrong, 161–76. Penticton, BC: Theytus Books.

Shoemaker, Adam. 1989. *Black Words White Page: Aboriginal Literature, 1929–1988.* Canberra: Australian National University Press.

Simpson, Matthew. 2021. "Fantasia '21 Interview: Thirza Cuthand on Their Film *Kwêskosîw* (She Whistles)." August 19. https://awesomefriday.ca/2021/08/interview-thirza-cuthand-kweskosiw-she-whistles/.

Skow, Bradford. 2015. *Objective Becoming.* Oxford: Oxford University Press.

Slade, Giles. 2013. "Flare Fatale: Dark Possibilities behind the Northern Lights." *Alternatives Journal* 39, no. 5 (September–October): 20–25.

Soop, Alex. 2022. *Midnight Storm Moonless Sky: Indigenous Horror Stories*, vol. 1. Calgary: Durvile and UpRoute Books.

Soop, Alex. 2023. *Whistle at Night and They Will Come: Indigenous Horror Stories*, vol. 2. Calgary: Durvile and UpRoute Books.

Spencer, Baldwin, and F. J. Gillen. (1899) 1968. *The Native Tribes of Central Australia.* Garden City, NY: Dover Books.

Steiner, George. 1998. *After Babel: Aspects of Language and Translation.* 3rd ed. Oxford: Oxford University Press.

Sullivan, Winnifred Fallers. 2005. *The Impossibility of Religious Freedom.* Princeton, NJ: Princeton University Press.

TallBear, Kim. 2018. "Making Love and Relations beyond Settler Sexualities." In *Making Kin Not Population*, edited by Adele E. Clarke and Donna Haraway, 145–64. Chicago: Prickly Paradigm Press. https://www.youtube.com/watch?v=zfdo2ujRUv8.

Thomas, Julia Adeney, Prasannan Parthasarathi, Rob Linrothe, Fa-ti Fan, Kenneth Pomeranz, and Amitav Ghosh. 2016. "*JAS* Round Table on Amitav Ghosh, *The Great Derangement: Climate Change and the Unthinkable.*" *Journal of Asian Studies* 75, no. 4 (November): 929–55.

Tuck, Eve, and C. Ree. 2013. "A Glossary of Haunting." In *Handbook of Autoethnography*, edited by Stacy Holman Jones, Tony E. Adams, and Carolyn Ellis, 639–58. Walnut Creek, CA: Left Coast Press.

Tuck, Eve, and K. Wayne Yang. 2012. "Decolonization Is Not a Metaphor." *Decolonization: Indigeneity, Education & Society* 1, no. 1: 1–40.

Unaipon, David. (1930) 2006. *Legendary Tales of the Australian Aborigines.* Edited by Stephen Muecke and Adam Shoemaker. Melbourne: Miegunyah Press.

UNESCO. 2019. "Budj Bim Cultural Landscape." World Heritage Convention. https://whc .unesco.org/en/list/1577/.

Vizenor, Gerald. 1999. *Manifest Manners: Narratives on Postindian Survivance.* Lincoln: University of Nebraska Press.

Vizenor, Gerald, ed. 2008. *Survivance: Narratives of Native Presence.* Lincoln: University of Nebraska Press.

Vizenor, Gerald Robert. 2016. *Treaty Shirts: October 2034—A Familiar Treatise on the White Earth Nation.* Middletown, CT: Wesleyan University Press.

Walkiewicz, Kathryn. 2021. "The Generative Refusal of Mixtape Narratives and Hybrid Monsters in Stephen Graham Jones's *Mongrels*." *ASAP/Journal* 6, no. 2 (May): 403–30.

Wallis, Keziah, and Miriam Ross. 2021. "Fourth VR: Indigenous Virtual Reality Practice." *Convergence* 27, no. 2: 313–29.

Whymper, Frederick. 1868. *Travel and Adventure in the Territory of Alaska.* London: John Murray.

Whyte, Kyle Powys. 2017. "Our Ancestors' Dystopia Now: Indigenous Conservation and the Anthropocene." In *The Routledge Companion to the Environmental Humanities*, edited by Ursula K. Heise, Jon Christensen, and Michelle Niemann, 206–15. Abingdon, Oxon., England: Routledge.

Wilson, William, artist. 2014. *Ojibwe Sky Star Map.* In *Ojibwe Sky Star Map: Constellation Guide; An Introduction to Ojibwe Star Knowledge*, by Annette S. Lee, William Wilson, Jeffrey Tibbetts, and Carl Gawboy. St. Cloud, MN: Native Skywatchers.

Yazzie, Melanie, and Cutcha Risling Baldy. 2018. "Introduction: Indigenous Peoples and the Politics of Water." In *Decolonization: Indigeneity, Education & Society* 7, no. 1: 1–18.

CHAPTER 4

WAYS OF THEORIZING IN PRACTICE (SECTION II)

NAOMI SIMONE BORWEIN

A growing Global cohort, or network, of Indigenous scholars, artists, film-makers, and writers wield Horror, as a tool, against a backdrop of sensation-alized and exoticized clichés of Indigeneity. These caricatures or simulations extend to representations of Indigenous culture, oral myth, and identity through the northern or southern lights: as spectacular dizzying arrays of spirals and streaks of light and energy painted onto the sky and reflected or refracted back onto the land (Cook 1777). The analysis in this chapter is an investigation into how self-identifying Indigenous authors view the conceptualization of their practice and product. Charting the horror echoes of speculative imagery and prose, I use semiopen qualitative interviews—based on a storying methodology advocated by Margaret Kovach (Nêhiýaw/Saulteaux) (2021, 166, 176) and others, alongside contemporary approaches that center Indigenous knowledges in a hybrid speculative genre (e.g., Topash-Caldwell 2020, 81; Shane Hawk, Dan Rabarts, and Gregory C. Loui interviews in this volume). The approach incorporates a storying style of analysis in two ways: (a) to explore transient phenomena through hor-ror—for example, aurorae (e.g., northern or southern lights), light and shadows, and particulate (matter) transactions of sky-land-water—and (b) to interrogate representative stereotypes of nature and eco-fictions in Indigenous literature. Similarly, in interrogating metaphor and genre tax-onomies within the shifting particulate of horror, there is freedom and flexibility to make space for a variety of Indigenous metaphysics and literary productions (Gates 2011; Shane Hawk interview in this volume).

What follows is, first, a synopsis of responses to a qualitative semiopen interview structured around set questions, gathered through online (email) exchanges with five self-identifying Indigenous speculative writers associated with the Horror Writers Association (HWA): (A) Shane Hawk, (B) Dan Rabarts, (C) Stephen Graham Jones, (D) Gregory C. Loui, and (E) Gina Cole (see Part 4 for the full interviews). An interactive exploration of meaning between critic-author responses highlights and commences the process of inspecting hurtful "stock tropes and expectations" (Jones, interview C), such as "'Indian Burial Ground' and 'Wise/Magical Indian'" (Hawk, interview A), projected onto critiques of, and reception to, Indigenous Horror. In the "Threads and Textualizations" section below, analyses of these tropes as literary artifacts are extended to the textualization of aurorae and other transient phenomena as "Comets of Knowledge" (Noori 2013, 35) interacting with those caricatures ("wicked glimpses") and other representative imagery. To extend this analysis, the reader should consider the aforementioned interviews that address the use of horror, light, and spectral a/effects.

At the level of critical discourse, and larger theoretical and epistemological frameworks, there is a disjunct between writer-interpretation and theorist/academic-interpretation of literary elements, as would be expected. Regardless, many ways of theorizing are visible within the interview responses: elements of conceptual visual models and units, aesthetic syntactic reimaginings, re(visioned) metaphors at the level of the (heterogeneous and hybrid) metaphysical mesh that binds a given narrative. Moving from Shane Hawk's assessment of Indigenous horror and Horror production, a vast diversity of stories and "lenses" exist through which writers attempt "to address their own fears or issues within their communities through the lens of horror," utilizing "differing subgenres of Horror" (interview A). A clear acceptance and engagement with Horror in Hawk's work encompasses the inescapable hybridity of contemporary Cheyenne and Arapaho Horror in America. The title of Hawk and Theodore C. Van Alst Jr.'s 2023 coedited volume *Never Whistle at Night* is a reference to a universal oral myth with many derivations across Turtle Island—never whistle at the ancestors, or the northern lights—as is the title of Alex Soop's 2023 collection. Hawk notes that with "all variables in mind, an Indigenous writer has a vast creative space to incorporate horror in their narratives to speak on social issues, past and present, or dream up a dystopian future that serves as a cautionary tale to entice immediate action and protest for change in today's landscape" (interview A). Interviewees navigate dark speculative fiction and the supernatural alongside surrealism, subgenres of futurism, culturally specific knowledges and terminologies (e.g., mana, matakite, iwi, and Māoritanga), and lived horror from a modern perspective—as a capture, a moment, of the transmission of horror and its recodified images, tropes, or elements. Cole's Pasifikafuturist, anticolonial rejection of the Horror genre resonates with Nalo Hopkinson's Afro-futurist perspective on the reactionary formation of antigenre (interview E). As "something more complex[,] and as the basis of Pasifika worldview" (interview D) in Loui's fictional world building, horror intensifies through the application of a "mana metaphysics model" because of external (non-Indigenous) perceptions that exhibit as the "[c]orruption of bodies and minds" in popular media, often read through contagion theories—part of the global eco-Horror trends. Stephen Graham Jones answers the most pointed question about theorizing, with an aesthetic example in action: "At first you see the toe, the shadow, the saliva left behind. And then, slowly, you become aware of more and more. And then you regret that you ever wanted to see the whole thing" (interview C), with implications of unsettling Horror lenses that telescope Native subjects and subject matter. This suggests a way of apprehending horror. Rabarts (interview B) posits that "[a]side from the use of the Aurora Australis (Southern Lights) as a symbol of impending planetary apocalypse, light becomes a weapon to battle the darkness"; "lenses of urbanisation and colonialism feature strongly" in Rabarts's work "when delving into the relationship between Māoritanga and fiction, and by extension the wider world being lensed accordingly"; then the horror realism is undergirded by supernaturalism "as a narrative lubricant" (interview B). Fluid relationships between elements of horror—speculative, structural, paradigmatic-theoretic—all underscore the need to center Indigenous knowledges in ways of knowing Horror.

THREADS AND TEXTUALIZATIONS

In the non-Indigenous world, there are many names for horror stories, and a diversity of approaches. "Whether you call them horror stories, griezelverhalen, historias de terror, skräckberättelser, racconti dell'orrore, or . . . spookstories, there's something universal about the telling and reading of a good, creepy tale" as "the international side of horror" (Jenkins and Cagle 2020, 10). But it is a global lens that warrants the question, "Whose universalism?" (Boscov-Ellen 2020). In the complex multirelational logic schemas of heterogeneous groups, what is Indigenous Horror and how do ways of knowing, ways of theorizing (in action), impact its constituent elements and transitions in form? *Na Viro* means "whirlpool" in Fijian, and the whirlpool metaphor or scaffolding is a holographic virtual grid that lived horror is projected onto in the narrative landscape. Spirals as in the "Spiral Galaxy–Vortex" of eco-fractals are another experimental embodied theoretical space-praxis with "the vortex radiance" (Hauk 2018, 30–34), where non-Indigenous and Indigenous logic systems and "metaphoric communication" (40) interact within nature, responding to "natural patterns" (30), gyre-like "regenerativity" (30, 41), and scale, expressed as "relentlessly nonlinear," underscoring a "sensibility that the universe moves along according to a plurality of nested and overlapping rules, rather than a single universal system" (Hauk 2018, 31; Davis 2008, 123). In the context of transient phenomena (as moving, transformative celestial and electrical phenomena), interpretations of narrative systems vacillate through culturally coded filters or lenses that touch the very structures and paradigms (praxes-foundations) of ways of theorizing. Yet "transient phenomena" viewed as (not)metaphor can be charted from the stars and spirals in cosmic mappings, read through oral myth and Creation, embedded in, for instance, the weaving elements of horror in work by Owl Goingback, as a way of knowing—beyond futurist discourses of the horrors of water wars, lived horror, and eco-apocalypse—moments of horror, strung together, also implicit in the transcelestial whirlpool (paradigm) of Cole, encompassing the compound structure of hybrid metaphors described by many authors. With Rabarts, such structures are visible in his work through scale/ratio, proportionality and time punctuating an apocalypse of light in the painted sky, a somewhat superficially similar manifestation to Loui's apocalyptic light (2017). Variations are visible in Jones's visceral abstractions of form and light, and as discussed in the introduction to *Anoka*, Hawk's a-no-ka-tan-han ("on both sides of the river")–based approach to star-mapped bioluminescent and phosphorescent horror elements is seen as navigating "collapsed stars" and green swirls (Hawk 2020, 58, 97). The permeable fluidity of an Indigenous interpretation of the aurora metaphor as a signpost to horror aesthetics (the otherwise of knowing apocalypse, ruptures in space-time structures, or transformative materialities) defies traditional genre categories.

Analyzing stories with horror elements (from self-identifying Indigenous authors of the broader international HWA community), reading textual elements, and then contextualizing meaning through author interviews and experiences helps evince the narrative systems extant in heterogeneous Indigenous approaches. Herein, fragmented parts of myths of aurorae exhibit within these narrative systems. The aforementioned approach to experientially engage with texts and contexts allows for a simultaneous "bringing together" of lenses and myths through linear, sequential, and cyclic concepts or elements from various traditions.[1] Assessing textual passages that represent theoretical or conceptual moments and/or metaphors such as aurora, light, display, color, intensity, spiral/s, ripple/s, wave/s, trajectories, particle/s, or atmosphere can be viewed and understood in different epistemological contexts. The function of "Indigenous metaphors" is equally formed through sequences of illusions; they must be taken as an entirety within the narrative fabric.

Take one illustrative example of what would be a speculative trope that functions within oral reality. An Anishinaabe elder "address[es] the issue of apocalypse" (White 2001, 223), which is often used to read Indigeneity, aesthetics, and nature (Leuthold 1998, 199) in eco-Horror criticism as one lens set within the sequencing of connections in the quotation: "That's what they talked about—how the white people were taking everything for this earth here—copper bullion, lead, uranium, anything and everything. They never put anything back in here. Then the old men, they say, 'what does this portend? Sometime maybe this earth will become light in weight. Then we'll just go flying off [into space] over there'" (White 2001, 223). He continues, "[W]e'll be weightless over there. . . . Many things shall come to be. And these animals will look [different,] too. . . . will come to do many things differently" (223). The wobbling/flying axis (orbit/pathway) as a function or action of the ontological lens (universe/otter/earth) is embedded in the elder's transcribed oral response: "That otter. I never see him jumping [as usual]. . . . He just hobbles along. . . . Then maybe their production are near fulfillment" (225). "Maybe it [the earth] is flying off its axis" (225, 223–27); "[I]t's hollowed out . . . that's why its orbit is altered. . . . [H]e enters a new realm when he blasts off and speeds up in the sky" (227). This way of knowing "apocalypse" suggests a shift in ontological perspective or "lens," questioning what is abnormal, what is expected, what is arresting—away from the apparatus and structure of mainstream Horror theory—that reframes, recenters its "I" and meaning, extended beyond the western stratosphere.

Ways of knowing apocalypse can be seen in Navajo tradition, within the hogan or domicile, where "a slight change of 2 degrees" seen in tracking the light passing through the hogan's aperture is understood as "[t]he shift of the earth, the axis that's causing climate change," offering a way to "readjust themselves to climate change" (Fowler 2021). This derivation suggests "apocalyptic" environmental implications read through the Navajo construction (Fowler 2021). Conversely, modern atmospheric apocalyptic devices are often skewed and mistranslated, like apocalypse itself from the Māori tradition, drawing on witness accounts in which Te Po (the unknown) is cosmogonic space, or the spirit world, and human figures are also celestial bodies. Te Ila-Roa (the

Milky Way) aligned with material and immaterial existence traverses atmospheric and celestial layers of a western (Einsteinian-Newtonian) universe that is filtered and distorted by, for example, the colonial anthropologist Elsdon Best in "UenUku and the Mist Maid," which describes the ethereal folkloric representation of the "Cloud house known as Ahoaho o Tukapua, wherein the Cloud Children abide when not roaming the vast realm of Watea (space)" (1929, 418). Non-Indigenous Horror, apocalyptics, futurisms, and the macabre often draw from such legends and myths. But authentic oral storytelling also tells of lived horror described through multilayered sensory experiences in the narrative landscape, which filters through on and beyond the land-sky-water, underscoring a way of knowing. The centrifugal lens of Horror ("lensed" by the west) is inherently distorted.

Pasifikafuturism in Gina Cole's 2022 novel *Na Viro*, set in Aotearoa (New Zealand), is an illustrative example of an actualized way of theorizing. The title means "whirlpool" in Fijian and binds the title/text (as paratext or relational context) to an Indigenous metaphysical lens projected between space and the land of long white cloud (Aotearoa). The complex metaphor of *Na Viro* can be read in conjunction with Cole's lens described in her PhD dissertation "Wayfinding Pasifikafuturism" as an "indigenous science fiction vision of the ocean" (2020, 87), where she states: "My dream envisions a fleet of Indigenous literary waqa [Fijian for boat] in oceanic space sailing through a continuum of the cosmos of the science fiction story" (87). Her 2020 critique has "not delved into" the "fertile" ground of "speculative fiction genres such as fantasy, horror" (87), or postapocalyptic, apocalyptic, or dystopian-utopian fiction. Privileging her agency while "Indigenizing" speculative genres and offering "a complete ontological shift" (Topash-Caldwell 2020, 81), *Na Viro* conjures allusions to standard apocalyptic themes and tropes of Sci-Fi futurist literature and the perceived horror of ecological collapse. In her novel, as a nod to the sixth extinction, "hive" ("water wars" and "data streams") is reinscribed through land-water-sky-based knowledge (8, 11), in which transient phenomena of the cosmos, or meteors like "Comets of Knowledge," interact with the pervasive and multilayered whirlpool image, extended to its virtual holographic dimensionality—as an alternative to entanglements of matter and meaning espoused by Karen Barad (2007). *Na Viro* offers a theoretical abstraction (way of theorizing) of the constituent elements of the whirlpool and the fabric of the stars, as souls, represented in the sky as Creation narratives that become a complex relational metaphor in which "stardust gathered in her bones, a live membrane on earth, a galactic harvest" (Cole 2022, 88) showing the deep constitutive connectivity of the universe from an Indigenous, Pasifika frame of reference.

The book offers a metacommentary on global Indigenous movements and contexts. Like The "Global Indigenous" "Alliance," the metaphysical or theoretical backbone of the text runs "on Indigenous principles, in harmony with nature," chaos, creativity, the cosmic order (Cole 2022, 17), where iris circuitry, a three-dimensional hologram of a whirlpool "pattern, a swirling movement" (50), "holographic maelstrom[s]" (49), interrelate the "virtual," "machine-like" ("consistent, precise" as empiricism) (50), and strange spinning currents. This imagery suggests systems reforming and colliding. The whirlpool's continuant function and parts are mirrored in gas, ocean, solar systems. Additionally, the iris, which could be oceanic or celestial waves (Cole 2022, 210), connects to astronomical transient phenomena: "spatial ebb and flow from the whirlpool," altering the "gravity satellites," the whirlpool deflecting "this meteor into Earth's orbit" (42), just as an older "cataclysm" had embedded "green peridot gems deep within the meteorite," which "shone from the synaptic web" of burnished rocks (23) like curtains of spectral light in Creation myths. Ways of theorizing weave through layers of being in transformative, phenomenological, nominally concrete and abstract forms.

In contrast to virtual worlds, those translated in David Chalmers's *Reality+* through the "problems of philosophy" in western consciousness and multimedia (2022), the vortex like "the x-ray style" of William Wilson's sky star map is used "to paint the Ojibwe constellations . . . an allegory for the material world and spirit world" (2014, 2), reflecting another way of simultaneously seeing. A Pasifika-specific derivation of this would be Cole's three-four-n-dimensional whirlpool projecting a "holographic maelstrom" of sparkling lights like an art installation (2022, 49). The many manifestations of the whirlpool in her text are used to imply an examination of different forms of reality, the dissonance between settler and Indigenous realities underscoring different ways of being and hybrid variations of Indigenous "metaphor." Recalling interactive Fourth Indigenous Virtual Reality, this suggests a way of reorganizing ways of theorizing (Wallis and Ross 2021, 313) through digitized knowledge and states of being, in a new metacognitive framework. In *Na Viro*, this is expressed as "a whirlpool virtual tour," smashing "virtual rocks with strikers" and skirting "massive gas clouds" (Cole 2022, 50). The whirlpool functions as a multidimensional sensory Indigenous speculative conceptualization that showcases how spectral phenomena transform within Cole's parameters.

A thread of horror, "ghostly" (Cole 2022, 51), "shock[ing]" (94), "scary, this new whirlpool" (57), "dreaded" (119, 126), in *Na Vira* is tied to the rupture or melding of Indigenous metaphysics and western science (fiction) and is represented by the living whirlpool(s), a braiding together of waves, currents, threads, of nodes and networks of relationality. This mixing is a manifestation of the appropriation (utilization), corruption or deterioration, and disruption of Indigenous knowledges (systems) through light, color, substance, materiality (or co-becoming) between projections of physicality (57). Time phases are distorted "around the dying whirlpool," where a "phosphorescent circle swam in a revolving mass," seemingly representative of the cosmos mirroring the rotation of iris circuitry (328). Manifested in abstract levels of being, this "gigantic swirling light pool in the water" floats above Aotearoa, land of the white clouds (328). The epilogue binds these cosmic and telluric layers of *being* together, floating with the current (like the whirlpool); "sky enclosed . . . iris [I/us] circuitry" seen in "long focus" is a "mapping array hung suspended" (335) in the field of vision between the water, the land, the sun, and the outer reaches of space. Equally, the fractal compound iris I/us circuitry suggests interaction or intersection of different epistemological systems.

Playing on an Indigenous (geomorphic) alternative to the materiality of dark matter, in *Black Ice Matter* (2016), Cole utilizes her earlier ontological lens, bound to corporeal life (like an actualization of material being that parallels the five sides of a prism). She is building a hybrid Indigenous prism theory, for instance, exploring light in its many relational states and (phenomenological) transformations, searching "for this [transformative] phenomenon" (Cole 2016, 109) apprehended in patterns of other "muted and less spectacular version[s]" of "blazing moments" and "blood hue[s]" (109). This way of theorizing is allied with heredity, elsewhere "a bloodline leading straight back to the Tanganyikan chiefs" (as "eerie red light . . . suspended in time" (14, 109). Consider how in the text rainbows "form a perfect circle of perfect colour" (109). In representations of experiential relationality, a "transformation" begins a "slow methodical breakdown" (110) of reality. Cole ties such visualization-conceptualization models to ice floes in rivers situated through the earth as it "shifted on its axis" and ecological water cycles (110, 119), reminiscent of the Inuit experimental lens in the short film *Three Thousand*, where the aurora borealis is mapped onto the glacial landscape (Asinnajaq 2017) and methodologically linked to ways of conceptualizing through ice/water in *Do Glaciers Listen?* (Cruikshank 2005). In Oceanic worldview, transformations as action of matter/phenomena are also anchored from the page to the stars (Cole 2020, 41, 46, 47; Ihimaera and Makereti 2017, 12): stars reflected/refracted against and through various surfaces and objects in the story "Till" or "Glacier" (144, 41, 46) and "ice floes at twilight" in the story "Grain Stack" (116). A person is like "a mere particle surrounded by frozen pack ice" (39) or "[a] thread of rainbow light" as a natural prismatic effect pulsating (165) with water-land-sky-cosmos. Radical relationality of water-ice-land-based knowledge offers moments of horror, dissecting the aurora as a lens for the unseeable of material exchange in telluric and ethereal interactions of constant and ostensibly transient phenomena.

Conversely, consider overtly Indigenous Horror. Shane Hawk's 2020 volume *Anoka* is a short story collection of Indigenous Horror that contains stories such as "Soilborne," "Wounded," "Orange," "Imitate," "Dead America," and "Transfigured." The epigraph for the edition is a juxtaposition of ways of seeing through two quotations: "We will be known forever by the tracks we leave" (drawing on a "Dakota proverb"), and "Everyone must leave something behind when he dies" (Ray Bradbury's *Fahrenheit 451*, quoted in Hawk 2020). This way of seeing is extended in Hawk's "Introduction: Why Anoka?": "Something rooted in real-life folklore intrigued me"; "The name Anoka originated from the Dakota word a-no-ka-tan-han, which means 'on both sides of the river,'" as an orientational coextant lens. As with other formative genres using prefaces and back matter to critique their genre, "Story Notes" lays out an aesthetic discourse. This form of co-being in hybrid Horror continues through multisensory aesthetics of hearing, scent, taste, vision, and the unseen: "Distant thunder" and the "smell of decay . . . assaulted his olfactory senses" (Hawk 2020, 51). He "became lost in the shifting spirals of various colors": "green spirals," "tiny spirals," "colored spirals" dancing around him as more than spectacle (36, 41). Elsewhere, the image of a celestial Ghost herd on the "horizon" implies Creation myths and the historical trauma of Indigenous lived horror through colonization. Representative of material agency (co-being and becoming), Hawk's use of the cosmic spider in a cosmogonic modern sense is a transitional moment when metaphors can be mistranslated or finessed for the horrific. In "Dead America," "[t]he dreamcatcher on his wall was a mere symbol. . . . apotropaic [protection] magic behind the Ojibwe's dreamcatcher legend. . . . [H]is dreamcatcher never protected him from the evil he experienced in recurring nightmares" where "spiders haunted him" (Hawk 2020, 66). The "spinning webs of lies" (81) in spiders' dreams and nightmares present as a hybridized image and actualization as a metaphor for the dreamcatcher, and a representation of horror in which "memoirs" (82) like Indigenous identities are knowingly falsified in dominant culture: Indigenous people transforming into spiders (84). "[H]ypnotic green swirls floating" (56) are paratextually and relationally trussed to these horror-imbued "creation" stories (61), with "glow-in-the-dark stars strewn across his ceiling" (41) like the northern lights etched in the sky as one hypnotic "symbol": "A large green swirl materialized and hovered over Main Street. . . . Every single child stopped . . . and gazed into the green swirl, mesmerized" (97), symbolically associating Creation, the stars, identity, oddities, and hypnosis with material experientiality.

While Hawk explores green swirling spectral Creation metaphors, in the 2017 young adult novel *21st Century Orc*, Gregory C. Loui's visual aesthetics create a multisensory scaffolding around moments of apocalyptic horror with a "mana metaphysics model" (interview D) from Native Hawaiian epistemologies using red tendrils that flow outward everywhere like an erupting volcano. However, Loui's "whirlwind of energy as spirits" extends "out of the earth around her" (2017, loc. 4884). He draws overt attention to the construction of an Indigenous way of experientially knowing a "storm of blood and darkness" that is "[n]ot a metaphorical storm" (loc. 4887). Lightning and the dusty spiraling of tornadoes consume the moons and stars (loc. 4883). The rise and fall of a doomed "civilization" and "horrors" "poisoned the world. . . . Then the final flashes of the Great War ignited the sky . . . [a]nd from the ashes . . . [c]oncrete rose up to replace the desert" (loc. 4901). The sempiternal and evanescent moment flew by "[o]ver five thousand years, in less than a second" (loc. 4893–901). The story emphasizes forms of time, a moment/sequence that contains "the entire history" of a people over "in the blink of an eye" (loc. 4899–900). Multidimensional readings of mana in Loui's horror metaphor complicate understandings of states of being and time phases, as much as relations between spirituality, practice, genealogy, and the elements and *naʻauao* (knowledge) at the core of mana (interview D; Shapiro 2017). In terms of metaphysics and the experimental lens/imagery applied to writing and world building, Loui, for example, uses "mana as the basis for one [fictional] world's reality":

I also base the entire metaphysics of one of my worlds off the concept of mana, and how perception can alter reality. . . . In that world, mana is the foundational energy that is functionally a more complex and Indigenous-influenced version of the Force. All things in the universe have mana and all interactions with other things are mana. A storm has mana. A blade cutting through flesh has mana. A birdsong has mana. However, mana is even more complicated when societies and relationships are involved, since mana can be transferred through these relationships, and perceptions can transfer mana. For example, believing someone is a monster gives them a poisonous mana that transforms them into a monster if their own internal mana or identity is not strong enough to resist external mana from their surroundings. Basically, I'm peeved about mana being just an energy source in much of pop culture and want to express it as something more complex and as the basis of Pasifika worldview. . . . [I]n the world where I use the mana metaphysics model, horror becomes even more horrific not only due to outside perception, but its very presence can infect others with its "evil" mana. I think that's relatively common, however. (Interview D)

Concepts like mana are often simplified, mistranslated, and relabeled as "Cosmic Horror" or animism through a western lens—but they represent one relational way of knowing and being. Consider how the sacred-land-place of Heiau (or temple) and Mauna Kea/Loa (from an aerial view, a circle) reveal a Hawaiian Indigenous lens. For instance, as Gregory Clark and Chelle Pahinui note, "Hāʻena," the name of a state park, "means 'red-hot' or 'burning'" (2015, 227). It is "a place where opposites come together," "a place of transitions" where "the two dominant volcanoes, Mauna Loa and Mauna Kea, have both flowed into the sea" without crossing paths (227). Yet "salt water and freshwater flow together . . . and the primordial mud is formed. Here, the black and white sands make elegant swirls together but do not mix" (227). Transformation of states of water and land filter through, and are constituted by, the being and becoming of the volcano.

Consider two short stories by Dan Rabarts in which there is a careful suturing of narrative elements based on knowledges and Ngāti Porou ways of knowing aligned with radical relationality on, for instance, water-based knowledge and orientational systems that traverse land-sky structures. This slippage is superficially reminiscent of transient phenomena as a theoretical paradigm. In his short story "The Silence at the Edge of the Sea" (2018b), Rabarts uses the phrase the "land of the long white cloud" (37). It is the only occurrence of the phrase in any short story in the 2018 anthology and is paratextually tied to the anthology's title: *Cthulhu: Land of the Long White Cloud*, one of whose coeditors is Bryce Stevens, who is of Māori descent. Framing the long white cloud as the multiconceptual space of Te Whanga Lagoon, where "the great empty eye-sockets of a leviathan" are *lensed*, "the tiny islands and their scatterings of sea-swept rocks emerge from the murky ocean. . . . [H]ere, at the edge of the world where the sun first rises, so too does the sun first set. The day is getting on, foreshortened . . . by the curvature of the earth. . . . From the air, the island resembles the profile of some beastly skull" (Rabarts 2018b, 33), focalizing the eye/socket/lens rotting on the ocean floor as a "remnant of its being" (33). "The sea is reflected in the glowering sky," the nuances of the landscape made insignificant "on the ocean's vast canvas" (33). The "vast canvas" with a scattering of points and a reconstruction of perspective and scaling is one spatial variation of an Indigenous (Ngāti Porou/Māori) metaphysical vision. Rabarts's short story "Mother's Milk" (2018a) offers a multisensory engagement with levels of being and co-becoming of "horror" elements and characters that resonate in spectral light and telluric phenomena: "a cloud fractured briefly, a lance of sunlight piercing its cloak" (80–85). Rabarts's passages imply two different aspects of ways of theorizing by (a) showcasing scale-ratio and space-time frames, and (b) interrelating perceived sensory horror(s) with positionality related to, for example, iwi or tribe-specific knowledges held by elders that equally impact Rabarts's editing process (interview B).

Now consider an approach by the iconic Indigenous Horror writer, Cherokee and Choctaw Owl Goingback, Bram Stoker Award winner and author of *Crota* ([1996] 2019), *Tribal Screams* (2018), and *Coyote Rage* (2019). Goingback comments in an HWA interview, "Indigenous Heritage in Horror," that "creating the same tingles of terror as the movies" and using Indigenous characters offer "a different way of looking at things," drawing on "oral storytellers" and "weaving a bit of teaching [elements] into the narrative" (Goingback 2021). This way of looking is seen in "twisted braid[s] of sweetgrass" and "twisting passages of the subterranean world," yarns mapped out across the sky, allied with the "sacred hoop," the "circle of tepees," and the use of the number four amplified through Creation stories in *Crota* ([1996] 2019, 39, 45, 170–71). The "Horror genre is constantly growing, evolving, reaching out to find new ways to scare an audience," drawing on "frights from formerly overlooked cultures and distant regions of the globe" (Goingback 2021). Although Goingback uses images, legends (and transformed myths), ways of knowing and storytelling, his engagement with Indigeneity in Horror from *Tribal Screams* to *Crota* is visible at various levels of the text, in line with a weaving metaphor-methodology.

Applying a highly visual writing style, Blackfoot writer Stephen Graham Jones, in his novels *The Only Good Indians* (2020) and *My Heart Is a Chainsaw* (2021), presents a spectrum of Indigenous Horror that pushes a western dipole of Native horror realism to Slasher Horror. Elsewhere, the sensory horrors of Jones's 2022 short story "Tiddlywinks" (242–50) is part of an inclusive depiction of *Other Terrors*. While nominally subsidiary to the plot, in these various texts, light, glass, spirals, and stars reflect metaphysical engagement with horror elements: "They're in there" (interview C). In *The Only Good Indians*, character Lewis "stares at the curtainless window" (window as a horror lens, lensed, as a way of being a horror trope), "trying to memorize each waver and imperfection in the glass so he can clock the reflection when it comes" (86). The warped lens created by "ripples in the window glass," permeated by another frame of reference, signposted by "one . . . finally smears with color, with motion" (87): as the resolution of the image/trope increases, you "regret that you wanted to see the whole thing" (interview C), suggesting sensory elements connected to horror as an alternative perception. In *The*

Only Good Indians, Jones uses spectral phenomena, natural rainbows, in a domestic setting, stating: "The whole backyard is shaking and loud and fast and dangerous . . . the kind of sensory trauma where . . . that iridescent sheet of color would collapse, turn to mist" in a violent clash (2020, 36). However, *My Heart Is a Chainsaw* starts with epigraph, "The slasher film lies by and large beyond the purview of the respectable" (Clover 2021), and equally so with writing (in the slasher subgenre). Suggestive of an aurora myth of the dead seeing "nothing but stars overhead, she drifts like that . . . imagining she's on a raft of the dead" (Jones 2021, 382, 298). This is tied to the action of swirling (instead of spirals), "the swirling flames" (Jones 2021, 16), the killer "at the swirling center" (124), and "blood swirling around her outstretched fingers" (382). Ways of knowing are a spectacular enrichment in the context of "slasher theories" and demon theory (Jones 2021, 169). Jones's prose style allows "Native Horror" tropes to be read as multivalent, or intersecting, simultaneous Horror that opens up space for the discussion of Indigenous Horror frameworks.

The analysis in this chapter emphasizes that shapeshifting "tropes" of theorizing in fiction have their own vitality and diaspora, independent of western genre critique and canon. Yet "transient phenomena" as a horror metaphor can be charted from the stars and spirals in cosmic mappings, or read through oral myth and Creation, or embedded in, for instance, the weaving elements of horror in work by Goingback, moving on to the way of knowing—beyond futurist discourses of the horrors of water wars, lived horror, and eco-apocalypse. These are moments of horror, strung together, implicit in the transcelestial Pasifika whirlpool (paradigm) of Gina Cole (2022), in the compound structure of hybrid metaphors described by Indigenous authors. For example, Rabarts employs organically mathematical dark speculative visualizations and use of aurora australis as apocalyptic light, while Hawk's *Anoka*, or a-no-ka-tan-han ("on both sides of the river")–based approach to star mapping showcases incandescent and bioluminescent horror elements that circumnavigate and personify Indigenous identity in "collapsed stars" and green swirls associated with aurorae (Hawk 2020, 58). Both the dynamic fluidity of Indigenous interpretations of the aurora metaphor, and associated metacommentary by authors, signpost the notion of being lensed, genrefied, while "unsettling" mainstream (western) horror aesthetics. These representations or manifestations can be understood as the other/wise of knowing apocalypse, space-time structures, and transformative states-of-being materialities, which ultimately defy traditional (non-Indigenous) genre categories.

Tracing spectral and celestial features through trends in theorizing Indigenous horror, or horror Indigeneity related to the cosmogonic and cosmological (as one global theory vogue), this chapter takes the example of transient phenomena (as part of myth, Creation, culture, and narrative practice) to disrupt standard metaphors that function like "comets of knowledge" within other systems/lenses. The analysis in this chapter offers a reevaluation of how one reads or recodes a theoretical lens with ways of knowing, expressed in the writing of Indigenous authors who selectively incorporate elements from, for instance, virtual reality and X-ray style to mana, to abstraction, borrowing from literary, artistic, performative, and oral-filmic forms (e.g., Loui and Goingback). The unraveling of horror into a visual codex of aesthetics in the writing of Indigenous authors suggests the complexity underlying literary criticism and theory of Indigenous Horror.

Contemporary visions of conceptual-metaphor symbolics used to develop frameworks—physical and metaphysical—suggest a nodal (radial, relational, interactional, "virtual," or simultaneous) metaphor structure within horror elements of the aurora in dark speculative fiction. What becomes clear is that, like the diaspora of genre from oral tales mirroring the movement of metaphor of the aurora as oscillatory phenomena, horror elements by self-identifying Indigenous writers traverse a spectrum of subgenres and use the horror aesthetic alongside heterogeneous ways of knowing, offering unique hybrid compositions that build a lattice upon which ways of theorizing can coexist in tension with non-Indigenous Horror theory.

NOTE

1. The Aboriginal Australian Horror writer Raymond Gates (2011: "The Little Red Man") has been a public advocate of Aboriginal horror metaphysics, and D. Bruno Starrs (2014) has equally embraced the Aboriginal Fantastic.

BIBLIOGRAPHY

Asinnajaq [Isabella Weetaluktuk], dir. 2017. *Three Thousand*. National Film Board. https://www.nfb.ca/film/three_thousand_inuktitut_version/.

Barad, Karen. 2007. *Meeting the Universe Halfway: Quantum Physics and the Entanglement of Matter and Meaning*. 2nd ed. Durham, NC: Duke University Press.

Best, Elsdon. 1929. "Uenuku and the Mist Maid." In *Maori Religion and Mythology*, part 2, 418. Wellington, New Zealand: P. D. Hasselberg.

Boscov-Ellen, Dan. 2020. "Whose Universalism? Dipesh Chakrabarty and the Anthropocene." *Capitalism Nature Socialism* 31, no. 1: 70–83.

Bradbury, Ray. 1953. *Fahrenheit 451*. New York: Ballantine Books.

Chalmers, David J. 2022. *Reality+: Virtual Worlds and the Problems of Philosophy*. New York: W. W. Norton.

Clark, Gregory, and Chelle Pahinui. 2015. "He Huaka'i ma Hā'ena: Treasured Places and the Rhetorical Art of Identity." In *Huihui: Navigating Art and Literature in the Pacific*, edited by Jeffrey Carroll, Brandy Nālani McDougall, and Georganne Nordstrom, 219–36. Honolulu: University of Hawai'i Press.

Clover, Carol J. 2021. Epigraph to *My Heart Is a Chainsaw*, by Stephen Graham Jones. New York: Simon and Schuster.

Cole, Gina. 2016. *Black Ice Matter*. Wellington, New Zealand: Huia Publishers.

Cole, Gina. 2020. "Wayfinding Pasifikafuturism: An Indigenous Science Fiction Vision of the Ocean in Space." PhD diss., Massey University, Manawatu, New Zealand. https://mro.massey.ac.nz/handle/10179/16334.

Cole, Gina. 2022. *Na Viro*. Wellington, New Zealand: Huia Publishers.

Cook, Captain James. 1777. *A Voyage towards the South Pole and Round the World*, vol. 1. London: W. Strahan and T. Cadell. https://gutenberg.net.au/ebooks/e00044.html.

Cruikshank, Julie. 2005. *Do Glaciers Listen? Local Knowledge, Colonial Encounters, and Social Imagination*. Vancouver: University of British Columbia Press.

Davis, Brent. 2008. "Interrupting Frameworks: Interpreting Geometries of Epistemology and Curriculum." In *Chaos, Complexity, Curriculum, and Culture: A Conversation*, edited by William E. Doll Jr., M. Jayne Fleener, Donna Trueit, and John St. Julien, 119–32. New York: Peter Lang.

Fowler, Henry H. 2021. "Indigenous Ways of Knowing." Paper presented at the Indigenizing University Mathematics session, Canadian Mathematical Society Winter Meeting, December 7, Simon Fraser University, Burnaby, British Columbia.

Gates, Raymond. 2011. "The Little Red Man." In *Dead Red Heart: Australian Vampire Stories*, edited by Russell B. Farr, 379–95. Greenwood, Australia: Ticonderoga Publications.

Goingback, Owl. 2018. *Tribal Screams*. Trieste, Italy: Independent Legions Publishing.

Goingback, Owl. (1996) 2019. *Crota*. Trieste, Italy: Independent Legions Publishing.

Goingback, Owl. 2019. *Coyote Rage*. Trieste, Italy: Independent Legions Publishing.

Goingback, Owl. 2021. "Indigenous Heritage in Horror: Interview with Owl Goingback." Horror Writers Association, October 11. https://horror.org/indigenous-heritage-in-horror-interview-with-owl-goingback/.

Hauk, Marna. 2018. "Ecofractal Poetics: Five Fractal Geometries for Creative, Sustainable, and Just Educational Design." In *Contemporary Environmental and Mathematics Education Modelling Using New Geometric Approaches: Geometries of Liberation*, edited by Susan Gerofsky, 29–46. Cham, Switzerland: Springer.

Hawk, Shane. 2020. *Anoka: A Collection of Indigenous Horror*. N.p.: Black Hills Press.

Hawk, Shane, and Theodore C. Van Alst Jr., eds. 2023. *Never Whistle at Night: An Indigenous Dark Fiction Anthology*. New York: Vintage Books.

Horror Writers Association (HWA) Interview Series. 2021. "The HWA Honors Indigenous Peoples Day." October 10. https://horror.org/the-hwa-honors-indigenous-peoples-day-2/.

Ihimaera, Witi, and Tina Makereti. 2017. Introduction to *Black Marks on the White Page*, edited by Witi Ihimaera and Tina Makereti, 8–13. Auckland: Penguin Random House New Zealand.

Jenkins, James D., and Ryan Cagle, eds. 2020. *The Valancourt Book of World Horror Stories*, vol. 1. Richmond, VA: Valancourt Books.

Jones, Stephen Graham. 2006. *Demon Theory*. San Francisco: MacAdam/Cage.

Jones, Stephen Graham. 2020. *The Only Good Indians*. New York: Simon and Schuster.

Jones, Stephen Graham. 2021. *My Heart Is a Chainsaw*. New York: Simon and Schuster.

Jones, Stephen Graham. 2022. "Tiddlywinks." In *Other Terrors: An Inclusive Anthology*, edited by Vince A. Liaguno and Rena Mason, 242–50. New York: William Morrow.

Kovach, Margaret. 2021. *Indigenous Methodologies: Characteristics, Conversations, and Contexts*. 2nd ed. Toronto: University of Toronto Press.

Lee, Annette S., William Wilson, Jeffrey Tibbetts, and Carl Gawboy. 2014. *Ojibwe Sky Star Map: Constellation Guidebook; An Introduction to Ojibwe Star Knowledge*. St. Cloud, MN: Native Skywatchers.

Leuthold, Steven. 1998. *Indigenous Aesthetics: Native Art, Media, and Identity*. Austin: University of Texas Press.

Loui, Gregory C. 2017. *21st Century Orc*. Kindle.

Noori, Margaret. 2013. "*Beshaabiiag G'gikenmaaigowag*: Comets of Knowledge." In *Centering Anishinaabeg Studies: Understanding the World through Stories*, edited by Jill Doerfler, Niigaanwewidam James Sinclair, and Heidi Kiiwetinepinesiik Stark, 35–57. East Lansing: Michigan State University Press; Winnipeg: University of Manitoba Press.

Rabarts, Dan. 2018a. "Mother's Milk." In *Te Kōrero Ahi Kā: To Speak of the Home Fires Burning*, edited by Grace Bridges, Lee Murray, and Aaron Compton, 75–86. Wellington, New Zealand: SpecFicNZ.

Rabarts, Dan. 2018b. "The Silence at the Edge of the Sea." In *Cthulhu: Land of the Long White Cloud*, edited by Steve Proposch, Christopher Sequeira, and Bryce Stevens, 33–46. Melbourne: IFWG Publishing.

Shapiro, Treena. 2017. "Cultivating Mana Lāhui." *Ka Wai Ola* 34, no. 12 (December): 14–15. https://issuu.com/kawaiola/docs/kwo1217_web.

Soop, Alex. 2022. *Midnight Storm Moonless Sky: Indigenous Horror Stories*, vol. 1. Calgary: Durvile and UpRoute Books.

Soop, Alex. 2023. *Whistle at Night and They Will Come: Indigenous Horror Stories*, vol. 2. Calgary: Durvile and UpRoute Books.

Starrs, D. Bruno. 2014. "Writing Indigenous Vampires: Aboriginal Gothic or Aboriginal Fantastic?" *M/C Journal* 17, no. 4. https://www.journal.media-culture.org.au/index.php/mcjournal/article/view/834.

Topash-Caldwell, Blaire. 2020. "'Beam Us Up, Bgwëthnënë!' Indigenizing Science (Fiction)." *AlterNative* 16, no. 2: 81–89.

Wallis, Keziah, and Miriam Ross. 2021. "Fourth VR: Indigenous Virtual Reality Practice." *Convergence* 27, no. 2: 313–29.

White, Hartley. 2001. "Ishkwaakiiwan: The Apocalypse." In *Living Our Language: Ojibwe Tales and Oral Histories*, edited by Anton Treuer, 223–27. Saint Paul: Minnesota Historical Society Press.

Wilson, William, artist. 2014. *Ojibwe Sky Star Map*. In *Ojibwe Sky Star Map: Constellation Guide; An Introduction to Ojibwe Star Knowledge*, by Annette S. Lee, William Wilson, Jeffrey Tibbetts, and Carl Gawboy. St. Cloud, MN: Native Skywatchers.

Part 2

Interrogating Discourse and Variations of Indigenous Horror

CHAPTER 5

BLAK HORROR, BLAK NARRATOLOGY, AND LISA FULLER'S *GHOST BIRD*

KATRIN ALTHANS

In the author's note to *Ghost Bird*, Wuilli Wuilli author Lisa Fuller explains that "[t]he creatures in this story are ones we believe exist" (2019, 278). For the novel, however, she "deliberately fictionalised some of their characteristics." Therefore, and to save them from misappropriation at the hands of white authors, the creatures remain unnamed. Through this strategy, Fuller opens up a reading of this monster that is not restricted to either the fictional or the nonfictional, the literary or the anthropological. Instead, the full potential of Blak Horror[1] as found in *Ghost Bird* can best be grasped if its monsters are read from a variety of angles, including Horror studies, monster studies (both cultural and anthropological), and postcolonial studies. Blak Horror, as I understand it, successfully merges Blak onto-epistemologies of the monstrous and the horrors of colonial invasion, and through this transgresses the boundaries of fiction and reality so carefully crafted in European discourses. It also enters into a creative and critical dialogue with the European tradition of Gothic Horror but decenters the European tradition by allowing Blak experiences, traditions, and epistemologies to take center stage. In *Ghost Bird*, these two important elements of Blak Horror are combined in the form of an unnamed monster on the one hand and the horrors of white male sexual violence against Blak women, past and present, on the other. As I will argue in this chapter, the combination of both creates a contemporary, postinvasion story of Horror reality, which makes us question Eurocentric approaches to Horror and monstrosity. At the same time, this instance of Blak Horror also asks us to reconsider issues of intertextuality, narratology, and fiction, such as the canonicity of the referenced texts and traditions, the Western-centric point of view prevalent in narratology, or the categorical dichotomy of fiction versus reality so prevalent in European thought. This chapter seeks to address these questions by introducing the idea of a contemporary Blak narratology, one that is firmly grounded in Blak storytelling traditions, and by critically examining matters of postcolonial intertextuality against the background of Horror fiction and monsters.

Thinking about traditionally Eurocentric approaches to culture, literature, and epistemologies in general for me also includes constantly reflecting my own position as a white, European, middle-class scholar whose only marginalization is gender based. My reading of *Ghost Bird* and any Blak cultural element represented and created in that novel is thus necessarily flawed and incomplete. It is that of an outside position. Therefore, I propose to understand my chapter as a critical engagement with the fictional quality of the novel, one which acknowledges that it is barred from fully understanding the Blak onto-epistemological content due to a deliberate opacity in the sense of Édouard Glissant, namely as "a right *not to be understood*" (Britton 1999, 19). Such a critical engagement necessarily also needs to question the frames of reference I mentioned earlier—monster studies, Horror studies, and, most of all, postcolonial studies—as they all have their origins in Western thinking. In order to do so, I will start with a discussion of monsters in Horror studies, anthropology, and monster studies and will review the current state of scholarship in (postcolonial) narratology and intertextuality. Here, I will focus on the ways in which theories of narratology and intertextuality still very much privilege a Western norm instead of including and engaging with non-Western forms. As I will argue, it is necessary to decenter this Eurocentric point of view and to interact with non-Western traditions of, for instance, storytelling, on an equal footing. By turning to elements of Indigenous methodologies to complement the postcolonial lens, I will offer a new approach to reading Blak literature within a matrix of postcolonial studies, Blak epistemologies, and non-Western narrative practices. Afterward, I proceed to read *Ghost Bird* against the background of these theoretical considerations as an instance of Blak Horror to show the ways in which the novel creates new stories through fusing fictional(ized) Horror and Horror reality.

Monsters at the Threshold of Knowledge

In his introduction to *The Monster Theory Reader*, Jeffrey Andrew Weinstock asks whether "something [is] still a monster if one believes in its existence and has a category to define it" (2020, 3). This neatly ties in with what Asa Mittman writes about the subjects of his research: "[M]onsters, of course, do not exist" (2013, 4). "To assert that they do," he goes on, "is to enter into the realm of cryptozoology" (2013, 4). Similarly, Noël Carroll, in his *The Philosophy of Horror*, starts from the premise of a "paradox of fiction . . . [i.e.,] the question of how we can be frightened by that which *we know does not exist*" (1990, 10, emphasis added). It is only logical that Carroll limits the subject matter of his discussion to "art-horror, that is, 'horror' as it serves to name a cross-art, cross-media genre whose existence is already recognized in ordinary language" (1990, 12); yet the way he, as a matter of course, does this, is disconcerting. These nonchalant presumptions of Horror as a genre, the characteristics of which are common parlance, allow him to evade a discussion of anything Horror apart from that of a very narrow fictional genre that is defined "by stipulation" rather than argument (1990, 13). For Carroll, the most important aspect of any definition of the Horror genre is not intrinsic but audience-related—the media of transmission are self-evident: "Members of the horror genre will be identified as *narratives and/ or images* (in the case of fine art, film, etc.) predicated on raising the affect of horror in audiences" (1990, 15, emphasis added). Similarly, Weinstock explains that "contemporary monster theory . . . prefers to focus on images of and narratives involving monsters (human and non-human) to tease out what such images and narratives say about their creators and their cultures" (2020, 26). Although Weinstock, unlike Carroll, does not explicitly limit those "images of and narratives involving monsters" to literary/visual fiction or art, he nevertheless makes clear that contemporary monster theory is interested in *representations* and the cultural work those representations do (and from which cultural anxieties those representations stem).

Although monsters, as Carroll (1990, 30) is inclined to concede, are a necessary, though not sufficient, intrinsic condition of the Horror genre, they exist as an idea only, which has no counterpart in formal reality. Consequently, he discusses them in fictional terms only, distinguishing Horror from fairy tales and myth (1990, 16). Both Mittman (2013, 4–6) and Weinstock (2020, 25–26) acknowledge how closely related to the real the unreal is when it comes to monsters and Horror and take great pains to explain their position on monsters as fictitious. However, it is not the existence (or nonexistence) of monsters that is most important for them, but the "social and cultural force" of what we call monsters (Mittman 2013, 6). Or, as Weinstock puts it, "monstrosity is a socially constructed category reflecting culturally specific anxieties and desires and often deployed . . . to achieve particular sociopolitical objectives" (2020, 25). Monsters here are mere metaphors for the abject, for that which is nonhuman within the human.

Monster anthropology, as endorsed by Yasmine Musharbash (Musharbash and Presterudstuen 2014, 2020; Musharbash 2021), on the other hand, considers "monsters as non-human *actors* who are other-than-the-norm" (Musharbash 2021, 2, emphasis added). Thus, Musharbash argues, anthropology fills a gap in monster studies in that it introduces the "empirical experiences of monsters . . . of 'living with monsters'" as the opposite of "understandings of monsters as fictional or part of folklore" (2021, 11). Both approaches to monsters, however, have one thing in common, which is a belief in taxonomic order: it is the act of transgressing the boundaries of the natural order that makes the monster monstrous, thus producing what Weinstock summarizes as "a sense of epistemological crisis" (2020, 3). However, it begs the question of whose epistemology is in crisis. Mittman also argues that "the monstrous is that which creates this sense of vertigo [in the sense of Massimo Leone], that which calls into question our (their, anyone's) epistemological worldview, highlights its fragmentary and inadequate nature, and thereby asks us . . . to acknowledge the failures of our systems of categorization" (2013, 8). Although he does not limit his definition of the monstrous to any particular understanding of the world but rather explicitly includes any epistemological worldview, his definition of the monstrous nevertheless requires taxonomies that differentiate between the natural and the unnatural. Jeffrey Jerome Cohen (1996, 6) makes a similar point in his seminal essay "Monster Culture (Seven Theses)," when elaborating his third thesis, "The Monster Is the Harbinger of Category Crisis," suggesting that the categories of Western thinking are the yardstick.

Yet what about epistemologies that have categories entirely different from those of European tradition or know no such categories at all? As Mittman (2013, 7–8) rightly concedes, categories of the monstrous are as much culturally intrinsic as they are imposed by cultural outsiders, especially in colonial contexts. Weinstock (2020, 26) draws our attention to Michel Foucault and his thoughts on categories and taxonomies, arguing that all categories are ultimately products of power relations. For Horror, Carroll's reasoning is a case in point, as he boldly draws a sharp line at what was considered natural following an Enlightenment agenda of scientific rationality on the one hand and superstition on the other when he pits an audience that "operates with a cosmology in which witches, demons, werewolves, and spectral forces are part of reality" against "[t]he scientific world view of the Enlightenment" (1990, 57). What Carroll idealizes here, Enlightenment rationality and a belief in the scientific naturalization of the world, is part and parcel of the imperial project, as Mary Louise Pratt ([1992] 2008, 32) explains: "[Natural history] extracts all the things of the world and redeploys them into a new knowledge formation." It was Carl Linnaeus, after all, who introduced the categories of *Homo sapiens* and *Homo monstrosus* (Pratt [1992] 2008, 32). Stephen T. Asma offers a more diachronic look at the categorization of monsters when he writes that although monsters "always disrupt the neat categories of taxonomy" (2009, 125), they over time either became absorbed into the classificatory system of natural history or challenged existing categories, as did, for example, the platypus. The idea of the horrific and of monstrous entities, of the real and the imaginary, it seems, heavily depends on the frames of references— and those frames more often than not have their origins in western Europe. Knowledge and the categorization of knowledge has long been a Western prerogative, as Palyku women Gladys and Jill Milroy succinctly point out:

> Western knowledge, as it is currently constituted, excludes or mar-ginalises many ways of knowing, including its own ancient ways. Western knowledge is increasingly problematic because of its domi-nance over other people's world knowledge and learning systems, its innate belief in its superiority over *all* forms of "knowing," and its claims to universality when it is only a "particular" way of knowing. (2008, 23)

Or, as Linda Tuhiwai Smith in the third edition of her seminal *Decolonizing Methodologies* puts it, "[k]nowledge and the power to define what counts as real knowledge lie at the epistemic core of colonialism" (2021, xii). Despite its historical complicity in accumulating said Western knowledge, it is again helpful to look at (contemporary monster) anthropology here. Although Musharbash agrees that monsters always transgress the boundaries of cat-egories, she considers categories themselves from an anthropological point of view and argues that "taxonomic systems are socio-culturally distinct" and that thus monsters are "equally socio-culturally distinct": "[M]onsters . . . depend on subverting the taxonomic schema of *the people they haunt*" (2021, 3, emphasis added). Weinstock concedes as much when he writes of "the relativity of the monstrosity" (2020, 3). Still, there is a fundamental difference when it comes to acknowledging the reality of the monster and of Horror—and thus to ontoepistemologies and which frames of reference to be applied.

Indigenous Methodologies, Postcolonial Narratology, and Blak Horror

Naomi Simone Borwein (2018, 63) has criticized postcolonial approaches to Blak Horror as insufficient and based on Western frames of references and has repeatedly proposed a reading firmly grounded in Blak ontologies and methodologies (2018, 62; 2020, 142). An analysis of texts featuring instances of Blak Horror, she writes, should be realized "through subaltern theories such as maban reality, Aboriginal fantastic, and Aboriginal totemism—read outside the postcolonial norm" (2018, 62). As much as I agree with both points she is making, that postcolonial approaches are ultimately still Western in concept and thought and that instead non-Western onto-epistemologies and methodologies should be foregrounded, I think she is wrong in rejecting the postcolonial lens altogether—both approaches, I would argue, are not mutually *exclusive*, but rather mutually *beneficial*. This, however, needs a recentering of postcolonial thinking, much in the sense of what Smith means when she urges us "to simultaneously work with colonial and Indigenous concepts of knowledge, decentring one while centring the other" (2021, xii). For literary analyses, this would include an entirely new take on narratology, which in postcolonial contexts has so far been only discussed in terms of well-established narratological categories, but not in terms of applying an entirely new set of narrative strategies, as Dorothee Klein (2022, 9–10) summarizes. When arguing for a dialogic reading of Blak literature, she draws on Donald Goellnicht in her book-length study of several Blak authors, who criticizes Western theory-led reading practices: "Such an encounter allows for a relational understanding of Aboriginal fiction in which different epistemologies and ontologies meet and collide, opening up new fields of knowledge but also problematising their accessibility" (2022, 11). My own reading of Blak Horror is informed by this idea of dialogue, as Blak Horror is, and here I disagree with Borwein on an important issue, informed by both Aboriginal and Western traditions and can best be discussed in terms of a critical understanding of postcolonial intertextuality. At the same time, what is needed is a particularly Blak narratology that takes into consideration the status of story in Aboriginal and Torres Strait Islander onto-epistemologies.[2] To quote Jill Milroy and Grant Revell: "Aboriginal peoples live, learn, and teach by stories" (2013, 2). Consequently, they begin their discussion of how story, mapping, and Country are intertwined "with a story to give [them] direction." Similarly, C. F. Black structurally follows the stories of Elders in her study of Indigenous jurisprudence, linking story, Country, and Law when she invites her reader to "[travel] through a series of camps and [sit] down at each camp to listen to the Law story conveyed there" (2011, 8–9). Story, after all, based in Country, is the defining element, and thus an Aboriginal and Torres Strait Islander narratology must necessarily be space- and place-based. Klein in her analyses of Kim Scott's *Benang* (1999) and *That Deadman Dance* (2010) proposes to read both novels as spatially structured, and as songlines, to grasp them fully. Through this, Klein modifies Western narratological conceptions of plot: "[P]lot needs to include spatial relations if it is to accurately describe contemporary Aboriginal narratives" (2022, 52). Her take on the spatiality of plot and the agency of space in Blak literature is thus a first step in the direction of developing a Blak narratology, yet she very decidedly makes clear that her position, like mine, is in no way authoritative. Instead, she respectfully acknowledges her outsider position and the texts' opacity (2022, 52). Similarly, this chapter is neither the place nor am I in any way entitled to authoritatively discuss matters of story in a Blak context, let alone develop a Blak narratology—instead, I write from the position of a reader trained in Western literary and cultural studies who relies on what Blak scholars have decided to share. And it is through this background together with new learning that I am approaching Blak Horror.

As Mykaela Saunders makes clear in her introduction to *This All Come Back Now: An Anthology of First Nations Speculative Fiction*, there is a discrepancy between Western and Aboriginal understandings of what constitutes the speculative in speculative fiction: "Spec fic, as a Western genre, employs devices that our cultural stories have dealt in for millennia—the difference is, to us these stories aren't always parsed out into fiction or fantasy, as they are often just ways we experience life" (2022, 8). The same holds true for Blak Horror, one of the "slippery types of stories" mentioned by Saunders (2022, 8) as being part of speculative fiction, which abounds in Aboriginal cosmological reality. To label this reality speculative is problematic in itself, but only as long as our frame of reference is a Western understanding of reality. If we acknowledge that there are a number of different realities, among them realities that accommodate the matter-of-fact existence of all sorts of (sometimes nonperceivable and as-yet-never-perceived) entities, then our reading may become a third reading, like the third archive described by Margo Neale and Lynne Kelly in their *Songlines* volume of the First Knowledges series: "In combination with the Western archive, this knowledge [the Aboriginal archive of knowledge embodied in Country] creates a third archive, available to all" (2020, 5). This third reading would then bring together a reading the background of which is in European literary traditions, and a reading the background of which is Blak storytelling traditions. This, in turn, would also benefit the fields of monster studies and monster anthropology and their elephant in the room, the reality of monsters.

One such reading practice with European literary traditions in mind is that of a postcolonial intertextuality. Originating in the well-known (and much criticized) concepts of writing back (see Ashcroft, Griffiths, and Tiffin 1989) and postcolonial counterdiscourse (see Tiffin 1987), the idea of a postcolonial intertextuality gained some currency in the early 2000s (see Caminero-Santangelo 2005) but has since lost its appeal, it seems. The problem is, as I summarize elsewhere, that "postcolonial reworkings of European originals need well-known sources in order to function properly and to help the reader participate in the game of similarities and modifications, yet on the other hand, this very dependency on and centrality of the Western literary canon and its characters, plots, and ideas is their greatest flaw" (Althans 2010, 21). Despite referencing Julia Kristeva's (1980, 66) idea of intertextuality as "a mosaic of quotations" in the course of my argument (Althans 2010, 23–24), in my summary I still privilege the imperial center, even in my criticism thereof—what is missing is a more comprehensive understanding of intertextuality, one that, in addition to literature, culture, and history, also takes into account different forms of knowledge. Explaining her choice of arranging the stories in *This All Come Back Now*, Saunders writes that "each of the stories is *in conversation* with its neighbours, bound to each other by through-lines of genre, character, setting, theme or trope" (2022, 15, emphasis added). This idea very much captures the concept of a postcolonial intertextuality I am proposing here: each text is in conversation with other texts and contexts, engaging with each other and bound to each other by a complex network of connections. In the case of Blak Horror, this means there's a need to look at Horror tropes from European traditions as well as at instances of Horror found in Aboriginal onto-epistemologies, storytelling, and the horrors of colonial legacies.

As such, my understanding of Blak Horror goes beyond the definition of Indighorror suggested by Borwein and adds a further layer. For Borwein, the "nightmares of the Dreaming" are key to Indighorror, and they go together with "horrorrealism," so that Indighorror blends "horrorrealism, the violence of assimilation and dispossession, [with] dark aspects of the Dreaming, Aboriginality through mythology, totemism, and animism" (2020, 143). As I would argue, however, the dark and horrifying elements of Aboriginal onto-epistemologies and the horrors of colonial violence with its trauma and ongoing legacies work within an intricate web of intertextualities, which also includes tropes stemming from the European tradition of Gothic Horror that have been adapted to the Australian landscape. I therefore

GHOST BIRD AND BLAK HORROR

Lisa Fuller's *Ghost Bird* is a case in point here, as it connects all three elements to create an example of contemporary, postinvasion Blak Horror. Those elements are not simply there for us to discover but emerge in what Derek Attridge calls the "singularity" of a literary work, that is "the *demand* that this specific collocation of words, allusions, and cultural references makes on me in the event of my reading, here and now, as *a member of the culture to whom these codes are familiar*" (2004, 67, second emphasis added). Meaning, therefore, lies in the eye of the beholder. Attridge here is only concerned with positive knowledge of cultural codes but ignores the willful opacity of different cultural codes, the right of meanings to not emerge for the individual reader. Blak Horror in *Ghost Bird* manifests itself through a number of uncertainties that have their origins in the text's willful opacity and the readings of which change depending on the reader's cultural position. This ambiguity is embodied in the character of Stacey: "I can pinpoint the second I started to believe science more than my own mob" (Fuller 2019, 24). She used to fully embrace Murri traditions while her Nan was still alive, but "turned [her] back on Nan's beliefs" after her death (24). In the course of the novel, however, Stacey gradually finds her way back to her traditional beliefs, but this is no linear pathway. She is constantly torn between different ways of interpreting events, trying to find reasonable, that is natural scientific, explanations for what happens: "[F]or God's sake . . . I'm letting a few nightmares completely mess with my head. . . . *Reason over superstition*" (69). It is important to note that the distinction between "Reason" and "superstition" here is drawn along the lines of a *Western* understanding of what constitutes (natural) science and what mere fantasies, a dichotomy imposed by the imperial project and internalized by Stacey. In much the same way, the reader is left wondering whether or not the monsters that grabbed Laney, Stacey's twin sister, early in the novel are nonhuman real or human real, a stand-in for white male sexual violence or actual monsters. This very much echoes Tzvetan Todorov's definition of the fantastic in that the reader is kept in a state of hesitation to the very end: "The fantastic is that hesitation experienced by a person who knows only the laws of nature, confronting an apparently supernatural event" (1973, 25). It is "the dividing line between the uncanny and the marvelous" (Todorov 1973, 27), and it is precisely this liminal space Blak Horror occupies.

In *Ghost Bird*, the catalyst for the events unfolding is a necklace with a pendant made from local stones, "'those' rocks" that "Nan and all the aunties and uncles warn us about," those that are "taboo" (Fuller 2019, 215). It is this pendant that connects two streaks of Horror as embodied in two different types of monsters, one a monster of Blak ontoepistemologies and one a human monster of colonial violence and brutality. The stone is the link, but the monsters are at once the embodiment of violence against Murri women, past and present, and the corporeal enforcers of taboo: "As the pendant hits air, a howling rolls around the camp, many voices" that sound "like women screaming in the dark" (234). The pendant is directly related to May Miller's trauma, as she was forced to wear it while being raped by a local white property owner (235–36). The voices May still hears are also an example of hesitation, as they can be read either as the voices of the monsters or as legacies of trauma.

The novel here also references classic exoticized Horror tropes appropriated by non-Blak authors (and filmmakers) for monetary reasons—the commodification of Blak onto-epistemologies. By linking this trope to both Blak cosmology and colonial violence, *Ghost Bird* both reclaims Blak culture and writes back to its appropriation at the hands of white people. The taboo stones are no longer mystic artifacts used by evil Black sorcerers to curse innocent white people, but are powerful parts of Blak onto-epistemology, and the monsters watching over them "are there to enforce the correct rules of behavior when it comes to certain situations [or] places" (Fuller, personal communication, June 16, 2022). At the same time, those stones have created another, colonial-based taboo in that the Murri community of the novel's fictionalized Eidsvold has decided to declare the mountain itself taboo to "keep the kids safe after what happened to me. Read it all wrong, . . . wouldn't listen to me," as May Miller says (Fuller 2019, 230).

Whereas May's trauma and the monsters are directly connected through the stone, there is also a colonial Horror connection of the second degree, that of how May's father was murdered. The story of her father is embedded within a time frame of ever past and ever present, as it is not entirely clear whether or not Oscar Miller is indeed May's father. In her visit to the local museum, Stacey comes across an old, undated photograph depicting a group of white men with "one man in chains sitting at their feet, like a prized dog. The old blackfulla's hands are chained in front" (Fuller 2019, 132). Written on the photograph is the name Oscar Miller. As the museum lady explains, the Murri man "was the first serial killer in Queensland," and his "killing spree" was catalyzed by a property dispute (132). The way Stacey describes the people in the picture, the white men dressed in "old-fashioned finery," Oscar Miller's "long white beard flow[ing] in a way that they'd banned long ago" (132), this photograph may well have been taken way earlier than the 1930s, when May must have been abducted. The story of May's father as told by the Murri community sounds alarmingly similar, though more recent: "Your grandfather on your father's side told me a story once, bout a woman [May] that disappeared." The rumor was that property owners abducted her, "and her father went after them" for retribution (61–63). Here, Blak Horror comes not only as a matter of content but also as a matter of form, as we are faced with the horrors of colonial violence in constant reiteration through a narrative strategy that privileges an ever-present.

Taking a closer look at the monsters themselves, we find ourselves in a dilemma in terms of the nature of Blak Horror. On the one hand, the monster's appearance clearly invokes the classical monster of European Horror imagination: "*The hands return to brush my face, a harsh texture to them, like a wolfhound's rough fur, but all over. . . . A slow reverberating growl begins and at first I think the world is shaking. Two bright red pinpricks of light appear . . . I realise what I am looking at just as the soft pinch of my chin turns to a bite and claws spike into my skin*" (Fuller 2019, 189–90). On the other hand, the monsters reveal the fallacies in my earlier writing on Aboriginal Gothic: it is not a monster of Blak onto-epistemology that is depicted in Gothic terms— this is just the way it appears to readers with a European background—and as such it is not "an imitation of the original European conventions of the Gothic" (Althans 2019, 279). Instead, it is both, Blak and European, at the same time, and one cannot be read without the other. As Fuller writes elsewhere, "these are beings we believe in. For us, their existence is fact" (2020). Their appearance may make me think of the monsters of Horror fiction, but seen from a different perspective, this reading changes. "Most Western people read them as simply evil," Fuller explained to me, "but they are more complex than that" (personal communication, June 16, 2022). They rather have their rightful place in the world; a right, even a duty, to exist.

Similarly, the monster's habitat is reminiscent of some stock elements of the European Gothic tradition. Horace Walpole's Isabella becomes Stacey when she tries to find her way through the dark subterranean passages: "I step into the dark. . . . A damp, musty smell fills my nose, reminding me of unwashed fur and earth," the light obliterated, the path through the cave system twisting and turning and sloping downward (Fuller 2019, 260). There also is the trope of a hostile nature that colonial Australian Gothic so frequently employs: the everyday practice of "[w]alking through bush . . . should feel natural. But the coolness of those trees enfolds me," and it is a reminder "that this place isn't home. It's taboo. . . . A heaviness pressing on me, a warning to turn back," trees "leaning in, grabbing at my clothes" (259). Accordingly, Laney's rescue at the hand of Stacey can also be read as an instance of rewriting the male hero in an act of feminist Gothic writing, restoring order in a slightly different way. The entire idea of a restoration of order, however, so vital for the Gothic novel proper, is ambiguous. How can order in the European generic sense truly be restored if the monster is left alive? How could it have been restored, from a Blak perspective, if the monster had not been given what was wrongfully taken and had the price not been paid properly?

The novel's position within an intertextual network is not limited to European or white Australian references, though. Although I am not familiar with the particular cultural tradition of the titular ghost bird, I cannot help but draw a connection to Nicole Watson's novel *The Boundary* (2011), which itself references Sam Watson's novel *The Kadaitcha Sung* (1990), not least through the use of feathers on the cover image and as delimiters between subchapters. The ghost bird is itself a strong cultural element, as is Red Feathers in *The Boundary*, and works in a similar way to reclaim Murri cultural heritage from the commodified misappropriation in Horror fiction. On the one hand, the ghost bird sits on the very same European-imposed liminal threshold of science and cultural beliefs Stacey is hovering in—Laney uses its (slightly teenagerized) cultural designation "a fucking ghost bird" and its zoological name "Tawny frog mouths" in the same breath (Fuller 2019, 21)—and it is depicted in Gothic terms when the "silver shape glides through the night air" (191) and lets Stacey experience the same kind of fright known from classic Gothic fiction. On the other hand, as May Miller explains, "[g]host birds ain't bad. . . . Not good either. They warn" (257). They are part of culture, and their appearance once more is an example of how Murri culture is reclaimed.

It all depends on the singularity of our reading, on the cultural codes we are familiar with, those we have grown up with or have been educated in. All the instances of Horror I have mentioned in this chapter can be read from various angles, and only if those angles are combined (as far as the individual reader is able to do so), can the wealth of meaning Blak Horror carries be accessed.

Ghost Bird is an example of how the three strands of what I have identified as constituting Blak Horror are intertwined and work together as much as against each other. It uses monsters of Blak onto-epistemologies as instances of cultural pride and respect, while at the same time they also feature as stock elements of classic Horror fiction. Furthermore, there are intertextual references to a number of literary traditions, both European and white Australian as well as Murri, if the definition of intertextuality is stretched. The centrality of the stone pendant and the taboo based in a certain locality may also be read with a Blak narratology in mind, which focuses on place and does not privilege a linear time frame of storytelling. All those issues I could touch upon only superficially in this chapter, and it is just the start.

This chapter started off in an entirely different fashion, with entirely different premises and entirely different outcomes in mind. In a private email conversation with Lisa Fuller, however, I became aware of my own cultural biases and ignorance, which I thought I would never fall prey to. When I tried to reconcile what I had learned through Lisa's words and explanations with how I had conceived of this chapter, I realized I had to completely revise my reading of the monsters. The chapter then took on a life of its own. Every day of writing, new impulses surfaced, all of which had their legitimate place in my discussion of Blak Horror. This chapter has become a living organism, one that is in conversation and constant negotiations with other texts and new learnings, one that will grow through critical discussion. The reading of *Ghost Bird* I have provided in this chapter is ultimately lacking; lacking the knowledge of a cultural insider. Much of the cultural and traditional knowledge needed to fully understand (and appreciate?) the cultural stories created in the novel remains opaque to me and therefore rejects being understood in Eurocentric terms—the other is not made an "*object* of knowledge" (Britton 1999, 19), but reclaims agency. Blak Horror is a shapeshifter in its own right, and my reading invites others to join the conversation.

NOTES

1. I am using the term "Blak" to refer to Aboriginal and Torres Strait Islander people in order to, following Jack Latimore's explanation, "differentiat[e] the Blak experience from the racialized experiences of non-Indigenous communities of colour" (2021).

2. In a personal email communication of June 16, 2022, Lisa Fuller drew my attention to the fact that the term "story" is "yet another English term that doesn't do the telling justice." My thoughts on the importance of stories within a Blak narratology in this chapter reflect the multifarious nature of this concept, which remains opaque in English.

BIBLIOGRAPHY

Althans, Katrin. 2010. *Darkness Subverted: Aboriginal Gothic in Black Australian Literature and Film*. Representations & Reflections, no. 2. Göttingen: V&R Unipress.

Althans, Katrin. 2019. "Aboriginal Gothic." In *Twenty-First-Century Gothic: An Edinburgh Companion*, edited by Maisha Wester and Xavier Aldana Reyes, 276–88. Edinburgh Companions to the Gothic. Edinburgh: Edinburgh University Press.

Ashcroft, Bill, Gareth Griffiths, and Helen Tiffin. 1989. *The Empire Writes Back: Theory and Practice in Post-Colonial Literatures*. London: Routledge.

Asma, Stephen T. 2009. *On Monsters: An Unnatural History of Our Worst Fears*. Oxford: Oxford University Press.

Attridge, Derek. 2004. *The Singularity of Literature*. Abingdon, Oxon., England: Routledge.

Black, C. F. 2011. *The Land Is the Source of the Law: A Dialogic Encounter with Indigenous Jurisprudence*. Abingdon, Oxon., England: Routledge.

Borwein, Naomi Simone. 2018. "Vampires, Shape-Shifters, and Sinister Light: Mistranslating Australian Aboriginal Horror in Theory and Literary Practice." In *The Palgrave Handbook to Horror Literature*, edited by Kevin Corstorphine and Laura R. Kremmel, 61–75. Cham, Switzerland: Palgrave Macmillan.

Borwein, Naomi Simone. 2020. "Synchronic Horror and the Dreaming: A Theory of Australian Aboriginal Horror and Monstrosity." In *Horror Literature from Gothic to Post-Modern: Critical Essays*, edited by Michele Brittany and Nicholas Diak, 141–63. Jefferson, NC: McFarland.

Britton, Celia M. 1999. *Edouard Glissant and Postcolonial Theory: Strategies of Language and Resistance*. Charlottesville: University Press of Virginia.

Caminero-Santangelo, Byron. 2005. *African Fiction and Joseph Conrad: Reading Postcolonial Intertextuality*. Albany: State University of New York Press.

Carroll, Noël. 1990. *The Philosophy of Horror; or, Paradoxes of the Heart*. New York: Routledge.

Cohen, Jeffrey Jerome. 1996. "Monster Culture (Seven Theses)." In *Monster Theory: Reading Culture*, edited by Jeffrey Jerome Cohen, 3–25. Minneapolis: University of Minnesota Press.

Fuller, Lisa. 2019. *Ghost Bird*. St. Lucia, Australia: University of Queensland Press.

Fuller, Lisa. 2020. "Why Culturally Aware Reviews Matter." *Kill Your Darlings*, October 5. https://www.killyourdarlings.com.au/article/why-culturally-aware-reviews-matter/?utm_content=buffer989c2&utm_medium=social&utm_source=twitter.com&utm_campaign=buffer.

Klein, Dorothee. 2022. *Poetics and Politics of Relationality in Contemporary Australian Aboriginal Fiction*. New York: Routledge.

Kristeva, Julia. 1980. "Word, Dialogue, and Novel." In *Desire in Language: A Semiotic Approach to Literature and Art*, by Julia Kristeva, translated by Leon S. Roudiez, 64–91. New York: Columbia University Press.

Latimore, Jack. 2021. "Blak, Black, Blackfulla—Language Is Important, But It Can Be Tricky." Reconciliation Australia, November 5. https://www.reconciliation.org.au/jack-latimore-blak-black-blackfulla-language-is-important-but-it-can-be-tricky/.

Milroy, Gladys, and Jill Milroy. 2008. "Different Ways of Knowing: Trees Are Our Families Too." In *Heartsick for Country: Stories of Love, Spirit, and Creation*, edited by Sally Morgan, Tjalaminu Mia, and Blaze Kwaymullina, 22–42. Fremantle, Australia: Fremantle Press.

Milroy, Jill, and Grant Revell. 2013. "Aboriginal Story Systems: Remapping the West, Knowing Country, Sharing Space." *Occasion: Interdisciplinary Studies in the Humanities* 5 (March 1). https://shc.stanford.edu/sites/default/files/2013-02/OCCASION_v05i01_MilroyRevell_032213_0.pdf.

Mittman, Asa Simon. 2013. "Introduction: The Impact of Monsters and Monster Studies." In *The Ashgate Research Companion to Monsters and the Monstrous*, edited by Asa Simon Mittman and Peter J. Dendle, 1–14. Farnham, Surrey, England: Ashgate.

Musharbash, Yasmine. 2021. "Monsters." In *The Open Encyclopedia of Anthropology*, edited by Felix Stein. https://www.anthroencyclopedia.com/entry/monsters.

Musharbash, Yasmine, and Geir Henning Presterudstuen, eds. 2014. *Monster Anthropology in Australasia and Beyond*. New York: Palgrave Macmillan.

Musharbash, Yasmine, and Geir Henning Presterudstuen, eds. 2020. *Monster Anthropology: Ethnographic Explorations of Transforming Social Worlds through Monsters*. Abingdon, Oxon., England: Routledge.

Neale, Margo, and Lynne Kelly. 2020. *Songlines: The Power and Promise*. First Knowledges, 1. Melbourne: Thames and Hudson Australia.

Pratt, Mary Louise. (1992) 2008. *Imperial Eyes: Travel Writing and Transculturation*. 2nd ed. New York: Routledge.

Saunders, Mykaela, ed. 2022. *This All Come Back Now: An Anthology of First Nations Speculative Fiction*. St. Lucia, Australia: University of Queensland Press.

Scott, Kim. 1999. *Benang: From the Heart*. Fremantle, Australia: Fremantle Press.

Scott, Kim. 2010. *That Deadman Dance*. Sydney: Pan Macmillan Australia.

Smith, Linda Tuhiwai. 2021. *Decolonizing Methodologies: Research and Indigenous Peoples*. 3rd ed. London: Bloomsbury Academic.

Tiffin, Helen. 1987. "Post-Colonial Literatures and Counter-Discourse." *Kunapipi* 9, no. 3: 17–34.

Todorov, Tzvetan. 1973. *The Fantastic: A Structural Approach to a Literary Genre*. Translated by Richard Howard. Cleveland: The Press of Case Western Reserve University.

Watson, Nicole. 2011. *The Boundary*. St. Lucia, Australia: University of Queensland Press.

Watson, Sam. 1990. *The Kadaitcha Sung*. Ringwood, Australia: Penguin Books Australia.

Weinstock, Jeffrey Andrew. 2020. "Introduction: A Genealogy of Monster Theory." In *The Monster Theory Reader*, edited by Jeffrey Andrew Weinstock, 1–36. Minneapolis: University of Minnesota Press.

CHAPTER 6

INDIGENOUS HORROR IN LATIN AMERICA

PERSEPHONE BRAHAM

Given the vast size, cultural diversity, and artistic production of the eighteen or nineteen countries we usually include under the rubric "Latin America"— a collection of modern political entities colonized mainly by the Portuguese and the Spanish—the categories contained within "Indigenous horror film in Latin America" all require some qualification. Today, there are several hundred Indigenous languages spoken in Latin America, the most widely used being Nahuatl (Mexico), various Mayan languages (Mexico and Central America), Tupí-Guaraní (Paraguay and parts of Argentina, Bolivia, and Brazil), Quechua and Aymara (Ecuador, Peru and Bolivia), and Mapuche (Patagonian Chile and Argentina). However, few of these groups have traditionally participated in mainstream media and cultural production, especially in Indigenous languages. Insofar as they are represented in national culture at all, they are relegated to museums, archaeological sites, and artisanal marketplaces.

Identifying specific cultural phenomena as "Indigenous" can itself be problematic given Latin America's history of conquest and colonization. The Spanish methodically extirpated Indigenous textual culture wherever they found it, so what we know of pre-Columbian history and traditions is largely from reconstructions created under Spanish religious supervision. Evangelizers worked to convince the Indigenous that their gods and local spirits were the Devil (Coluccio 1984, 22). The prolonged evangelization campaign waged throughout Latin America from 1492 forward, in addition to popular traditions brought by adventurers from the Iberian Peninsula and other parts of Europe, left few Indigenous customs and beliefs free of syncretic influence.

Our knowledge of nonliterate cultures is similarly compromised. The advent of philology and folklore studies in the early nineteenth century coincided with Latin American independence (1810–1825), and the presence of European and US anthropologists at critical junctures shaped Latin American ethnological practices within the larger framework of nation building. In this context, it is not unlikely that the monsters and myths of Western antiquity, introduced in the chronicles of conquest and reinforced through evangelization, were again injected into descriptions of Indigenous and syncretic belief by mythographers and folklorists trained in the structuralist and comparatist traditions. Popular horror figures such as La Llorona (the Crying Woman) may have roots in pre-Columbian belief, but we only know their stories through mediated reconstructions and cannot avoid comparisons with figures of Western myth such as Medea.

The Iberian Americas also experienced a much longer process of racial mixture than English and French colonies, and many Latin American cultures are predominantly ethnically mixed (mestizo), or at least advertised as such in official discourse. These so-called myths of *mestizaje* elide and further marginalize the "unmixed" Indigenous, while making a fetish of their more spectacular beliefs and practices. As an example, twentieth-century Mexican horror film appropriates motifs from pre-Columbian cultures without lending any particular dimension to contemporary Indigenous interests or identities.

REGISTERS OF INDIGENEITY

Taking into consideration all of the above, we find it useful to limit the application of the concept of "Indigenous horror" to a few films that demonstrate the diverse registers of Latin American Indigeneity while foregrounding salient movements and tendencies. In countries like Peru where there are sizeable, segregated Indigenous communities, movements like *cine regional* and categories like *cine de terror andino* allow us to consider an autochthonous corpus defined by its geographical, cultural, and ethnic separation from the mestizo culture of the capital. By the same token, important horror films by metropolitan filmmakers would be left out if we limited this study to films made by Indigenous filmmakers, on Indigenous topics, in Indigenous languages, for Indigenous audiences. In Mexico or Colombia there is a less clear-cut "100% Indigenous" body of filmmaking, but many substantial films focus on the horror of specific Indigenous experiences or use Indigenous lore as a source for horror. "Registers of Indigeneity," in this context, refers to the gamut of representations arising from the Indigenous origins or characteristics of a given film narrative; the degree to which the narrative represents particularly Indigenous problems or histories; the cultural attributes of the filmmakers; the target audience; and the tools and techniques brought to bear in the creation of the cinematic illusion.[1]

LA LLORONA: CONQUEST, "AZTEC HORROR," AND GENOCIDE

Latin American *cine de terror*, or horror film, has deep roots. The story of La Llorona, one of Latin America's most enduring horror legends, is captured in one of Mexico's first horror films, Ramón Peón's *La Llorona* (The Crying Woman, 1933). As mentioned above, our knowledge of the Indigenous sources is secondhand. The figure of the Crying Woman is described in three postconquest histories: Dominican friar Diego Durán's (c. 1537-1588) *Historia de las Indias de Nueva España e islas de la Tierra Firme* (composed between 1576 and 1581, also known as the *Códice Durán*); Diego Muñoz Camargo's (c. 1529-1599) *Historia de Tlaxcala* (1591); and Franciscan friar Bernardino de Sahagún's (c. 1499-1590) *Historia general de las cosas de la Nueva España* (1540–1585, also called the *Códice Florentino*). The last was written in Nahuatl (in Roman transliteration), Latin, and Spanish. According to these accounts, La Llorona appeared in the sixth of eight "fateful portents" (*presagios funestos*) revealed to Moctezuma II, the Aztec emperor destined to be conquered by the Spaniards under Hernán Cortés. This is the version presented by Muñoz Camargo:

> The sixth wonder was this: the people heard in the night the voice of a weeping woman, who sobbed and sighed and drowned herself in her tears. This woman cried: "O my sons, we are lost . . . !" Or she cried: "O my sons, where can I hide you . . . ?" (León-Portilla 2006, 7)

> El sexto prodigio y señal fue que muchas veces y muchas noches, se oía una voz de mujer que a grandes voces lloraba y decía, anegándose con mucho llanto y grandes sollozos y suspiros: "¡Oh hijos míos! del todo nos vamos ya a perder . . ." e otras veces decía: "Oh hijos míos ¿a dónde os podré llevar y esconder . . . ?" (Muñoz Camargo 2007)

Whether or not the La Llorona myth is of wholly Indigenous origins,[2] the Mexican version of her legend became bound up with the story of another Indigenous woman, Malintzin/Malinalli, who was sold as a slave to the Spaniards and became Cortés's companion. Malintzin became known as Doña Marina or La Malinche, and she was a brilliant strategist and linguist; without her interpretation and deep knowledge of Indigenous political tensions, Cortés's project might have had an entirely different outcome. Like Helen of Troy, Eve, Pandora, La Cava, and other ill-fated women of myth and history, La Malinche was blamed for betraying her people to the Spanish. The quintessential "bad mother," she was both victim and author of the Mexican condition.

Versions of the Llorona myth in various parts of Latin America describe her as a woman dressed all in white, with long, black hair, who weepingly accosts passersby. As one folklorist puts it, "When someone stops to help her, she uses the opportunity to rob them of all their possessions, and sometimes even takes their clothing, causing the victim to have a nervous breakdown from which it takes a long time to recover" ("Cuando alguien detiene su paso para socorrerla, aprovecha la circunstancia para quitarle todo lo que posee, y en algunas ocasiones hasta la ropa, originando en la víctima una crisis nerviosa de la que ha de tardar en reponerse") (Coluccio 1984, 255).[3] Sometimes La Llorona wanders along riverbanks and other waterways, and any encounter with her is fatal, especially for men.

Peón's *La Llorona* is a modern tale framed around two long, historical flashbacks. The first is the tale of a young "Indian princess"[4] in colonial Mexico who kills herself and her young son when her Spanish lover refuses to marry her. A second flashback tells the story of Doña Marina and Cortés. Malintzin's betrayal has earned the hatred of the Indigenous population (*la raza vencida* or vanquished race), and, fearful for the life of their young son, Cortés takes him away from her. Malintzin goes mad and then commits suicide, swearing vengeance on all his descendants. The "curse of La Malinche" is thus integrated into the figure of the crying woman whose wanderings presaged the conquest. In both historical episodes, the Indigenous women wear a mysterious ring that carries the curse from generation to generation and stab themselves in the heart with an obsidian knife, symbolically performing the ritual Aztec sacrifice that so horrified the original conquistadors. In each death scene, the spirit of the dead woman is shown rising from her corpse, accompanied by eerie wailing.[5]

Peón's *La Llorona* was made one year after Soviet filmmaker Sergei Eisenstein's *¡Que viva México!* (1932), which amplified Indigenous and folk motifs—stark countryside, serape-draped peasants, nopal cactus, carved stone skulls from an Aztec temple, and the *calavera* masks of the Day of the Dead—into an iconographic shorthand for *la mexicanidad*, or the condition of being Mexican. Peón's film, in which an ancient "Indigenous curse" menaces a present-day bourgeois family, draws on Eisenstein's theme of an *other, deeper* Mexico that simultaneously exists within, and resists, the modern. The notion of a powerful, potentially violent, Indigenous ("Aztec") element within the rational, developed Mexican nation guided interpretations of *la mexicanidad* for many decades. At the same time, the Mexican state exercised a politics of *mestizaje* (in which, as the cliché goes, even the elites who send their dry cleaning to Paris have an Indigenous *abuela* somewhere) through patronage and control of the arts, film, museums, and mass media, which we now recognize as a politics of "de-Indianization" or *desindianización* (Rojas 2017). The actor/director Emilio "El Indio" Fernández (whose Indigenous origins were never proven) made his fortune on visual clichés of idealized Indigeneity in films like *María Candelaria* (1943), where patently white, European actors (in this case Dolores del Río, who had just returned from a career in Hollywood and a broken affair with Orson Welles) played humble Indigenous peasants.[6]

In contrast to (and in tension with) the suppressive whitewashing of Indigenous and rural populations in mainstream Mexican film, the B-movie "Aztec horror" genre propagated a vocabulary of gruesome themes and motifs such as ritual sacrifice, *tzompantli* (walls or racks of skulls on display), mummies, the Day of the Dead, and so on. "Aztec" (*azteca*) was a general term used by the Nahuatl-speaking Mexica people of Tenochtitlan to describe a military alliance that included many groups in central Mexico. It came into common use among Europeans in the eighteenth century. Today, the term *mexica* or *mexika* is preferred. However, the term "Aztec" functions as a sign or construct, much like the racist term "voodoo," connoting extreme, violent, and/or occult practices. As one critic observes, in Aztec horror film, the "idyllic landscapes and tragically noble Indians are replaced by human sacrifice, decaying corpses, and maniacal scientists" (Gunckel 2007, 122). An early example of this genre, Chano Urueta's *El signo de la muerte* (The Mark of Death, 1939), revolves around an ancient codex that holds the key to resurrecting the Aztec race (which, as we know, never disappeared) through the ritual sacrifice of four virgins. This sets the tone for the genre, which mixes Aztec motifs with Hollywood tropes and techniques. Mexican actors and filmmakers frequently worked or trained in Hollywood during the 1930s and 1940s, and Hollywood horror blockbusters such as *Dracula* (Tod Browning, 1931) were filmed simultaneously with Spanish-speaking casts for Latin American distribution. The attitude of the films reflects the educated public's view of Indigenous culture as "an important aspect of national patrimony and identity" (Gunckel 2007, 126), but simultaneously it seeks to elicit a prurient enjoyment of violent spectacle and ritual barbarity that is entirely *other*. Aztec horror reached its peak in the late 1950s and 1960s, with Rafael Portillo's Momia Azteca series; Chano Urueta's massive opus; the numerous superhero-horror films featuring *lucha libre* hero El Santo; and so on.

There are many, many films about the Llorona myth, and, as we see in the conflation of the filicide Llorona with the mad witch Medea; the violated, reviled Malinche; sensual, man-hungry river spirits or sirens; and Eve, the author of Man's expulsion from the Garden of Eden, she comes to embody a generalized, multivalent monstrous femininity. In horror film, the Llorona figure becomes increasingly detached from Indigenous tradition or belief. René Cardona's *La Llorona* (1960), like the 1933 film, is the story of Luisa del Carmen/La Llorona (played by María Elena Marqués), an "Indian princess" with no specific connection to Doña Marina/Malinche, who betrayed her people for the love of a rather generic Spanish conquistador and is reincarnated in the present day as a nanny to a descendent of her lover. Rafael Baledón's *La maldición de La Llorona* (The Curse of the Crying Woman, 1963), a very well-known Gothic take on the legend, barely alludes to its Indigenous connection through the vengeful ghost of the witch Marina.

Jayro Bustamante's *La Llorona* (Guatemala, 2019) is the most truly "Indigenous" of the Llorona films to date; in fact, it is a momentous, authentic testimonial to the historical and present-day horrors experienced by Latin America's Indigenous peoples. The film centers on the fundamental fact of postcontact Indigenous experience: the horror of genocide—both general, in the course of the conquest and ensuing enslavements, and particular, as a recurring pattern of mass violence visited upon Indigenous communities by their governments and other powers. It was nominated for more than sixty awards and has garnered twenty-eight prizes to date from international critics' associations (IMDb n.d.). It is the first film from Central America, not to mention Guatemala, to be nominated for the Golden Globe (2021). Bustamante's previous film, *Ixcanul* (Volcano, 2015) was filmed mostly in the Kaqchikel Mayan language, by native Kaqchikel speakers, and parts of *La Llorona* are also presented in Mayan.

Bustamante's *La Llorona* deploys the legend of a grieving woman searching for her children as a metaphor for the collective and individual trauma suffered by Guatemala's Indigenous at the hands of the US-backed Guatemalan government and armed forces. Sometimes rather cynically called a "civil war," the violence that took place between 1960 and 1996 is also referred to as the Guatemala or Maya Genocide. A military campaign of massacres, disappearances, tortures, and rapes, the war was nominally waged against leftist guerrilla insurgents—as in the case of Peru, discussed below—but was really motivated by movements toward land reform and Indigenous suffrage: in short, challenges to Guatemala's feudal economy and social structure. According to a 1999 United Nations report, the violence was almost entirely one-sided, leaving more than two hundred thousand mostly Maya victims dead and forty-five thousand missing (Amnesty International 2012). The report stated that the army was responsible for most of the crimes. Although General José Efraín Ríos Montt, the political and military force behind the worst atrocities, was tried and sentenced to prison for his crimes, his sentence was overturned and he was never punished, dying in 2018 at the age of ninety-one. La Llorona is also the name of a tiny village that was "disappeared" in 1981 following one of the early massacres (reckoned to be over six hundred people killed).

La Llorona is Bustamante's first horror picture. The main character, Alma, is played by Mayan Kaqchikel actress María Mercedes Coroy (of *Ixcanul*), with a large supporting Mayan cast. The film takes place mostly in the residence of retired general and former president Enrique Monteverde (a stand-in for Ríos Montt, played by Julio Díaz), who is on trial for his role in the genocide. His family, who represents the elites who support the dictatorship, is starting to unravel: his wife, Carmen (Margarita Kenéfic), convenes fanatical Catholic prayer circles, and his daughter Natalia (Sabrina De La Hoz) gradually realizes that her husband may have been disappeared by her own father's order. When Monteverde is found guilty but then goes free, a growing mob of protesters surrounds the house, demanding justice for their missing family members. One night, Monteverde is awakened by the sound of a woman crying; he arms himself with an old service weapon but only finds a dripping faucet. He becomes so agitated that he discharges his weapon when Carmen comes upon him, slightly wounding her. Recognizing La Llorona's curse in the eerie episode, the servants abandon the house, leaving only the housekeeper, Valeriana (María Telón), who quickly brings in a new servant, Alma, from her town.

The turning point of the film is when Alma emerges from the protesting crowd dressed in white, looking directly up into the eyes of the cowering family within the house as she passes through the police barriers toward them. Little by little, we learn through fragmented flashbacks that appear in Carmen's dreams that Alma's children were drowned in front of her twenty years previously at Monteverde's personal direction.[7] Alma, whose name means soul or spirit, is closely associated with water and is often shown bathing, washing, or simply drifting submerged in the garden pool, her black hair floating in long tentacles around her. The uncanny behavior of water in its various forms invokes La Llorona's association with seductive, malevolent water spirits, and Monteverde, coming upon her submerged in a bath, becomes aroused even as he tries to kill her. Captivated by Alma's spiritual influence, the general's granddaughter, Sara (Ayla-Elea Hurtado), follows her into the pool and almost drowns. The sound of dripping water and tears disturb the general when he tries to rest; rooms inexplicably flood; a stack of flyers with the faces of the missing fills the garden pool like water lilies (and then turn into frogs); when Alma emerges from the pool bathed in moonlight and wearing a white dress, it is impossible to tell if she is real or a specter.

Alma embodies the collective spirit of Guatemala's Indigenous victims, particularly all the women who were raped by soldiers and saw their children murdered (recalling the story of La Malinche). At the same time, she is a siren, a spirit of collective denunciation and even vengeance. By the film's end, we realize that the roiling protesters from whose midst she first emerged are actually the ghosts of Monteverde's victims, and we can surmise that Alma manifests as a physical being through their will.

The filming of *La Llorona* was obstructed by a former exterior minister, and Guatemala's elites complained that the film showed the country in a bad light ("no mostraba a la sociedad guatemalteca bajo una luz favorable") (*Diario las Américas* 2021). Fearing further interference, Bustamante shot the film at the Mexican and French embassies in Guatemala City, as that was international territory, and rushed to complete the film within a year from pre- to postproduction. The story goes that Bustamante chose horror for its marketing advantage as a genre that would appeal to younger audiences. However, horror is the only genre that could possibly convey Guatemala's recent history. In telling this story in Indigenous voices through the frame of an Indigenous legend, re-presenting the testimony of Ríos Montt's Indigenous victims, Bustamante gives voice to the ghosts of generations.

CIRO GUERRA'S *EMBRACE OF THE SERPENT*: EXTRACTIVIST HORROR

Like Jayro Bustamante, Ciro Guerra is an award-winning filmmaker whose *El abrazo de la serpiente* (Embrace of the Serpent, 2015) is acclaimed among international audiences, critics, and film organizations. It was the first Colombian film to be nominated for an Oscar (2016). Guerra similarly directs his cinematic eye to Indigenous and rural experience, privileging nonmetropolitan voices and histories, although he does not identify as a member of an Indigenous community. In terms of registers of Indigeneity, both filmmakers, while definitely metropolitan (European/mestizo/ladino) in terms of class, training, and phenotype, have acquired significant credibility as interpreters of Indigenous landscapes. *El abrazo de la serpiente* was shot on location in the Colombian Amazon region, employing local Indigenous (nonprofessional) actors representing multiple linguistic groups.

However, as Charlotte Gleghorn observes, the recent centering of Indigenous stories by metropolitan filmmakers "has taken place largely in parallel to circuits of Indigenous filmmaking across Latin America" (2020, 32): that is, it should not be mistaken for "Indigenous filmmaking" per se. Furthermore, Bustamante and Guerra are not exempt from criticism for what one critic rather scathingly describes as their "indigeneity-oriented cinematic productions" (Gonzalez Rodriguez 2022, 144). Questions about the deployment of Indigenous language, identity, or history in such films as a kind of imagological virtue signaling rather an authentic mode of communication are certainly worthy of scrutiny. As another critic notes, these works enjoy a weighted symbiotic relationship with their subjects:

> The work of Jayro Bustamante, like that of Ciro Guerra, shows how the audiovisual medium makes possible a greater visualization of Indigenous peoples, amplified by the hegemonic institutional and cultural backing that international film festivals bring with them.

> Tanto la obra de Jayro Bustamante como la de Ciro Guerra muestran cómo el medio audiovisual ha posibilitado una mayor visualización de los pueblos originarios, amplificada por el hegemónico respaldo institucional y cultural que conllevan los festivales internacionales de cine. (González de Canales Carcereny 2020, 10)

Unlike *La Llorona*, *El abrazo de la serpiente* is not explicitly a horror film. There are no ghosts or other supernatural phenomena. However, both films portray the traumas arising from a historical horror visited on Indigenous peoples. Indigenous populations were devastated by the rubber extraction fever that burned through the Amazon Basin between 1879 and 1912, and again during World War II. So-called rubber barons enslaved Indigenous peoples (many from previously uncontacted groups), using involuntary transportation, forced labor, abusive economic practices, rape, torture, and murder in the pursuit of rubber for predominantly US and British markets. Epidemics and border conflicts among the affected nations added to the holocaust. The horrors of "rubber fever" were famously exposed in Colombian writer José Eustasio Rivera's novel *La vorágine* (The Vortex, 1924), which depicts a ravaged jungle consuming its despoilers.

Guerra's film is framed by the personal and racial history of the Indigenous shaman Karamakate (played by Nilbio Torres and Antonio Bolívar), focused through his encounters with German ethnographer Theodor Koch-Grünberg (played by Jan Bijvoet, called Theo von Martius in the film) in 1909 and US ethnobotanist Richard Evans Schultes (played by Brionne Davis, called Evan Schultes in the film) in 1940. Karamakate is a remnant: the last of his tribe and sole surviving custodian of Indigenous knowledge, language, and tradition on the threshold of extinction. Guerra initially framed the story around the two anthropologists' journals and photographs, but he quickly realized that Western "knowledge" of Indigenous cultures is entirely inadequate:

> As I started working with the Amazonian communities, I realized that their point of view regarding this story had never been told. . . . In order for the film to be true to that, I had to stop being faithful to the "truth" because, to them, ethnographic, anthropological, and historical truths were as fictional as imagination and dream, which for them was valid. (Casey 2016)

Ultimately, the film seems to argue that the ethnographic "production" of non-Western cultures has always served colonialism. Both anthropologists are seeking the rare, sacred *yakruna* flower, von Martius to cure his illness and Schultes ostensibly to find spiritual enlightenment via its hallucinogenic properties but actually because it grows alongside a desirable rubber plant. Each expedition takes place on the eve of a world war provoked by rampant Western imperialism. When von Martius photographs Karamakate early in the film, Karamakate describes the photographic image as *chullachaki*, or dehistoricized remnant, explaining a that a *chullachaki* (written or photographic) is similar to us, but captures us.[8] The photographic *chullachaki* is emptied of time and memories. The capture of the *chullachaki* via the technology of ethnographic archive is therefore a spiritual analog to the extraction of the natural resources of the Amazon and the cannibalistic transmutation of enslaved Indigenous bodies into rubber wealth. When Schultes encounters Karamakate in 1940, the shaman describes himself as *chullachaki*. The film itself is in black and white, alluding to the extractivist nature of ethnographic knowledge production (Pare 2022, 186) and Karamakate's condition as ghostly remnant.

El abrazo de la serpiente portrays Western education and evangelism as similarly cannibalistic, and here is where horror comes into play. The Spanish and Portuguese colonial enterprise was bolstered by a discourse of civilization and evangelization that focused on the eradication of cannibalism and rhetorically associated "barbaric" practices such as polyamory, sodomy, and nakedness, as documented in the protoethnographic lore of the day. Isabel of Castille's 1503 "Cannibal Law" exempting noncannibal peoples from despoliation was followed in 1510 by a papal decree expressly permitting enslavement of cannibals, and the imputation of cannibalism became a license to enslave and murder Indigenous peoples.[9]

In *El abrazo de la serpiente*, von Martius and Karamakate stop at a Capuchin mission in Colombia's Vaupés region. The missionaries are running a school for Indigenous orphans of various rubber massacres, to save them from "cannibalism and ignorance" through the rigors of deculturation. A plaque at the mission entrance explicitly links the evangelical mission with rubber exploitation:

> In recognition of the value of the Colombian rubber pioneers, who, risking their lives and fortunes, bring civilization to lands of cannibals and savages, showing them the way of the Lord and His Holy Church. (Rafael Reyes, President of Colombia, 1907)

> En reconocimiento del valor de los pioneros colombianos del caucho, quienes, arriesgando su vida y bienes, traen la civilización a tierras de caníbales y salvajes, mostrándoles el camino del Señor y de su santa Iglesia. (Rafael Reyes, presidente de Colombia 1907)

The priests are running a kind of wholesale *chullachaki* production line, stealing the children's "pagan" names and erasing their language and cultural memory. Karamakate tells a rapt group of boys about their culture and ecology, and slyly admonishes them not to believe the Christians' "crazy tales about eating the body of their gods." In the night, the visitors witness the Gothic torchlight spectacle of Father Gaspar ceremonially whipping one of the boys, who is tied to a post, solemnly observed by the other orphans. Some thirty years later, when Schultes and Karamakate return to the area, the way is marked by a crucified corpse. They are taken to the mission, called "our Eden" and run by a self-appointed Brazilian "Messiah" whose acolytes are the grown-up boys. The acolytes are variously styled as old-fashioned tonsured monks, and hooded henchmen in grass skirts.[10] Various scenes of horror follow: a crucified boy shot through with arrows (à la Saint Sebastian) is surrounded by penitent monks scourging themselves and walking on their knees; Karamakate performs a healing ritual on the Messiah's companion; and the hallucinating acolytes devour their Messiah, now calling himself "Redeemer of the Indians," during the ensuing orgy of celebration.

To my knowledge, no one has yet commented on Guerra's obvious debt to the Italian exploitation films of the 1970s and 1980s, in particular the subgenre "Cannibal Horror." These films usually involve a scientific or ethnographic expedition that disappears into the jungle and gets eaten by cannibals. The best known of these is Ruggero Deodato's 1980 film *Cannibal Holocaust*, summarized as follows in IMDb:

> 1979. Determined to make a documentary about the Indigenous cannibalistic tribes of the virgin Amazon rainforest, a small American film crew sets foot in the unexplored, peril-laden jungle. Instead, the team disappears without a trace. Six months later, noted anthropologist Harold Monroe and his seasoned guides embark on a mission to locate the missing documentarians in the heart of the Green Inferno. Before long, unsettling evidence about their fate comes to light. Now, a desperate battle to recover the raw footage begins. (Riganas 1985)

This setup is quite similar to that of Rivera's *La vorágine* and Guerra's *El abrazo de la serpiente*, in which white outsiders, the self-appointed arbiters of civilization, penetrate the "dark" jungle, and the story of the first party drives a second expedition, retracing their path. Both films use Indigenous nonactors as the "cannibal" cast. In *Cannibal Holocaust*, it turns out that the "civilized" documentary crew were the real savages, torturing, raping, and burning villages to make sensational footage, until they met their gruesome and well-deserved cannibal fate.[11] As the "exploitation" nomenclature suggests, the film is an orgy of grotesque violence and gore that thematizes the cannibalistic nature of Western exploitation of the Amazon and its peoples. Both the structure and the theme of *El abrazo de la serpiente* reveal a visual and thematic kinship with the Cannibal Horror genre.

PISHTACOS AND *JARJACHAS*—ANDEAN HORROR

Among the films that exemplify the many registers of Indigenous horror, Andean regional horror cinema (*cine de terror andino*) is by far the "most" Indigenous. The genre is created by Indigenous directors specifically seeking to communicate Indigenous culture, traditions, and history to an Indigenous audience. As Milton Gonzalez notes, "Peruvian *Cine regional* (Regional Cinema), [is] an unsupported, overlooked and peripheral but thriving Andean cinematic tradition, unique in several respects" (Gonzalez Rodriguez 2022, 9). The most important aspect of Andean regional cinema is that its creators produce it "on their own terms" ("en sus propios términos") (Rivera Cusicanqui 2015, 88). Filmed in small towns and screened in modest community spaces, *cine regional* invites active public participation and audience feedback. As filmmaker Lalo Parra Bello says, his audiences "want to see themselves, the landscape, the people, the Quechua language, the traditions that are no longer told in the city" ("quieren verse a ellos mismos, los paisajes, la gente, el quechua . . . las tradiciones que ya no se cuentan en la ciudad") (Velásquez Núñez and Becerra Heraud 2011). In contrast to Bustamante's and Guerra's films, *cine regional andino* is not driven by a problematics of ethnicity. As Mary Weismantel observes, centuries of extreme racism toward Andean peoples have resulted in an avoidance of race terms such as the extremely pejorative *indio*, with a preference for terms such as *autóctono* or *natural* (Weismantel 2001, xxxiv). The term *nativo* is sometimes used to mark a character such as a shaman as imbued with specifically Indigenous expertise. Rather than ascribing certain traits or characteristics to Indigeneity, regional filmmakers take it as a default, allowing individuality and nuance to emerge.

Andean horror films often feature monstrous figures from Quechua and Aymara popular culture. Such figures sometimes, though not always, refer to the violence of colonial history or the fact that people suffered in Peru's civil conflict. The motif of the body snatcher, the vampirical fat stealer, or the soul stealer is common, reflecting the legacy of the colonial extractivist paradigm. While not all Andean horror film centers on Indigenous monster lore, this chapter focuses on figures of Indigenous origin rather than more generic ghost or possession stories.[12]

The fat-stealing Andean *pishtaco* and its analogues ñakaq, *lik'ichiri*, and Bolivian *kharisiri* are striking in their reversal of the Christian imputation of cannibalism to Indigenous peoples. Andean names for the fat stealers—the Quechua *pishtaku*, from *pishtay*, "to cut into pieces, to slaughter"; ñakaq, "to butcher"; *lik'ichiri*, "fat remover"; and the Aymara *kharisiri*, "to cut with a knife or razor"—all denote butchery, and popular art represents the *pishtaco* in the act of rendering butchered victims' fat. Fat stealers are generally portrayed as male, white or mestizo, and affiliated with modern technology. Andean rumors about fat-stealing priests began with the arrival of Europeans, and they were first documented in fray Cristóbal de Molina's *Account of the Fables and Rites of the Incas* (*Relación de las fábulas y ritos de los Incas*, 1575) in connection with coercive evangelization. A monster of the Ayacucho region, the Niño Ñakaq is a statue of the Christ child who leaves his niche by night to steal fat (Weismantel 2001, 199). The *pishtaco* would have also syncretized with the Spanish *sacamanteca* (fat taker), a bogey invoked to enforce good behavior in children. Fat is sacred to Andean cultures and is associated with a person's spirit or essence. Pagan souls were coveted by evangelizing priests, who themselves were notorious for gluttony and avarice, as we know from Felipe Guamán Poma de Ayala's *Nueva corónica y buen gobierno* (1615), a history of the Incas and manual for good government addressed to King Philip III of Spain. Part of Guamán Poma's purpose in the *Buen gobierno* was to curb the excesses of "the psychopath Father Juan Bautista de Albadán" (Ouweneel 2017, 116), a notorious torturer whose behavior alone seems sufficient to support reports of priests rendering Indigenous bodies for their fat.

During the colonial period, the stolen fat was reputed to be used variously as holy oil or to grease church bells; the *kharisiri* traditionally appeared as a Franciscan monk who stole fat from his victim's liver for holy oil (Crandon-Malamud 1991, 120). Modern fat stealers are believed to sell the fat to lubricate sugar mills and jet engines (Scheper-Hughes 1993, 236); to make luxury cosmetics and bath soaps; or, worst of all, to pay off the external debt to international banks. Tales of *pishtacos* and *kharisiris* multiply around US-affiliated development projects and in the context of Peru's long civil conflict (1980–2000), as portrayed in Mario Vargas Llosa's *Death in the Andes* (*Lituma en los Andes*, 1993). In November 2009, a *"pishtaco"* scandal in the Peruvian press was used to cover up the disappearance of sixty people in the region of Huánuco (Whalen 2009). There is no better metaphor than cannibalism for extractivist systems like mining, which converts enslaved bodies to silver or copper. The Bolivian Cerro Rico de Potosí, a silver mine in operation since 1547, is popularly known as the "the mountain that eats men" (Forero 2012). Films featuring the fat stealer include José Antonio Martínez Gamboa's *Pishtaco* (2003); José Gabriel Huertas's *Nakaq* (2003); Henry Vallejo's *El misterio del Kharisiri* (The Mystery of the Kharisiri, 2004); and Nilo Inga's *Sangre y tradición* (Blood and Tradition, 2005).

Other monstrous popular figures that appear in Andean horror are the *uma* (a decapitated, flying witch's head), subject of two films by Lalo Parra Bello; and the *jarjacha* (or *qarqacha*), a half-human, half-llama that is produced through an incestuous relationship. The *jarjacha* makes a diabolical "qar-qar-qar" sound and immobilizes its victims by spitting on them.

Mélinton Eusebio's 2002 *Qarqacha: El demonio del incesto* was the first *jarjacha* film. The film takes place in the town of Ayawilka, where three anthropology students arrive from Lima to conduct research in poverty. When a local man holds a mirror up to the strangers, it becomes clear that he thinks they may be soul stealers. The villagers' true hostility, however, is aimed at a pair of cousins (Rosita and Avelino) and the woman with whom the students are staying, who turn out to be in incestuous relationships. The young cousins are rounded up in their llama form, and in the morning they turn out to be Rosita and her father, Macario, the mayor. The villagers stone them to death, but Macario comes back from the dead and wreaks more havoc. The film's setup, in which metropolitan technocrats enter an Indigenous space, is familiar from cannibal horror and mondo horror, and particularly the film *El abrazo de la serpiente*. However, the students here are merely witnesses to the villagers' story (although one does die at the hands of back-from-the-dead Macario). The real horror is incest, and harsh church teachings on the subject. Palito Ortega Matute's *Incesto en los Andes: La maldición de los Jarjachas* (Incest in the Andes: The Curse of the Jarjachas, 2002) was produced the same year, followed by *La maldición de los Jarjachas 2* (The Curse of the Jarjachas 2, 2003); *Jarjacha 3* (2012); and *El demonio de los Andes* (The Demon of the Andes, 2014), the last of which features professional actors.

It is evident that *jarjachas* and *pishtacos* are something of a staple in Andean *cine de terror*. In a 2019 documentary on Andean horror film, when a taxi driver asks whether his passengers are filming a *pishtaco* or *jarjacha*, the director replies: "No, something more Inca-like [*incacucha*]" (Dietrich 2019). *Jarjacha vs. Pishtaco: La batalla final* (Jarjacha vs. Pishtaco: The Last Battle, 2011), directed by Nilo Escriba Palomino, is a battle "between two evils." By pitting the *pishtaco* against the *jarjacha*, this film seems to suggest a longing that Western demons would fight each other to the death.

The *condenado* (the damned, the accursed), often linked to the *jarjacha*, is perhaps the most common monster in Andean horror (Bustamante and Luna Victoria 2017, 71). Alluding again to the historical violence of Christianization, the *condenado* sometimes appears in Franciscan robes. The *condenado* may be the progeny of an incestuous liaison, as in Miler Eusebio's *Supay, el hijo del condenado* (2010), in which a boy returns after death to wreak vengeance on his killers. As Emilio Bustamante and Jaime Luna Victoria point out, the behavior of the *condenados* in films like the above-mentioned *Qarqacha: El demonio del incesto* and *La maldición de los jarjachas 2* appears to draw on the cannibalistic zombies introduced in George Romero's 1968 *Night of the Living Dead*.

The *jarjacha* and *condenado* represent "normal" members of the community who either only show their monstrous form at night or masquerade as living beings to get close to their victims. The violation of community norms by incest transforms them into cannibalistic brain hunters, manifesting a sense of internal social destabilization under conditions of terror. By contrast, the *pishtaco* clearly externalizes the source of evil and terror to white foreigners: the evangelizing clergy of the colonial era, foreign technocrats and extractivist corporations, and the armed conflict in which many Indigenous Andeans were murdered and disappeared.

Metropolitan filmmakers like Jayro Bustamante and Ciro Guerra visualize Indigenous perspectives and histories to denounce the impact of Western imperialism on Indigenous communities. Both filmmakers, despite critiques, contribute to a broader conversation about Indigenous representation and storytelling in cinema, acknowledging the complexities of their roles as non-Indigenous directors interpreting Indigenous experiences. Andean regional horror cinema is a wholly different project, which represents Indigenous matters in Indigenous registers to Indigenous audiences. However, both kinds of Indigenous horror cinema reflect the violence at the heart of the Western colonial and extractivist enterprise.

NOTES

1. See Milton Fernando Gonzalez Rodriguez (2022) for a complete discussion of Indigeneity in Latin American film.

2. Scholars such as Thomas Janvier (1910) and Eduardo Matos Moctezuma (2013) argue that the figure can be traced to Mexica deities Coatlicue and Cihuacóatl. For an analysis of Indigenous Mesoamerican and other sources for the legend, see Kirtley 1960; for regional variations, see Coluccio 1984.

3. All translations are the author's unless otherwise indicated.

4. This was a common descriptor applied to Indigenous women who became noteworthy through intimate connection (willing or otherwise) with a Spaniard. It may be true of Malintzin/Malinalli; it also exalted the conquistadors by association, and would strengthen their claims to titles of nobility (*hidalguía*) and lands.

5. Luis Buñuel's *Los olvidados* (The Young and the Damned, 1950) used Peón's spirit-rising visual effect in a famous dream sequence, in which the young protagonist Pedro's callous, promiscuous mother floats to him in her nightgown to offer him a slab of raw meat. Pedro is the result of her rape, alluding to the primordial rape of Indigenous Mexico by the Spanish conquistadors and their descendants. In the film, Pedro's mother's character and history allude to the condition of La Malinche as the "bad mother": both victim and author of the Mexican condition of cosmic orphanhood.

6. *Ánimas Trujano* (Ismael Rodríguez, 1961) went to the other extreme, with Japanese film star Toshirō Mifune playing a dissolute Oaxacan (presumably Zapotec) Indian who aspires to be the majordomo of his village fiesta.

7. Ríos Montt was known for his personal supervision of many such actions, even staying for the cleanup and disposal of bodies (Gardeazábal Bravo 2022, 70).

8. The concept of *chullachaki* advanced in Guerra's film is quite different from the Andean *chullachaki*, a shape-shifting trickster said to protect the forest or jungle.

9. Cannibalism has also been the bread and butter, so to speak, of ethnographers from 1492 forward. For more on the uses and functions of cannibalism in Latin America, see Barker, Hulme, and Iversen 1998; Schreffler 2005; Jáuregui 2008; Braham 2012; and Dalton and Potter 2018.

10. The costumes are possibly taken from a well-known engraving "The Dance of the Bayenté among the Yahua Indians of Peru," published in the French naturalist Paul Marcoy's 1869 *Voyage à travers l'Amérique du Sud* (Travels in South America), captioned in the English translation "The dance of the Bayenté, or dance of the devil, among the Yahua Indians of Peru."

11. *Cannibal Holocaust* was remade (sort of) as *The Green Inferno* by Eli Roth in 2013, featuring a bunch of white-savior types, a plane crash (a nod to Frank Marshall's 1993 cannibal classic *Alive*), and the tag line "No good deed goes unpunished." The theft of the *yakruna* seeds in *El abrazo de la serpiente* mirrors the story of nineteenth-century British adventurer George Wickham in *Kautschuk* (The Green Hell, 1938) by Eduard von Borsody, an Austrian in service to the Nazis. *Kautschuk* means *caucho* (rubber). Another possible inspiration for Guerra's film is Nelson Pereira dos Santos's 1971 film *Como era gostoso o meu frances* (How Tasty Was My Little Frenchman), which centers on the capture of a Frenchman by the Tupinamba tribe (who practiced ritual cannibalism) and foreshadows their impending despoliation by European extractivist powers.

12. See Weismantel (2001) for a discussion of race and monstrosity in the Andes, E. Bustamante and Luna Victoria (2017) on Peruvian regional cinema, and Eljaiek-Rodríguez (2018, ch. 6) on Andean horror film, particularly the *Qarqacha* films.

BIBLIOGRAPHY

Amnesty International. 2012. "Guatemala: Former Head of State's Trial for Genocide One More Step against Impunity." January 27. https://www.amnesty.org/en/latest/news/2012/01/guatemala-general-s-trial-genocide-one-more-step-against-impunity/.

Baledón, Rafael, dir. 1963. *La maldición de La Llorona*. Cinematográfica ABSA.

Barker, Francis, Peter Hulme, and Margaret Iversen. 1998. *Cannibalism and the Colonial World*. Cambridge: Cambridge University Press.

Braham, Persephone. 2012. "The Monstrous Caribbean." In *The Ashgate Research Companion to Monsters and the Monstrous*, edited by Asa Simon Mittman and Peter J. Dendle, 17–47. Farnham, Surrey, England: Ashgate.

Browning, Tod, dir. 1931. *Dracula*. Universal Pictures.

Buñuel, Luis, dir. 1950. *Los olvidados*. Ultramar Films.

Bustamante, Emilio. 2020. "Peruvian Regional Cinema: Transtextuality, Gender and Violence in *Bullying maldito, la historia de María Marimacha*." In *Peruvian Cinema of the Twenty-First Century: Dynamic and Unstable Grounds*, edited by Cynthia Vich and Sarah Barrow, 65–83. Cham, Switzerland: Palgrave Macmillan.

Bustamante, Emilio, and Jaime Luna Victoria. 2017. *Las miradas múltiples: El cine regional peruano*. Lima: Universidad de Lima, Fondo Editorial.

Bustamante, Jayro, dir. 2019. *La Llorona*. El Ministerio de Cultura y Deportes de Guatemala; La Casa de Producción, Les Films du Volcan.

Cardona, René, dir. 1960. *La Llorona*. Producciones Bueno.

Casey, Nicholas. 2016. "'Embrace of the Serpent,' Ciro Guerra's Searching Tale about Invaded Amazon Cultures." *New York Times*, February 15. https://www.nytimes.com/2016/02/16/

movies/embrace-of-the-serpent-ciro-guerras-searching-tale-about-invaded-amazon -cultures.html.

Coluccio, Félix. 1984. *Diccionario de creencias y supersticiones: Argentinas y Americanas.* Buenos Aires: Ediciones Corregidor.

Crandon-Malamud, Libbet. 1991. *From the Fat of Our Souls: Social Change, Political Process, and Medical Pluralism in Bolivia.* Berkeley: University of California Press.

Dalton, David, and Sara Potter. 2018. "Introduction: The Transatlantic Undead; Zombies in Hispanic and Luso-Brazilian Literatures and Cultures." *Alambique: Revista Académica de Ciencia Ficción y Fantasía / Jornal Acadêmico de Ficção Científica e Fantasía* 6, no. 1.

Deodato, Ruggero, dir. 1980. *Cannibal Holocaust.* F. D. Cinematografica.

Diario las Américas. 2021. "Bustamante ignora advertencias y triunfa con 'La Llorona.'" February 27. https://www.diariolasamericas.com/cultura/bustamante-ignora -advertencias-y-triunfa-la-llorona-n4217538.

Dietrich, Martha-Cecilia, dir. 2019. *Horror in the Andes.* Royal Anthropological Institute.

Eisenstein, Sergei, dir. 1932. ¡Que viva México! Moss Film; Mexican Film Trust.

Eljaiek-Rodríguez, Gabriel. 2018. *The Migration and Politics of Monsters in Latin American Cinema.* Cham, Switzerland: Palgrave Macmillan.

Escriba Palomino, Nilo, dir. 2011. *Jarjacha vs. Pishtaco: La batalla final.* Inka Llacta Producciones.

Fernández, Emilio, dir. 1944. *María Candelaria.* Films Mundiales.

Forero, Juan. 2012. "Bolivia's Cerro Rico: The Mountain That Eats Men." NPR, September 25. https://www.npr.org/2012/09/25/161752820/bolivias-cerro-rico-the-mountain-that -eats-men.

Gardeazábal Bravo, Carlos. 2022. "Espectros subversivos y miedos neoliberales en *La Llorona* de Jayro Bustamante." In *Violencia, poder y afectos: Narrativas del miedo en Latinoamérica*, edited by Marco Ramírez Rojas and David Rozotto, 65–86. Martlesham, Suff., England: Boydell and Brewer.

Gleghorn, Charlotte. 2020. "Filmic Disciples and Indigenous Knowledges: The Pedagogical Imperative in *El abrazo de la serpiente* (Ciro Guerra, 2015)." *Diálogo* 23, no. 1 (Spring): 31–45.

González de Canales Carcereny, Júlia. 2020. "Películas en lenguas indígenas producidas en países hispanohablantes: *Ixcanul* y *El abrazo de la serpiente.*" *Diálogo* 23, no. 1 (Spring): 7–19.

Gonzalez Rodriguez, Milton Fernando. 2022. *Indigeneity in Latin American Cinema.* New York: Bloomsbury Academic.

Guamán Poma de Ayala, Felipe. 1993. *Nueva corónica y buen gobierno.* Edited by Franklin Pease G. Y. Translated by Jan Szemiński. Mexico City: Fondo de Cultura Económica.

Guerra, Ciro, dir. 2015. *El abrazo de la serpiente.* Buffalo Films; Caracol Televisión.

Gunckel, Colin. 2007. "*El signo de la muerte* and the Birth of a Genre: Origins and Anatomy of the Aztec Horror Film." In *Sleaze Artists*, edited by Jeffrey Sconce, 121–43. Durham, NC: Duke University Press.

Huertas, José Gabriel, dir. 2003. *Nakaq.* Magnum Producciones.

IMDb. n.d. "*La Llorona* (2019)." Awards. https://www.imdb.com/title/tt10767168/awards /?ref_=tt_ql_op_1.

Inga, Nilo, dir. 2005. *Sangre y tradición*. Inti Films.

Janvier, Thomas A. 1910. *Legends of the City of Mexico*. New York: Harper and Brothers.

Jáuregui, Carlos A. 2008. Introduction to *Canibalia: Canibalismo, calibanismo, antropofagia cultural y consumo en América Latina*, 13–46. Madrid: Iberoamericana Vervuert.

Kirtley, Bacil F. 1960. "'La Llorona' and Related Themes." *Western Folklore* 19, no. 3 (July): 155–68.

León-Portilla, Miguel. 2006. *The Broken Spears: The Aztec Account of the Conquest of Mexico*. Boston: Beacon Press.

Marcoy, Paul. 1869. *Voyage à travers l'Amérique du Sud de l'Océan Pacifique à l'Océan Atlantique*. Paris: Librairie de L. Hachette.

Marshall, Frank, dir. 1993. *Alive*. Touchstone Pictures; Paramount Pictures; Kennedy/Marshall Company.

Martínez Gamboa, José Antonio, dir. 2003. *Pishtaco*. Magnum Producciones.

Matos Moctezuma, Eduardo. 2013. "¿La leyenda de La Llorona es de origen prehispánico?" *Arqueología Mexicana* 21, no. 122: 5.

Molina, Cristóbal de. (1575) 2010. *Relación de las fábulas y ritos de los Incas*. Edited by Paloma Jiménez del Campo. Madrid Iberoamericana. https://archive.org/details/relacion-de-las -fabulas-y-ritos-de-los-incas/mode/2up.

Molina, Cristóbal de. 2011. *Account of the Fables and Rites of the Incas*. Translated by Brian S. Bauer, Vania Smith-Oka, and Gabriel E. Cantarutti. Austin: University of Texas Press.

Muñoz Camargo, Diego. 2007. *Historia de Tlaxcala*. Edited by Alfredo Chavero. Biblioteca Virtual Miguel de Cervantes. https://www.cervantesvirtual.com/obra-visor/historia-de -tlaxcala-0/html/.

Ortega Matute, Palito, dir. 2002. *Incesto en los Andes: La maldición de los Jarjachas*. Peru: Roca Films; Fox Perú Producciones.

Ortega Matute, Palito, dir. 2003. *La maldición de los Jarjachas 2*. Roca Films; Fox Perú Producciones.

Ortega Matute, Palito, dir. 2012. *Jarjacha 3*. Perú Movie; Fox Perú Producciones.

Ortega Matute, Palito, dir. 2014. *El demonio de los Andes*. Perú Movie; Fox Perú Producciones.

Ouweneel, Arij. 2017. "Buen Gobierno: Chronicles of Violence Committed against Amerindians in the Andes." *Revista Europea de Estudios Latinoamericanos y del Caribe*, no. 104 (December): 113–20.

Pare, Gwendolen. 2022. "El abrazo de la serpiente: Ecología de saberes y mundo chullachaqui." *A Contracorriente: Una revista de estudios latinoamericanos* 20, no. 1 (Fall): 172–201.

Peón, Ramón, dir. 1933. *La Llorona*. Eco Films.

Riganas, Nick. 1985. "Cannibal Holocaust." IMDb, June 21. https://www.imdb.com/title/ tt0078935/.

Rivera, José Eustasio. 1924. *La vorágine*. Bogotá: Pontifical Xavierian University.

Rivera Cusicanqui, Silvia. 2015. *Sociología de la imagen: Miradas ch'ixi desde la historia andina*. Buenos Aires: Tinta Limón Ediciones.

Rodríguez, Ismael, dir. 1961. Ánimas Trujano (El hombre importante). Azteca Films.

Rojas, Rafael. 2017. "El mito del estado mestizo." *Letras Libres*, July. https://letraslibres.com/ revista/el-mito-del-estado-mestizo/.

Roth, Eli, dir. 2013. *The Green Inferno*. Worldview Entertainment; Dragonfly Entertainment; Sobras International Pictures.

Ruétalo, Victoria, and Dolores Tierney. 2009. *Latsploitation, Exploitation Cinemas, and Latin America*. New York: Routledge.

Sahagún, Bernardino de. 2000. *Historia general de las cosas de Nueva España*. Edited by Alfredo López Austin and Josefina García Quintana. 3rd ed. Mexico City: Consejo Nacional para la Cultura y las Artes.

Scheper-Hughes, Nancy. 1993. *Death without Weeping: The Violence of Everyday Life in Brazil*. Berkeley: University of California Press.

Schreffler, Michael J. 2005. "Vespucci Rediscovers America: The Pictorial Rhetoric of Cannibalism in Early Modern Culture." *Art History* 28, no. 3 (June): 295–310.

Urueta, Chano, dir. 1939. *El signo de la muerte*. CISA.

Vallejo, Henry, dir. 2004. *El misterio del Kharisiri*. Pioneros Producciones.

Vargas Llosa, Mario. 1993. *Lituma en los Andes*. Barcelona: Editorial Planeta.

Vargas Llosa, Mario. 1996. *Death in the Andes*. Translated by Edith Grossman. New York: Farrar, Straus and Giroux.

Velásquez Núñez, Sofía, and Javier Becerra Heraud, dirs. 2011. *El otro cine*. Mercado Central.

Waddell, Calum. 2017. *Cannibal Holocaust*. Liverpool: Liverpool University Press.

Weismantel, Mary J. 2001. *Cholas and Pishtacos: Stories of Race and Sex in the Andes*. Chicago: University of Chicago Press.

Whalen, Andrew. 2009. "Peru Villagers Murdered to Make Anti-Wrinkle Cream." *Toronto Star*, November 20. https://www.thestar.com/news/world/2009/11/20/peru_villagers _murdered_to_make_antiwrinkle_cream.html.

Part 3

Indigenizing Gothic-Horror Aesthetics?

CHAPTER 7

FROM SILENCE TO EXCESS

INDIGENOUS EDUCATIONAL GOTHIC

JADE JENKINSON

In *Solar Storms* (1994), protagonist Angel yearns for "an unbroken line between me and the past," wanting it "not to be fragments and pieces left behind by fur traders, soldiers, priests and schools" (Hogan 1994, 77). However, the novels I discuss in this chapter spotlight educational experiences in which no unbroken line exists between past and present—when education itself disrupts knowledge transference. Angel is removed from her mother at a young age, and it is only in learning of the haunting history of her homeland that she can complete her reeducation into her ancestral knowledges and channel this into activism. Likewise, Lisamarie in *Monkey Beach* (2000), and Ivy, Mary, and Jessie, three generations of the Koopundi family at the center of *Plains of Promise* (1997), also face hardship because land removal, residential schooling, child removal, and fostering disrupt their childhoods. Linda Hogan's (Chickasaw) *Solar Storms*, Eden Robinson's (Haisla/Heiltsuk) *Monkey Beach*, and Alexis Wright's (Waanyi) *Plains of Promise* can all be considered Indigenous Educational Gothic. In this chapter, I define the Indigenous Educational Gothic and examine this mode by focusing on two key tropes: silence and excess.

Historically, control of education has served as a tool for settler states to assimilate and acculturate those who challenged hegemonic power. In the latter part of the nineteenth century, boarding schools in the United States, known as residential schools in Canada and mission schools in Australia, were promoted as instruments for the "improvement" of Indigenous peoples by settler-colonial governments. In the 1980s, testimony, life writing, and scholarship exposed these schools as assimilationist institutions contributing to Indigenous genocide, and often sites of violence, disease, and neglect, offering little or no educational benefit. However, the true impact of these educational histories only began to be acknowledged in the mainstream in the 1990s. Landmark reports such as "Bringing Them Home" (Australian Human Rights Commission 1997) in Australia detailed the forced removal of Indigenous children.[1] In Canada, the last residential school closed in 1997, with a high-profile apology not occurring until 2008 under Prime Minister Stephen Harper.[2] Brenda J. Child (Red Lake Ojibwe) notes that the "Indian boarding school . . . like the Trail of Tears or Wounded Knee" is an institution that is "symbolic of American colonialism at its most genocidal" (2018, 38). While boarding schools in the United States closed earlier than Canadian ones, ending in the 1930s, US mission schools continued until the 1970s (Child 2018). Although Child warns against oversimplifying these educational histories, she recognizes the comparable aims of boarding schools in both countries and the lack of attention paid to this history in the United States. Undoubtedly, American acknowledgment has been less pronounced, especially at a political level, with President Barack Obama signing a formal apology in 2009.[3] However, in the period between 1990 and 2000, the time my chosen novels were published, all three governments demonstrated reluctance to acknowledge Indigenous rights or make substantive amends.

Indigenous Educational Gothic works respond to this history by interrogating the historical use of education in Canadian, US, and Australian settler states, narrating its effect on individual protagonists and their wider communities. While Gothic may be a flawed label to apply to Indigenous works, I follow theorizations of Indigenous Gothic by scholars including Warren Cariou (Métis), Michelle Burnham, and Katrin Althans. These scholars have been instrumental in uprooting the Gothic genre from its Western ascendancy by tracing its presence in specific Indigenous narrative traditions, exploring the genre's cross-fertilization with Western Gothic, and analyzing how Indigenous writers and filmmakers repurpose and revitalize Gothic, often for political purposes.[4] Furthermore, recent work on Residential School Gothic[5] enables scholars to consider responses to this particular history in works including Tomson Highway's (Cree) novel *Kiss of the Fur Queen* (1998), Georgina Lightning's (Cree) film *American Evil* (2008),[6] and Jeff Barnaby's (Mi'gmaq) film *Rhymes for Young Ghouls* (2013). However, none of these scholarly explorations has been able to encompass the ways that creatives across the United States, Canada, and Australia have used Gothic as a reaction to the educational violence within settler colonial nations with comparable educational policies concerning Indigenous peoples. In addition, there has been no scholarship that looks more widely at abusive state education as it relates to both political agendas and biopolitical mechanisms and examines the imposition of the settler-colonial project into the home as well as in institutional settings. My work positions Indigenous Educational Gothic as a mode within the wider Indigenous Gothic genre,[7] and I theorize that the Gothic institution reoccurs as a means of depicting and interrogating violent educational histories within these three countries, particularly when they are not present in the official rhetoric. The work here contributes to my wider doctoral thesis, which interrogates both Indigenous and settler depictions of education in the Gothic genre.

In this chapter, I argue that in *Solar Storms*, *Monkey Beach*, and *Plains of Promise*, excess (as that which points to a multiplicity of meanings and the play of signifiers to the point of dissolution) and silence (as an absence of knowledge) both destabilize reader positioning and upset dichotomous thinking in the 1990s, a time in which "recognition politics" delimit these conversations (Coulthard 2014, 3). Instead of "ushering in an era of peaceful coexistence grounded on the ideal of reciprocity or mutual recognition," argues Glen Sean Coulthard (Yellowknives Dene), recognition politics in settler-colonial nations is seen as an end in itself (3). For example, in Australia, the United States, and Canada, the 1990s was a period of small-scale apologies for state policies, such as residential and mission schooling. However, the recognition politics at the core of these apologies became apparent as governments were less than keen to make material amends or revise official histories. These three novels are therefore important interventions in the climate of the 1990s, specifically demonstrating that educational abuses are not historical and reinforcing the detrimental effects that the intersection of environmental, social, and educational state policies have had on Indigenous communities. In addition to their depiction of abusive educations, these works may also be read as exemplifying "grounded normativity" (Coulthard 2014, 13). Coulthard positions grounded normativity as a means of resistance to the reproduction of "colonialist, racist, patriarchal state power" at the heart of recognition politics. As an alternative, he calls for "modalities of Indigenous land-connected practices and longstanding experiential knowledge that inform and structure . . . ethical engagements with the world and . . . relationships with human and nonhuman others over time" (3, 13). While Coulthard's work is political in focus, Leanne Betasamosake Simpson (Michi Saagiig Nishnaabeg) explores grounded normativity[8] in relation to Indigenous (specifically Nishnaabeg) pedagogy, ethics, and storytelling. Simpson's work takes a closer look at the "heteropatriarchal and colonial gendered violence" within Western education tradition and calls for a return to "land as pedagogy": an education by which coming to know "requires complex, committed, consensual engagement" rather than an education based on "dominance and nonconsent" (Simpson 2017, 14, 15). The novels I define as Indigenous Educational Gothic address the profound impact of a historical past of abusive, nonconsensual educations on bodies, land, and animals and highlight acts of neocolonialism that continue to erode Indigenous rights and resources. At the same time, these novels also demonstrate Indigenous resurgence through the perseverance of grounded normativity in consensual reeducation within Indigenous communities and methodologies.

The use of an intersectional approach enables authors of Indigenous Educational Gothic to expand political dialogues. However, these novels are also creative outputs that broaden the parameters of horror. Indeed, Western Gothic and testimonial life writing often exhibit certain levels of binarism, which can delimit these works.[9] Silence and excess offer a means to open dialogues and bypass the restrictions implicit within generic forms. In fact, the effects of silence and excess may be more akin to terror, famously described by Ann Radcliffe (1826) as experience-expanding dread or apprehension rather than horror—which she understood as freezing repulsion. However, Radcliffe's definition of horror as shocking but also providing a cathartic moment intersects considerably with criticism surrounding how the Gothic genre capitalizes on Indigenous pain by placing Indigenous peoples into victimry paradigms;[10] furthermore, such concepts arise in a social and cultural milieu that eventually informs Settler Gothic writing. Instead, I examine the effects of silence and excess within the context of representing Indigenous histories by employing the terminology "aesthetics of horror" versus "ethics of horror." My use of these two terms is indebted to my reading of Warren Cariou's, David Garneau's (Métis), Susan Sontag's, and Kait Pinder's discussions of aesthetics; and Michelle Burnham's, Julia V. Emberley's, and Fred Botting's discussions of ethics. However, my reading extends these varied interpretations by means of a dialogic approach, which shapes these theories within the specific context of Indigenous literatures.

In my definition, an "aesthetics of horror" relies on visual effects to provide the reader with the satisfactory thrill of fear, whereas an "ethics of horror" alludes to the germination of fear without release to provoke deeper engagement.[11] To engage with the "ethics of horror" is to be denied the shock and following cathartic release the spectator experiences in watching horror films. Instead, the reader's ontological certainties are unsettled, as is their place regarding another's pain from a safe distance.[12] Burnham suggests that by turning away from the "recuperative politics of traditional gothic" and instead providing a "fearful collapse of self and knowledge," authors may engage in an ethical Gothic (2011, 12–16). Cariou's call for an "aesthetics of action" in opposition to one "of fear" (2006, 733) and Garneau's work on colonial cultures' "scopophilia" (2016, 23)—in which asymmetrical power relationships are reinforced through the empathetic settler and suffering Indigenous person(s)—emphasize why Indigenous Educational Gothic works move away from an "aesthetics of horror."

I argue that Hogan, Robinson, and Wright engage in a far more ethical horror by contrasting their work with a flagrant horror that trades on pain by using tropes of silence and excess. A study of silence and excess enables me to illustrate how these writers move away from using horror as a cathartic entertainment form in which "anxieties and other negative emotions towards the world or the society one inhabits [can] be released safely" (Cherry 2009, 12). Instead, Indigenous Educational Gothic is more unsettling by drawing our attention to Indigenous experiences in settler nations in which horror is an everyday reality, for, as Black and Ohkay Owingeh Pueblo author Rebecca Roanhorse states, "horror in so much Indigenous literature . . . is not rooted in the idea that 'something has been forgotten.' It's rooted in very material things, like the lived remembrance of massacres, for example" (Schoonover 2022, 299). Mainstream horror often elicits an identification with an Other as a means of belaying guilt, for example Carol Clover's influential reading of cross-gender identification with the "final girl" in 1970s and 1980s slasher films to alleviate fears about male violence in society (1987).[13] As publications aimed at a mainstream audience in the context of a climate of "recognition politics," Hogan's, Wright's, and Robinson's works are shaped by the imperative to prevent settler "over-identif[ication] with the other," which can "collapse the distance that might otherwise . . . challenge [reader] complicity in ongoing colonialism"— often a purview of Settler Gothic (Robinson and Martin 2016, 12). Indeed, Grace Dillon (Anishinaabe) makes clear that "Native intellectual traditions encompass this need to speak out and uncover situated historical moments, not as superficially applied universal truths or outlets allegorizing the broad human condition, *but as a means of chronicling real events and encouraging accountability*" (2007, 223, my emphasis). Dillon's statement invites me to consider an "ethics of horror" within the context of Indigenous Educational Gothic literature. This exploration involves scrutinizing the deployment of horror in narrating historical events through disrupting reader expectations, avoiding the distant observation of another's pain, and unsettling ontological certainties. I examine the utilization of horror as both an affective form and as a means of aligning with the aims of grounded normativity. This alignment involves fostering an exchange rooted in "heterogeneous knowledges" rather than the "transactional exchange" typical of reconciliation politics (Emberley 2014, 72).

"God, You Can Be So Dense": Silence in *Monkey Beach* and *Solar Storms*

Monkey Beach and *Solar Storms* are coming-of-age stories narrated by female protagonists. In *Monkey Beach*, Lisamarie is dissatisfied with her school's Eurocentric pedagogy and receives an alternative education from her rebellious uncle, as well as knowledge of Haisla traditions from her Ma-ma-oo. Angel, the main character in *Solar Storms*, returns to the land of her relatives after social services removes her at an early age. Upon returning to her family, Angel learns of her tribal history, valuable survival skills, and how to harness her gift as a plant healer. "Bildungsroman" may therefore be a convenient label for both works as they perform acts of mediation by creating a "dialogic relationship" between Indigenous cultures and non-Indigenous readers to "maneuver" the reader into different ways of knowing (Ruppert 1995, ix, x). Yet, Gothic elements resist the order, chronology, and knowledge accumulation of the bildungsroman—a resolutely "Eurocentric and patriarchal form" (Ruppert 1995, 12). If the bildungsroman "make[s] integration into the existing social order legitimate by channeling individual energy into socially useful purposes," the genre is antithetical to the context of assimilatory Indigenous educational policies both authors depict (Bolaki 2011, 12). Silence within these texts denies the reader easy access to a digestible version of Indigenous culture; at the same time, silence can provoke reader dislocation and terror.

Lisamarie's return to school at the end of *Monkey Beach* demonstrates her perseverance, despite the psychological and physical trauma that causes her to drop out prematurely. However, the hope and closure promised by this ending are undermined by the death of Lisamarie's brother—an occurrence for which additional information is eventually provided—and her friend Pooch's suicide, for which no explanation is offered. Pooch may not be a central character, but his suicide is important in providing the reader with a glimpse into occurrences just out of view of our narrator—unresolved pain that escapes the cause-and-effect logic of the main plot. Lisamarie's friends Frank and Karaoke begin to discuss the reasons behind the suicide but are cut off midsentence: "'[W]e all know why he did it,' Karaoke said. 'Shut up,' Frank said. 'Just shut up.' 'Yes, let's not talk about it. Josh didn't—' 'Shut. Up'" (E. Robinson 2000, 319). This exchange leaves the reader frustrated and in the dark. Unlike the other deaths in the book, which appear to be accidents or the result of unseen forces, Pooch's death is at his own hands. The silence behind the incident feeds into an "ethics of horror," generating terror as a shocking incident with no revelation of a cause or a resolution. Pooch's death affects readers differently from the more aesthetic sense of horror the reader experiences when hearing of the accidental deaths of Ma-ma-oo in a house fire and Mick drowning after being caught in a fishing net.[14] Lisamarie describes the horrifying image of "Mick's empty eye sockets in his lipless face, the fishing net embedded in his skin" and Ma-ma-oo's remains being pulled out of the house fire: "[She] had no hair, no skin. She was charred" (274, 293). Pooch's death provokes terror when the reader realizes it is not just some outside, unknown Gothic force or accident that brings death to the community, but instead the very real intersections of oppression to which Pooch is subject.

Pooch is raised by his grandmother after the death of his parents; his brother is in jail, and the family has little money. He is also a nephew of Josh, who sexually abuses Pooch's cousin Karaoke: a repetition, Robinson hints, of the abuse Josh himself experienced at a residential school.[15] The reader does not find out if Pooch is another one of Josh's victims. Here, silence disturbs the satisfaction of a revelatory or confessional praxis, often present in autobiographical works and the sense of sublime and ensuing catharsis in the Gothic genre.[16] Silence provokes deeper reflection about the reasons behind the event and the intersection of poverty, residential schooling, and lack of opportunity within this peripheral community—all of which may have some part to play in the suicide. The reader must ruminate on the terror of abuse without visceral detail; thus, silence fails to provide the sense of release or onward movement provoked by revelation. Silence is tricky in a climate that requires the sharing of the self as evidence for reparation, and that at the same time only allows space for oppressed people to speak of their pain. Eve Tuck's (Unangax) open letter has highlighted the dangers of "damage-centered research," in particular its "pathologizing effect" by which "oppression singularly defines a community" (2009, 413). In accordance with Tuck's stance, silence in *Monkey Beach* fails to provide enough detail to invigorate "the fantasies of outsiders"—outsiders, in this case, are the readers (Tuck 2009, 412). Yet, the use of silence is not without its criticisms. For example, when the young Lisamarie asks her Uncle Mick about his former role as an American Indian Movement (AIM) activist, Mick attempts to recount his experiences with suitable brevity and language for Lisamarie's young age: "This old lady had told the police about what the Goons were doing and the police had told the Goons what she said, and so the Goons came over to her house while we were having tea and they shot at us" (E. Robinson 2000, 51). The apparent act of reframing performed by Mick is a conscious reminder of the implications of his silence.

Mick's editing of the story leads us to reflect on how the media narrates Indigenous voices, cultures, politics, and histories in a reductionist manner to ensure that the non-Indigenous reader is entertained or even enraged. However, nuance and detail are omitted, as Tuck discusses in her open letter (2009). Although Mick is obviously committed to the movement, his focus on events rather than the causes when narrating the story to Lisamarie draws attention to the ways mainstream media reports Indigenous activism. For example, Sophie McCall notes how the media portrayal of the Kanehsatà:ke Resistance (Oka Crisis) reinforced "Manichean stereotypes of violent Natives versus besieged settlers, while eliding the historical roots of the conflict" (2011, 77). This kind of reporting is also noted by Angel when she protests state-sponsored damming in *Solar Storms*: "[T]hey called us terrorists" (Hogan 1994, 283). Nevertheless, Kit Dobson remarks of *Monkey Beach* that "these sorts of interventions"—Mick's reframing and Frank's silencing of Karaoke when she tries to discuss Pooch's death—"leav[e] Lisa (and the novel's readers) with a diminished sense of the stakes of being Haisla in Canada" (2009, 13). Dobson's frustration is understandable as AIM was certainly pivotal in the late 1960s and 1970s. AIM was organized around the "principles of political and cultural sovereignty from the U.S. government"—values shared by their counterparts in Canada and some regions of Latin America (Horton 2017, 22). However, factionalism catalyzed the demise of the larger movement around 1978.[17] Mick's use of reductionist language to depict this historically significant grassroots organization is disappointing. Yet, Robinson's silence here draws attention to the pressures put on Indigenous writers not only to represent particular histories but also to share their pain with readers, as a means of pedagogical exchange. In this instance, the use of silence reveals that there is a line to be drawn between literature and politics, between artistic creation and representation, as well as revealing the limitations implicit within the novel as an entertaining story versus its broader aspect as a political device in its own right.

Robinson's own words in her work on protocols and modern storytelling also shed light on silence in *Monkey Beach*. The treatise draws our attention to the fact that some things simply cannot go down in print—elements of what Robinson calls "Haisla copyright" (E. Robinson 2011, 30–31). "Haisla copyright" refers to the laws that dictate what can be published and the protocols surrounding clan stories owned by individuals and families that require "permission and a feast in order to be published" (30–31). In musing on her own editing process, Robinson notes her uncertainty in including scenes of a potlach and her decision to focus on a different story because she is told that "traditional people were uncomfortable talking about the potlach itself" (32–33). Robinson's discussion demonstrates that as well as preventing digestible readings of pain that distance us from the effects of catharsis, silence also takes us out of the pages of the narrative to remind us of our distance from the text. Silence demonstrates that it is not the purpose of Indigenous literature to provide an insight into Indigenous cultures or reduce Indigenous stories into easily understandable proverbs. Silence enables Robinson to engage with painful histories in a manner that does not minimize distance but utilizes ambiguity to provoke deeper thought.

Linda Hogan's work may also be read as an example of Indigenous Educational Gothic, for it explores how girls' education is disrupted by the effects of historical abuses reemerging in the present, and employs silence to provoke terror and to distance her readers from an "aesthetics of horror." *Solar Storms'* protagonist, Angel, is removed from her family after her mother, Hannah, violently assaults her as a child. Hannah has also been abused as an infant, yet we hear nothing of Hannah's life before she is "blown in" to Adam's Rib via a storm (Hogan 1994, 34). Hogan's silence denies access to the horrors of torture Hannah is subject to during this period. Instead, as Irene S. Vernon points out, the reader is left with a "sense of the transmission of trauma [as] an intergenerational passing whereby Hannah's life choices and behaviors mimic her mother's" (2012, 38). However, silence here moves from an "aesthetics of horror" to an "ethics of horror." In *Solar Storms*, we do not see the violence that Hannah is subject to, only its aftereffects. Therefore, our engagement with her character is not one of ontological certainty, often found in the Gothic genre. Hogan further complicates Hannah's character, as she is neither good nor evil—although she is an abuser, she has also been abused. Indeed, Fred Botting's (2012) discussion of the two strands of ethics in contemporary society is applicable here. The first strand is the "contemporary media-managerial form that polarizes good and evil, reinforcing the parameters of Western capitalism," and the second, the "more troubling ethics of excess and horror" (Botting 2012, 26). The latter strand is troubling because it sits on the border between "pleasure, violence and consumption" (26). Hogan's portrayal of Hannah uses silence in the form of distance to broaden the dichotomous characterizations of the Gothic genre as it is enmeshed within Western capitalism. Like Botting's description of the second strand of ethics, Hannah's portrayal is troubling, for, in line with an "ethics of horror," Hannah's violent acts must be read within the context of the cultural devastation she has faced; they cannot be attributed within the Manichean paradigm often found in the Gothic genre.

In *Solar Storms*, Hannah's story explores both historical and contemporary educational abuses, demonstrating the nuanced and intersectional approach through which the Indigenous Educational Gothic mode addresses traumatic histories. Hannah remains silent despite her centrality to the narrative—her clouded past is mirrored in her muted present. Silence encourages the reader to think more deeply about Hannah and her experiences. It would be easy to demonize Hannah, and indeed, many scholars compare her to the windigo: a cannibalistic and greedy ice figure appearing in many Algonquian-speaking cultures. Summer Harrison suggests that, like the windigo, Hannah "no longer understand[s] [her] responsibility to the larger community" (2019, 20). Vernon goes further, stating that Hannah is the windigo itself because she "feels nothing, she tortures others, she is born of the storm, she has a heart of ice, and people fear her" (2012, 43). Yet, Bush, the ex-wife of Hannah's father, attempts to help Hannah through a ceremony by journeying into Hannah's mind. Bush describes how Hannah was "a body under siege, a battleground. But she herself never emerged. The others, with their many voices and ways, were larger than she was. She was no longer there" (Hogan 1994, 99). Bush soon realizes that "[t]hey came awake at night, those who'd hurt her. Them. Those who walked the floor in her skin" (100). Bush's description emphasizes Hannah's haunting and her lack of agency. Indeed, an elder later confirms that Hannah is a "meeting place" for others; she is testament to their voices and the historical violence of the past (101). Through Hannah's silence, Hogan refuses to use trauma as means of pedagogical exchange and provides a perspective on haunting that extends beyond the Western ontological framework of symptomatic reading.

Symptomatic reading finds its roots in the work of Freud and Marx, and, because modern readings of the Gothic and first-wave trauma studies emerge from Freud's work on repression, both evidence similar strategies for "reading" trauma. Paul Ricoeur's "hermeneutics of suspicion" demonstrates how Freud's method of interpretation used symbolic language to proffer a double meaning (1970). Such practices, Ricoeur argues, stem from Freud's theory of the unconscious, specifically the notion that our unconscious actions relate to our repressed subconscious. Repressed subconscious memories must, in turn, be recovered if the subject is to become psychologically whole and, in the realm of literary criticism, for a text's "true" meaning to be found. Consequently, these reading practices have become prevalent in texts and films employing Gothic tropes to address historical trauma. However, in *Solar Storms*, the ghosts that congregate within Hannah suggest that her haunting does not fit within this Western framework. Instead, Hannah's haunting refers to a community trauma. This is the trauma of colonists and fur traders who hunted the animals to extinction, regarded "Native women as objects for temporary sexual gratification," and allowed

Indigenous communities to starve when resources were used up (Vernon 2012, 39). With this history in mind, Kathleen Brogan's work on cultural haunting may shed light on Hannah's condition. Brogan writes: "[I]n the literature of cultural haunting, such haunting potentially leads to a valuable awareness of how the group's past continues to inhabit and inform the living" (1998, 8). Therefore, "the exorcism of all forms of ghostliness" is not necessarily useful or beneficial, as in the Christian tradition, for this "could result in a historical amnesia that endangers the integrity of the group" (Brogan 1998, 8). Hannah demonstrates how the colonial past continues to haunt the present as an example of "the memory of genocide . . . made visible" and charges the reader not to forget the intersectional nature of abuse (Castor 2006, 170).

In the case of violent educations, dispossession is often followed by a repossession—whether that be a haunting or, more sinisterly, the overwriting of the dispossessed's story. In death, Hannah's overwritten body materializes the effects of acculturation. Angel and Bush are alone in preparing Hannah's body for burial, because the authorities charge for help due to the remoteness of the location. Consequently, the two must use available materials, such as newspaper, to wrap the body. Newspaper not only evidences the material poverty resulting from Indigenous disenfranchisement under settler colonialism but also makes apparent Hannah's "overwritten" status in the novel. Angel narrates:

> How appropriate it was to place her on words of war, obituaries, stories of carnage and misery, and true stories that had been changed to lies. It seemed the right bed for her. Some of the words stuck to her body, dark ink, but we did not wash them off; it was a suitable skin. Then Bush took down the cloth curtain partition and we wrapped my mother inside it. She wound the sheet around that, rolling Hannah from side to side as if she were merely a bolt the fabric had been wrapped around. (Hogan 1994, 253)

Even in death, we cannot access Hannah, for just as her scars bear witness to the violence that she was subject to as a child, the "war," "carnage," "misery," and "lies" that imprint on her skin overwrite Hannah's body with the violence of words (253). Hannah is only a trace of a life written upon by the brutality of others. Her story is one of colonization, of gender inequality, of hunger and of greed. Although Hannah is a perpetrator of violence and abuse, she is not the source of this darkness; she is instead the "fire [that] burns itself away, uses itself as a fuel" (252). Angel describes her conflicted feelings in this moment of death with poignancy: "Hannah had been my poison, my life, my sweetness and pain, my beauty and homeliness. And when she died, I knew I had survived in the best of ways for I was filled with grief and compassion" (251). Angel's cathartic description demonstrates how Hogan continually redefines Hannah and continues to reshape and redeploy Gothic and Indigenous intersections within the Indigenous Educational Gothic mode to story trauma without reducing the narrative to one of victimry. Indeed, even in this last moment, Hannah continues to resist definition.

In her analysis of silence in Sherman Alexie's *Indian Killer* (1996), Michelle Burnham suggests that it is "the absent presence of Native ghosts and Native stories . . . [that] encourages a fearful collapse of self and knowledge" that makes the novel disturbing (2011, 16). Burnham continues that Indigenous Gothic writing aptly envisions the loss of self through its refusal to grant absolution. As well as being an antiliberal novel, the loss of self in *Indian Killer* may also make it ethical in a Levinasian sense[18] because it responds to trauma in ways that refuse domestication or mourning, and thus refuse incorporation into the self (Burnham 2011, 6–8). A similar disavowal is present in both *Monkey Beach* and *Solar Storms*, in which silences deny the reader and some characters—such as Pooch and Mick in the former novel and Hannah in the latter—complete and digestible knowledge of their subjects. Unlike the confessional style that characterizes life and residential school writing, these characters pose more questions than answers. In addition, characters' undefinable aspects prevent the creation of a self/Other binary often employed to distance the reader from another's pain. Yet, Indigenous Educational Gothic goes further than Burnham's conception of an Indigenous Gothic, for it explores the intergenerational effects of abusive educations and looks to state policy in the present. This mode refuses to disassociate the carving up and destruction of land from violence wrought on the body, or to divide poverty from racial and gendered oppression. While Indigenous Educational Gothic works may share similarities with residential school life writing, they differ from these earlier narratives as their Gothic stylings mean they are unbound from the realist conventions of autobiography and can look at a wider picture of education under settler-colonial governments. Intersectionality and a time/space collapse attest to how the novels move away from historicizing Indigenous disenfranchisement as being both "past" and located only within residential schooling, distinguishing Indigenous Educational Gothic from Residential School Gothic.

"Must Have Been Goats, That's All": Excess in *Plains of Promise* and *Monkey Beach*

At the center of the mission complex in *Plains of Promise*—Alexis Wright's novel detailing the impact of white colonization on four generations of Indigenous women in Australia—is a rather unsettling tree. The tree, a poinciana, is not native to the setting. We are told that the poinciana is a "thirsty greedy foreign tree intruding into the bowels of their [the Indigenous inhabitants'] world" (Wright 1997, 4). This imported parasite sucks the nutrients from the land and, in Françoise Král's words, is "a vegetal vampire" (2002, 9). It is not difficult to see how the tree is a blatant Gothic metaphor for the ways European colonialism thrives through the theft of resources and subjugation of people in the lands it takes root within. The tree demonstrates that it is the settlers—white Christian missionaries—that haunt this setting. This reversal is a fitting example of Indigenous Gothic, a genre characterized as "overturning the kinds of possessive acts (possession by ghostly spirits, but also possession of material land) established by . . . Gothic tradition" (Burnham 2014, 228). This genre had been a fruitful means of expanding the boundaries of the Gothic by rethinking its "narrative conventions" and "cultural assumptions" (Burnham 2014, 235). However, we must be mindful of viewing Indigenous Gothic as merely a reversal of Settler Gothic, for this delimits its creative potential and encourages the kind of binary thinking that both perpetuates Othering and simplifies literature written by the colonized as merely writing back.

This section will pass over the vampiric tree and refocus on the crow that sits within it and "draw[s] the cards of death" to examine how Indigenous Educational Gothic confronts the reader with the unknowable and goes further than the act of writing back (Wright 1997, 4). The crow is the means through which I will explore the trope of excess. Rather than Botting's (1996) definition of Gothic excess as that which exceeds Enlightenment morality and rationality, I reference film scholar Kristin Thompson's (1982) definition of the term, and my analysis is also influenced by examinations of the trickster figure found in various Indigenous storytelling traditions, as I will elaborate on shortly.[19] Instead of a philosophical excess, Thompson emphasizes the visual qualities of excess as an "image that goes beyond the narrative structures" (288). Arising from the conflict between the "material" and the "unifying structures," excessive elements "do not participate in the creation of narrative or symbolic meaning" (290). While the excess Botting is referring to suggests a deeper ideological reading of the narrative, Thompson, following Roland Barthes and Stephen Heath, looks at excess as both "counternarrative" and "counterunity" (293). In this context, excess generates horror effects by providing too much meaning, to the point that the symbol loses its integrity, denying the reader certainty.

The repetition of a device that exceeds its initial function is another means by which Thompson determines the presence of excess (1982, 293). Wright's use of crows may adhere to this definition, for while the crow is initially introduced to add atmosphere to the setting, narrative emphasis on the crow and its unstable symbolic repetition confuses meaning.[20] First, when Ivy is incarcerated at Sycamore Heights, a group of crows "appear[s] at precisely the same time every year—the anniversary of Ivy's arrival," sitting "on a tree outside Ivy's ward" where they "stay . . . for weeks" (Wright 1997, 173). Here, the reappearance of the crows undermines their earlier association with death, for the crows' position outside Ivy's window suggests hope. The crows' return indicates that, despite Ivy's incarceration and unresponsiveness, she will be free again, and there are higher forces at work than the institution. Second, the narrative moves ahead in time, and Ivy's lost daughter, Mary, makes friends with a crow. This exchange suggests that the crow must surely be a familial link. Yet Jessie, Ivy's granddaughter, hates crows and throws stones at them. Third, as Mary and Jessie return to the mission to hunt for Ivy, crows are associated with Indigenous rights. Mary states: "No Land Rights. No Crow Rights. Stereotypes the same. Black is negative. Stands for no. Crows are negative" (258). Despite this, the children in the mission revere the crows and ask Jessie to stop throwing stones at them. Finally, in the epilogue, crows are "greedy and evil" and always "need to live in new places," recalling European settlement (303).

The lack of fixed meaning defies the unifying impulse of the crow motif. Instead, the crow enables a vertical rather than a horizontal opening of the narrative; they haunt a symbolic, digestible, and specific interpretation of Wright's Gothic form. Are crows the haunting return of the past or the traces of Indigeneity in the present? Are they symbolic of settler greed or Indigenous survivance? Crows take on multiple meanings as the story progresses. Unlike the explicit symbolism of the tree, the crows resist a "hermeneutics of suspicion" in which we read between the lines to reveal a deeper, unified truth; instead, they expand meaning (Ricoeur 1970). Excess as a narrative device is not so dissimilar from the role of the trickster in Indigenous storytelling traditions. In fact, the crow, as a trickster figure, enables a closer look into this link.

The crow and the raven are often associated with the trickster in some Australian Indigenous cultures. Tricksters are known for "emptying out" specific meaning, particularly when meaning evolves from entrenched binaries (such as good and evil) associated with a Judeo-Christian worldview. Gerald

FROM SILENCE TO EXCESS: INDIGENOUS EDUCATIONAL GOTHIC   177

Vizenor talks of both ravens and crows as "native tricksters, a union of pushy, avian mongrels, trust breakers, thieves, and astute healers" (2009, 13), while Lee Maracle (Stó:lō) insightfully discusses, in relation to her own character, Raven,[21] how the trickster is an "oversimplification" of an agent that is often a "harbinger of social transformation" (Kelly 1994, 85). Mudrooroo (Colin Johnson)[22] notes that crows, as "trickster character[s]," are most popularly known for their role in the story of how fire came to humans (Mudrooroo 1994, 35–36). In this story, tricksters are respected but not entirely trustworthy figures. As an archetype within Native American and First Nations' storytelling—indeed across many storytelling practices—tricksters are neither "moral [n]or functional": they do not "prove the values that we live by, nor do they prove or demonstrate the responses to domination by colonial democracies" (Vizenor 1995, 70). In their multiplicity of meaning, tricksters generate a response that "take[s] pleasure in a language game and imagination, a noetic liberation of the mind" that, in the context of *Plains of Promise*, may be read as the pedagogical impulse to broaden overdetermined depictions of Indigeneity (Vizenor 1995, 70).

Excess also disturbs the reader's expectations of learning about Haisla traditions in *Monkey Beach*. In this novel, excess contrasts with the explanatory narration. At the start of the novel, Robinson describes Lisamarie finding a tortured dog in a ditch:

> I stood beside a ditch, looking down at a small, dark brown dog with white spots. I thought it was sleeping and climbed down to pet it. When I was near enough to touch it, I could see that the dog's skin was crisscrossed by razor-thin cuts that were crusted with blood. It had bits of strange cloth tied to its fur. The dog whimpered and its legs jerked. Someone tsk-tsked. I looked up, and a little, dark man with bright red hair was crouching beside me. "Your doggie?" I said. He shook his head then pointed towards my house. (E. Robinson 2000, 19)

Although Robinson may include this description to generate an atmosphere of violence and threat, the details of the description point to its excessive traits. For instance, if the dog stands for violence against the innocent, why have strange pieces of cloth been tied to its fur, almost in a gesture of care or ritual? It is also unclear to the reader whether the incident is a dream, a vision, or reality. This section seems to mark the first appearance of the little red-haired man, but the sentence that follows, in which Lisamarie's mother calls her in for her dinner, has all the semblance of normality. It is strange that the little man suggests that the dog is Lisamarie's, even though it clearly is not. Furthermore, the scene is structurally cut off from the rest of the chapter via page breaks in the form of a wave icon, suggesting its importance—to an outsider reading the material, Haisla epistemology evoked through this passage might be missed. Additionally, neither Lisamarie's actions within the novel nor Robinson's writing explicitly explain the scene, which without culturally specific context has no clear relevance to the plot, except perhaps to foreshadow the upcoming deaths in the novel. Yet even these deaths bear no resemblance to the torture of the dog. Likewise, Robinson's depiction of the B'gwus (Sasquatch) and the T'sonoqua (a Haisla female monster) are also examples of how Robinson distorts our onto-epistemological uncertainties by continually redefining these monstrous figures throughout the novel.[23] I read these moments of excess as significant to Robinson's distancing from a tell-all or consciously explanatory mode. Instead, such instances purposefully make the reader step back and redefine their expectations of the novel and of Robinson's Gothic form.

Jodey Castricano (2006) examines Robinson's debunking of a psychoanalytic understanding of First Nations' culture via a close reading of Lisamarie's encounter with a therapist. The therapist attempts to diagnose Lisamarie with a psychological disorder; at the same time, Lisamarie sees the therapist being fed on by her own demons, "the thing that was beside her whispering in her ear" (E. Robinson 2000, 272). Castricano also examines how Robinson's Gothic form has been critically received. The witty observation that "what goes bump in the night in one context is the sound of a paradigm clash in another" demonstrates the dangers of applying a psychoanalytically inflected Gothic reading to the book and indicates how Robinson seems to be writing purposefully against this type of Gothic interpretation (Castricano 2006, 809). Robinson's use of excess supports this reading, for excess, which is consciously counternarrative, prevents a metaphorical or symbolic reading inherent in the psychoanalytic mode. In moving away from a definitive explanation for unreal elements, Robinson demonstrates how two competing epistemologies can and do exist side by side in Haisla lives. Additionally, these incidents create an ominous tone that darkens the book but does not reduce educational experiences to mere victimry paradigms. Like Wright's use of crows, excess in *Monkey Beach* draws our attention to the materiality of the text, disturbing our ontological certainty by narrating events that seem to exist beyond the narrative progression.

Excess within Educational Gothic texts complicates psychological or metaphorical readings. In line with the "aesthetics of horror," excess focuses on generating effect and sensorily impacting the reader. Unlike the "aesthetics of horror" and moving toward an ethical horror, the Gothic surface that these authors purposely create confounds easy interpretation by forming surface rather than depth, leaving a radical ambiguity present when we attempt to attach a deeper meaning to these elements.[24] This ambiguity allows authors to move away from the "methodological individualism"[25] in which Indigenous experiences are reduced to paradigmatic structures of evil perpetrators and innocent victims, ignoring institutional bodies; and, on the other end of the political spectrum, allows them to avoid the kind of neoliberal progressivism in which Indigenous culture must be seen as an "ethical disruption of post-colonial discourse" (Henderson 2009, 188). Excess disrupts the perfunctory clarity settler culture needs from Indigenous texts by means of a focus on surface and ambiguous meaning.

In an era in which horror has become so oversaturated that it ceases to be shocking and is instead a form of entertainment or voyeuristic pleasure subsumed into "the flows of monetary exchange and performance optimism," silence and excess demonstrate an ethical Gothic response to historical trauma (Botting 2001, 173). In textual rather than narrative excess, and in silence that is signposted but not answered, we can rediscover the disturbance without the pleasure that horror, in its most affective form, provokes. In these three novels, silence and excess enable authors to move beyond an "aesthetics of horror" in which pain and shock make audiences recoil, but ultimately entertain them, to something that requires deeper engagement. Together, silence and excess make us revisit our expectations of these texts. Silence prevents easy identification with the "Other" and opens up a space for thought; excess precludes the metaphorical and moralistic readings we expect from Gothic literature by providing too much detail and confounding meaning. These tropes are vital when we consider the content of the texts, the dark histories and abusive educations authors depict, for both empathy and ontological certainty can limit our engagement through overidentification. Indeed, Sontag notes that while sympathy is unhelpful, it "proclaims our innocence as well as our impotence"; sentimentality also fails to incite action, for it is "entirely compatible with a taste for brutality and worse" (2003, 35–36). Instead, it seems vital that these texts make us encounter strangeness.

"Strangeness" is a term that Shoshana Felman and Dori Laub employ to describe texts that testify to violence (1992, 7). Strangeness is important, for it makes us acknowledge the "limits of [our] epistemological unities" (40). This topic is explored by Julia V. Emberley, who demonstrates how testimonial norms emerge from a Western post-Enlightenment ideology and are thus limited in their acknowledgment of the heterogeneity of "knowledges and knowledge formations," particularly in relation to the divergent "cultural construction of the 'self'" in an Indigenous epistemological framework (2014, 40). Therefore, a sense of strangeness is vital in "defamiliarizing" the reader so that "listening and learning are transformed into knowledge, but just what that knowledge is, is not always evident" (55). In other words, the strange site generates multiple meanings and is dependent on factors of greater consequence than the reader. Thus, silence and excess not only close down empathetic relationships but also open up the possibility for alternative knowledges in the texts and an ontological uncertainty that is action inducing rather than freezing. In this way, these texts enable a more ethical engagement with the horrors of the past while also looking to the survivance of the present.

Indigenous Educational Gothic works present more nuanced pictures of the hardships their protagonists face in an era of recognition politics, in which Indigenous writing is expected to only perform the function of testimony in certain ways—to be "clearly and cleanly 'other' to settler culture" (Henderson 2009, 188). Indigenous Educational Gothic works also demonstrate a creative response to trauma in the ways authors establish the "active sense of presence" Gerald Vizenor (1999, vii) calls for when he talks of survivance, as well as broadening the parameters of what we understand Gothic and Indigenous writing to be, in line with Leanne Betasamosake Simpson's call for "resurgence as a mechanism" for Indigenous continuance (2017, 25). These novels are grounded in earlier testimonial traditions but written several decades later, often by descendants of survivors, and thus demonstrate a new wave of writing that tackles the intergenerational effects of abusive educations and looks at a broader and more intersectional picture of education Indigenous girls receive in settler nations.

NOTES

1. The report detailed the forced removal of Indigenous children, particularly those deemed to be of mixed descent (the term "half-blood" or "half-caste" was used at the time), and concluded that this practice was tantamount to genocide.

2. Continuous pressure from Indigenous activists and communities resulted in the Indian Residential Schools Settlement Agreement in 2005, which was supposed to provide survivors with compensation. However, recent discoveries of unmarked graves at Canadian residential school sites highlight the need for further investigation.

3. Added to a defense appropriations spending bill, the Apology Resolution (2009) was "watered down," indirect, and apolitical, according to Ojibwe journalist and writer Rob Capriccioso (2010).

4. Louis Owens (Choctaw/Cherokee) and Alan Velie first applied the term "Indigenous Gothic" to the work of Anishinaabe writer Gerald Vizenor to characterize his revision of the "Frontier Gothic" (Velie 1991–1992, 75). Since then, scholars including Burnham, Cariou, and

Althans have expanded this genre in line with a plethora of creative outputs (Burnham 2014; Cariou 2006; Althans 2010).

5. Jennifer Henderson (2018) examines how Residential School Gothic films instead demonstrate the horrors of state educational policies toward Indigenous peoples. However, in stressing the genre's recycled aspects, Henderson critiques the "distance and containment" Gothic generates by confining the evils of the schooling system to a past era, while the focus on individual perpetrators detracts from state fault (44). That said, the films that Henderson critiques are settler productions.

6. The original release title for this film was titled *Older than America*. Although set in America, the film looks more broadly at these institutions in both the United States and Canada.

7. I follow John Frow, who defines "mode" as a "thematic and tonal qualification or 'colouring' of genre," whereas genre is "a more specific organisation of texts with thematic, rhetorical and formal dimensions" (2006, 67).

8. Simpson uses the term "grounded normativity" interchangeably with "Nishnaabeg intelligence."

9. While the Gothic employs the binary of good and evil, life writing, which has often had a testimonial function and therefore must stand up as "truth," has little room for nuance.

10. Victimry, a term coined by Gerald Vizenor, connotes the opposite of survivance. While survivance is "an active sense of presence, the continuance of native stories, not a mere reaction, or a survivable name," victimry instead describes the roles Indigenous peoples are accorded within historical accounts of genocide rather than how they define themselves (Vizenor [1994] 1999, vii). It is therefore vital to examine how these authors use the mode to explore the horrors of the past in ways that resist reinstating the pain and erasure that Settler Gothic trades on.

11. I employ the term "aesthetics" in a Kantian sense, which positions aesthetics in terms of a judgment of the sublime and the beautiful by a disinterested observer rather than Alexander Gottlieb Baumgarten's pre-Kantian understanding of aesthetics as the sensory engagement of the lower faculties. To confuse matters, Baumgarten's definition of aesthetics would feed into the idea of an ethical response I put forward, and it is to save confusion (and to emphasize the principled nature of these constructions) that I have used the term "ethics of horror" rather than "aesthetics of horror." However, Pinder's term "aesthetics of care" (2019) and Cariou's understanding of "aesthetics of action" (2006, 733) all use aesthetics in a pre-Kantian sense and influence my term "ethics of horror."

12. Susan Sontag discusses this at length in *Regarding the Pain of Others* (2003).

13. Clover writes, "Cinefantastic horror, in short, succeeds in the production of sensation to more or less the degree that it succeeds in incorporating its spectators as 'feminine' and then violating that body—which recoils, shudders, cries out collectively—in ways otherwise imaginable, for males, only in nightmare" (Clover 1987, 213).

14. Although this is unclear, because Robinson also suggests that these deaths are the result of an unseen force that Lisamarie must appease to save herself from drowning at the end of the novel.

15. In *Monkey Beach*, Robinson links the sexual abuse Karaoke is subjected to by her Uncle Josh to the residential school legacy. Josh, it appears, repeats the abuse he is himself a victim of at the hands of his residential schoolteacher, Father Archibald.

16. The sublime usually emanates from natural scenes that are beautiful yet terrifying spectacles, evoking awe but also inspiring fear. A classic example of the sublime and ensuing catharsis in the Gothic genre is the fire at the end of Charlotte Brontë's *Jane Eyre* (1847), in which Bertha Mason sets fire to Thornfield Hall. This event is both terrifying and awesome via the spectacle of the rational, patriarchal manor being consumed by the natural, untamed, and Other, represented by the fire and by Bertha.

17. Yet many local AIM groups continued, and some are still active.

18. French philosopher Emmanuel Levinas believes that ethics emerge from contact with an Other, which results in a questioning of the self. See *Totality and Infinity: An Essay on Exteriority* (1969) and *Otherwise than Being; or, Beyond Essence* (1981).

19. Thompson redefines the term "excess" in her classic 1982 study of Sergei Eisenstein's *Ivan the Terrible* (produced in 1944).

20. Crows and ravens, with their eerie caws and their tendency to feast on carrion, appear in the Gothic genre often as harbingers of death, such as in *Hamlet* (1601) and *Macbeth* (1623), where ravens appear before acts of destruction. The raven is also the subject of Edgar Allan Poe's American Gothic poem "The Raven" (1845), in which the speaker slowly descends into madness because of a lost love. Crow-like birds also appear in J. R. R. Tolkien's *Lord of the Rings* trilogy (1954–1955), as spies of the evil wizard Saruman, and in Robinson's *Monkey Beach*—to warn protagonist Lisamarie of impending dangers.

21. Raven is a character from Maracle's work *Ravensong* (1993).

22. Mudrooroo is a figure whose Aboriginal identity has been convincingly challenged but whose work gathering Indigenous Australian storytelling archetypes is nonetheless still useful.

23. For more on Robinson's portrayal of these "monsters," see Andrews (2001) and Appleford (2005).

24. Stephen Best and Sharon Marcus explain surface reading using the example that such a practice would view "ghosts as presences, not absences and lets ghosts be ghosts, instead of saying what they are ghosts of" (2009, 13). Surface reading practice thus aims to dispel psychological interpretation (depth reading) by paying attention to what is there in the text.

25. The term "methodological individualism" is defined by Roland D. Chrisjohn, Sherri L. Young, and Michael Maraun (2006).

BIBLIOGRAPHY

Althans, Katrin. 2010. *Darkness Subverted: Aboriginal Gothic in Black Australian Literature and Film.* Göttingen: V&R Unipress.

Andrews, Jennifer. 2001. "Native Canadian Gothic Refigured: Reading Eden Robinson's *Monkey Beach.*" *Essays on Canadian Writing*, no. 73 (Spring): 1–24.

Appleford, Rob. 2005. "'Close, Very Close, a B'gwus Howls': The Contingency of Execution in Eden Robinson's Monkey Beach." *Canadian Literature*, no. 184 (Spring): 85–101.

Australian Human Rights Commission. 1997. "Bringing Them Home: Report of the National Inquiry into the Separation of Aboriginal and Torres Strait Islander Children from Their Families." April. Sydney: Australian Human Rights Commission. https://humanrights.gov.au/our-work/projects/bringing-them-home-report-1997.

Best, Stephen, and Sharon Marcus. 2009. "Surface Reading: An Introduction." *Representations* 108, no. 1 (November): 1–21.

Bolaki, Stella. 2011. *Unsettling the Bildungsroman: Reading Contemporary Ethnic American Women's Fiction.* New York: Brill.

Botting, Fred. 1996. *Gothic.* The New Critical Idiom Series. London: Routledge.

Botting, Fred. 2001. "Candygothic." In *The Gothic,* edited by Fred Botting, 133–52. Cambridge: D. S. Brewer.

Botting, Fred. 2012. "Love Your Zombie: Horror, Ethics, Excess." In *The Gothic in Contemporary Literature and Popular Culture: Pop Goth,* edited by Justin D. Edwards and Agnieszka Soltysik Monnet, 19–36. New York: Routledge.

Brogan, Kathleen. 1998. *Cultural Haunting: Ghosts and Ethnicity in Recent American Literature.* Charlottesville: University Press of Virginia.

Burnham, Michelle. 2011. "Sherman Alexie's *Indian Killer* as Indigenous Gothic." In *Phantom Past, Indigenous Presence: Native Ghosts in North American Culture and History,* edited by Colleen E. Boyd and Coll Thrush, 3–26. Lincoln: University of Nebraska Press.

Burnham, Michelle. 2014. "Is There an Indigenous Gothic?" In *A Companion to American Gothic,* edited by Charles L. Crow, 223–37. Chichester, W. Susx., England: John Wiley and Sons.

Capriccioso, Rob. 2010. "A Sorry Saga: Obama Signs Native American Apology Resolution; Fails to Draw Attention to It." Indian Law Resource Center, January 13. https://indianlaw .org/node/529.

Cariou, Warren. 2006. "Haunted Prairie: Aboriginal 'Ghosts' and the Spectres of Settlement." *University of Toronto Quarterly* 75, no. 2 (Spring): 727–34.

Castor, Laura Virginia. 2006. "Claiming Place in Wor(l)ds: Linda Hogan's 'Solar Storms.'" *MELUS* 31, no. 2 (Summer): 147–58.

Castricano, Jodey. 2006. "Learning to Talk with Ghosts: Canadian Gothic and the Poetics of Haunting in Eden Robinson's *Monkey Beach.*" *University of Toronto Quarterly* 75, no. 2 (Spring): 801–13.

Cherry, Brigid. 2009. *Horror.* Abingdon, Oxon., England: Routledge.

Child, Brenda J. 2018. "The Boarding School as Metaphor." *Journal of American Indian Education* 57, no. 1 (Spring): 37–57.

Chrisjohn, Roland David, Sherri L. Young, and Michael Maraun. 2006. *The Circle Game: Shadows and Substance in the Indian Residential School Experience in Canada.* Rev. ed. Penticton, BC: Theytus Books.

Clover, Carol J. 1987. "Her Body, Himself: Gender in the Slasher Film." *Representations* 20 (October): 187–228.

Coulthard, Glen Sean. 2014. *Red Skin, White Masks: Rejecting the Colonial Politics of Recognition.* Minneapolis: University of Minnesota Press.

Dillon, Grace L. 2007. "Miindiwag and Indigenous Diaspora: Eden Robinson's and Celu Amberstone's Forays into 'Postcolonial' Science Fiction and Fantasy." *Extrapolation* 48, no. 2 (Summer): 219–43.

Dobson, Kit. 2009. "Indigeneity and Diversity in Eden Robinson's Work." *Canadian Literature,* no. 201 (Summer): 54–67.

Donaldson, Laura E. 1988. "The Miranda Complex: Colonialism and the Question of Feminist Reading." *Diacritics* 18, no. 3 (Autumn): 65–77.

Emberley, Julia V. 2014. *The Testimonial Uncanny: Indigenous Storytelling, Knowledge, and Reparative Practices*. Albany: State University of New York Press.

Felman, Shoshana, and Dori Laub. 1992. *Testimony: Crises of Witnessing in Literature, Psychoanalysis, and History*. New York: Routledge.

Frow, John. 2006. *Genre: The New Critical Idiom*. Abingdon, Oxon., England: Routledge.

Garneau, David. 2016. "Imaginary Spaces of Conciliation and Reconciliation." In *Arts of Engagement: Taking Aesthetic Action in and beyond the Truth and Reconciliation Commission of Canada*, edited by Dylan Robinson and Keavy Martin, 21–41. Waterloo, ON: Wilfrid Laurier University Press.

Harrison, Summer. 2019. "'We Need New Stories': Trauma, Storytelling, and the Mapping of Environmental Injustice in Linda Hogan's *Solar Storms* and Standing Rock." *American Indian Quarterly* 43, no. 1 (Winter): 1–35.

Henderson, Jennifer. 2009. "'Something Not Unlike Enjoyment:' Gothicism, Catholicism, and Sexuality in Tomson Highway's *Kiss of the Fur Queen*." In *Unsettled Remains: Canadian Literature and the Postcolonial Gothic*, edited by Cynthia Sugars and Gerry Turcotte, 175–204. Waterloo, ON: Wilfrid Laurier University Press.

Henderson, Jennifer. 2018. "Residential School Gothic and Red Power: Genre Friction in *Rhymes for Young Ghouls*." *American Indian Culture and Research Journal* 42, no. 4 (October): 43–66.

Hogan, Linda. 1994. *Solar Storms*. New York: Scribner.

Horton, Jessica L. 2017. *Art for an Undivided Earth: The American Indian Movement Generation*. Durham, NC: Duke University Press.

Kelly, Jennifer. 1994. "Coming Out of the House: A Conversation with Lee Maracle." *ARIEL* 25, no. 1 (January): 73–88.

Král, Françoise. 2002. "Re-Surfacing through Palimpsests: A (False) Quest for Repossession in the Works of Mudrooroo and Alexis Wright." *Commonwealth Essays and Studies* 25, no. 1 (Autumn): 7–14.

Levinas, Emmanuel. 1969. *Totality and Infinity: An Essay on Exteriority*. Translated by Alphonso Lingis. Pittsburgh: Duquesne University Press.

Levinas, Emmanuel. 1981. *Otherwise Than Being; or, Beyond Essence*. Translated by Alphonso Lingis. New York: Springer.

McCall, Sophie. 2011. *First Person Plural: Aboriginal Storytelling and the Ethics of Collaborative Authorship*. Vancouver: University of British Columbia Press.

Mudrooroo [Colin Johnson]. 1994. *Aboriginal Mythology: An A–Z Spanning the History of the Australian Aboriginal People from the Earliest Legends to the Present Day*. London: Aquarian.

Pinder, Kait. 2019. "View of Action, Feeling, Form: The Aesthetics of Care in Tracey Lindberg's Birdie." *Studies in Canadian Literature / Études en Littérature Canadienne* 44, no. 2: 218–38.

Radcliffe, Ann. 1826. "On the Supernatural in Poetry by the Late Mrs. Radcliffe." *New Monthly Magazine and Literary Journal* 16, no. 1: 145–52.

Ricoeur, Paul. 1970. *Freud and Philosophy: An Essay on Interpretation*. Translated by Denis Savage. New Haven, CT: Yale University Press.

Robinson, Dylan, and Keavy Martin. 2016. "Introduction: 'The Body Is a Resonant Chamber.'" In *Arts of Engagement: Taking Aesthetic Action in and beyond the Truth and Reconciliation Commission of Canada*, edited by Dylan Robinson and Keavy Martin, 1–20. Waterloo, ON: Wilfrid Laurier University Press.

Robinson, Eden. 2000. *Monkey Beach*. Boston: Houghton Mifflin Harcourt.

Robinson, Eden. 2011. *The Sasquatch at Home: Traditional Protocols and Modern Storytelling.* Edmonton: University of Alberta Press.

Ruppert, James. 1995. *Mediation in Contemporary Native American Fiction*. American Indian Literature and Critical Studies Series, no. 15. Norman: University of Oklahoma Press.

Schoonover, Madelyn Marie. 2022. "Indigenous Futurisms and Decolonial Horror: An Interview with Rebecca Roanhorse." *Gothic Studies* 24, no. 3: 295–303.

Simpson, Leanne Betasamosake. 2017. *As We Have Always Done: Indigenous Freedom through Radical Resistance*. Minneapolis: University of Minnesota Press.

Sontag, Susan. 2003. *Regarding the Pain of Others*. London: Hamish Hamilton.

Thompson, Kristin. 1982. *Eisenstein's "Ivan the Terrible": A Neoformalist Analysis*. Princeton, NJ: Princeton University Press.

Tuck, Eve. 2009. "Suspending Damage: A Letter to Communities." *Harvard Educational Review* 79, no. 3: 409–28.

Velie, Alan R. 1991–1992. "Gerald Vizenor's Indian Gothic." *MELUS* 17, no. 1 (Spring): 75–85.

Veracini, Lorenzo. 2015. *The Settler Colonial Present*. Basingstoke, Hants., England: Palgrave Macmillan.

Vernon, Irene S. 2012. "'We Were Those Who Walked Out of Bullets and Hunger': Representations of Trauma and Healing in *Solar Storms*." *American Indian Quarterly* 36, no. 1 (Winter): 34–49.

Vizenor, Gerald Robert. 1995. "A Trickster Discourse: Comic and Tragic Themes in Native American Literature." In *Buried Roots and Indestructible Seeds: The Survival of American Indian Life in Story, History, and Spirit*, edited by Mark Allan Lindquist and Martin Zanger, 67–83. Madison: University of Wisconsin Press.

Vizenor, Gerald Robert. (1994) 1999. *Manifest Manners: Narratives on Postindian Survivance*. Lincoln: University of Nebraska Press.

Vizenor, Gerald Robert. 2009. *Native Liberty: Natural Reason and Cultural Survivance*. Lincoln: University of Nebraska Press.

Wright, Alexis. 1997. *Plains of Promise*. St. Lucia, Australia: University of Queensland Press.

CHAPTER 8

INDIGENIZING GOTHIC COMICS

UNSETTLING THE COLONIAL SPECTER

SABRINA ZACHARIAS

Indigenous creators have always existed in society; however, historically, most mainstream depictions of Indigenous peoples in the Western canon have been presented, produced, and shaped by settler and colonial ideology. In short, settler-created depictions of Indigenous peoples serve and feed into negative stereotypes that perpetuate colonial attitudes and racism, which work to undermine Indigenous peoples and conciliatory efforts (Skinner 2018).[1] Indigenous writers and creators speak back to these narratives and representations, deconstructing and resituating—or in Rebecca Roanhorse's words, a lawyer and speculative fiction author of Ohkay Owingeh descent, "re-imagin[ing]" (2018)—Indigenous portrayals across media forms, including comics and popular culture. Indigenous characterizations by Indigenous creators demonstrate the continued resilience that Indigenous peoples must uphold in the face of racism and inequality in contemporary society.

Indigenous peoples across North America, and worldwide, have survived and continue to withstand the apocalypse of colonialism and racism that began with the first explorers and settlers. Roanhorse states in her article "Postcards from the Apocalypse" that "Native folks have already experienced an apocalypse. All the sort of dystopian tropes you see in movies, we've experienced those—our land lost, our children taken away, sent to schools and things like that. And we've survived" (2018). The Indigenous Gothic is an act of survivance against and within colonialism and settler-centric society; it is a "call for awareness" (LaPensée 2017) of Indigenous identities and issues by unsettling the Gothic from its traditional European settler origins and reviving it with Indigenous cultures and worldviews. The Indigenous Gothic centers narratives on Indigenous peoples and issues, dismantling settler constructions of Indigenous peoples. This chapter identifies and traces the Indigenization of the Gothic and the less discussed deployment of the Indigenized Gothic *in comics*, aiming to better define the genre of texts known as Indigenous Gothic. Both mode and form are critical to the function of the text as a representation of Indigenous issues and resistance against settler narratives and ideology. Traditional literary forms are more entrenched in colonialism as the English language itself remains a tool of colonization and cultural genocide (Milloy 1999, 46; Griffith 2019, 68). Thus, the "comics form," with its visual and image-based narratives, distances storytelling practices from colonial traditions and enables more alternative and Indigenous-based narrative expressions.

Furthermore, visual-based narratives ask of the reader a deeper level of engagement with the text, requiring the reader to participate in the process of storytelling through involvement in interpreting the images, bringing their own cultural knowledge and understandings to inform their readings of the text. The reader takes on two forms specifically in this type of reading: Indigenous readers or those who bring prior awareness of Indigenous culture and practice to their reading; and readers who carry little or no prior knowledge and understanding of Indigenous culture. For both, the text represents and articulates Indigenous experiences; separately, one will have prior knowledge and experience, with access to and understanding of layers of the text and narrative informed by their cultural awareness, while the other will have the opportunity to learn from and appreciate the texts as they engage with them.

To demonstrate the function of the Indigenous Gothic in comics and the process of Indigenizing the Gothic mode, this chapter engages with Indigenous Gothic comics representing the Missing and Murdered Indigenous Women, Girls, and Trans and Two-Spirit peoples (MMIWGT2S) epidemic in Canada and North America more widely. A focus on the MMIWGT2S crisis and depictions of experiences from survivors and family members in comics such as *Sixkiller* (2018) by Lee Francis IV and Weshoyot Alvitre, and *Will I See?* (2016) by David Alexander Robertson, Iskwē, Erin Leslie, and G. M. B. Chomichuk, provides an opportunity to raise awareness of the ongoing crisis of the MMIWGT2S. Further, these comics demonstrate how the Indigenous Gothic becomes both an act of survivance[2] in an apocalyptic world and an unsettling of settler conceptions of Indigenous peoples in a nontraditional literary form.

It is imperative that I acknowledge and locate myself within this discussion before going further, both to express my appreciation for the land I reside on, to honor the Indigenous people who have worked and lived on this land historically and presently, and to acknowledge the worldview and experience I am bringing to this discussion and analysis. I am a settler scholar. I grew up in Treaty One Territory, the Heart of the Homeland of the Red River Métis. Currently, I reside on the traditional territory of the Haudenosaunee and Anishinaabe peoples, where I continue learning of and from Indigenous scholars, writers, and creators. As a settler scholar at a colonial institute, Queen's University, I recognize that my experience, education, and worldview shape my interpretations of the texts I engage with and the research I am doing. I hope that my work may add to the ongoing discussions about and around Indigenous literature, comics, and decolonizing efforts.

Indigenous Comics: *Sixkiller* and *Will I See?*

The texts this chapter focuses on are written or created by Indigenous writers and artists: *Sixkiller*, published by Native Realities, written and created by Lee Francis IV and Weshoyot Alvitre; and *Will I See?*, published by HighWater Press, written and produced by David Alexander Robertson, Iskwē, Erin Leslie, and G. M. B. Chomichuk. *Sixkiller* and *Will I See?* proffer an understanding of how the Indigenous Gothic itself functions as part of the Gothic genre but, further, how the Indigenous Gothic is an act of resistance, the rewriting and unsettling of settler narratives.

Sixkiller is an Indigenous retelling of Lewis Carroll's *Alice's Adventures in Wonderland* (1865). What is significant about this retelling is not only that it centers around a young Cherokee woman, but the story itself is framed as a Gothic tale: the reader joins Alice, a young Indigenous woman, on her journey for revenge; she is institutionalized and must deal with schizophrenia and the murder of her sister. The failure of the justice system drives Alice's efforts to seek revenge. The comic engages in the larger conversation that centers on and brings attention to the MMIWGT2S crisis by directly addressing the ongoing crisis's effects on families and individuals, and the lack of repercussions for those who harm. There is no justice for Alice's older sister's murder, so Alice intends to get it for herself.

Will I See? follows the narrative of another young Indigenous woman, May, identified within the comic as Cree. May moves through the city she lives in—an unnamed urban space—collecting items from Missing and Murdered Indigenous Women. The geographical ambiguity acknowledges that the MMIWGT2S crisis is not defined by imaginary geographical lines; it is an issue across North America (Rifkind and Fontaine 2020, 343). In the narrative, May experiences a brush with the violent threat of existing in a North American urban space as a young Indigenous woman. Casting May, a Cree teen, as the main character demonstrates more clearly the "emotional and social effects of the MMIWGT2S epidemic" (Rifkind and Fontaine 2020, 341). Young Indigenous women are one of the most vulnerable populations in society because of the MMIWGT2S epidemic, and by casting a young Indigenous woman as the main character, *Will I See?* (and *Sixkiller*) powerfully demonstrate the degree to which this issue is affecting Indigenous communities.

Sixkiller and *Will I See?* are two works arising from the flourishing genre of Indigenous comics, more specifically Indigenous comics that address the MMIWGT2S epidemic. However, these texts in particular serve as fascinating examples of the Indigenous Gothic as a genre rather than simply engaging with aspects of the Gothic or the Gothic mode as some other comics do. *Sixkiller* and *Will I See?* engage with and appropriate the Gothic mode and genre to blend and restructure it through a lens of Indigenous culture and spirituality, ultimately unsettling settler tradition and understanding and telling stories of resistance and survival.

The Emergence of the Indigenous Gothic —Exercising the Colonial Specter

The Indigenous Gothic takes the familiar devices of Gothic landscapes, figures, and expressions of anxiety and trauma and reestablishes them within an Indigenous understanding and worldview. Indigenous writer Alicia Elliott posits that the emerging prevalence of Indigenous Horror texts—a genre directly related to the Gothic—from Indigenous creators enables the exploration of colonialism's ongoing reality at a safe distance (2019). Indigenous Gothic and Indigenous Horror texts provide "comfort in witnessing a world where the horror eventually stops—even if that world is fictional" (Elliott 2019). This need is reflected in the rise of Indigenous speculative fiction, with depictions of Indigenous sovereignty "imagin[ing] and mobiliz[ing] projects to actualize alternative futures" (Topash-Caldwell 2020, 35). The provided comfort from these imagined futures and spaces where the horror ends emphasize the need for the expression and expulsion of trauma and traumatic experiences, because "what more is there to fear when you've already faced governments who have tried for centuries to wipe you out, who have used biological warfare and forced starvation to create apocalypse for your people?" (Elliott 2019). The Indigenous Gothic provides a space to express the trauma of living in a colonial (apocalyptic) world.

The emergence of the Indigenous Gothic highlights the former (and in many ways continued) lack of non-colonial- or non-settler-influenced representations of Indigenous peoples and issues; this willful exclusion is a common characteristic of a settler-controlled society. Gina Wisker's scholarship on the Postcolonial Gothic and Horror is beneficial in identifying how this subgenre of the Gothic emerges from "the need to explore, reimagine, and record in literature the magical, the historical, and the still contemporary, everyday mythical that is frequently overlooked, denied, and invisible in culturally dominant forms of literary expression" (2007, 401). The need for representation of culture, beliefs, and ethnic backgrounds has been historically lacking due to the dominating voice of the settler creator in most genres and forms. Diversified narratives, visual or otherwise, oppose and correct culturally dominant ideas, replacing the cultural fictions with the Indigenous writers' "acknowledg[ment of] the mundane horror of living in a country that dehumanizes you" (Elliott 2019). However, while there are instances in which Wisker's theory of Postcolonial Gothic aligns with Indigenous Gothic, the Postcolonial Gothic has marked differences from the Indigenous Gothic, the foremost being that settler creators cannot write texts categorized as "Indigenous Gothic." The subgenre emerges through the need to express these Othered worldviews, experiences, and beliefs; because settler creators, or those who are part of the dominant culture, do not have Indigenous worldviews, experiences, and beliefs, settler creators fundamentally cannot create these texts.

Furthermore, Wisker states that the Postcolonial Gothic "reinhabits and reconfigures, it reinstates and newly imagines ways of being, seeing, and expressing from the points of view of and using some of the forms of people whose experiences and expressions have . . . largely been unheard of and even discredited" (2007, 402). While the idea that Wisker purposes of the "reinhabit[ing] and reconfigur[ing,] . . . reinstat[ing] and newly imagine[d] ways of being, seeing, and expressing" (402) is in line with the necessity of Indigenizing the Gothic genre to better express the Indigenous community's experiences, it is necessary to contest Wisker's argument in two places. First, the terminology that Wisker employs, "postcolonial," is unsuitable due to the fraught nature of the idea of the world being a "postcolonial" one (it is not). Second, "using some of the forms of people whose experiences and expressions have . . . largely been unheard of and even discredited" is a problematic approach at best and, in some instances, identified as a practice of active colonization at worst. "*Using . . .* the forms of people" (my emphasis) implies that those creating or constructing the Postcolonial Gothic text need not be part of the cultural group the narrative centers around (402). This suggested use of Indigenous cultures and identities as literary tools for the settler creator echoes the enslavement, mistreatment, and misuse of Indigenous and various Othered groups in the past, which in some ways continue to be standard practices of colonialism. Thus, this departure from the Postcolonial Gothic returns us to the assertion that the settler creator cannot create Indigenous Gothic texts. The use of Indigenous cultures and identities by settler writers and creators is an inherently colonizing act.

The critical framework I am suggesting recognizes and necessitates that Indigenous Gothic texts and narratives be produced by Indigenous creators or writers. As Angela Elisa Schoch/Davidson points out, scholarship surrounding the Indigenous Gothic has not yet been concerned with tracing a historical pattern of Indigenous creators employing the Gothic mode (2020, 143). Instead, the study surrounding the Indigenous Gothic has primarily focused on individual studies of singular texts (Castricano 2006) rather than a survey of the Indigenous Gothic (Schoch/Davidson 2020, 143). Historically, this individually based critical tradition has been influenced by the lack of representation or attention given to Indigenous authors writing in the Gothic mode.[3] There have been other forms of study that approach or engage with ideas similar to the Indigenous Gothic that I will here lay out; however, they engage with the literature, much as Davidson gestures to, as an individual literary study or as something separate (and often fraught, depending on its categorization) from the Indigenous Gothic. Voices that are related to this conversation about the Indigenous Gothic also emerge from the fields of Postcolonial and Canadian Gothic; they include Jodey Castricano, who presents a reading of Eden Robinson's work as a primarily Canadian (Indigenous) Gothic work (2006); Amy Elizabeth Gore, who grapples with defining the Indigenous Gothic novel (2011); and Michelle Burnham, who approaches an American Indigenous Gothic not as an intervention against settler-controlled and constructed representations of Indigenous peoples but rather as a subgenre that adds to an overarching American Gothic (2014). I meet these readings—acknowledging the scholarship of American, Postcolonial, and Canadian Gothic, working with and building from it—and posit that the Indigenous Gothic is a separate expression of the Gothic that, as Wisker says so clearly, is an effort to "explore, reimagine, and record in literature the magical, the historical, and the still contemporary" from an Indigenous perspective, awash in Indigenous culture and worldviews. Furthermore, I analyze the deployment of the Indigenous Gothic in comics and how the form magnifies this Indigenous expression of experience and worldview.

Several scholars such as Angela Elisa Schoch/Davidson (2020), Ken Gelder (2014), and Cynthia Sugars (2014) have pointed out how the terminology "Indigenous gothic" is problematic for Indigenous writers and creators through the "gothic's" connection to the colonial past. "Indigenous gothic" functions not dissimilarly from the way that "postcolonial" does, implying and necessitating the colonizer to the creative process: the Indigenous Gothic would not have emerged if not for colonialism, as the Gothic is an inherently European artistic tradition (Schoch/Davidson 2020, 148). I wonder, however, if it is possible to think differently about the term "Indigenous Gothic." The Indigenous Gothic engages with familiar aspects and devices of the Gothic, adopting and blending them into Indigenous understandings and worldviews. Indigenizing the Gothic tradition is a dynamic gesture of resistance that decenters the settler from the text and refocuses on Indigenous peoples, communities, issues, and worldviews. Colonialism remains an inexorable specter haunting the Indigenous Gothic text, but it is being contained and mediated by the Indigenous worldview it is filtered through.

With the specter of colonialism in mind, the Indigenous Gothic functions on two levels of understanding within a text. First, in the visual and literary aspects of a text, the creator will engage with the typical figures and landscapes of the Gothic through their cultural lens. Second, the history of colonialism, ongoing racism, intergenerational trauma, and oppression haunt the texts. Settler narratives and the peoples who were—and are—silenced and erased by colonialism emerge through the texts as an ever-present phantom. The physical text is inherently Gothic. It is "haunted by the ghosts of those who were hidden and silenced in the colonial and imperial past and those who now still might occupy a parallel universe, unheard, unspoken, unwritten" (Wisker 2007, 402). These two functions, the text's content and its haunting, are inextricable. The discussions exploring racism, ongoing oppression, trauma, and colonialism transfer the specter of colonialism's victims to the physical text.

Indigenous Gothic takes up the characters, spaces, and themes of the Gothic we are familiar with and resituates these elements through an Indigenous lens. The Gothic has standard features and figures that invoke historical and cultural anxieties (Botting 1996, 1–2). These figures and features are taken up and reframed with an Indigenous perspective. No longer is it the madman, skeletons, or supernatural demons: the Gothic figure becomes the real threat of colonialism, the settler, the perpetrator of the MMIWGT2S crisis. Another key feature of the Gothic being Indigenized is the narrative landscape. The narrative is not set in the crumbling castles and abbeys that construct Romantic Gothic settings (Botting 1996, 2); the story world takes shape in the spaces and places significant to Indigenous history and experiences. We see the emergence of Gothic landscapes as spaces that the traumas experienced by Indigenous Peoples haunt. The Indigenous Gothic alters each of these aspects of the Gothic according to Indigenous worldviews and experiences.

This Indigenizing can also manifest through the act of rewriting settler texts. *Alice's Adventures in Wonderland* is not traditionally categorized as a Gothic text: the choice to retell the story through an Indigenous perspective that employs the Gothic within it functions as a complex metaperformance of the text itself. Because the story is traditionally one of settler origin, the specter of colonialism hovers over the narrative, shaping the text into a Gothic one through that connection. Moreover, the writer and creator make an active choice to lend the narrative a darker tone, one that assists in telling a weightier story about the experiences and implications of the MMIWGT2S epidemic. The text becomes Gothic through its settler origins and the inclusion of the Gothic mode in its retelling. The choice to reframe the story complicates our understanding of the text and how we read it. The Indigenization of the text asks the reader to recognize the specter of colonialism while functioning to exercise it. Appropriating the narrative and reframing it within the cultural context of Indigenous worldviews is an overt act of resistance against settler ideology, especially as Alice moves through settler-dominated spaces and continues to push back against settler norms and understandings.

Reading Gothic Comics:
The Visual versus the Literary

The Gothic in comics functions similarly to and distinctly from the Gothic in more traditional literary texts. Excess, a common element of Gothic texts, plays a significant role in graphic Gothic storytelling. Thus, there is the aesthetic of excess, "multiple points of view, coexisting storylines, alternate realities, self-conscious fictionality structure" (Round 2014, 57); and the excess of seeing, which is the color, style, and use of embodied or disembodied perspectives. The reader's perspective also becomes a necessary tool in the storytelling process in graphic Gothic texts. Gothic comics require an active reader who "resurrects the creator, who is not dead, but rather undead" (Round 2014, 58) and who interprets the narrative in the gutters of the comics. The active reader is necessary for the two final elements of Gothic comics to function correctly. These elements find their forms as the haunting, the information inferred from one panel and the knowledge gained from the next; and the encrypting, the active assignment of information to the gutter in reading both panels. The reader *must* see both panels to fill in the gap of the gutter. Active readers "resurrect" the writers while breaking down the narrative, assigning events and actions in the gutter spaces (encrypting that information) to reach what the creators are presenting to them (Round 2014, 57–58).[4]

The comic form allows writers and readers to unsettle settler narratives and beliefs through nontraditional storytelling methods. With more traditional forms of literature such as prose writing, novels, and poetry, there is a legacy of colonialism that cannot be separated and that becomes difficult to challenge—the language that these texts are written with has been a tool in the cultural genocide of Indigenous tribes throughout history. Telling these stories in a nontraditional format allows creators to tell their stories in unexpected ways. There is room for experimentation and the ability to work more traditional Indigenous storytelling into the texts themselves. This experimentation and unsettling of settler storytelling practices extend to the ordering of the narrative through the comics' sequential art. The comic form allows for greater opportunities to disrupt reader expectations of how we read and how we tell stories. Scott McCloud, in his book *Understanding Comics*, underscores that sequential art storytelling from different cultures, geographical locations, and historical periods orders narratives in different ways (1994, 11, 14), demonstrating that sequential art does not need to be read left to right, top to bottom. Comics are not beholden to the Western traditions of linear narrative storytelling and reading practice. Thus, the form makes itself particularly useful when it comes to nonlinear Indigenous styles of storytelling.

Furthermore, the comic form creates access to larger audiences. Sarah Henzi discusses the ways the form enables storytellers to reach a broader audience, identifying that "the strength of the comic book is how it uses minimal text with graphic art to tell the story, making it more accessible not only for youth, but for those who may not want to, or cannot, read at length about the history of colonialism"[5] (2016, 25). The alternative form of the visual narrative makes the issues addressed more accessible for many groups of people and thus allows for a broader audience to engage with and learn from the knowledge and experiences being shared.

The comic form is becoming more frequently used by Indigenous creators, becoming "a new space of diffusion and discussion" (Henzi 2016, 28) for various topics that affect Indigenous communities. The comics and the narratives they present are a "vehicle through which to educate others and a means to restore a voice to memory. . . . In this sense, the stories become complex artistic performances that emphasize the visual, adding to, and complementing, the textual, and enabling exploration of different means to reconnect the elements of the past with those of the present and the future" (29). Henzi's conclusion to her article "'A Necessary Antidote': Graphic Novels, Comics, and Indigenous Writing" (2016) addresses whether or not the comic form is appropriate to present and convey stories that deal with issues like the MMIWGT2S crisis. The answer she provides is yes, that through the different textual and visual aspects, narratives are made more authentic, and the

> images speak beyond linguistic, cultural, and generational gaps—an element that is becoming increasingly important given those gaps, caused by shame, lack of education and, more importantly, governmental assimilation policies. . . . [T]hey enable a form of transdisciplinarity, for they touch upon the political, the social and the cultural. . . . These works partake in the creation of a new space to voice, create and resist, as well as to restore and reaffirm experiences, histories and memory, and to rectify the falsity of colonial imagery. (36–37)

Ultimately, the nontraditional literary form encourages and invites, if not *demands*, of its readers, throughout the reading process, that they engage consciously and actively with the narrative and information being expressed, to "reflect on the representation itself, [their] imaginative engagement with that representation, and [their] relationship to the content" (Polak 2017, 20). With *Will I See?* and *Sixkiller*, readers are asked to engage thoughtfully with the content, bringing their knowledge and understandings, approaching the texts respectfully, and recognizing their situational relationship to the represented experiences of the MMIWGT2S crisis.

SIXKILLER AND *WILL I SEE?*: EXAMPLES OF INDIGENOUS GOTHIC COMICS

Sixkiller opens to the shattered view of Alice's sister's murder scene, employing both the aesthetic of excess and the excess of seeing (Round 2014, 57) through the broken perspective and overlay of the narrative boxes reciting Carroll's poem. The complex imagery asks the reader to take on the role of an *active* reader, to infer the information needed to piece together the narrative told through the panels. As the reader moves forward with the narrative visually and textually, they learn that they have implicated themself in witnessing the murder scene. By reading into the shattered panels, the reader becomes haunted by the information gathered, encrypting the gutter space with the events and actions necessary to reanimate the narrative presented.

The reader becomes "haunted" by the knowledge they have gained through the images, and the act of witnessing the murder scene carries profound implications. The situation echoes the real experience of the public's implication in the ongoing genocide of the MMIWGT2S epidemic through the lack of action taken to bring justice to the families of the victims. The reader is informed that Alice's sister's killer would not be facing justice for his crime, fortifying these implications of guilt and bridging fiction and reality. From the beginning, through the Indigenization of Carroll's story, the text becomes haunted by the Missing and Murdered Indigenous Women and Girls. It is locatable in the conversation of the ongoing genocide, grappling with the lack of justice for the MMIWGT2S by giving it a significant role in the narrative, pointedly shaping Alice's life. By engaging with such a topic, the text becomes fundamentally Indigenous. The narrative, much like Alice, is shaped by the murder, dealing with an issue that widely affects Indigenous communities.

Sixkiller recasts familiar characters from Carroll's story and mediates them through an Indigenous lens. The role of the rabbit shifts and takes up new meaning in *Sixkiller*. Rabbit is a catalyst in Alice's decision to embark on her journey to seek revenge, although it is unclear if Rabbit in *Sixkiller* is meant to function as the White Rabbit or the March Hare. However, what seems to make the most sense is Rabbit embodying both characters. Indeed, visually, Rabbit resembles the Hare in coloration, and the back-and-forth manner of their exchange with Alice Sixkiller calls back to the way that Carroll's Alice and the March Hare exchange remarks:

> ". . . you and I are in this same world **together**, girl."
> "I am not sure that's **true**. My world exists **behind** this fence."
> "And mine behind **this** fence."
> "What are you saying? You're on the **outside**?"
> "Maybe. Or could be the **other** way 'round." (Francis 2018)

The nature of Rabbit's speech acts as a callback to the March Hare in the original *Alice's Adventures in Wonderland*:

> "Have some wine," the March Hare said in an encouraging tone.
> Alice looked all round the table, but there was nothing on it but tea.
> "I don't see any wine," she remarked.
> "There isn't any," said the March Hare.
> "Then it wasn't very civil of you to offer it," said Alice angrily.

"It wasn't very civil of you to sit down without being invited," said the March Hare." (Carroll [1865] 1991)

There is a similarity in the tone and pacing of the exchange when each Alice engages with her respective hare. Alice Sixkiller's Rabbit goes on to invoke the concept of time to her, echoing the White Rabbit as well: "Oh, girl, justice comes in its **own** time. You just have to have an **eye** on the clock. . . . Be strong and remember when **justice** is ready, don't be late" (Francis 2018). This statement from Rabbit invokes, for readers familiar with Carroll's story, the White Rabbit that begins Alice's journey into Wonderland, worrying over time and the possibility of being late. Ultimately, the Rabbit's role and riddlesome way of speaking in *Sixkiller* do more than simply tie the character back to the White Rabbit and March Hare. Rabbit takes up the Cherokee identity of Trickster (Native Languages of the Americas 2020). Rabbit manifests the trickster identity, verbally through their speech and physically through an unsettling expression of the double: their physical appearance shifting between a familiar representation of a rabbit to something more uncanny, almost skeletal looking. The shifting of the physical appearance evokes the duplicitous nature of the trickster figure of Rabbit, as "among Cherokee stories, Rabbit is always a trickster; he's always getting into trouble" (Guess 2016, 177).

Three of the most notable locations that Alice moves through are a graveyard, a mental institution, and a church. Each of these places haunts the narrative through the significant roles they've played throughout history as tools of the colonizer. We observe the pathetic fallacy at play here as well. Alice's emotional state is mirrored in the natural environment in the graveyard, later resulting in the flooding caused by her grief. The flooding that leads to Alice's removal from the mental institution functions as another point of reference to Carroll's story—Alice floods the rabbit hole she follows the White Rabbit into: "She went on shedding gallons of tears, until there was a large pool all 'round her and reaching half down the hall" (Carroll [1865] 1991). However, in Carroll's story, the flooding hinders the protagonist's progress rather than assisting her. The flooding helps Alice Sixkiller by removing her from the settler-controlled institution that prevents her from moving forward in her story.

The church Alice enters after she has left Rose Creek provides an even more complex interaction in the text and its use of Gothic landscape, drawing upon the long history of the church's involvement with colonialism and genocide. The text acknowledges the history of the church harming Indigenous peoples and communities. By having Alice take the objects she needs for her journey from this space, the text bestows the power in the current relationship between Alice and the church, with Alice. She controls how she interacts and moves through the space; she dictates her relationship with the landscape. Further, Alice engages in an internal monologue acknowledging her Creator in the narrative boxes overlaying the panels. The monologue invokes her belief system, a system not structured or influenced by the colonizer, further evacuating the symbolic power that might have remained in the church landscape and further solidifying Alice's power and sovereignty in the narrative landscape.

Sixkiller's other aspects add to the Gothic mode and mark it as an Indigenous Gothic comic, particularly the engagement with spirituality and cultural beliefs. Alice's relationship with the totems she keeps in her room and the one-sided conversation she has with her sister in the narrative boxes as the flood sweeps her out and away from Rose Creek echoes what Jodey Castricano refers to in her writing on Eden Robinson's *Monkey Beach* as "a means of 'learning to live.' . . . [T]alking with ghosts is transformational because . . . it involves the recollection as well as the reintegration of a spiritual dimension of Haisla culture in spite of its negation in the wake of European contact" (2006, 812). While Alice is not Haisla, a similar process happens in *Sixkiller* for the protagonist. Not only does she speak with Rabbit and the totems she keeps in her room, but she also speaks directly to her sister. By centering ghosts and spirits in an Indigenous worldview, the settler-centric traditions of the Gothic are troubled and questioned; indigenizing these spectral figures challenges how the Gothic is conceptualized. Thus, the ghost or spirit of Alice's sister is not the typical threatening figure so often posed by the ghostly characters in Gothic texts. Instead, the spirit takes on new meaning; Alice's conversations become transformational acts, amounting "to a transgenerational affirmation of an inheritance, thus involving a call to responsibility" (Castricano 2006, 812). Putting her spirituality and beliefs into practice, Alice shifts her world, creating the opportunity for the protagonist to seek justice for her sister and herself.

Will I See? differs from *Sixkiller* in that it is not a retelling of a traditional settler-colonial narrative but a collaborative narrative explicitly created to engage with the issue of the MMIWGT2S crisis. Candida Rifkind and Jessica Fontaine engage with both the comic and the connected animated music video "Nobody Knows" to discuss the intermedial text(s) as exemplary of the "Indigenous created comics that Sarah Henzi argues 'partake in the creation of a new space to voice, create and resist, as well as to restore and reaffirm experiences, histories and memory, and to rectify the falsity of colonial imagery'" (Rifkind and Fontaine 2020, 342). Rifkind and Fontaine address the Gothic aspects of the comic, identifying the different ways the Gothic is at play and being appropriated by the creators. Their reading of the text is influenced by Eve Tuck's idea of desire-centered research and education

(Tuck 2009). Rifkind and Fontaine posit that *Will I See?* presents an "educative narrative about MMIWGT2S and Indigenous culture, for both settler and Indigenous audiences" (2020, 342), and Amber Dean calls for readers to "inherit what lives on from the disappearance of so many women" (2015, 7). Rifkind and Fontaine identify and acknowledge that the text itself is complex and inherently Indigenous, functioning to address the issue of the Missing and Murdered Indigenous Women and Girls without separating the issue from its colonial root (2020, 342).

Will I See? opens with panels depicting aerial and wide shots of an urban landscape, locating the reader within the text in the unnamed North American city where the main character, May, resides. The city images are overlayed with Cree syllabics, and May takes up the space on the right-hand side of the page, spanning the four horizontal panels, not limited by the gutters that separate them.[6] These images, read together, assert that "Indigenous girls, women, Trans, and Two-Spirit persons are being disappeared from cities across these lands now known as North America" (Rifkind and Fontaine 2020, 343). Moreover, this page in particular sets the tone and expectation for what type of text the reader is engaging with, centering on Indigeneity and the Indigenous experience, "point[ing] to the past sovereignty of Indigenous languages and Indigenous bodies across the continent[,] and express[ing] the desire for sovereignty in the future" (345). *Sixkiller* appropriates a settler narrative to resist and destabilize settler understanding and sovereignty further; *Will I See?* follows its own narrative, centering the reader's attention on the experience of the Indigenous woman or girl and the threat that follows her through these haunted lands.

Reading *Will I See?* with Julia Round's theory of Gothic comics in mind, the reader can easily see that the text has both the aesthetic of excess and excess of seeing at play throughout the visual narrative. As the reader moves through the landscape with May and her feline companion, multiple points of view come into play: a third-person point of view in which May and the black cat are visible walking across a playground; a second, alternative third-person perspective, a past moment from when an Indigenous woman was violently disappeared; and the final perspective, the earring that belonged to this now missing woman. The object is viewed through May's first-person perspective as she muses, "I guess somebody lost it" (Robertson et al. 2016). These perspectives, amid the splashes of red interrupting the images, drawing the eye to certain areas and symbolizing the violence enacted there, demonstrate this aesthetic of excess and excess of seeing, urging a sense of foreboding in the reader as we know what May does not yet know—that the owner lost more than her earring on that playground.

As for Gothic characters in *Will I See?*, the traditional Gothic figure of the madman/criminal appears and takes up new meaning in the man who kidnaps and attempts to harm May. To the reader, his physical presence evokes the fear and threat posed to May and young Indigenous women like her by colonially influenced gender- and race-based violence. His ever-shifting appearance forces the reader to accept that this violence comes in many shapes and sizes. Perhaps more identifiable among traditional Gothic figures in the text is May's feline companion, whom she names Chípiy (Ghost). The black cat is often an ominous symbol in Gothic texts—the Indigenization of this figure, however, foils these expectations. Chípiy becomes a significant guiding figure for May throughout her journey in the narrative—Rifkind and Fontaine make the connection that May and the reader, in following May through her story, are mirroring what Dean proposes, that "following ghosts, as a practice of inheriting what lives on from the disappearances of so many women, might work to provide a more widespread grappling of the ways we are all differently implicated in those disappearances" (Amber Dean, quoted in Rifkind and Fontaine 2020, 350). May's journey includes following Chípiy through spaces that are haunted by the specters of the Missing and Murdered Indigenous Women and Girls; readers, in following this process, are faced with the responsibility of "grappling" with the inheritance of gender- and race-based violence both within and beyond the text, and their own implication in that violence. Chípiy is a "spirit animal born from one of the disappeared women" (Rifkind and Fontaine 2020, 353), assisting May through her journey as she "inherits" the lives of the other disappeared women who haunt the spaces she engages with by collecting the objects that belonged to them. May moves through this process of inheritance by following one spirit (Chípiy) and embracing the rest (through the objects), asking the reader to recognize the continued presence of Indigenous peoples and worldviews and, further, "the ways Indigenous deaths have also come at the hand of intentional violence. They [Indigenous peoples] are forced to disappear by colonial systems and forceful actions" (Rifkind and Fontaine 2020, 350).

These spirits or specters are an essential part of May's spiritual journey: by existing within the text, the specter also exists in the narrative and beyond it—taking part in conversations about and evoking the MMIWGT2S crisis, transferring the voices of the women and girls who have been silenced to the physical text, haunting it. These specters take on different shapes tied to the Seven Sacred Teachings (Robertson et al. 2016).[7] Having the ghostly figures appear around May in the seven forms connects them to Cree spirituality, reminding the reader that the narrative is being presented through an Indigenous lens and that the Gothic conventions are Indigenized. These spirits are not the ghostly stock figures recognized in European settler Gothic but are rooted in Indigenous spirituality and culture, framing the Gothic in an Indigenous worldview.

These ghostly figures further lend themselves to the Gothic conventions the creators engage with in the text, literally haunting the landscape throughout the comic. The superimposed images in the landscape of May's city, where women and girls have been kidnapped or murdered, make their presence inexorable from the land and space they were disappeared from. These spaces are quite literally haunted by trauma—instead of "[harking] back to a feudal past associated with barbarity, superstition and fear" (Botting 1996, 2), the narrative calls up racially and sexually fueled violence, a direct result of colonialism. In many ways, this trauma is inescapable; there are very few instances in which May moves through a space that is *not* haunted by the violence Indigenous women face. This inescapable haunting asks the reader to recognize and acknowledge the fear and threat entrenched in the feminine, queer, and two-spirit Indigenous experience in a colonized space.

Castricano's idea of "learning to live" (2006, 812) through the spirituality and hauntings of those passed is also explored in *Will I See?* May interacts with the items that belonged to missing and murdered Indigenous women and, with the help of her Nohkom, or grandmother, May makes a necklace out of the found objects. May is engaging with, at a safe distance, the ongoing genocide. Through conversation about what happens to the spirits of those who pass, May can understand and deal with the fear of being a young Indigenous woman in the city. May takes the conversation to heart; after having her own traumatic experience with kidnapping, she relays what her Nohkom explained about the spirits of those who have passed to Chípiy. In recognizing the spiritual teachings that her Nohkom shares with her, May can deal with her own traumatic kidnapping experience and recognize the women and girls who were disappeared in the natural world around her. Through her spirituality, May experiences this "learning to live" and simultaneously exercises resistance against settler colonialism, living her life with her Indigenous beliefs, from the earth, and returning to the earth (Robertson et al. 2016).

THE INDIGENOUS GOTHIC COMIC: ALTERNATIVE SURVIVANCE, REVIVAL, AND RENEWAL

In "Postcards from the Apocalypse" (2018), published in *Uncanny Magazine*, Rebecca Roanhorse demonstrates what Indigenous peoples and communities have experienced and lived through—scenarios that seem like dystopic fiction to the white settler. The legacy of colonialism is an ongoing, everyday horror that Indigenous communities face; the Missing and Murdered Indigenous Women, Girls, and Trans and Two-Spirit peoples epidemic is a symptom of that colonial horror. Thus, Indigenous artists create alternative realities where the horror finally stops (Elliott 2019). The Indigenous Gothic text, and in the case of *Sixkiller* and *Will I See?* the Indigenous Gothic *comic*, create a space in which colonialism is addressed and exorcised. By appropriating a Euro-American literary Gothic mode and recasting, reshaping, and repurposing it in an Indigenous worldview and experience, the settler and colonialism, while still present within the text, are decentered and destabilized. The Indigenous Gothic comic provides a space for alternative storytelling in its form and narrative focus. Different stories can be told with the emphasis shifted from English language–reliant storytelling to a more visually based narrative structure.

Expressions of the unspeakable have historically been a common trait of the Gothic. Indigenous Gothic comics take that articulation to a new level: what might be inexpressible in other forms become accessible and visible to both knowledgeable and unknowledgeable readers. These experiences haunt the reader; they become inescapable, just as the spirits of the disappeared women are inescapable in the landscape of *Will I See?* Indigenous Gothic comics are objects of survivance: they are objects of renewal and revival, and for some, objects of haunting. Readers cannot look away from the experiences and worldviews expressed in the texts, nor can they ignore their implications, demanding that readers recognize and reflect upon their role in the horrors conveyed. The Indigenous Gothic is an act of survivance against and within colonialism and settler-centric society; it is a "call for awareness" (LaPensée 2017) to Indigenous identities and issues. The Indigenous Gothic exists as a separate version of the Gothic genre, complex and necessary in its deployment—identifiable through its creation by an Indigenous artist or writer and through the Indigenous worldviews and experiences expressed within. The comic form takes the expression of the Indigenous Gothic one step further; the implementation of the Indigenous Gothic in a nontraditional literary form engenders the ability to express the unspeakable and shows what might otherwise be inaccessible. Both mode and form are critical to the function of the text as a representation of Indigenous issues and resistance against settler narratives and ideology. Traditional literary forms are more entrenched in colonialism, as the English language itself remains a tool of colonization and cultural genocide. Thus, the comic form distances the storytelling practices from colonial traditions and enables alternative, Indigenous-based narrative expressions. Ultimately, both the Indigenous

Gothic and the Indigenous Gothic in comics fulfill the desire to investigate and reimagine both the fantastic and the mundane, past and present experiences and expressions that have been historically silenced and ignored in settler media (Wisker 2007, 401), providing a space to express the trauma of living in a colonial (apocalyptic) world. The Indigenous Gothic in comics gives voice to and represents Indigenous culture, experiences, and issues in ways its readers cannot avoid.

Notes

1. I use the term "conciliatory" following Jesse Wente's example in his talk at Mount Allison University, as quoted by Laura Skinner (2018). The idea that "we've never really had a functioning relationship so what we need is conciliation, the building of that functioning relationship, not repairing what was there" (quoted in Skinner 2018) is fundamental and should be acknowledged by larger players in efforts of (re)conciliation—that there was never any conciliation to being with, at least not on the part of the settlers.

2. Gerald Vizenor coined the term "survivance," identifying it as "moving beyond our basic survival in the face of overwhelming cultural genocide to create spaces of synthesis and renewal" (1994, 53). It does not mean to simply exist; rather, survivance is a dynamic act of continuing to create and assert the Indigenous presence, worldviews, beliefs, and so on, despite the continued efforts of cultural genocide Indigenous communities face.

3. This is not a static fact, however, as there is a growing number of authors in Gothic-adjacent genres such as Horror, Science Fiction, and Fantasy. Historically there has been a lack of representation, but more presently this has shifted; studies in the Indigenous Gothic presently and moving forward will have a great deal more to work with and approach critically, as more and more Indigenous writers' work is receiving the attention and acknowledgment it rightfully deserves.

4. Candida Rifkind and Jessica Fontaine also discuss the Gothic aspects of comics that are at play in communicating the MMIWGT2S epidemic (2020, 345–46).

5. Henzi is here referring to Gord Hill's use of the comics form to depict the centuries of ongoing resistance Indigenous peoples have and continue to exercise under the settler Canadian government; it is an adept point that is applicable to Indigenous writing at large in the comics form and fits well with this discussion of representing the MMIWGT2S crisis.

6. This inclusion of Cree syllabics is arguably a significant piece of the text in that it is also participating in the ongoing movements for Indigenous language revival, both through the depiction of the syllabics and through the use of Cree words such as "Chípiy," the name May gives her black cat companion. Language revitalization is incredibly important, and a further act of resilience, resistance, and survivance.

7. The Seven Sacred Teachings are "natural virtues that form a foundation to achieve Mino-Pimatisiwin, the good life" (Robertson et al. 2016).

Bibliography

Botting, Fred. 1996. *Gothic*. The New Critical Idiom Series. London: Routledge.

Burnham, Michelle. 2014. "Is There an Indigenous Gothic?" In *A Companion to American Gothic*, edited by Charles L. Crow, 223–37. Chichester, W. Susx., England: John Wiley and Sons.

Carroll, Lewis. (1865) 1991. *Alice's Adventures in Wonderland*. Project Gutenberg. https://www.gutenberg.org/files/11/11-h/11-h.htm.

Castricano, Jodey. 2006. "Learning to Talk with Ghosts: Canadian Gothic and the Poetics of Haunting in Eden Robinson's *Monkey Beach*." *University of Toronto Quarterly* 75, no. 2 (Spring): 801–13.

Dean, Amber. 2015. *Remembering Vancouver's Disappeared Women: Settler Colonialism and the Difficulty of Inheritance*. Toronto: University of Toronto Press.

Elliott, Alicia. 2019. "The Rise of Indigenous Horror: How a Fiction Genre Is Confronting a Monstrous Reality." CBC Arts. https://www.cbc.ca/arts/the-rise-of-indigenous-horror-how-a-fiction-genre-is-confronting-a-monstrous-reality-1.5323428.

Fontaine, Lorena Sekwan. 2017. "Redress for Linguicide: Residential Schools and Assimilation in Canada." *British Journal of Canadian Studies* 30, no. 2: 183–204.

Francis, Lee, IV. 2018. *Sixkiller*, no. 1. Albuquerque, NM: Native Realities.

Gelder, Ken. 2014. "The Postcolonial Gothic." In *The Cambridge Companion to the Modern Gothic*, edited by Jerrold E. Hogle, 191–207. Cambridge: Cambridge University Press.

Gore, Amy Elizabeth. 2011. "The Indigenous Gothic Novel: Tribal Twists, Native Monsters, and the Politics of Appropriation." Master's thesis, Montana State University.

Griffith, Jane. 2019. *Words Have a Past: The English Language, Colonialism, and the Newspapers of Indian Boarding Schools*. Toronto: University of Toronto Press.

Guess, Sequoyah. 2016. "Rabbit and Possum Look for Wives." In *A Listening Wind: Native Literature from the Southeast*, edited by Marcia Haag, 176–82. Lincoln: University of Nebraska Press.

Henzi, Sarah. 2016. "'A Necessary Antidote': Graphic Novels, Comics, and Indigenous Writing." *Canadian Review of Comparative Literature / Revue Canadienne de Littérature Comparée* 43, no. 1 (March): 23–38.

LaPensée, Elizabeth. 2017. Introduction to *Deer Woman: An Anthology*, edited by Elizabeth LaPensée. Albuquerque, NM: Native Realities.

McCloud, Scott. 1994. *Understanding Comics: The Invisible Art*. New York: HarperCollins.

Milloy, John Sheridan. 1999. *A National Crime: The Canadian Government and the Residential School System, 1879 to 1986*. Winnipeg: University of Manitoba Press.

Native Languages of the Americas. 2020. "Native American Legends: Trickster Rabbit (Jistu)." http://www.native-languages.org/trickster-rabbit.htm.

Polak, Kate. 2017. *Ethics in the Gutter: Empathy and Historical Fiction in Comics*. Columbus: Ohio State University Press.

Rifkind, Candida, and Jessica Fontaine. 2020. "Indigeneity, Intermediality, and the Haunted Present of *Will I See?*" In *Graphic Indigeneity: Comics in the Americas and Australasia*, edited by Frederick Luis Aldama, 340–60. Jackson: University Press of Mississippi.

Roanhorse, Rebecca. 2018. "Postcards from the Apocalypse." *Uncanny Magazine*, no. 20, January 2. https://www.uncannymagazine.com/article/postcards-from-the-apocalypse/.

Robertson, David Alexander, Iskwé, Erin Leslie, and G. M. B. Chomichuk. 2016. *Will I See?* Winnipeg: HighWater Press.

Round, Julia. 2014. *Gothic in Comics and Graphic Novels: A Critical Approach*. Jefferson, NC: McFarland.

Schoch/Davidson, Angela Elisa. 2020. "Indigenous Alterations." In *The Palgrave Handbook of Contemporary Gothic*, edited by Clive Bloom, 143–62. Cham, Switzerland: Palgrave Macmillan.

Skinner, Laura. 2018. "What Canada Needs Is Conciliation, Not Reconciliation." *The Argosy*, November 28. https://www.since1872.ca/news/what-canada-needs-is-conciliation-not-reconciliation/.

Sugars, Cynthia. 2014. *Canadian Gothic: Literature, History and the Spectre of Self-Invention*. Cardiff: University of Wales Press.

Topash-Caldwell, Blaire. 2020. "Sovereign Futures in Neshnabé Speculative Fiction." *Borderlands Journal* 19, no. 2 (October): 29–62.

Tuck, Eve. 2009. "Suspending Damage: A Letter to Communities." *Harvard Educational Review* 79, no. 3: 409–28.

Vizenor, Gerald Robert. 1994. *Manifest Manners: Postindian Warriors of Survivance*. Middletown, CT: Wesleyan University Press.

Wisker, Gina. 2007. "Crossing Liminal Spaces: Teaching the Postcolonial Gothic." *Pedagogy* 7, no. 3 (Fall): 401–25.

CHAPTER 9

THE BAYONET SCAR

JUDY WATSON'S ABORIGINAL GOTHIC ARTS PRACTICE

JAYSON ALTHOFER

This chapter contains the names of people who have died.

As an artist I seek to reveal layers beneath the ground, within objects, their history, their making and their taking, to rattle the bones of the museum, to wake the dead who are not dead but alive to all of us.
—JUDY WATSON, 2015

The English imperial museum system, including its collecting and keeping outposts in Australia, is so far steeped in Australian Aboriginal blood that bloody marks spill, pool, and whirl across the oeuvre of the Waanyi woman and Brisbane-based contemporary artist Judy Watson (b. 1959).[1] In her etching *the holes in the land 5* (2015),[2] a red wash representing "spilt blood stains the plan of the drains and water-pipes of the British Museum. The orderly conduct of fluids and waste around the building is disrupted, flooded by the huge stain of blood-like ochre" (Best 2018, 21). The blood-like layer, leakage, or splatter, a leitmotif of Watson's practice, indicts that museum and its agents as accomplices to and beneficiaries of the Indigenocide haunting the political and cultural unconscious of White Australia. Indigenocide, as conceptualized by Raymond Evans and Bill Thorpe, "refers to those actors (governments, military forces, economic enterprises or their agents, private individuals etc.) who carry out destructive actions, policies and practices on Aboriginal individuals, families and groups *mainly because of their perceived indigeneity or 'Aboriginality'*" (2001, 34; original emphasis).

Watson marks the museum's bowels with signs of blood spilled by the spread of criminogenic settler colonialism across Australia, to unsettle acceptance and perpetuation of Indigenocidal culture. "It is intensely discomforting to conceive of an Australian social order where the mass murder of certain people, identifiable by their ethnicity, was a way of life," Evans and Thorpe attest (29). Indigenocide was, and remains, a deadly lifeway, "tolerated by the settler majority, and winked at by a state which, in other settings, upheld the precepts of British culture, law and justice" (29). Given the quotidian violence of British invasion and occupation, "the overwhelming sense is that of abomination rendered commonplace" (33). That Australian settler society was established in "the context of acceptable terror [is] the historical truth" (29).

Museum collections of Aboriginal bodily remains and material culture arose from unexceptionable terror, too. "Museum building in Britain in the nineteenth century was a direct consequence of war, colonialism and missionary expeditions, which returned with 'exotic' objects. In London, museums were built after successful colonial ventures with displays of empire and the hope that such displays, like the empire itself, would be a lasting achievement" (Duthie 2011, 16). Blood ties museum to massacre. Moreover, museums embedded in Indigenocide are redolent of Gothic spaces (dungeons, secret cabinets, fortified towers); their conventions—holding, keeping, cataloging—appear analogous to horrific punishments: captivity, vivisepulture, dismemberment. Regarding the Wellcome Historical Medical Museum in London, which is a concern of Watson's video work *skullduggery* (2021), David Punter has evoked the "Gothic spaces of a museum [where artifacts] are enjoying, or suffering, a secret afterlife of their own" (2008, 241). While Watson has called the museum and the gallery "fantastic place[s] for objects to be cared for," they present as fearsome edifices: "I didn't go into a gallery until I was seventeen. It's just getting over that fear of the institution, the big, big building. Then one of the elders was talking about how a museum is just like a cave, it's where you put your stuff so it's safe" (Watson 2010, 68). In the colonial museum, however, Indigenous materials are largely alienated from and inaccessible to the people from whose home, or Country, they have been removed. Watson's reparative Gothic practice concerns the lives and afterlives of First Peoples' heritage locked in collections such as the British Museum and the Wellcome Collection.

As a "superb interpreter . . . of the horrors of the frontiers" (Marr 2023, 415) and of those frontiers' bloody presence in museums, Watson draws on and contributes to Western art traditions and contemporary international cultural forms. Her practice evinces kinship with various aesthetic modes, including Abstract Expressionist and Color Field painting (Helen Frankenthaler and Mark Rothko are direct influences) and the Splatter and Slasher subgenres of Horror cinema—films whose moving-image violence, involving a "graphic sense of physicality" and "Body-horror" (Brophy 1986, 8–10), partly evolved from Abstract Expressionism's "violence of image," which culminated in Jackson Pollock's canvases: "true precursors to Splatter movies and their intense abstraction of bodily violence into a state of action" (Brophy 1988). Formally, the blood effects that characterize many of Watson's works about Australian and international colonial history recall drip, pour, and splatter paintings by Pollock, Kay WalkingStick, and Hermann Nitsch, among others. In terms of horrific subject matter, her works evoke, for example, Francisco Goya's, Francis Bacon's, and Anselm Kiefer's artistic explorations of structural bloodlettings and blood-soaked histories.

Here, splatters, pools, and washes of blood-effect signify not only "imaginative kinship" between painterly and cinematic representations of gore (Skal 1994, 313) but also a historical, generative articulation between gory representational art and capitalism's production of real gore—"splatter capital" (Steven 2017)—not least through imperialism and colonialism: "engines of horror that render asunder social, religious, and economic structures as well as bodies" (Höglund 2018, 328). The Splatter mode, due to its very constitution by motifs of violence and gore, can be remarkably political and critical. "It reminds us of what capital is doing to all of us, all of the time—of how predators are consuming our life-substances," for instance; "the particular brand of horror mobilized in splatter . . . promotes an extant truth: capitalist accumulation is and always has been a nightmare of systematized bloodshed" (Steven 2017, 13). Watson's bloody mark-making reminds us of how the predatory Australian colony protractedly mutilates and devours Indigenous lives, her practice being extremely responsive to the systematic development of colonial blood feasts. Similarly, as the Slasher mode "pries open the fleshy secrets of normally hidden things" (L. Williams 1990, 191), Watson probes and exposes the secrets of colonial massacres, museums, and memories, revealing the slash-and-dispersal modus operandi of colonialism itself, from killing fields on her matrilineal Country to hidden stores of stolen objects in the British Museum (Althofer 2023).

Watson's oeuvre expresses "a shared sensibility with Indigenous experience on a global basis" (Watson and Martin-Chew 2009, 15). This chapter focuses on Australian colonial horrors but references American authors Edgar Allan Poe, Mark Twain, and the Laguna Pueblo Indian woman Leslie Marmon Silko, because the colonization of the United States has long interested Watson and informed her understanding of British colonialism in Australia. She studied American literature as well as printmaking at university, and some of her early prints allude to Manifest Destiny: *trail of tears* (1978) concerns the violent removal of Cherokee people—"thinking about the dispossessed Native Americans who are forced to walk away from their country onto somebody else's country," and, Watson says of Australia, "that happened here" (Love n.d., 5)—while *burning ghosts* (1979) appropriates and juxtaposes a historical image of American settlers with covered wagons and a 1974 photograph of Nubian people by Leni Riefenstahl. Intensely abstracted body-horror and the open, fleshy secret of state violence connect her painting about a New York police shooting of an unarmed Black Guinean immigrant man, *41 stoppages—amadou diallo* (2000), with her group of paintings *a complicated fall*, *memory bones*, and *palm cluster* (all 2007) about the bashing to death in Palm Island, Queensland, police custody of Aboriginal man Mulrunji Doomadgee. Watson's *experimental beds* (2012), a suite of six colored etchings, incorporates architectural drawings by Thomas Jefferson and her sketches of artifacts unearthed and produce grown in Jefferson's "experimental beds": gardens of American imperial botany at Monticello, used to test the acclimatization of plants from around the world. The title *experimental beds* also connotes Jefferson's relationship with enslaved woman Sally Hemings: "The union between a white man and a black woman was one of many parallels that Watson identified between her own Aboriginal family and the enslaved people in Jefferson's household" (Kluge-Ruhe Aboriginal Art Collection n.d.). The series' multilayered form and its artifactual investigation of Monticello anticipated another suite of six colored etchings, *the holes in the land* (2015), two of which depict the ichnography of the British Museum splattered with blood.

This chapter highlights the Gothic horror of Watson's practice, particularly of those works made through close engagement with colonial collections that have incorporated, or incarcerated, stolen First Peoples' heritage, heritage that she has listened to and symbolically liberated and repatriated. It regards her oeuvre through the prism of "Aboriginal Gothic," which exposes ever-present colonial horrors and their aftermaths: "[A]s the Other speaking back to white people," Aboriginal Gothic "can provide alternate views about the brutal past, the silencing and the voiding of Aboriginal history which ghosts the land" (Wisker 2021, 390). The chapter outlines Watson's distinctive Aboriginal Gothic and educes Gothic characteristics of her works' reception.

It relates Watson's practice to other expressions of Aboriginal Gothic and frames salient Australian contexts for her Gothicism by the conceit of drawing together two contemporary images that recall Poe's "The Pit and the Pendulum" (1842): former Australian prime minister John Howard's race-based "pendulum" (Howard 1997b), designed to swing against Aboriginal land rights and, thus, human rights for Aborigines, and what the Gungalu and Birri Gubba (Wiri) woman Lilla Watson calls "the pit of the colonial mentality" (2021, xv). The chapter's final section scans Gothic patterns in selected works from Judy Watson's oeuvre from the mid-1990s to the present.

The works by Watson examined here manifest "the key Gothic pattern" identified by Gilda Williams's survey of Gothic aesthetics in contemporary visual art: "[A] lost history or an uninvited force impose[s] itself on the present as a kind of haunting, demanding our urgent attention and resolution" (2014, 415). Besides this pattern of temporal oppression and obligation, Watson's works evoke "spatial discomfort," which forms another insistent Gothic pattern, "whether from entrapment in dungeons or buried in a premature grave, [to] the disorientation of labyrinths" (Luckhurst 2014, 62). However, her works are not unreflectively grounded in Western phenomenologies of either stable or unstable time and space. They imply, rather, "an immersive timelessness outside of a linear chronology" (Perkins 2020), known as, poetically, the "Dreaming," which translates various Aboriginal words. Dreaming cannot be fixed "*in*" time: it was, and is, everywhen" (W. E. H. Stanner, quoted in Perkins 2020; original emphasis). It alludes to spatially precise perceptions and experiences of intimate interconnectivity between Country, community, and culture: "[I]n Aboriginal tradition, Dreaming maps ancestral epistemology, passed down through oral tradition, onto the land" (Borwein 2018, 62). Whereas modern history presents as a terrible burden—in Karl Marx's summation, "[t]he tradition of all the dead generations weighs like a nightmare on the brain of the living" (Marx and Engels 2010, 11:103)—Dreaming affirms that the dead generations are not dead but alive, so that, "in Indigenous Gothic, ghosts just might deliver psychological wholeness and healing" (Burnham 2014, 234). Watson's lithograph *the guardians* (1990) centers a group of spectral humanoid figures, about which she wrote in 1993: "I can feel the presence of the guardians here [on Country] / connecting me with my ancestors" (2003, 56).

Watson's works trace her forensic exploration of the labyrinths, dungeons, and graves, premature and plundered, of Australia's colonial and museal pasts, which are not past but present. A premise of this study of her practice is the salience of Marx's Gothic critique of capitalism and its global processes of imperialist exploitation, extraction, and extermination. These processes are also identified and resisted by practitioners of Indigenous Gothic around the world. In her novel *Almanac of the Dead* (1991), Leslie Marmon Silko draws on Marx's treatment of monstrosity, not least capital's "vampire thirst" (Marx and Engels 2010, 35:263), to reimagine "the clash of native peoples in the Americas with capitalist modernity" (McNally 2011, 114). Marx, Silko wrote, "recited the crimes of slaughter and slavery committed by the European colonials who had been sent by their capitalist slave masters to secure the raw materials of capitalism—human flesh and blood" (quoted in McNally 2011, 115). His graphic portrayal of colonial-capitalist monsters—vampires and werewolves who manufacture "slaughtered remains of indigenous peoples"—reveals "the real terrors of modern social life" and "give[s] voice to suffering" (115). For Massimiliano Tomba, "spectres, vampires and the living dead became constituent elements" of Marx's writing through "the deathlike scenario of capitalist modernity" (2013, 47). Gothic Marxism and Aboriginal Gothic engage, expose, and undermine capitalism's monstrous formation of a totalizing Gothic reality.

Throughout this chapter, I posit the colonial museum as a vital embodiment of capitalism's "deathlike scenario" and a spectacularly monstrous microcosm of Indigenocide: an undead body subserving a complex of Indigenocidal values and activities. The museum's fearsome vitality derives, vampire-like, from First Nations' lifeblood. As Watson has spoken of the plans of the British Museum as its bones (Best 2018, 13), its skeleton is arrayed in displays that are trophies of dispossession and murder. So long as the museum is taken to be the legitimate "home" of stolen human remains and objects, it is doomed to remain one of the unhomely/haunted houses of the Indigenocidal society.

TENDER TRAP

Judy Watson's matrilineal family is from Waanyi Country, Boodjamulla (Lawn Hill Gorge), in the Gulf of Carpentaria, Queensland. Since the 1990s, she has faced the terror acceptable to White Australia, sat with discomfort and trauma, both personal and communal, and situated a significant part of her practice in response to horrific lived experiences and legacies. In 2007, at the funeral of her grandmother Grace Isaacson, she learned from family that her great-great-grandmother Rosie had been bayoneted in her upper body during a massacre at Lawn Hill in the mid-1880s. Rosie and the only other survivor were both aged about twelve or thirteen years.

Reflecting on the bayonet scar that Rosie carried for the rest of her life, Watson has spoken of "haunting" and "living presences": Rosie's scar "is the open wound with the salt in it," "[a] trans-generational trauma throughout history and our families" (quoted in Balla 2018). Terror, trauma, and the whitewashing of their transgenerational force affect all First Peoples. "Every Aboriginal person is basically a survivor of massacres in their area," says Watson, who aims to "peel back layers" and "push back the whitewash and look at what is actually there because no matter where we are from, if we live here, this is Aboriginal land, so that history is going to be the basis of everybody's story" (quoted in Caddey 2016, 24). Unpeeling whitewashed layers of historical experience reveals the Indigenocidal dismemberment of Australia's First Nations as well as the morbidly fragmented state of Australia's unreconciled national body.

Watson meets the horrors of dispossession and colonial collections with her signature style of Aboriginal Gothic, which mixes seduction and violence. As if giving a positive, political complexion to John Ruskin's infamous dismissal of James A. M. Whistler for "flinging a pot of paint in the public's face" (Ruskin [1877] 1895, 73), Watson has praised Goya's "commentary about the political situation and what was happening on the ground in Spain [in the early 1800s]. When I see Goya's work it's like he's spitting pigment across centuries" (2010, 73). Her own métier is to comment on the disasters of the Australian wars, on murder considered as one of the colonizers' arts, and on present-day denial and diminishment of commonplace abomination by, in effect, pitching buckets of blood on her works and thereby her viewers.

Yet viewer reception of the horrors of her work can be serpiginous rather than sudden. "In my momentary daze, I almost miss the violence—the images of pins, spines, hooks, and the dashes of red," writes one reviewer. "This is Watson's secret weapon; she seduces us with mesmeric forms and then hits us with the heavy stuff" (Clugston 2020). Arrernte and Kalkadoon curator Hetti Perkins calls Watson's work a "tender trap," luring viewers into a Gothic experience of entrapment and live burial that has a visceral impact; "like a Venus flytrap," its attractiveness "get[s] people in there and snap! The trap shuts. It's often the least strident-looking works that can pack the most powerful punch because you don't see it coming" (quoted in Reich 2020). For Watson, art that contributes to "social change [can be] hard, in-your-face confrontational, or subtle and discreet." She prefers "the latter approach for much of [her] work, a seductive beautiful exterior with a strong message like a deadly poison dart that insinuates itself into the consciousness of the viewer without them being aware of the package until it implodes and leaks its contents" (quoted in TarraWarra Museum of Art 2020). Creepingly or starkly, the horrors will grip and gore your gaze: "Once in the trap, or king hit, or caught with a poison dart, you are forced to face dark and uncomfortable histories that thrum beneath the surface of the work" (Reich 2020). Gina Wisker argues that "nuanced social justice insight [is] a major feature of the Gothic, since by destabilizing cover-ups and dangerous complacencies, it might be possible to move forward acknowledging without repeating the delusional and often destructive past" (2021, 391). Watson's seductive pushing back of the whitewash impels viewers to develop and act upon such insight.

Goya, "Spain's foremost Gothic painter" (Aldana Reyes 2017, 1), bore witness to *el desmembramiento d'España*—Spain's dismemberment. His etchings and "black paintings" "evoke dark horrors from folklore, historical experience and imagination" (Myrone 2020, 424). Likewise, Watson elicits, layers, and reveals horrors from her people's oral stories, settler records, and museum collections. "I'm commenting on things that are happening. But I'm also layering this with other memories from my past and from this country's past" (Watson 2010, 73). Her practice implies that the sleeplessness of settler reason—its incessant anxiety, paranoia, and guilty conscience—dreams up Indigenous monsters. Monstrous Black activists and organizations stake land claims to White Australians' suburban homes! This rabid fear displaces and projects settler land hunger onto the dispossessed. "An obsession with dispossession, of having wealth stolen from you that you stole—what for Australians does this inevitably evoke if not the confiscation of a continent from its Aboriginal inhabitants?" (Eipper 1999, 205). Settler ideology denies, distorts, and disremembers settler society's basis in massacre culture. Watson's practice slops the blood of true stories in the face of settler indifference and inurement to carnage.

THE PIT AND THE PENDULUM

"Is there such a thing as Aboriginal gothic?" asks the Bandjalung man, curator, and art historian Djon Mundine (Mundine and Browning 2014). Critical study of Australian Aboriginal Gothic has burgeoned in recent years (e.g., Althans 2010, 2019; Clark 2013; Borwein 2018; Araluen 2019a, 2019b). Whether or not Mundine was riffing on Michelle Burnham's notable essay "Is There an Indigenous Gothic?" (2014), his question is rhetorical. He had already foregrounded horrifying Gothic imagery from first contact to its phantasmogenetic fallout:

> The Ngarrindjarri, at the mouth of the Murray River, called the first Europeans they saw Kraingkari (krink for short) rotting corpse. In their experience, after death the outer skin rots away taking away

black skin leaving a pink-white layer of flesh. They saw them as having no colour, of being similar in appearance to rotting corpses of the dead, as ghosts. Aboriginal people then became the ghosts either as victims of colonial massacres or as shadowy figures on the edge of the national psyche, neither really citizens nor aliens—ghost citizens who refuse to go away. (Mundine 2012; see also Mundine and King 2013)

Haunting, as the Bandjalung descendent, poet, and cultural critic Evelyn Araluen observes, has become "a generative philosophy in the work of Indigenous researchers and creative practitioners, conceptualizing radical forms of engagement and refusal of settler-colonial spaces and conventions. Aboriginal gothic—whether it operates as a mode, genre, or aesthetic . . . plays out these practices of haunting in resistance to what Michael Griffiths calls the artifactuality of settler-colonial imaginings of Aboriginality" (Araluen 2019b). In this regard, Watson's receptivity to ancestral ghosts, secrets (buried, open, familial, national), and artifactual afterlives is exemplary. Michael Griffiths (2018) extends Tom Griffiths's studies (1996, 1998) of settler collections of "curiosities." Collectors, the latter demonstrates, "did not want to recognise living Aborigines because it would turn their detached 'science' into a disturbing humanities. [Their] interest in the culture was as a dead culture, a relic, ornamental culture [to be] displayed like a trophy" (1998, 5, 7). Frantz Fanon called colonialist collecting and display conventions "cultural mummification" (1967, 34), an aptly Gothic designation that summons "the mummies wrested from their tombs by explorers, [transported] back to Europe for display" (Wynne 2021, 693). For Fanon, the preexisting "culture, once living and open to the future, becomes closed, fixed in the colonial status, caught in the yoke of oppression. Both present and mummified, it testifies against its members. It defines them in fact without appeal" (34). "Mummification" renders Australian Indigenous culture—the world's oldest continuous living culture—dead; it defines First Nations bodies and objects as bizarre, curious, exotic, and primitive.

Australian Aboriginal Gothic critique frequently recalls Jack D. Forbes's classic *Columbus and Other Cannibals: The Wétiko Disease of Exploitation, Imperialism, and Terrorism* (1979). Burnham suggests that Native American Gothic stories about *wétiko*/windigo cannibalism "might be seen to expose the windigo unconscious of [Euro-American understandings of Frontier Gothic], to reveal its disavowed dependence on a destructive logic of excessive consumption" (2014, 235). For Araluen, White Australian settler culture is constituted by—*cannibalizes*—Aboriginal bodies: "The horror slips sublime as you build house and fence and church. . . . Our bones mortar your buildings and your poems but all the while we're away in fringes and reserves. Don't look at me. Cover up the earth that knows me but leave wells so you can drain it. Take our language from our bleeding mouths and give it to your songs" (2019a). Settler culture suffocates and consumes Aboriginal people and Country in Araluen's poems, too. In "The Trope Speaks," "[t]he trope feels a ghostly spectre haunting the land, but smothers it with fence and field and church" (2021, 32). Her anthology *Dropbear* (2021) is "a razor-sharp gothic reclamation that peels back the layers of colonialism and what we call Australia" (Adelaide Festival 2022). This encomium also fits Watson's commitment to peeling back layers of the Indigenocide that bayoneted children, yet, rubbing salt in the wound, whitewashes its infliction of physical and psychological torture.

Watson's artworks and Mundine's and Araluen's literary parallels demonstrate that corporeal bodies as much as ghostly traces are central to Aboriginal Gothic, as they are to Gothic per se. "Gothic," as Punter states, "provides an image language for bodies and their terrors" (1998, 14). Regarding the 1700s, Yael Shapira defines the subject of a discrete Gothic motif—the corpse—as "an image of a dead body rendered with deliberate graphic bluntness in order to excite and entertain" (2018, 1). From invasion in 1788, Aboriginal people's heads were hunted, their bodies dismembered, and their bones dispatched to England for sale, study, and display, typifying a ruling-class carnival of "enlightened" cruelty. Watson's Aboriginal Gothic renders their blood with a blunt graphic force that has a sharp political edge.

For Indigenous activists, artists, and writers, to remember ancestors and to self-represent, or visibilize, survival of invasion, massacre, and still-present colonialism is a political act. Perkins explains: "Many Aboriginal people living in the more evidently colonized zones of Australia have experienced a form of ethnocide that has attempted to dispossess us of our history, our culture and even our identity. To counter her 'invisibility' as an urban-based Aboriginal woman, Watson embarked on a journey of self-enlightenment by travelling back to her grandmother's country in remote northwest Queensland" (1997, 12). Watson's self-enlightenment, arts practice, and Gothic stylings have developed in multilayered national, political, and existential conditions whose time span from the 1990s to now may be framed and whose effects figured by metaphors that conjure Poe's "The Pit and the Pendulum."

In *Wik Peoples v. the State of Queensland* (1996), the High Court of Australia found that the statutory pastoral leases under its consideration did not bestow rights of exclusive possession on the leaseholder (Stevenson 1996).

Native title rights could coexist, depending on the character and terms of each lease. Given a conflict of rights, however, the rights under the pastoral lease would extinguish the remaining Native title rights. The federal and state governments, in concert with varied capitalist interests, propagandized that much of Australia, including suburban backyards, were threatened by Indigenous land rights. Prime Minister John Howard's federal government drew up the Native Title Amendment Bill (1997), allegedly to reinstate certainty of (White) land ownership. Howard hectored: "What has happened with native title is that the pendulum has swung too far in one direction. [This legislation] brings the pendulum back to the middle . . . from the absurd point it reached after the *Wik* decision" (1997b). In fact, Howard's "pendulum" was honed to swing only around the extremes of his racist legislation and the extrajudicial Indigenocide incited by his "dog-whistling" government. The pendulum repeatedly hit its targets, Aboriginal people. "Historic observation reveals," to turn Fanon's insight onto this Australian story, "that the aim sought is rather a continued agony than a total disappearance of the pre-existing culture" (1967, 34). The year before, 1996, Howard had envisioned "an Australian nation that feels comfortable and relaxed about three things. I would like to see them comfortable and relaxed about their history[,] . . . the present [and] the future" (interviewed in Jackson 1996). The moral vacuum of Howard's vision was sounded by the thrumming of his telltale pendulum. The relaxation and comfort of those he interpellated as fellow, "fair"-minded White Australians depended not only on "them" being oblivious to "their history" in its full-blown, racist horror and terrorism, but also on the past and present agonies of Aboriginal Australians persisting into the future. Howard starkly epitomized Australian national-colonial rituals that "call Aboriginal people into a morbid dance in which death and continuity are required" (Rose 2001, 149).

"The true monster of Australian Gothic fiction," Katrin Althans writes, "was the white settlers' dark Other, Australian Indigenous people" (2019, 277). This "true monster" recurs in a Gothic strain of Australian political discourse, mobilized to shore up support for Indigenocidal policy and law. Howard's amendment to the Native Title Act (1992) was passed in 1998. Deputy Prime Minister Tim Fischer mangled the government's rationale with the oxymoron that their legislation would underwrite "bucket loads of extinguishment and bucket loads of native title" (McKenna 2004). Conflicting horror stories welled up: Fischer traduced Aboriginal land councils as "bloodsucking bureaucracies" (quoted in Boland 2000), and an Aboriginal leader, Noel Pearson, declared that the amendment "'ripped the heart out' of the original legislation, giving away 80 per cent of Aboriginal people's position" (McKenna 2004). No land council had vengeful designs on any backyard—a false horror story; but—a truly horrific history—every settler house and fence and church is built, bought, or inherited through the blood and bones of the dispossessed.

Reflecting on *Another Day in the Colony* (2021), an essay collection about commonplace and structural racism by the Munanjali and South Sea Islander woman Chelsea Watego, Lilla Watson likens Watego's book to a horror script replete with zombies, somnambulists, and victims of live burial. Watego's story "is the story of many of her mob," and she tells it "so well because she has lived it her whole life and at times it must be like a living nightmare, where you can't wake up [and be kept] from falling into the pit of the colonial mentality to become one of the 'walking dead' (people who don't think)" (L. Watson 2021, xv). A real, whole-of-life nightmare: in one of the "guises Aboriginal Gothic takes when engaging with its European counterpart[,] . . . the Gothic is stripped of its fictional quality and assumes the form of Gothic realities" (Althans 2019, 279). The Gothic resonance of Lilla Watson's wording chimes with Achille Mbembe's theorization of "necropolitics" (2019). Australia's colonial and federal governments have exercised "necropower" by "creating *death-worlds*" for Australia's First Peoples: forms of social existence in which they are "subjected to living conditions that confer upon them the status of the *living dead*" (Mbembe 2019, 92, original emphases).

In his prose poem "The Grounding Sentence" (2014), Samuel Wagan Watson, who is of Munanjali, Birri Gubba, German, and Irish descent, describes being possessed by the colonial mentality and trapped in its pit:

> For too long I have complacently existed on these killing fields and built a house of straw in the down-wind of the enemy. My ancestors' tongues are sealed and delivered trophies on the shelves of the invaders' sterile museums . . . [. . .]
>
> I have hunted for trophies of my own and fallen into the snares of what the invader prides most of all, and that is the ability to turn blood against blood. (2020, 46, 48)

Watego, having escaped the pit, "knows white Australians so much better than they know themselves because, consciously or unconsciously, white Australians through acts of racism are so willing to expose to Aboriginal people the very worst parts of their nature" (L. Watson 2021, xv). Those worst parts manifest an Indigenocidal structure of feeling, aiming to monster Aboriginal people into the pit where the pendulum swings put them in extremis.

"The Pit and the Pendulum" dilates on the sensation of a moment via the intense lens of terror. Poe has long been a tutelary spirit of the Gothic in Australia due to his influence on the Melbourne writer Marcus Clarke, whose 1876 Gothic musing on the Australian landscape under the appellation "Weird Melancholy" makes him one progenitor of the "monsters that fill the pages of Aboriginal horror" (Borwein 2018, 66). Like Poe's fiction, Aboriginal experience of White Australian history is a Gothic tale, "only" real, as defined by Chris Baldick: "For the Gothic effect to be attained, a tale should combine a fearful sense of inheritance in time with a claustrophobic sense of enclosure in space, these two dimensions reinforcing one another to produce an impression of sickening descent into disintegration" (1992, xix). Aboriginal people live with the pit and the pendulum as constant presences. In the colony, enclosure of Country and inheritance of trauma are everywhere and everywhen.

The terrors enacted by monstrous settlers can be elaborated via another American writer, Mark Twain, who had some awareness of those monsters and terrors. In *A Connecticut Yankee in King Arthur's Court* (1889), Twain reflects, contra Edmund Burke, that France had "two 'Reigns of Terror.'" *La Terreur* swept away the prolonged reign of terror of *l'Ancien* Régime "in one swift tidal wave of blood." The French Revolution represented "a settlement of that hoary debt in the proportion of half a drop of blood for each hogshead of it that had been pressed by slow tortures out of that people in the weary stretch of ten centuries of wrong and shame and misery." All France, Twain imagined, "could hardly contain the coffins filled by that older and real Terror—that unspeakably bitter and awful Terror which none of us has been taught to see in its vastness or pity as it deserves" ([1889] 1917, 105–6). His profundity about seemingly unending, unspeakable terror resonates with Aboriginal people's experience of both the swift, serial, individual moments and the slow, multiplicative, intergenerational momentum of over two centuries of Indigenocidal terror.

During his 1895–1896 lecture tour of the Australian colonies, Twain heard about Australia's fatal frontiers. In *Following the Equator: A Journey around the World* (1897), he relayed the settler novelist Rosa Praed's anecdote about Aboriginal people killed by being fed arsenic-laced Christmas pudding. He concluded, however, that "Australian history is almost always picturesque"— rather than sublime in the sense of inducing dread and delivering death. "It does not read like history, but like the most beautiful lies. . . . [B]ut they are all true, they all happened" (169). Characterizing Australian history as picturesque obviates its unspeakable Indigenocide. The horror, to adapt Araluen, is sublime. As against the beautiful lies and necessary illusions of whitewashed history, Watson has us learn to see settler terror in its everydayness and vastness, as it deserves.

Atrocity Exhibition

A kind of horror show awaited visitors to Watson's 2022–2023 survey exhibition, *skeletons*, curated by Wakka Wakka and Kalkadoon woman Amanda Hayman and hosted by the Queensland State Archives in Brisbane. This exhibition opened, according to the venue's website, "the closet doors to Australia's skeletons" and discovered "buried evidence within the state's archives" (Queensland State Archives 2022). The exhibition, one reviewer thought, would make viewers' skin crawl and horripilate because of its exposé—"The inequity that remains in 'the bones' of governance in Queensland is laid bare"—and would even "chill some viewers to the bone with its accounts of atrocities imposed upon her people" (See 2022). An expressed intention of the exhibition was to make its host "more inviting to First Nations people," but it also served "to unsettle their Second Nations counterparts by immersing them in a grief and dispossession that is ever-present" (See 2022). It was a wading into Australia's inland sea of blood.

The entry point to *skeletons* was marked by the two textile works *butcher's apron series, flag #1* and *flag #2* (1994). They hung like parted doors and symbolized "a threshold to truth" (Hayman 2022), as if to warn: abandon false naïveté, all settlers who enter here. They beautifully veiled, and bluntly revealed, the modern Inferno of Indigenocide. Although "butcher's apron" is a queasy dysphemism for the Union Jack, "its thick and thin lines of red symbolising the blood shed from British colonisation" (Hayman 2022), Watson's flags' "seductively sheer red muslin [enticed] visitors into the exhibition space" (See 2022). The text on the flags became legible only upon nearing them. The inscription on *flag #1* is a 1994 statement by a member of the "Save Our Flag" organization: *My main aim is that we retain our monarchy; it is a part of our heritage and we have to leave our country as we received it.* On *flag #2* is Watson's riposte: *rape slaughter dispossession.*

The title *butcher's apron* travesties the rosy-fingered dawning of British settlement of the multitudinous lands of Australia as a drowning in blood. Some settler writers acknowledged this Indigenocidal incarnadining. The memoirist William Stamer observed in the mid-1860s: "No device by which the race [Aborigines] could be exterminated had been left untried. They had been hunted and shot down like wild beasts—treacherously murdered whilst sleeping within the paddock rails, and poisoned wholesale by having arsenic or some other substance mixed with the flour given to them for food" (1866, 2:98). So-called civilizing recipes, Stamer ironized, were flaunted under "our blood-red flag" (2:99). On some frontiers, the "act of poisoning whole communities of Aborigines with arsenic or strychnine-laced milk or rations—the so-called 'death pudding'—[was] almost a commonplace occurrence" (Evans, Saunders, and Cronin 1993, 49–50). Massacre by poisoning is encoded in Norman Lindsay's ultraviolent children's book *The Magic Pudding* (1918). Lindsay's Australian classic has encouraged White Australia, intergenerationally, to sublimate and celebrate its daily disposal of the First Nations as a Cockaigne-like myth of magically unending consumption (Althofer and Musgrove 2022). Twain claimed, dubiously, that "the use of poison was a departure from custom" (1897, 211), but there is no denying that it was customary at the time of his tour. In a double twist of White anxiety and arrogance, he excoriated massacre exposers more than massacrers: "It takes hold upon morbid imaginations and they work it up into a sort of exhibition of cruelty, and this smirches the good name of our civilization" (211). By "our civilization," Twain meant "the White man's," which should not be smirched by the blood it has poisoned or burdened by culpability for its toxic terrors.

Since the outbreak of Australia's "History Wars" in the 1990s, massacre deniers have fantasized "an unsullied Union Jack proudly flying over the Australian continent" (Evans and Thorpe 2001, 21). Massacre diminishers mitigate the scale and structural significance of slaughter. Slaughter is a settler building block, but Prime Minister Howard figured it as relatively superficial, a blemish: "[T]he treatment accorded to many indigenous Australians over a significant period of European settlement represents the most blemished chapter in our history" (1997a). Truth seekers and tellers like Judy Watson feel compelled to find the realities of what the flag hides or sometimes vaunts with its blood-red lines. Evans and Thorpe discern "a chilling glimpse of Nietzsche's 'festival of cruelty'" (2001, 21). The "joy in cruelty" psychologized by Nietzsche (1969, 68) describes the sardonic kicking of Aboriginal bodies by the journalist who reported that rations given by a squatter to the local people "contained about as much strychnine as anything else and not one of the mob escaped. When they awoke in the morning they were all dead corpses" (quoted in Evans, Saunders, and Cronin 1993, 49). Flying the butcher's apron in contemporary Australia confirms Nietzsche's theory that "the ever-increasing spiritualization and 'deification' of cruelty" both permeate "the entire history of higher culture" and "in a significant sense actually [constitute] it" (1969, 68). It is also confirmed by the artifactuality of colonial collections, which spiritualizes, or launders, the museum's role in massacre by reconstituting the dismemberment of the First Nations as material culture fit for repeated visual consumption. The collecting of Indigenous bodily remains occurred not only "in the wake of frontier violence" (Turnbull 2017, 295) but also in its vanguard. Settler desire to collect motivated murder as well as the posthumous violence of grave robbery.

Watson's video work *skullduggery* (2021) remembers the desecration of the grave of an Aboriginal man, Tiger, at Lawn Hill in the 1930s, the theft of his skull and breastplate, and their acquisition by the Wellcome Historical Medical Museum. Tiger's skull and breastplate were assimilated into what's been called "a truly Gothic curiosity . . . the enormous collection of bizarre artefacts amassed by Henry Solomon Wellcome from across the globe" (Horner and Zlosnik 2008, 9). But a person's skull is not "bizarre" (very strange, unusual). Nor was collecting skulls bizarre. As intimated by Henry Lawson's Gothic-realist short story "The Bush Undertaker" (1892), whose title character digs up a "blackfellow's grave" to steal and sell "'payable dirt,' or, rather, a skeleton" (Lawson [1892] 1894, 59), grave robbery was endemic on the frontiers and, for the metropolitan centers, a macabre yet infra-ordinary means to build "scientific" collections of mummified cultures. Lawson used Gothic tropes "to describe the potential for injustices committed against Indigenous Australians to come back to haunt colonial oppressors" (Gildersleeve 2021, 210). Watson's haunting video features a map, blood-stained paper, and manuscript letters, with voice actors reading correspondence between a Matron Kerr from Burketown Hospital and curators at the Wellcome. The work peels back their correspondence and commerce in Tiger's plundered bodily remains—it desublimates their sangfroid—to unearth the exhibitionist joy in cruelty that both masqueraded as and actually made up the high culture of museology. All Australia contains cases of civilized skullduggery. For Watson, this commonplace abomination should be uncontainable common knowledge.

From *butcher's apron series* to *skullduggery*, Watson has conjured many bloody ghosts at the feasts of White Australia. Thomas More, writing of a place where sheep eat people, anticipated a global history of "geographic imperialism with pastoralism as its core" (Evans and Thorpe 2021, 34). Watson pictures Australia as a demesne for colonialist cannibalism. Settler forces carve up, consume, and squander Indigenous lands and lives. Here, as elsewhere, imperial power was and is insatiable. "European hunger for resources," Watson and her coauthors state in an article about a work discussed below, *the names of places* (2016), "led to the denial of Indigenous sovereignty and culture [and the] violent rush for land-hunting and flag-planting" (Hooper, Richards, and Watson 2020, 193). Capital, as Marx showed, "appears as a Moloch demanding the whole world as a sacrifice belonging to it of right" (Marx and Engels 2010, 32:453). The foundational violence inherent to English-capitalist Empire in Australia drove the sacrifice of whole First Nations worlds. The capitalist Moloch incessantly predates Aboriginal worlds of art, too. Its Gothic orality— or "horrorality," to adapt Philip Brophy's coinage (1986)—is evoked by Hetti

Perkins: "[T]his voracious appetite in the commercial art world for devouring Aboriginal art. I see that as very much in parallel to the devouring of people, or the devouring of the body" (Perkins and Norman 2022). Watson's practice grapples with the cannibalistic comportment of art viewers steeped in settler culture's all-consuming monstrosity.

Marx adverted to capital's drive to sacrifice the whole world for its self-reproduction in the opening sentence of *Capital*, volume 1 (1867): "The wealth of those societies in which the capitalist mode of production prevails, presents itself as 'an immense accumulation of commodities'" (Marx and Engels 2010, 35:45; Marx was quoting himself). Although "an immense accumulation of commodities" is the standard translation of Marx's phrase *eine ungeheure Warensammlung, ungeheure* also means "monstrous" (35:45). He pictures an immense *and* monstrous accumulation of commodities. His imagery recalls a subgenre of still-life painting, the *Pronkstilleven*. The *Pronk* (rich, sumptuous, ostentatious) still life emblematized the rise of Dutch mercantilism, the ascendant middle class, and their proclivity to exhibit their riches, accumulated, as Marx outlines, by barbaric exploitation and extraction, especially in the Dutch colonies. By a harrowing account of commodity production as a Moloch feasting on workers' bodies, *Capital* demonstrates that commodities are made with "human brains, nerves, and muscles" (35:54). Reviewing the opening sentence, *eine ungeheure Warensammlung* appears as an acutely grotesque satire on the *Banketje* (banquet) subject of still-life painting. The accumulation of commodities is monstrous because it comprises an immense mass of eaten and expended human bodies, the feast and waste of Moloch.

A society's wealth presents itself as an immense accumulation of commodities that is constituted by the structural enormity of capital's monstrous cannibalism of workers. Homologously, a museum's rich holdings of Indigenous artifacts, such as in Wellcome's "enormous collection" accumulated from around the world, are grounded in the murder of people whose bodily remains and belongings are stolen for display. In Susan Best's reading of *the holes in the land 5*, quoted above, "the huge stain of blood-like ochre" disrupts, even floods, the "orderly conduct of fluids and waste around" the British Museum (2018, 21). The blood's disruptive appearance at the museum is preceded, however, by its constitutive role in the digestive flow of "collectibles" into the museum. Watson's print insinuates the normal ordering of things at the museum—the daily accession, storage, and display of human remains and other trophies—as based on the immense bloodshed of the colonial killing fields. The print is a palimpsestic trap. Superficially, the blood-like wash that transgresses the drainage appears sanguinary yet seductive. Underneath lies Watson's strong message, like a deadly poison dart, embedded in the primary image of the colonial museum having drained and transfused the blood of Indigenous victims: its voracious appetite is vampire-like.

The rush to devour Aboriginal people and culture concerns a series of etchings made by Watson in 1997: *our bones in your collections*, *our hair in your collections*, and *our skin in your collections*. Each print "refers to the systematic dispossession and institutionalisation of Indigenous people and culture, catalogued in the ethnographic collections of museums around the world" (Perkins 2004, 168). Watson based the prints on her drawings of museum-held objects, some taken from Waanyi country. She was "careful not to exactly replicate the objects and even concealed them behind a veil of chine collé. In so doing, she respectfully acknowledged their cultural significance, while enfolding these disenfranchised objects in a protective 'skin'" (Perkins 2004, 168). Watson actively resisted the Western viewer expectation of feeding the eyes with exotic human remains, the trophies of Indigenocide: "I didn't want them to be feasted upon too easily" (Watson 2010, 68). She represented ancestors' bones, hair, and skin, not as if still-life edibles but as still alive and powerful: "[B]ecause some of the objects are really potent [it's] always good having a bit of skin in between. The skin of the paper that I use, but also the skin of overlay. I see it as veiling" (68). Watson gave veiling, a generic marker of Gothic (Sedgwick 1986, ch. 4), an Indigenous dimension or inflection. Gothic can be evidenced by "the subtle but consistent uses of skin to signal monstrosity" (G. Williams 2014, 420), but here Watson applies skin as a subtly protective surface against settler monsters getting an eyeful. Her paper-skin veils are reparative auras, gently cast to protect ancestors' remains from penetrative, extractive, all-consuming settler visuality and voyeurism.

Watson's practice involves "rattling the drawers of the archives" as well as the bones of the museum (Watson, quoted in Hooper, Richards, and Watson 2020, 194). She shakes up archival papers and visibilizes the blood that spectrally stains and sticks them together in silent testament to White Australia's totalizing controls, death-worlding, over Aboriginal people's lives and life choices. For Aboriginal women, as the Narungga woman, poet, and activist Natalie Harkin shows, "the spectres of the archive do not rest" (2014, 4). Attuned to the archive as a site of bloodshed and genealogy, Harkin writes: "My family's records provide a chilling and intimate snapshot of lives lived under extraordinary surveillance from the 1920s to the 1950s" (4). The snapshot is encircled, engorged, by "both visceral-reality and created-imagined fantasy,"

> something that anchored and centred and pulsed to and from the heart of it all. And that was *blood*. The revered and repulsed colonial obsession, written into the record. *Flowing. Stirring. Spilling. Dripping.*

Mixing. Blood. Aboriginal blood and white blood. Full-blood and mixed-blood. Half-caste and quarter-caste. Quadroon and octoroon. Sub-human and fully-human. The racialised assumptions underpinning a so-called real and true Aboriginality became absolute on the colonial blood-dilution-scale, and reinforced the actions of government. *Blood everywhere . . . everywhere blood on the record.* (Harkin 2014, 4–5, original emphases)

Harkin's "spectropoetics of the archive" sounds like an ekphrasis of Watson's artist's books; indeed, her poetics is inspired by Watson's "journey through heritage as she learns from the ground up, poetically integrating body, emotion and country in her work" (6). Watson's integrative, decolonializing journey is antipodal to the sickening katabasis into the pit of the colonial mentality, dismemberment, and disintegration.

Archived specters pervade Watson's two artist books: *a preponderance of aboriginal blood* (2005, republished 2019) and *under the act* (2007). Her books exemplify Aboriginal Gothic interventions that "both haunt, and are haunted by colonial visions" (Araluen Corr 2018, 500). They recall Walter Benjamin's thesis, "There is no document of civilization which is not at the same time a document of barbarism" ([1968] 2007, 256), and Fred Wilson's germinal installation, *Mining the Museum* (1992–1993), at the Maryland Historical Society. Wilson reflected:

I created one vitrine of repoussé silver with the label, "Metalwork 1793–1880." But also made of metal, hidden deep in the storage rooms at the historical society, were slave shackles. So I placed them together, because normally you have one museum for beautiful things and one museum for horrific things. Actually, they had a lot to do with one another; the production of the one was made possible by the subjugation enforced by the other. (Karp and Wilson 1996, 183)

In the archive, Watson was rapt in the dialectical contrast and unity between the "beautiful and old fashioned" aesthetic of the documents and their "horrible content" (quoted in Fritsch 2015). As the beautiful paperwork aestheticized the subjugation and slaughter of Aboriginal people, *a preponderance of aboriginal blood* presents copies of official documents splashed with red ink, evoking blood splatter, "as if a remnant from a crime scene" (Helmrich 2019, 19), and symbolizing dehumanization, living death, and murder. The documents bloodied by Watson include electoral enrollment statutes from the Queensland State Archives that defined a person as a "full-blood Aborigine" (ineligible to vote) or a "half-caste" (eligible). These and other shocking categories, "quadroon" and "octoroon," were key ideological constituents of the legal discrimination, or mummification, experienced by Aboriginal Australians into the 1960s (Watson and Martin-Chew 2009, 76). Responsive to the archival material's "latent power" (Watson 2005), she kept the documents legible by using chine collé to convey the impression of Aboriginal blood spilled on or, perhaps, sprung from each page. For the springing, or violent letting, of Aboriginal blood was productive: it conditioned and sustained, among other things, the careers of settler archons and archivists.

The work *under the act* features Watson's family photographs as well as materials held in the Queensland State Archives, all related to her great-grandmother and grandmother being forced to live under Queensland's Aboriginal Protection and Restriction of the Sale of Opium Act of 1897. Watson reanimated the death-worlds encoded by the archival documents with ghostly but familial presences, layering two of them with photographs of relatives: "Peering out from the formality of the official letters, and washed over with blood-coloured pigment, are the strikingly animated faces" of Watson's great-grandmother Mabel Daly, her mother's cousin Mavis Pledger, and Mavis's son David (Luker 2016, 92). While Watson's practice often involves "concealing with layers those things too painful or raw to expose" (Watson and Martin-Chew 2009, 19), her layering of official papers with bloody marks gestures to raw and painful experiences of terror and trauma. Watson's *détournement* of colonial visions and archives re-presents, to borrow Naomi Simone Borwein's evocative phrase, "a muliebral terrorscape" (2018, 70). The documents and demeanor of "civilization" are streaked, ineffaceably, with blood. While Watson's artist's books serve to remember ancestors, in her words, "who are not dead but alive to all of us," they could carry the acid dedication of Octave Mirbeau's Gothic-anarchist novel *Le jardin des supplices* (The Torture Garden, 1899): "To the priests, to the soldiers, to the judges, and to the men who educate, lead and govern mankind I dedicate these pages of murder and blood" (Mirbeau [1903] 2008, 3). Watson's incarnadined pages reflect White Australia's own dedication to Indigenocide.

Watson's practice has exposed settler joy in the raw pain and trophying consumption of Indigenous people with the graphicness of Goya and the Grand Guignol (a Parisian theater in the Pigalle district), not for grisly entertainment but to induce viewers to listen for their ghostly voices. After learning that her great-great-grandmother had survived a massacre, she enlisted fellow artists and family members to help her make and install *40 pairs of blackfellows' ears, lawn hill station* (2008): lifelike sculptures of eighty ears, cast from beeswax, nailed to a wall inside the TarraWarra Museum of Art (in the work's first iteration), referencing "a frontier home décor of ghastly dimensions," slashed and assembled by "one of the most violent men on the northern frontier in the 1880s and 90s" (Rose 2001, 149). The primary source of Watson's installation was Emily Creaghe's account of visiting Lawn Hill Station in the period of the massacre. The station manager, Jack Watson, was a scion of a wealthy Anglo-Irish family and educated at an elite Melbourne grammar school. On February 8, 1883, Creaghe wrote in her diary: "Mr. Watson has 40 pairs of blacks' ears nailed round the walls collected during raiding parties after the loss of many cattle speared by the blacks" (1882–1883). To quote one of Goya's mordant titles, *Grande hazaña! Con Muertos!* A heroic feat! With dead men! Watson was romanticized as "The Gulf Hero," despite his butchery of Aboriginal people. Or, more likely, because of it: hero-worship of a killer of "blacks" is an everyday function when settler culture spiritualizes and deifies depravity.

Jack Watson's display of wanton cruelty was less a furioso performance, more in calculated conformity with decades of official terrorism and spectacles of Indigenocidal power. On April 10, 1816, in the decade when Goya created *Los desastres de la guerra*, the governor of New South Wales, Lachlan Macquarie, ordered a punitive expedition against "Hostile Tribes." Dead Aboriginal adults were to be "hanged up on Trees in Conspicuous Situations, to Strike the Survivors with the greater Terror" (quoted in Connor 2005, 51). The wax ears made by Watson and her collaborators "are a chilling reminder of the crimes perpetrated against Aboriginal people since the invasion. They represent a gruesome shrine . . . to the memory of all Aboriginal people mutilated by troopers and pastoralists" (Leffley et al. 2015, 18–19). Watson's installation asks viewers to hear and learn the stories of the silenced, the slaughtered. The forty pairs of ears in this torture garden are attentive, too: "The drooping flesh appears in all sorts of shapes and sizes like the individuals they were torn from. In the gallery they listen for the remorse of the oppressors, asking us to account for their treatment" (Clugston 2020). Dante's understanding of most new characters and circles of hell first came through the ear. Watson's silent re-creation of a sickening descent into Indigenocide requires us to listen deeply for the individuals who lost their ears and lives and to their living descendants. Reciprocated deep listening, not a mutual earful, creates paths out of the infernal pit.

In Native American Gothic, "Indians are threatened with extermination [by a monstrous] cast of dangerous imperialists and capitalists who haunt the landscape of Native America" (Burnham 2014, 228); conventions of Euro-American Settler Gothic othering are thereby inverted or reversed. Likewise, Watson's practice exemplifies Althans's point that Aboriginal Gothic contests "mechanisms of othering" (2019, 279). In White Australian Gothic fiction, the true monster or "dark Other" is the Indigene (277). In Aboriginal Gothic, settler massacrers are real-life monsters. The likes of Jack Watson, Governor Macquarie, and the 145 other perpetrators listed in Judy Watson's *the names of men* (2017), which also features the ghostly silhouettes of a bayonet and rifle, acted as if to fulfill the directive of Kurtz in Joseph Conrad's *Heart of Darkness*: "Exterminate all the brutes!" (Conrad [1899] 1996, 208). In Aboriginal Gothic, the monsters have names and faces, as also clearly articulated and envisioned in the photographic series *Horror Has a Face* (2017) by the Badtjala woman, artist and writer Fiona Foley. Foley's title alludes to the cinematic adaptation of Kurtz in the film *Apocalypse Now* (1979). Colonel Kurtz's squalid but honest philosophy—"Horror has a face and you must make a friend of horror. Horror and moral terror are your friends" (Coppola 1979)—encapsulates the Indigenocidal structure of feeling that possesses White Australia and dispossesses the First Nations globally.

Indigenocidal torture gardens in Watson's work appear not only on stolen land, such as those ears crucified at a pastoral station on Waanyi Country, but also in the museum built and filled with stolen objects. As part of "the hellish Antipodes" (Borwein 2018, 62), Australia has been othered as a site of confinement, live burial, and torture: "The Antipodes was a world of reversals, the dark subconscious of Britain. It was, for all intents and purposes, Gothic *par excellence*, the dungeon of the world" (Turcotte 1998, 10). Massacre culture turned Indigenous Australians' own Country into a dungeon where they were chained, tortured, mutilated, and slaughtered. The taking of their plundered bodily remains and objects also made the colonial museum into a dungeon from which release is an unnatural curiosity.

Watson was an artistic fellow at the British Museum in 2013, given privileged access to the labyrinthine stores of the paragon of "the institution, the big, big building" that affrighted her teenage self. She researched Aboriginal cultural material held in its collections since the nineteenth and early twentieth centuries and reworked her research drawings to produce a suite of six color etchings, *the holes in the land* (2015). In each one, treasured objects and lithographic washes of bright, shimmering, even haunting color are overlaid onto an architectural floor plan of the museum. The objects, which include a hair-string skirt, a paddle, clubs, and pituri bags, "are liberated from storage" (Best 2018, 10) and "remind us of the holes left by their absence in Aboriginal culture" (grahame galleries + editions 2015). They "are all rendered in black so that they register as shadows, or perhaps it would be better to say shades of their former selves," which are mourned (Best 2018, 10). The washes of brilliant color mostly suggest aerial views of Country, but the red-ochre marks of *the holes in the land 1* and *the holes in the land 5* recall blood stains and the Indigenocidal acts by which people's garb, utensils, and weapons were dismembered from Country and appropriated as museum pieces.

Watson sees "the plans of the museum being the bones of the work and the objects being shadows floating across the top of them" (quoted in Best 2018, 13). As against the nightmare of the objects kept captive by the museum in perpetuity, the etchings are dream visions of their release and repatriation. While Watson's "works often refer to specific events, their enigmatic and often intimate forms, gestures and marks also imply an immersive timelessness outside of a linear chronology" (Perkins 2020). In *the holes in the land*, the shadow-objects escape, haunt, defy, and confound the timebound artifactuality of settler treatments of Aboriginality. Floating free over and above the museum floor plans and purposefully drifting across the picture plan, virtually restored to their songlines, the objects are not "deadened museal objects" (Best 2018, 20) but vital elements in the synchronic immersiveness of the Dreaming. Here, Aboriginal culture is no longer trapped in the museum qua dungeon: it is returned and resutured to Country.

Watson's practice forms a cumulative body of evidence that epitomizes how Aboriginal Gothic embodies "the violence of a barbarous colonial reality" (Borwein 2018, 61). For Watson, evidence of settler barbarism is painfully plain, especially in the names of places: "We have so many places on our maps like Massacre Inlet or The Leap, Skeleton Creek, Skull Hole, etc. As we drive through the country we ask: 'How did these places get these names?'" (Hooper, Richards, and Watson 2020, 194). Watson collaborated with historians and other researchers to identify and map massacres sites for her multimedia and multiscalar work *the names of places* (2016). This work extended the established Indigenous practice of making art to record and remember massacres. When *the names of places* was displayed at the National Gallery of Australia, Canberra, in 2017, a high-definition video (duration 21:59 minutes) slowly scrolled an alphabetical list of hundreds of massacre sites, "in an ascending reel like a movie" (Lebde 2020), superimposed on a map of Australia shown with tremulous, uncertain, and so unsettled boundaries. Next to the video, a touchscreen allowed viewers to read historical documents associated with each massacre. Watson wanted viewers "to be aware that any map is a slippery, contested artifact, and also to have a bodily response to the work" (Dovey 2017). After watching the video, a relative turned to Watson in anguish and exclaimed in horror, "Where *wasn't* there a massacre?" (quoted in Dovey 2017, original emphasis). "I watched, entranced as the list went on and on," one reviewer recalled, "the chills climbing up my body as each minute went by, like how the credits climbed up the screen. There are easily hundreds of sites named, with thousands of lives lost. The extent of the loss is a terrifying reality"; underlying the list, "Watson's use of vein-like lines that transition to darker, redder shading that seeps inwards from the margins of the screen to the epicentre of the map, is symbolic of the genocidal bloodshed and the penetrative depth of generational trauma" (Lebde 2020). The video acts on viewers like a splatter film about real colonial horrors.

In *the names of places*, Watson points to blood and bones being everywhere. Everywhere bones in and under house and fence, church and parliament. "Mapping colonial violence forces readers to acknowledge that empires and modern nations are often built on the bones of the dispossessed" (Hooper, Richards, and Watson 2020, 193). The work contributes to local, national, and multidirectional remembrance of settler violence from Indigenous perspectives (Kennedy and Graefenstein 2019). It illustrates Borwein's contention: "Aboriginal horrors are concrete and multiplicative, linked through the body, spirit, sacred space, symbol, and reality—the construction of a nonsequential order" (2018, 71). Although the hundreds of massacre sites indicate the chronological, multifrontier spread of criminogenic settler colonialism across Australia, their nonsequential plotting subverts linear temporality. Watson's massacre map makes the settler perspective shudder with temporal and spatial discomfort. As Jeanine Leane says of such rattlings of "the settler mythscape," it disturbs settlers' "sense of familiarity with a place and history that they knew and brings to the fore a time, that they consider 'the past' that is still unresolved" (2020)—a consideration whose false consciousness is an archetypal Gothic plight and plot device.

On Watson's slippery map, the horror "slips" sublime. By the ambivalent abstraction of cartography, which reveals and veils at once, it emanates an overwhelming visceral sense of massacred corpses everywhere in the ground. The sites are signs that the horror and grief are not past, but ever-present; that haunting is embodied and multiplied through intergenerational transmission; but also that haunting is not necessarily horrifying. To unearth and represent the bones in the museum, the archive, and the map is to honor the dead. Watson's tender traps and poison darts savage Indigenocidal beliefs and abominations, but exposing and facing these horrors also helps to reveal and heal holes in the land, the spirit, and the songlines. "By opening up the map, looking at and beyond 'the names of places,' we attempted to unravel the past and repair the gaps within our ancestral lines. If Rosie hadn't escaped the massacre, my family and I would not be here" (Watson, in Hooper, Richards, and Watson 2020, 194). Drive your car and plant your house on the bones of the dead—*the names of places* subtly visualizes this proverb of the White Australian circle of the worldwide inferno of Indigenocide.

Watson's Aboriginal Gothic challenges her settler viewers and interlocutors to acknowledge that they, we, I, would not be here, in the way we are now/I am now, without mass butchery of the lands and lives of the First Peoples.

CONCLUSION

In *The Kadaitcha Sung* (1990), a novel by the Wangerriburra and Birri Gubba man, activist, and writer Sam Watson, the spirit of a murdered Aboriginal woman appears "screaming to all those of the blood to avenge her" (quoted in Borwein 2018, 70). In this scene from "a cellar of colonial depravity," Borwein writes, "Watson's Aboriginal chamber of horrors resembles the horror pornography of Marquis de Sade" (70). Similarly, Judy Watson's visual explorations of White Australia's massacre culture recalls Mirbeau's dissection of colonialist horror pornography in *The Torture Garden*. Like Mirbeau, Watson bears witness to the pendulum of "civilized" society swinging between "joy in cruelty" (Nietzsche 1969, 68) and its attendant "exhibition of cruelty" (Twain 1897, 211)—epitomized by Jack Watson and re-presented in *40 pairs of blackfellows' ears, lawn hill station*—and the hiding or whitewashing of its barbarous realities.

Mirbeau satirized the imperial fantasy of massacring colonized peoples and leaving no trace of the crime by basing his characterization of an English artillery officer on the inventor of the expanding or "dum-dum" bullet. "I sometimes ask myself if it's not a tale by Edgar Allan Poe," the officer reflects—Poe's "The Man That Was Used Up" (1839) is an apt intertext here—then effuses:

> But no [. . .] the marvellous little Dum-Dum worked wonders. Of twelve Hindus not one remained standing! The bullet had gone through their twelve bodies which were afterwards no more than twelve heaps of mangled flesh and literally crushed bone. [But I'm looking for] a little bullet which would leave nothing of anyone it hit ... nothing ... nothing ... nothing ... (Mirbeau [1903] 2008, 35)

By the insistent "nothing," Mirbeau emphasized the mania of the officer's murderous will to conquer and insinuated the impossibility of leaving "nothing," especially as the murderer's own mind is filled and possessed by evidence of criminal desire. He also anticipated Edmond Locard's Exchange Principle of 1920, which speaks to Watson's practice of visibilizing the bloody traces of the ongoing terrors of invasion and dispossession. As Katrina Davidson wrote of Watson's exhibition *memory scars, dreams and gardens* at Tolarno Galleries, Melbourne, in 2020: "Like the closing of a wound, the works simultaneously engulf the artist's immediate concerns and the shared trauma of national and international events beyond our control. In *Locard's Exchange Principle*, 'every contact leaves a trace' and in the case of Judy Watson's work her memories and experiences have become impregnable to her artistic practice" (2020). The Gothic surface, "seething with its unhealthy history," contrasts with a sanitizable one, "wipe-clean, bearing no trace of the past" (G. Williams 2014, 423). Watson's practice testifies to the denialist toxicity of whitewashed layers and demonstrates the justice of taking hold of "unhealthy history" and working to remedy it. Prescribed by the ancient pharmacy of her ancestors, Watson's poison darts implant antidotes to massacre culture's still-circulating ideological poison.

While Watson's subtle and discreet approach is reparative, repair can also occur by way of the hard, confrontational depiction of bloody wounds that remain open, psychically and spiritually, as opposed to denying their existence or claiming that "closure" means health. The pure horror and bloodiness of multiple works in Watson's oeuvre are not just a slap in the face of settler taste: they jump out and scream in that face. For settler culture, it is intensely discomforting, a monstrous aberration even, to awaken to an Australian social order where First Nations peoples, survivors of mass murder, instead of being "ghost citizens," express their voice and visibilize their presence as living people who have the right to monster up to the monstrosity of White Australia.

Notes

1. My thanks to Judy Watson for reading and correcting earlier drafts of this chapter. I'm responsible for any remaining errors. The artist is not related to any of the three other people named Watson who are mentioned in the chapter. "Indigenous Australians" and "Aboriginal and Torres Strait Islanders" are common general terms for Indigenous peoples of Australia. Watson has stated, "I am an Aboriginal artist, as distinct from being an artist from the Torres Strait Islands. The term 'Indigenous Australian' can apply to both groups of people" (Lewandowska and Watson 2016, 5). Thus, I use "Aboriginal" rather than "Indigenous" in the title. Throughout the chapter, I use both currently acceptable terms as well as "First Nations" and "First Peoples."

2. Reproductions of most artworks discussed here are available online.

Bibliography

Adelaide Festival. 2022. "Once and Future: With Evelyn Araluen and Jazz Money, Chaired by Natalie Harkin." Podcast. https://2022.adelaidefestival.com.au/events/2022-writers-week/once-and-future/.

Aldana Reyes, Xavier. 2017. *Spanish Gothic: National Identity, Collaboration and Cultural Adaptation*. Basingstoke, Hants., England: Palgrave Macmillan.

Althans, Katrin. 2010. *Darkness Subverted: Aboriginal Gothic in Black Australian Literature and Film*. Göttingen: V&R Unipress.

Althans, Katrin. 2019. "Aboriginal Gothic." In *Twenty-First-Century Gothic: An Edinburgh Companion*, edited by Maisha Wester and Xavier Aldana Reyes, 276–88. Edinburgh: Edinburgh University Press.

Althofer, Jayson. 2023. "The British Museum Has Fallen Down." *Imprint* 58, no. 4: 32–37.

Althofer, Jayson, and Brian Musgrove. 2022. "Nursery Atrocities: The Australian Children's Classic *The Magic Pudding*." In *Representing Childhood and Atrocity*, edited by Victoria Nesfield and Philip Smith, 273–96. Albany: State University of New York Press.

Araluen, Evelyn. 2019a. "Snugglepot and Cuddlepie in the Ghost Gum." *Sydney Review of Books*, February 11. https://sydneyreviewofbooks.com/essay/snugglepot-and-cuddlepie-in-the-ghost-gum-evelyn-araluen/.

Araluen, Evelyn. 2019b. "Aboriginal Gothic: Haunting and Artifactuality." Paper presented at the Indigenous Sovereignties, Identities, Histories conference, History House, Sydney, October 10.

Araluen, Evelyn. 2021. *Dropbear*. St. Lucia, Australia: University of Queensland Press.

Araluen Corr, Evelyn. 2018. "Silence and Resistance: Aboriginal Women Working within and against the Archive." *Continuum* 32, no. 4: 487–502.

Baldick, Chris. 1992. Introduction to *The Oxford Book of Gothic Tales*, edited by Chris Baldick, xi–xxiii. Oxford: Oxford University Press.

Balla, Paola. 2018 "The Names of Places: A Conversation with Judy Watson." Royal Melbourne Institute of Technology Gallery, April 17. https://rmitgallery.com/news/the-names-of-places-a-conversation-with-judy-watson/.

Benjamin, Walter. (1968) 2007. *Illuminations*. Edited by Hannah Arendt. Translated by Harry Zohn. New York: Schocken Books.

Best, Susan. 2018. "Anger and Repair: The Art and Politics of Judy Watson's *the holes in the land (2015)*." *Third Text* 32, no. 1: 2–22.

Boland, Sue. 2000. "The Death of Reconciliation?" *Green Left*, no. 397, March 15. https://www.greenleft.org.au/content/death-reconciliation.

Borwein, Naomi Simone. 2018. "Vampires, Shape-Shifters, and Sinister Light: Mistranslating Australian Aboriginal Horror in Theory and Literary Practice." In *The Palgrave Handbook to Horror Literature*, edited by Kevin Corstorphine and Laura R. Kremmel, 61–75. Cham, Switzerland: Palgrave Macmillan.

Brophy, Philip. 1986. "Horrality—The Textuality of Contemporary Horror Films." *Screen* 27, no. 1 (January–February): 2–13.

Brophy, Philip. 1988. "The Corpse of Modernism and the Blood of Jackson Pollock." https://www.philipbrophy.com/projects/essaysA/corpseofmodernism/essay.html.

Burnham, Michelle. 2014. "Is There an Indigenous Gothic?" In *A Companion to American Gothic*, edited by Charles L. Crow, 223–37. Chichester, W. Susx., England: John Wiley and Sons.

Caddey, Kate. 2016. *Judy Watson: A Case Study*. Booragul, Australia: Lake Macquarie City Art Gallery.

Clark, Maureen. 2013. "Out of the Shadows: Aboriginal Gothic, 'Race,' Identity and Voice in Tracey Moffatt's *beDevil*." In *Gothic Topographies: Language, Nation Building and "Race,"* edited by P. M. Mehtonen and Matti Savolainen, 105–17. Farnham, Surrey, England: Ashgate.

Clugston, Hannah. 2020. "Judy Watson Review: Pain and Persecution in a Lush and Stunning Landscape." *Guardian*, March 5. https://www.theguardian.com/artanddesign/2020/mar/05/judy-watson-review-pain-and-persecution-in-a-lush-and-stunning-landscape.

Connor, John. 2005. *The Australian Frontier Wars, 1788–1838*. Rev. ed. Sydney: University of New South Wales Press.

Conrad, Joseph. (1899) 1996. *Heart of Darkness and Other Tales*. Edited by Cedric Watts. Oxford: Oxford University Press.

Coppola, Francis Ford, dir. 1979. *Apocalypse Now*. Omni Zoetrope.

Creaghe, Emily Caroline. 1882–1883. *Diary, 22 Dec. 1882–5 Sept. 1883*. State Library of New South Wales, Sydney, call no. MLMSS 2982.

Davidson, Katina. 2020. "Catalogue Essay." In *memory scars, dreams and gardens*, by Judy Watson, exhibition catalog, Tolarno Galleries, Melbourne, November 13–December 12. https://tolarnogalleries.com/judy-watson-memory-scars-dreams-and-gardens-room-sheet/.

Dovey, Ceridwen. 2017. "The Mapping of Massacres." *New Yorker*, December 6. https://www.newyorker.com/culture/culture-desk/mapping-massacres.

Duthie, Emily. 2011. "The British Museum: An Imperial Museum in a Post-Imperial World." *Public History Review* 18, no. 12 (December): 12–25.

Eipper, Chris. 1999. "The Magic in the *Magic Pudding*." *Australian Journal of Anthropology* 10, no. 2 (August): 192–212.

Evans, Raymond, Kay Saunders, and Kathryn Cronin. 1993. *Race Relations in Colonial Queensland: A History of Exclusion, Exploitation, and Extermination*. 3rd ed. St. Lucia, Australia: University of Queensland Press.

Evans, Raymond, and Bill Thorpe. 2001. "Indigenocide and the Massacre of Aboriginal History." *Overland*, no. 163 (June): 21–39.

Fanon, Frantz. 1967. *Toward the African Revolution: Political Essays*. Translated by Haakon Chevalier. New York: Grove Press.

Foley, Fiona. 2017. *Horror Has a Face*. Exhibition catalog. Bowen Hills, Australia: Andrew Baker Art Dealer.

Forbes, Jack D. 1979. *Columbus and Other Cannibals: The Wétiko Disease of Exploitation, Imperialism, and Terrorism*. Davis, CA: Deganawidah-Quetzalcoatl University Press.

Fritsch, Lena. 2015. "Judy Watson, *a preponderance of aboriginal blood* 2005." Tate Modern. https://www.tate.org.uk/art/artworks/watson-a-preponderance-of-aboriginal-blood-p82511.

Gildersleeve, Jessica. 2021. "Terror in Colonial Australian Literature." In *The Palgrave Handbook of Steam Age Gothic*, edited by Clive Bloom, 203–16. Cham, Switzerland: Palgrave Macmillan.

grahame galleries + editions. 2015. *the holes in the land*, by Judy Watson. https://grahamegalleries.com.au/judy-watson-exhibition-the-holes-in-the-land/.

Griffiths, Michael R. 2018. *The Distribution of Settlement: Appropriation and Refusal in Australian Literature and Culture*. Crawley, Australia: University of Western Australia Publishing.

Griffiths, Tom. 1996. *Hunters and Collectors: The Antiquarian Imagination in Australia*. Melbourne: Cambridge University Press.

Griffiths, Tom. 1998. "The Haunted Country." In *Land and Identity: Proceedings of the 1997 Conference Held at the University of New England Armidale New South Wales, September 27–30, 1997*, edited by Michael Deves and Jennifer A. McDonell, 1–12. Armidale, Australia: Association for the Study of Australian Literature.

Harkin, Natalie. 2014. "The Poetics of (Re)Mapping Archives: Memory in the Blood." *Journal of the Association for the Study of Australian Literature* 14, no. 3: 1–14.

Hayman, Amanda. 2022. "*skeletons*: Curator's Essay." In *skeletons*, exhibition catalog. Brisbane: Blaklash; Queensland Government.

Helmrich, Michele. 2019. "The Wounds of the Repressed." In *a preponderance of aboriginal blood*, by Judy Watson, rev. ed., 16–23. Brisbane: grahame galleries + editions.

Höglund, Johan. 2018. "Imperial Horror and Terrorism." In *The Palgrave Handbook to Horror Literature*, edited by Kevin Corstorphine and Laura R. Kremmel, 327–37. Cham, Switzerland: Palgrave Macmillan.

Hooper, Greg, Jonathan Richards, and Judy Watson. 2020. "Mapping Colonial Massacres and Frontier Violence in Australia: 'the names of places.'" *Cartographica* 55, no. 3 (Fall): 193–98.

Horner, Avril, and Sue Zlosnik. 2008. Introduction to *Le Gothic: Influences and Appropriations in Europe and America*, edited by Avril Horner and Sue Zlosnik, 1–11. Basingstoke, Hants., England: Palgrave Macmillan.

Howard, John. 1997a. "Opening Address to the Australian Reconciliation Convention, Melbourne." PM Transcripts, May 26. https://pmtranscripts.pmc.gov.au/release/transcript-10361.

Howard, John. 1997b. "Television Interview with Kerry O'Brien, the 7.30 Report." PM Transcripts, September 4. https://pmtranscripts.pmc.gov.au/release/transcript-10469.

Jackson, Liz, presenter. 1996. "An Average Australian Bloke." *Four Corners*, ABC TV, February 19.

Karp, Ivan, and Fred Wilson. 1996. "Constructing the Spectacle of Culture in Museums." In *Thinking about Exhibitions*, edited by Reesa Greenberg, Bruce W. Ferguson, and Sandy Nairne, 180–91. London: Routledge.

Kennedy, Rosanne, and Sulamith Graefenstein. 2019. "From the Transnational to the Intimate: Multidirectional Memory, the Holocaust and Colonial Violence in Australia and Beyond." *International Journal of Politics, Culture, and Society* 32, no. 4 (December): 403–22.

Kluge-Ruhe Aboriginal Art Collection, University of Virginia. n.d. "Judy Watson: *experimental beds*." https://kluge-ruhe.org/collaboration/judy-watson-experimental-beds/.

Lawson, Henry. (1892) 1894. "The Bush Undertaker." In *Short Stories in Prose and Verse*, 55–71. Sydney: L. Lawson.

Leane, Jeanine. 2020. "*Living on Stolen Land*: Deconstructing the Settler Mythscape." Review of *Living on Stolen Land*, by Ambelin Kwaymullina. *Sydney Review of Books*, November 6. https://sydneyreviewofbooks.com/review/kwaymullina-living-on-stolen-land/.

Lebde, Nadine. 2020. "Art Review: *Terra inFirma*." Exhibition, Leo Kelly Blacktown Arts Centre, September 5–November 7, 2020. StoryCasters. https://storycasters.net/review-terra-infirma/.

Leffley, Jessica, Carol Carter, Joanna Davies, and Debbie Abraham. 2015. *(in)visible: The First Peoples and War*. Booragul, Australia: Lake Macquarie City Art Gallery.

Lewandowska, Marysia, and Judy Watson. 2016. "Conversation with Judy Watson." May 2–10. 40years.ima.org.au/assets/pdf/CiF_JWatson_Full_Conversation.pdf.

Love, Wendy. n.d. *Where I Belong*. Episode 9: Judy Watson. Podcast transcript. https://www.museumofbrisbane.com.au/wp-content/uploads/2022/04/EP-9_Judy-Watson_Transcript.pdf.

Luckhurst, Roger. 2014. "Gothic Colonies, 1850–1920." In *The Gothic World*, edited by Glennis Byron and Dale Townshend, 62–71. Abingdon, Oxon., England: Routledge.

Luker, Trish. 2016. "Animating the Archive: Artefacts of Law." In *Law, Memory, Violence: Uncovering the Counter-Archive*, edited by Stewart Motha and Honni van Rijswijk, 70–96. Abingdon, Oxon., England: Routledge.

Marr, David. 2023. *Killing for Country: A Family Story*. Collingwood, Australia: Black Inc.

Marx, Karl, and Friedrich Engels. 2010. *Collected Works*. Digital edition, 50 vols. London: Lawrence and Wishart.

Mbembe, Achille. 2019 *Necropolitics*. Translated by Steven Corcoran. Durham, NC: Duke University Press.

McKenna, Mark. 2004. "Blackfellas, Whitefellas and the Hidden Injuries of Race." *The Age*, April 17. https://www.theage.com.au/entertainment/books/blackfellas-whitefella-and-the-hidden-injuries-of-race-20040417-gdxov8.html.

McNally, David. 2011. *Monsters of the Market: Zombies, Vampires and Global Capitalism*. Leiden: Brill.

Mirbeau, Octave. (1903) 2008. *The Torture Garden*. No translation attribution. Washington, DC: Olympia Press.

Mundine, Djon. 2012. "Ghost Citizens." In *Ghost Citizens: Witnessing the Intervention*, catalog of an exhibition curated by Djon Mundine and Jo Holder. Sydney: The Cross Art Projects.

Mundine, Djon, and Daniel Browning. 2014. "The Creature from the Freudian Id." *AWAYE!*, ABC Radio National, Australia, March 15.

Mundine, Djon, and Natalie King. 2013. "Conversations with a Shadow." In *Shadowlife*, catalog of an exhibition curated by Djon Mundine and Natalie King, 4–9. Parkville, Australia: Asialink; Bendigo, Australia: Bendigo Art Gallery.

Myrone, Martin. 2020. "Gothic Art and Gothic Culture in the Romantic Era." In *The Cambridge History of the Gothic*, vol. 1, *Gothic in the Long Eighteenth Century*, edited by Angela Wright and Dale Townshend, 406–24. Cambridge: Cambridge University Press.

Nietzsche, Friedrich. 1969. *On the Genealogy of Morals / Ecce Homo*. Edited by Walter Kaufmann. Translated by Walter Kaufmann and R. J. Hollingdale. New York: Vintage Books.

Perkins, Hetti. 1997. *Fluent: Emily Kame Kngwarreye, Yvonne Koolmatrie, Judy Watson; XLVII Esposizione Internazionale d'Arte La Biennale di Venezia*. Exposition catalog. Sydney: Art Gallery of New South Wales.

Perkins, Hetti. 2004. *Tradition Today: Indigenous Art in Australia*. Sydney: Art Gallery of New South Wales.

Perkins, Hetti. 2020. "Looking Glass: Judy Watson and Yhonnie Scarce." NETS Victoria. https://netsvictoria.org.au/essay/looking-glass/.

Perkins, Hetti, and S. J. Norman. 2022. "Blak People Just Do That Stuff Innately. We Know How to Make Family for Each Other.." *The Australian*, March 17. https://www.theaustralian .com.au/life/qa-sj-norman-and-curator-hetti perkins-bond-through-art-and-identity/ news-story/23de2c30a91e68e0493723f4f1b6f80f.

Poe, Edgar Allan. (1842) 1982. "The Pit and the Pendulum." In *The Complete Tales and Poems of Edgar Allan Poe*, 246–57. London: Penguin Books.

Punter, David. 1998. *Gothic Pathologies: The Text, the Body and the Law*. Basingstoke, Hants., England: Palgrave Macmillan.

Punter, David. 2008. "A Voyage through the Phantom Museum." In *Le Gothic: Influences and Appropriations in Europe and America*, edited by Avril Horner and Sue Zlosnik, 219–41. Basingstoke, Hants., England: Palgrave Macmillan.

Queensland State Archives. 2022. "*skeletons*: New Exhibition by Judy Watson." https://blogs .archives.qld.gov.au/2023/05/29/skeletons-an-exhibition-by-judy-watson/.

Reich, Hannah. 2020. "Australian History Put through the Looking Glass by Aboriginal Artists Judy Watson and Yhonnie Scarce in New Exhibition." ABC Arts, December 4. https://www.abc.net.au/news/2020-12-05/australian-history-aboriginal-art-judy-watson -yhonnie-scarce/12943274.

Rose, Deborah Bird. 2001. "Aboriginal Life and Death in Australian Settler Nationhood." *Aboriginal History* 25: 148–62.

Ruskin, John. (1877) 1895. *Fors Clavigera*. New York: Merrill and Baker.

Sedgwick, Eve Kosofsky. 1986. *The Coherence of Gothic Conventions*. New York: Methuen.

See, Pamela. 2022. "Exhibition Review: *skeletons*, Judy Watson." Arts Hub, December 6. https://www.artshub.com.au/news/article/exhibition-review-skeletons-judy-watson -2599468/.

Shapira, Yael. 2018. *Inventing the Gothic Corpse: The Thrill of Human Remains in the Eighteenth-Century Novel*. Basingstoke, Hants., England: Palgrave Macmillan.

Skal, David J. 1994. *The Monster Show: A Cultural History of Horror*. London: Plexus.

Stamer, William. 1866. *Recollections of a Life of Adventure*. 2 vols. London: Hurst and Blackett.

Steven, Mark. 2017. *Splatter Capital: The Political Economy of Gore Films*. London: Repeater Books.

Stevenson, Brian. 1996. "The Wik Case." Wik vs. Queensland. https://www.wikvsqueensland .com/case.html.

TarraWarra Museum of Art. 2020. *Looking Glass: Judy Watson and Yhonnie Scarce*. Media release, September 14. Healesville, Australia: TarraWarra Museum of Art.

Tomba, Massimiliano. 2013. *Marx's Temporalities*. Translated by Peter D. Thomas and Sara R. Farris. Leiden: Brill.

Turcotte, Gerry. 1998. "Australian Gothic." In *The Handbook to Gothic Literature*, edited by Marie Mulvey-Roberts, 10–19. Basingstoke, Hants., England: Macmillan.

Turnbull, Paul. 2017. *Science, Museums and Collecting the Indigenous Dead in Colonial Australia*. Cham, Switzerland: Palgrave Macmillan.

Twain, Mark. 1897. *Following the Equator: A Journey around the World*. Hartford: American Publishing Company.

Twain, Mark. (1889) 1917. *A Connecticut Yankee in King Arthur's Court*. New York: Harper and Brothers.

Watson, Judy. 1995. Artist's Statement. In *Möet and Chandon Touring Exhibition Catalogue*, 14. Melbourne: Möet and Chandon Australian Art Foundation.

Watson, Judy. 2003. *sacred ground beating heart: works by Judy Watson 1989–2003*. Edited by Kate Hamersley. Bentley, Australia: John Curtin Gallery.

Watson, Judy. 2005. Artist's statement. In *a preponderance of aboriginal blood*. https://grahamegalleries.com.au/judy-watson-a-preponderance-of-aboriginal-blood-2005/.

Watson, Judy. 2010. Artist's statement. In *Art + Soul: A Journey into the World of Aboriginal Art*, by Hetti Perkins, 68–73. Carlton, Australia: Miegunyah Press.

Watson, Judy. 2015. Artist's statement. In *Unsettled: Stories Within*. Exhibition at the National Museum of Australia, November 27, 2015–March 28, 2016. https://www.nma.gov.au/exhibitions/unsettled/judy-watson.

Watson, Judy, and Louise Martin-Chew. 2009. *Judy Watson: blood language*. Carlton, Australia: Miegunyah Press.

Watson, Lilla. 2021. Foreword to *Another Day in the Colony*, by Chelsea Watego, xv–xvi. St. Lucia, Australia: University of Queensland Press.

Watson, Samuel Wagan. (2014) 2020. "The Grounding Sentence." In *Fire Front: First Nations Poetry and Power Today*, edited by Alison Whittaker, 46–48. St. Lucia, Australia: University of Queensland Press.

Williams, Gilda. 2014. "Defining a Gothic Aesthetic in Modern and Contemporary Visual Art." In *The Gothic World*, edited by Glennis Byron and Dale Townshend, 412–25. Abingdon, Oxon., England: Routledge.

Williams, Linda. 1990. *Hard Core: Power, Pleasure, and the "Frenzy of the Visible."* London: Pandora Press.

Wisker, Gina. 2021. "Shadows in Paradise: Australian Gothic." In *The Routledge Companion to Australian Literature*, edited by Jessica Gildersleeve, 384–92. New York: Routledge.

Wynne, Catherine. 2021. "Victorian Stage Magic, Adventure and the Mutilated Body." In *The Palgrave Handbook of Steam Age Gothic*, edited by Clive Bloom, 691–710. Cham, Switzerland: Palgrave Macmillan.

Part 4

Actualization-Conceptualization: h/Horror Interviews with Dark Speculative Writers Self-Identifying as Indigenous

INTERVIEW A

SHANE HAWK

NAOMI SIMONE BORWEIN

Shane Hawk is an award-winning Cheyenne and Arapaho editor and author. His works include the coedited volume *Never Whistle at Night* and *Anoka*, a short story collection.

NAOMI SIMONE BORWEIN: How would you describe your own understanding of what horror is?

SHANE HAWK: At the micro and denotational level, horror is our visceral reaction to threatening stimuli; it's a raw, unthinking emotion innate to our human wiring. Zooming out, horror encompasses everything we fear, tangible or not. Horror as a genre (fiction, film, play, etc.) is a playground for us to vicariously confront fears behind a bulwark.

BORWEIN: How do you employ it in your writing?

HAWK: I employ horror in my writing to address my personal fears and issues with which I've struggled since childhood. For instance, being mixed race, the adrenaline rush I get from writing a creepy sequence while confronting my identity issues is therapeutic. The buildup and release are addicting. I've also used horror to examine mental health issues I've experienced for extended periods of my life. Horror writing is therapy.

BORWEIN: This question relates to the use of light and shadow in passages or moments of horror in your writing. Can you describe some specific uses of light, contrast, shadow in your fiction, and how these might punctuate sensory moments—moments of sensory impact?

HAWK: In a recent story I wrote, a boy is checking the backyard because the patio door slammed. It's a moonless night, and they're in Utah near a Ute rez, with the closest neighbor being acres away, no lights. The boy is taken in by the sheer blackness of the windows, and out of curiosity, he flicks on the back-porch light. The light is so blinding that he immediately turns it back off, but swears he sees something near the dog pen. As the overbearing light pulses in his vision, he turns the light back on to inspect the yard, but nothing is there. He's unsure whether to believe his eyes because he's also experiencing insomnia. The use of light and shadow in this sequence was deliberate to show he's comfortable in the darkness and fears the light despite the opposite being true for boys his age.

BORWEIN: Along these lines, how are sensory elements connected to moments of shock, horror, terror—that representational conjunction of, for instance, auditory, olfactory, touch?

HAWK: Shock is much more effective in Horror movies than on the written page. Shock employs sensory elements insofar as immediate, gut-wrenching action, usually at the intersection of sight and sound. A reader of Horror fiction must be unsuspecting, and it's usually from either fiery or indifferent passages where an uncanny visual takes hold of the narration, combined with rapid descriptions of the event's sound, taste, and feel. If a writer can meet that conjunction smoothly, they have a highly memorable scene on their hands; think the motorcycle scene from Stephen Graham Jones's *The Only Good Indians*.

Horror is like shock in that it's fleeting, but it has the buildup as if it's the climactic moment to the rising action of both dread and terror. Though, unlike the climax of a typically structured story, there are numerous moments of horror instead of a singular event. Those moments are often a mixture of both visual and auditory elements. In Horror cinema, visuals are immediate, and they are paired with abrupt-yet-related sound effects, or emotionally jarring music score effects, e.g., plucks on a violin. In Horror literature, the same sensory elements conjoin to make effective sequences, though writers can add the taste of blood, or the rancid stench of decaying flesh, or how the wriggling lumps on someone's arm feels.

Terror is separated from the previous two in that it's a reaction rooted in both emotion and intellect. Terror is when a character is faced with an imminent threat, and they mentally process how they will face it and what the consequences will be. Terror can come in many forms, sensory wise, but in my experience, it's commonly been linked to auditory senses, i.e., discovering their drastic situation by listening to other characters, or hearing an inevitable threat approaching. It requires mental processing, and these characters can be hit by all senses: a metallic taste in their mouth, sweat accumulating in their palms, the smell of fire and ash as it approaches, etc.

BORWEIN: How are those patterned in the narrative landscape or setting?

HAWK: The best thing writers can do is give life to the setting the characters are in before tackling characterization. Effective Horror writers employ all five senses, or a majority of them, in every scene so readers can put themselves in the characters' shoes. If readers can't suspend their disbelief, they can't get into narratives, and if they can't connect with the characters, there won't be any emotional impact. Without fostering empathy between readers and characters, writers would not be able to create effective Horror.

BORWEIN: How do you view, or what are your understandings of, the reception to Indigenous Horror and dark speculative writing?

HAWK: Speaking only from my experience, readers have a great reception to Indigenous Horror or dark fiction. I am asked daily for recommendations, but there aren't a lot to give now, with the most prominent being Stephen Graham Jones and Owl Goingback. This is changing, though, and I'm glad to be a part of it by coediting an all-Indigenous dark fiction anthology titled *Never Whistle at Night* with Theodore C. Van Alst Jr. The reception to its concept was overwhelming, so much so that Ted and I held many conference calls with Big 5 imprints interested in the project and sold the rights to three imprints of Penguin Random House both in the US and in Canada. We are glad that they see the potential of Indigenous dark fiction and spreading it to the masses. People are curious to explore different Indigenous nations' folklore and modes of storytelling. There is an honest curiosity and excitement that is discernibly separate from a sense of exoticizing or fetishizing that is known to too many Natives. Additionally, I've heard only positive things from Natives and non-Natives alike concerning Indigenous Horror films like Jeff Barnaby's *Blood Quantum*. There just need to be more producers willing to take a risk on creating new stories from Indigenous folks rather than rehashing old, safe stories. I've recently spoken to some Indigenous writers who have books or stories ready to adapt, even with well-known directors ready to go, but there's just no financing available for these projects. Despite this being the case, I remain hopeful to see more Indigenous Horror on the screen.

BORWEIN: How does—if at all—your self-identification as Indigenous affect your horror aesthetics?

HAWK: Perhaps my being Indigenous affects my horror aesthetics to the extent that my horror intermingles with narratives that include the folklore, traditions, and issues of my tribes and others. While I am inspired by the

Horror greats, much of my work is also informed by my own connection to (and concern for) nature and the things I find important like belief, meditation, fasting, praying, respect for elders and the community at large, etc.

BORWEIN: Do you actively engage with the knowledges, conventions, belief systems, metaphysical conditions of your culture(s)?

HAWK: Yes. I am enrolled in the Cheyenne and Arapaho Tribes of Oklahoma, and I am also of Hidatsa descent. I engage daily with the conventions of my tribes, which can extend to religious beliefs, medicinal knowledge, language acquisition, etc. (I am currently learning to read and speak Arapaho.)

BORWEIN: Can you describe in general terms the construction of "monstrous" or sinister figures in your narrative landscapes—if possible, using an example?

HAWK: As you know, there are so many Indigenous nations across Turtle Island and the rest of the world, and they all have distinct cultures and views down to the individual level. Indigenous dark fiction writers must be wary of what and how they write sinister figures, especially if they are borrowing legends and lore from tribes other than their own. I had this in mind when I included a w*nd*go in my short story "Transfigured." This beyond-sinister entity originates from Algonquin-speaking nations which include my own (Cheyenne and Arapaho), but not the Siouan-speaking nations like the Dakota found in my collection *Anoka*. I personally believe in this entity and wanted to tread lightly for those who are Dakota and don't wish to engage with it. For this reason, I constructed this monster in my story indirectly and don't really call it by its name. I used exaggerated imagery in this version of the entity to not summon the actual ones. I wrote it as a cannibalistic figure as tall as a tree, giving it glowing red eyes and mind control over the town's children to kill their parents for it to collect their flesh. There are others, but this monster in Indigenous lore requires walking on eggshells when writing or should be avoided altogether. I'm unsure if I will interface with this entity ever again in my writing.

In an unreleased tale, I also constructed an antagonist from a Cheyenne legend, Hestovatohkeo'o (Two-Face). This humanoid monster has a second face on the back of its head, and all those who glimpse it either die immediately or are paralyzed until he comes back to finish the job. Allowing my imagination to run wild, I wrote a grim story wherein this creature controls a small town in South Dakota by demanding a child sacrifice every winter (Christmas), and if it doesn't get what it wants, it goes on a rampage. The town is in a drugged stupor because their water supply is tainted by a liquid secreted by Two-Face after consuming a child. The only thing that kills it is the Cheyenne Sacred Arrows from the nearby Black Hills. With this creature,

I felt like I had more liberty to change it to my liking. Depending on who you ask, legends should either never be touched or should be altered enough to not interfere with their original telling.

BORWEIN: As an editor, can you offer insight into the use of horror in Indigenous speculative fiction?

HAWK: Ted and I had the amazing opportunity to read about one hundred submissions for *Never Whistle at Night*, all from Indigenous writers around the globe. It was interesting to see how writers approached their stories. The open call was wide open, no specific theme, just dark fiction from Indigenous writers. Some were written in traditional narratives akin to their tribe's stories, some were modernized retellings of age-old moralistic warning tales, and many wrote about issues faced by the Indigenous community: identity, racism, climate change, sovereignty, body autonomy, conservation, foster care systems, etc. All these writers attempted to address their own fears or issues within their communities through the lens of horror, and they chose differing subgenres of Horror as well, e.g., Body Horror, Quiet Horror, Psychological Horror, Haunted House Horror, etc. With all variables in mind, an Indigenous writer has a vast creative space to incorporate horror in their narratives to speak on social issues, past and present, or dream up a dystopian future that serves as a cautionary tale to entice immediate action and protest for change in today's landscape.

BORWEIN: Is there anything else you would like to speak about?

HAWK: I would like to say that I'm glad hurtful tropes like the "Indian Burial Ground" and "Wise/Magical Indian" are leaving cinema and books. There's still room to grow (I have *Antlers* directed by Scott Cooper in mind), but at least there are more Indigenous writers taking the reins and telling their own stories. Spooky stories have been shared between Natives from time immemorial, and likewise, non-Natives have been appropriating folklore, legends, and symbols for their non-Native storytelling—usually in an awkward or offensive manner. Things are changing for the better, and I am extremely optimistic and excited for what's to come from Indigenous creatives around the world. And on top of that, I am eternally grateful for being able to be a tiny sliver of that change. Onward and upward.

Interview B

DAN RABARTS

NAOMI SIMONE BORWEIN

Dan Rabarts is an award-winning Ngāti Porou writer, editor, and narrator. A multiple recipient of the Australian Shadow Awards, and multiple recipient of the Sir Julius Vogel Award, his works include the Path of Ra series and the award-winning steampunk podcast *Tales from the Archives*.

NAOMI SIMONE BORWEIN: How would you describe your own understanding of what horror is? How do you employ it in your writing?

DAN RABARTS: Horror is a lens through which reality can be examined, which we apply to the art we create through a variety of techniques, some more obvious than others. It is a reflection of the disturbing or terrifying, laid over expressions of either imaginary worlds or the world we know in order to create a sense in the audience of being unsettled, disquieted by the potential for these representations to possibly come about, in some way, in the real world.

For this reason, the idea of Horror as a genre is at best a gross oversimplification of the purpose of horror in the execution of the arts, and at worst a deliberate effort to undermine the fact of horror as it appears throughout all art in its many forms. To box horror into a genre label, capturing such obvious forms as the slasher film, the haunted house novel, or the creature feature, is to deny that horror also intrudes into the wider artistic landscape, including literary fiction, romance, and the Horror genre's closer cousins: crime, science fiction, and dark fantasy.

To expand upon the above, consider the example of literary historical fiction set against the backdrop of war, and the disturbing elements which may unsettle the reader which draw upon this context, even if the work in question lacks some of the more obvious signifiers which most consumers associate with horror. By drawing on subject matter which has the effect on the reader of creating an atmosphere that the reader may find upsetting, and where that sense of disquiet is reinforced by the potential or the fact of that horror taking place in reality, then Horror has been overlaid on the work aesthetically, even if not generically. Similarly, romance novels may have a premise including elements such as domestic abuse as a narrative catalyst, which may indeed trigger strong negative emotional responses in the reader. Again, Horror is found in its polar opposite genre by simply being laid over the surface, or woven into the fabric, of the text.

Horror, therefore, is a frame of reference and can found far beyond the generally accepted bounds of what might be deemed the Horror genre.

In my own work, horror takes many forms, whether in the form of supernatural otherworldly intruders, such as Makere in the Path of Ra series (cowritten with Lee Murray), or the brutal and sadistic murders and injuries which occur in the otherwise comedic fantasy series Children of Bane, or the horror of personal grief and mental illness and the terrible acts these may lead to in my short story "Riptide." In each of these instances, horror serves as an emotional driver for the main characters and the narrative, yet each work does so in a different way.

In the Path of Ra novels, the monsters working to break through to our world from beyond the veil provide a traditional concrete villain for the characters to strive against, while delivering opportunities for action and adventure as expected of the supernatural thriller genre. In Children of Bane, sudden moments of physical brutality punctuate the generally absurdist text to throw the reader out of their comfort zone and reinforce that despite the story's flippant tone, the characters are indeed journeying through a harrowing and dangerous narrative.

In "Riptide," the horror cuts much closer to the real world, suggesting that the monsters of the story may be nothing more than the manifestation of the narrator's fragmenting grip on reality, and that the experiences of the characters in this story could very closely reflect the struggles that many people live through, dealing with mental illness and personal loss.

BORWEIN: This question relates to the use of light and shadow in passages or moments of horror in your writing. Can you describe some specific uses of light, contrast, shadow in your fiction, and how these might punctuate sensory moments—moments of sensory impact? Along these lines, how are sensory elements connected to moments of shock, horror, terror, surprise—that representational conjunction of, for instance, auditory, olfactory, touch? How are those patterned in the narrative landscape or setting?

RABARTS: In *Hounds of the Underworld* (Path of Ra, book 1), we are introduced to the world of the villainous monsters when Matiu enters a space where the sunlight is corrupted and refuses to enter, as if he is stepping through a veil into another place, where what is good becomes tainted: "The sunlight falling on the dog's golden hide drains away, leaving shades of grubby yellow, old dirt, rotting corn." The deeper he gets, the more the light flees, refusing to be drawn into the darkness within the building:

> Even without his sunglasses, Matiu can't see Hanson, despite the light spilling in from the front room. . . . Matiu takes another small step towards the room, straining against the unnatural gloom to see something, anything, through that black doorway. . . . [H]e needs to get a light on in that room. And at the same time, he doesn't think he wants to see. Because there beyond the doorframe, in that sucking darkness, all is not well.

In this passage, light and dark are used both in the traditional manner of defining good versus evil, but also to drive the emotional thread of the scene, that what Matiu doesn't know, but which he fears, lies just beyond the light, out of sight, but he is not out of reach of whatever lurks in the shadow: "Vague shapes continue to bend and twist in the dark behind Hanson, and the sound of something slick and liquid drowns out the baying of the dogs." Matiu reacts to this fear, reflected in his physicality: "Matiu's stomach lurches, his legs suddenly burning with the urge to run, . . . but he's paralysed. He can't look away from the horror that is Hanson, inching forward from the darkness. He can hardly breathe, yet he manages to summon words from his dry throat."

In another example, light and darkness are used as a visual signifier foreshadowing that not only our characters, but the city as a whole, are in danger. "Sunlight bleeds down the tenements and high-rises that march gaunt and unyielding across the Auckland skyline. Matiu stares through the windscreen as the canyons of glass and concrete, flaring on one side, dark on the other, swell upon the horizon like gravestones in the setting sun's harsh rays." This is a significant moment as Matiu realises that the narrative is about more than just him but could affect many thousands of people.

This fear is realised in the third book of the series, *Blood of the Sun*. "Like a curtain of darkness has been thrown across the land, the lights of the city blink out."

Aside from the use of the aurora australis (southern lights) as a symbol of impending planetary apocalypse, light becomes a weapon to battle the darkness. "His palms are open, and spread between them is a ball of light, too bright to gaze upon, a miniature sun whorled around with coiling patterns. Its heat burns him. Surely, it will burn the beast as well."

The line between light and dark is often indistinct, but the shadows represent the front line of the battle between good and evil. "Fractured sunlight splinters Erica's features, promising the fall of night. . . . Like hell will Erica let Sandi Kerr lay so much as a finger on her sister again. This night will be long, and dark, and terrible."

This dichotomy is overturned in the latter part of the third book, however, as we learn that evil is not always darkness, but can also be present in the light we thought was safe. "Although the hour has barely gone midnight, in this other place of roaring time the sun is rising. Ra's glow is bright and angry in the east, lifting above the horizon, the eye of the god peering into this fractured world." In this way, we come full circle and raise the unsettling possibility that what we think is good and right, the light, may in fact be as corrupt and dangerous as the darkness we fight so hard against.

BORWEIN: How do you view, or what are your understandings of, the reception to Indigenous Horror and dark speculative writing?

RABARTS: Putting aside the fraught space of cultural appropriation, Indigenous fiction (by which we mean fiction written by a person of a particular nonhegemonic cultural identity and centred around themes or concepts which draw strongly on that culture) has a tendency to lend itself to dark or horrific themes, primarily due to the nature of folklore to draw on primal fears as a source of inspiration for many of the fundamental foundations of cultural narratives.

Western cultures have largely sanitised the darker roots of the original mythologies which underpin foundational storytelling, as can be seen by any number of studies into the often bloody and disturbing histories upon which many fairy tales and nursery rhymes are based. Indigenous cultures may not have experienced this same distancing of these founding narratives from their origins, although the influence of colonialism and hegemonic religion can be seen altering the modern iterations of many Indigenous mythologies as a result.

This is to establish that the baseline for the normative standards for Indigenous dark fiction differ from those upon which non-Indigenous dark fiction is based, resulting in a market wherein the reader who brings a degree of expectation to a work when they start to consume it may find, upon entering that work, that the signposts they expect are absent, and they are without a guide entering a strange land. This is because consuming fiction is a learned experience. We learn to suspend our disbelief and separate reality from falsehood, and in so doing to accept falsehood (fiction) as a sort of reality. We learn from what we consume, an unspoken contract with the creator of the work in which there is a shared understanding of the rules of the fiction in question, which are in turn founded on a thoroughly ingrained set of cultural biases, assumptions, and predetermined narrative norms.

Through the underlying structure of these assumed shared understandings, the creator and the consumer of a work of fiction therefore share an identification with the work and the narratives upon which that work is based. When a reader steps into a story without that shared identification, the result can be mixed, falling somewhere between two extremes: either the reader is disoriented and unable to relate to the work and therefore their reception is negative, because the work is failing to meet the assumed contract between author and reader; or the reader is adrift in a work which defies their expectations, and they find this experience refreshing, rewarding, edgy, and innovative.

Indigenous Horror, therefore, draws a fine line between alienating its potential audience or capturing new audiences by breaking away from the norm. In most cases, it will do both. Where it draws criticism, this criticism is often directed not so much at the work itself but at the creator, which in turn has a tendency to lend itself to other social biases including, to one extent or another, racism or classism. On the other hand, different audiences who are hungry for something that breaks the tired, repetitive old frameworks are highly supportive of new voices creating fiction from different moulds, and this support can be seen in shifting attitudes toward recognising fiction in the awards field. One example would be *Black Cranes*, a collection of Horror fiction from Asian women writers, which won the Bram Stoker Award for Superior Achievement in a Fiction Collection in 2021 (Omnium Gatherum, edited by Lee Murray and Geneve Flynn).

BORWEIN: How does—if at all—your self-identification as Indigenous affect your horror aesthetics? Do you actively engage with the knowledges, conventions, belief systems, metaphysical conditions of your culture(s)?

RABARTS: Being of Māori descent, part of my journey as a writer has been to find my voice as a Māori writer as well as being an author of speculative fiction. I draw on Māoritanga in many of my works, including the Path of Ra series and several short stories and novellas. When I do so,

I maintain a healthy respect for the cultural and spiritual elements I'm drawing on, and go through a review process with more knowledgeable cultural leaders.

In the first instance, I will write with a piece of folklore or mythology in mind, bringing this into the work, usually researching the material using internet resources such as Te Ara (teara.govt.nz) to clarify my own understanding, and will also look to find the *iwi* (tribe) to whom a particular folk story is attributed, and try to learn the original interpretation and origin of the story as well. Care is taken to avoid appropriating narratives which are held sacred by any particular *iwi*, if I do not *whakapapa* (trace lineage) to those *iwi*. To take the stories of another *iwi* and use them as my own would be disrespectful to those who maintain the care of those narratives.

Where a source is more generic, care is then taken not to attribute specific story elements to any particular *iwi*; in fact, in many cases I have fictionalised *iwi* names to allow a story element to work without creating disrespect to any *iwi*. The core of the Māoritanga must, however, remain consistent with the spirit of the mythology, and must respect the source of that narrative.

Once I've completed a draft of a story, I then forward it first to my father, who holds a great deal of knowledge of the history and folklore of our *iwi* and of many of the peoples with whom our *iwi* have interacted historically, as well as having a wealth of knowledge of Māoritanga both general and *iwi*-specific. He will read and review, and make notes about any errors, inconsistencies, or use of Māoritanga which may cause disrespect. I'll have a chance to review, and then he will send the story on to others who may have more specific knowledge of particular elements used in the story, for their feedback. All of this comes back to me, and I use this to rework the story to make sure that what I have used in the narrative is doing so from a place of understanding and respect, while still telling the story, or a story that resembles, the one I set out to tell. In particular, any use of Māori language, whether in text or dialogue, is reviewed by a fluent speaker, and this is one area where the most changes will come out of a draft. Once these steps have been completed, I can have confidence that the work I'm sending out into the world has been checked and approved by those more knowledgeable than I, and in the process, I learn a great deal about my own history and the narratives of my people.

BORWEIN: Can you describe in general terms the construction of "monstrous" or sinister figures in your narrative landscapes—if possible, using an example?

RABARTS: How monstrous a figure might be in one of my works will depend on how far from reality the story is willing to go. For a story set close to the real world, the horror lies in things which are just a little off from what we recognise as normal; in fact, if the wrongness is conceivable and believable, this makes the horror all the more likely to impact the reader. As per my comment above, the writer and the reader share a contract, and this contract can dictate the extent to which the horror of a monstrous figure can distort our accepted reality. Genre expectations are a major driver of this, although given the chance genre can always be defied or subverted (and as a creative, I am always presenting myself with the opportunity to defy genre).

For the Path of Ra series, our villains include a megalomaniacal cultist bent on sacrificing her followers to some darker power to achieve immortality, a metaphor not far off from what we often see in the real world among subculture personalities, particularly in religion and politics. We also have humans, or figures much like humans, with attributes which draw on alien or Lovecraftian imagery, corruptions of the human form with features like tentacles and claws.

In my short story "Floodgate" (published in *The Mammoth Book of Dieselpunk* [edited by Sean Wallace], 2015), a group of Māori soldiers and an Australian pilot fighting in northern Africa during an alternate history of the First World War discover that the Kaiser has a new weapon to turn on the allied naval forces in the Mediterranean: the Loch Ness Monster (and its young). In this story, I draw on the horrors of war (recalling the history of Carthage and by association humankind's centuries-long love affair with bloody conflict) and also take a mythical beast and twist it slightly, while barely revealing the monster itself, in the same way the mythical Nessie is so rarely seen. In this story, the monster itself is not the true horror, compared to the horrors to which humans will sink to achieve their dark ambitions, the final exposition of which is continent-spanning warfare.

BORWEIN: There is a discourse in relation to various Indigenous metaphysics on patterning, orientation, somatic/holistic experience, and ways of knowing. The Inuit artist Asinnajaq creates an encapsulated cinematic universe (in a 2017 short film) to inspect their ontological lens, and it is narrated in Inuktitut and incorporates manifestations of pattern moving between states, alongside the use of old ethnographic propaganda films, newsreels—as horror realism—landscape, and throat singing. Can you offer a representation of your lens or vision? How do your representations of moments of horror relate to such a lens, within the constraints of the written word/world?

RABARTS: The lenses of urbanisation and colonialism feature strongly in my work when delving into the relationship between Māoritanga and fiction, and by extension the wider world being lensed accordingly. Representations of Māori in my work walk a line between exploring the challenges and pressures faced by Māori coexisting in a country run by the colonial majority, in particular the impact of modernisation and rationalism on the spiritualism of the *tangata whenua* (people of the land). In the Path of Ra series, we see this in the way that Matiu's ability as a *matakite*, to see into the spirit realm and into the future, has isolated him from others and contributed to his involvement in crime. Māori are overrepresented in New Zealand in both mental health and crime statistics, so this series presented an opportunity to unpack some of that social dilemma by using the supernatural as a narrative lubricant.

INTERVIEW C

STEPHEN GRAHAM JONES

NAOMI SIMONE BORWEIN

A *New York Times* best-selling and Bram Stoker Award–winning Blackfoot Horror writer, Stephen Graham Jones has written dozens of works including *The Only Good Indians*, *My Heart Is a Chainsaw*, and *The Angel of Indian Lake*.

NAOMI SIMONE BORWEIN: How would you describe your own understanding of what horror is?

STEPHEN GRAHAM JONES: Horror is that which disturbs. Doesn't have to be supernatural. It just has to mess your sleep up.

BORWEIN: How do you employ it in your writing?

JONES: If I'm not getting nervous writing this, then I know I'm probably not in horror terrain, yet, need to push a bit farther.

BORWEIN: This question relates to the use of light and shadow in passages or moments of horror in your writing. Can you describe some specific uses of light, contrast, shadow in your fiction, and how these might punctuate sensory moments—moments of sensory impact?

JONES: Ever since the midnineties I've been using "halflight" to describe a kind of liminal space. A space in which things can emerge.

BORWEIN: Along these lines, how are sensory elements connected to moments of shock, horror, terror, surprise—that representational conjunction of, for instance, auditory, olfactory, touch?

JONES: Got to use them all if you want to creep people out.

BORWEIN: How are those patterned in the narrative landscape or setting?

JONES: Not patterned for me. Just as they come up.

BORWEIN: How do you view, or what are your understandings of, the reception to Indigenous Horror and dark speculative writing?

JONES: Seems people are receptive. Trick is, to tell them Indigenous horror stories without leaning on the stock tropes and expectations about us.

BORWEIN: How does—if at all—your self-identification as Indigenous affect your horror aesthetics?

JONES: No clue. I know I'm scared of everything. That could be it.

BORWEIN: Do you actively engage with the knowledges, conventions, belief systems, metaphysical conditions of your culture(s)?

JONES: I don't know about "actively." But, yeah, I'd guess they're there.

BORWEIN: Can you describe in general terms the construction of "monstrous" or sinister figures in your narrative landscapes—if possible, using an example?

JONES: At first you see the toe, the shadow, the saliva left behind. And then, slowly, you become aware of more and more. And then you regret that you ever wanted to see the whole thing.

BORWEIN: There is a discourse in relation to various Indigenous metaphysics on patterning, orientation, somatic/holistic experience, and ways of knowing. The Inuit artist Asinnajaq creates an encapsulated cinematic universe (in a 2017 short film) to inspect their ontological lens, and it is narrated in Inuktitut and incorporates manifestations of pattern moving between states, alongside the use of old ethnographic propaganda films, newsreels—as horror realism—landscape, and throat singing. Can you offer a representation of your lens or vision?

JONES: Not really, I don't think.

BORWEIN: How do your representations of moments of horror relate to such a lens, within the constraints of the written word/world?

JONES: No clue.

BORWEIN: Is there anything else you would like to speak about?

JONES: We need more and scarier monsters, always.

Interview D

GREGORY C. LOUI

NAOMI SIMONE BORWEIN

Gregory Loui is a Kānaka Maoli speculative Pasifikafuturist writer. His works include *21st Century Orc*.

NAOMI SIMONE BORWEIN: How would you describe your own understanding of what horror is?

GREGORY C. LOUI: My understanding of the best horror elicits a very visceral reaction of fear and disgust in the reader. Some horror can be therapeutic or is simply a way for people to get a small adrenaline high.

BORWEIN: How do you employ it in your writing?

LOUI: I'm not primarily a horror writer. I am primarily a fantasy writer with some elements of sci-fi and horror sprinkled into my writing for flavor. I employ horror in my writing as a way to raise tension and the stakes for the characters. Usually, most instances of horror in my writing have two distinct origins. Either horror occurs due to human error and miscalculation in some kind of forbidden process, or the horror comes from beyond human understanding, often from an Eldritch Abomination that slumbers under the ocean. I like to think that this horror is drawn from Japanese influences such as Studio Ghibli films or the Dark Souls series. I also use horror to convey loss and tragedy arising from some atrocity or calamity in the past that still ripples through into the present. Often, world-shifting events in my stories leave scars on the landscape itself or monsters that haunt such places.

BORWEIN: This question relates to the use of light and shadow in passages or moments of horror in your writing. Can you describe some specific uses of light, contrast, shadow in your fiction, and how these might punctuate sensory moments—moments of sensory impact?

LOUI: I enjoy using light, contrast, and shadow a lot in my fiction because I'm a very visual person and I tend to think of my fiction almost as if it were a movie. I like very dramatic lighting to set the mood for specific scenes and often use low-light or single-color situations for horror. I've been working on a scene where a monster/god literally steps out of the shadows into the light as a major revelation and climax to the story. In this instance, the shadows are actually empty air so the monster/god fully materializes into this reality once the light hits it.

BORWEIN: Along these lines, how are sensory elements connected to moments of shock, horror, terror, surprise—that representational conjunction of, for instance, auditory, olfactory, touch?

LOUI: I like to try to use horror as a layered experience as the horror approaches. Auditory and olfactory elements come first to build the tension with the horror still in the shadows or in the distance, then visual elements as the horror reveals itself and touch elements once the action starts.

BORWEIN: How are those patterned in the narrative landscape or setting?

LOUI: It's important to note that within Hawaiian culture, darkness is not strictly evil. In fact, in oral histories, the universe is said to have arisen from a primordial and gentle darkness. As stated previously, I try to avoid pure horror when using darkness as a theme but instead try to use horror with a sense of majesty. As such, most horror places are patterned as dirty or corrupted by human influences. These are split into two semidistinct categories: pollution or experimentation by sentient creatures. I also think these kinds of horror are more compelling than a creature in the dark.

BORWEIN: How do you view, or what are your understandings of, the reception to Indigenous Horror and dark speculative writing?

LOUI: I think Indigenous horror and dark speculative writing has been eye-opening to many people who aren't aware of the history of colonization and genocide that Indigenous peoples have gone through. As a person of Hawaiian descent, I think Indigenous horror is often used and seen as a way to educate people who may not be as familiar with Indigenous history. Some of the Indigenous horror writings that I've read focus on the experiences of Indigenous boarding schools. I also think that there is a desire to see things outside of familiar tropes. Our current generation of readers have already read the classics and want to find something fresh. Indigenous horror and speculative writing in general is fresh for western audiences.

BORWEIN: How does—if at all—your self-identification as Indigenous affect your horror aesthetics?

LOUI: My self-identification as Indigenous has affected my horror aesthetics by trying to incorporate both mythological stories from my Indigenous background and the horrors of historical colonization. Loss of identity is a major theme in my work, so I tend to write monsters that were once human as horrific, while monsters that are just wild fauna are majestic.

BORWEIN: Do you actively engage with the knowledges, conventions, belief systems, metaphysical conditions of your culture(s)?

LOUI: As mentioned previously, Hawaiian culture doesn't see the dark as pure evil; instead, it is the original state of the universe. In fact, the dark is considered divine in comparison to the day, which is associated more with humanity than with the gods. I also base the entire metaphysics of one of my worlds off the concept of mana, and how perception can alter reality. I speak more to this in a later question. And of course, I try to incorporate as many Indigenous "monsters" as possible into my works, either as natural fauna or cursed beings. Most of them are exaggerated versions of animals in our reality. As for in daily life, however, I do not practice many traditions from Native Hawaiian culture. I try my best to learn Hawaiian language and culture, but I was never adept at integrating it into my daily life.

BORWEIN: Can you describe in general terms the construction of "monstrous" or sinister figures in your narrative landscapes—if possible, using an example?

LOUI: I try to avoid completely irredeemable monsters that have no sympathetic qualities. Instead, I prefer to construct tragic monsters that elicit a sense of melancholy. I have four main categories that I work with: the tragic monsters; predators that hunt only for their biological needs; human monsters that are not physically monstrous but monstrous through their actions; and then finally, Eldritch horrors from beyond our reality. Of these four, I like using the latter two the most for actual "horror" scenes and plots. One example is my current project: the Tyrant Khagan and Eshaka are two of the previously mentioned categories. The Tyrant is a cursed immortal from an age long past, twisted into a half-monster that can only kill, but a sympathetic character. In his backstory, he chose to become a monster to save his people and his beloved. Now, after his side lost, the Tyrant is left behind, a shattered shell of himself, left to roam the wastes. In the story, he is just a tool for Eshaka, the truly monstrous figure, to manipulate. Heavily inspired by *Bloodborne* in his design, where the Tyrant Khagan is crossed between a horse and a man. Meanwhile, Eshaka is an all-too-human "monster," a powerful man who runs a human trafficking ring and who has gaslit the main character of that specific story into believing she is worthless without him. I made sure he never physically assaults another, but his actions drive the entire plot of the story and cause an immense amount of suffering. I modeled him after the many "scholars" (mostly anthropologists and archaeologists) who dissected Indigenous cultures and people for the sake of so-called enlightenment and progress. In summary, Eshaka is monstrous not because of what he is but what he does.

BORWEIN: There is a discourse in relation to various Indigenous metaphysics on patterning, orientation, somatic/holistic experience, and ways of knowing. The Inuit artist Asinnajaq creates an encapsulated cinematic universe (in a 2017 short film) to inspect their ontological lens, and it is narrated in Inuktitut and incorporates manifestations of pattern moving between states, alongside the use of old ethnographic propaganda films, newsreels—as horror realism—landscape, and throat singing. Can you offer a representation of your lens or vision?

LOUI: I'm not sure what you mean by this question. I'm not especially focused on metaphysics nor experimental lens/imagery for my writing other than using mana as the basis for one world's reality as mentioned earlier. In that world, mana is the foundational energy that is functionally a more complex and Indigenous-influenced version of the Force. All things in the universe have mana, and all interactions with other things are mana. A storm has mana. A blade cutting through flesh has mana. A birdsong has mana. However, mana is even more complicated when societies and relationships are involved, since mana can be transferred through these relationships, and perceptions can transfer mana. For example, believing someone is a monster gives them a poisonous mana that transforms them into a monster if their own internal mana or identity is not strong enough to resist external mana from their surroundings. Basically, I'm peeved about mana being just an energy source in much of pop culture and want to express it as something more complex and as the basis of Pasifika worldview.

BORWEIN: How do your representations of moments of horror relate to such a lens, within the constraints of the written word/world?

LOUI: Unless horror is explicitly from beyond our reality, I try to make most horror constrained to the realistic and our world's laws. That being said, in the world where I use the mana metaphysics model, horror becomes even more horrific not only due to outside perception, but its very presence can infect others with its "evil" mana. I think that's relatively common, however. Corruption of bodies and minds is often used in horror and is justified through different means, such as biological agents in most zombie media.

BORWEIN: Is there anything else you would like to speak about?

LOUI: One thing I've noticed about Indigenous horror and speculative fiction is that there's a particular emphasis on disease as a source of horror due to the history of disease and Indigenous peoples. I recently saw an Indigenous zombie film, and there was a clever twist that only the Indigenous people were immune. I expect there to be more after COVID-19.

INTERVIEW E

GINA COLE

NAOMI SIMONE BORWEIN

Gina Cole is an award-winning Pasifikafuturist writer of Fijian, Welsh, and Scottish descent. Cole incorporates Pasifika epistemologies and anticolonial approaches in her work, such as *Black Ice Matter* and *Na Viro*.

NAOMI SIMONE BORWEIN: How would you describe your own understanding of what horror is?

GINA COLE: Horror engenders fear and terror in the audience.

BORWEIN: How do you employ it in your writing?

COLE: For effect at crucial moments in plot. As background menace.

BORWEIN: Can you describe some specific uses of light, contrast, shadow in your fiction, and how these might punctuate sensory moments—moments of sensory impact?

COLE: For creating suspense. Hero versus villain. Like the story of Antigone. Although the villain is a nuanced character, they are always defeated.

BORWEIN: Along these lines, how are sensory elements connected to moments of shock, horror, terror, surprise—that representational conjunction of, for instance, auditory, olfactory, touch?

COLE: Through the visceral—gory, hacking, bloody.

BORWEIN: How are those patterned in the narrative landscape or setting?

COLE: See above.

BORWEIN: How do you view or what are your understandings of the reception to Indigenous Horror and dark speculative writing?

COLE: Horror is part of Indigenous people's history over the past five hundred years of colonialism and our present-day lives. This horror is well understood by Indigenous peoples. Not so sure about white settlers and their descendants, who have directly benefitted from colonialism and suffer from cultural amnesia regarding the horrific deeds of their ancestors.

BORWEIN: How does—if at all—your self-identification as Indigenous affect your horror aesthetics?

COLE: Colonisation visited horror upon Indigenous peoples. It is a horror that carries on today via intergenerational post-traumatic stress and current systems of colonial hegemony that we live under and that continue to visit colonial horror upon us, e.g., nuclear testing and ICBM testing in the Pacific, the prison industrial complex, the capitalist industrial complex, the patriarchy, racism, theft of our lands and resources, destruction of language and culture, the Anthropocene, climate change. I live this horror every day. So does every body on the planet. And I write about it.

BORWEIN: Do you actively engage with the knowledges, conventions, belief systems, metaphysical conditions of your culture(s)?

COLE: Yes.

BORWEIN: Can you describe in general terms the construction of "monstrous" or sinister figures in your narrative landscapes—if possible, using an example?

COLE: You only have to look to colonialism. For example, Captain James Cook is a figure of horror for us. He is a murderer, a purveyor of disease and fear. He paved the way for wholesale colonisation and the horror that came with it for Indigenous Pacific peoples and still pervades our lives today— massacre, death, destruction. The monstrosity of such figures, the horror of the many festivals and statues that continue to celebrate them as heroes in our lands and the rewriting of history that erases their horrific deeds, is a continuing state of horror for us.

BORWEIN: There is a discourse in relation to various Indigenous metaphysics on patterning, orientation, somatic/holistic experience, and ways of knowing. The Inuit artist Asinnajaq creates an encapsulated cinematic universe (in a 2017 short film) to inspect their ontological lens, and it is narrated in Inuktitut and incorporates manifestations of pattern moving between states, alongside the use of old ethnographic propaganda films, newsreels—as horror realism—landscape, and throat singing. Can you offer a representation of your lens or vision?

COLE: Colonisation sought to annihilate us. It failed.

BORWEIN: How do your representations of moments of horror relate to such a lens, within the constraints of the written word/world?

COLE: As Nalo Hopkinson wrote, our stories "take the meme of colonizing the natives and, from the experience of the colonizee, critique it, pervert it, fuck with it."

BORWEIN: Is there anything else you would like to speak about?

COLE: No.

EPILOGUE

DIS/INSP/SECTING GLOBAL INDIGENOUS HORROR

*NAOMI SIMONE BORWEIN, JUNE SCUDELER,
KRISTA COLLIER-JARVIS, AND KATRIN ALTHANS*

This epilogue functions as a conversation between select contributors to the volume. It is meant to *open up* an academic discussion about "Global Indigenous Horror" literature as a uniquely hybrid genre visible in this exploratory volume. Here, said contributors consider the "nature" of Horror as "genre," assessing its theorizing, actualization, and variations on approaches as well as the politics of certain popular trends, alongside heterogeneous or multifarious Indigenous ways of knowing—thus, exploring what "Indigenous h/Horror" looks like, and how it actually exists, from culturally specific perspectives. As outlined in the introduction, this book is at the intersection of some lively academic disputes surrounding, for instance,

1) approaches like de-Westernizing and decolonizing;
2) appropriation by white academics;
3) the labeling of Indigenous Horror through genre appellations, glossaries, and categorizations;
4) the use of Horror metaphors or translation concepts in relation to Indigenous culture(s), groupings, and frames of reference;
5) cross-cultural, hybrid "genre" analysis;

6) the cultural taboo of Horror subjects and respectful engagement with horror and stories via the genre;

7) the universalization of minority voices (as a Western construct); and

8) Eco-Horror, Folkloric Horror, Cosmic Horror, Apocalyptic Futurism, and Anthropocene discourses—which can situate, and fragment, Indigeneity within Global Horror criticism.

Explicitly addressing such terms, trends, and debates is meant to productively explore, utilize, and move beyond such controversies related to reading h/Horror across Indigenous and non-Indigenous epistemological structures. The volume *Global Indigenous Horror* is not "ethnographic" but seeks to evince ways of knowing Indigenous Horror in its entirety: from oral tradition to anthropological engagements and witness testimonies to Indigenous Modernity and contemporary production by Indigenous Horror writers/ creators. While others use Horror as a toolbox, here it is also applied to catalyze discussion, to actualize a field, and to access and share knowledges.

In line with its title "Dis/insp/secting *Global Indigenous Horror*," this epilogue asks, "What is Global Indigenous Horror?" in the contemporary moment, as a corollary to scholarly chapters, as critiques (Parts 1–3), and author interviews in Part 4. Thus, using a semiopen qualitative email interview method, Naomi Simone Borwein poses four questions (Q1–Q4) of Métis scholar June Scudeler, Mi'kmaw scholar Krista Collier-Jarvis, and Katrin Althans.

Q & A

BORWEIN Q1. What do you feel are the most relevant issues, contentions, debates (e.g., genre, de-Westernization, decolonialism, "white academics" [Cole 2006, 29], and cultural taboos) to address when discussing Global Indigenous Horror as a field, and particularly within literary studies? Are there effective ways to redress some of these tensions?

SCUDELER A1. First, I like Horror because it is a sneaky genre. It lures in people but can also pack a wallop of politics. *Get Out*, which has been placed under the umbrella of "smart horror," is the example that springs most readily to mind (Peele 2017). My students are excited to read Indigenous horror texts and watch Indigenous horror films because people don't usually think of Indigenous people working in the genre. For me, it is essential to situate Indigenous texts and films in their Nation-specific context. Eden Robinson

(Haisla/Heiltsuk) situates her novel *Monkey Beach* within Haisla ways of knowing but is also influenced by Stephen King; there isn't a dichotomy between the two. As Indigenous scholars, we are constantly battling the idea that all Indigenous people are the same, so it was important for me to write about the Métis rougarou. The rougarou is not only a scary creature but also a way to teach lessons about respect and the continuance of traditions.

ALTHANS A1. I think that those issues you mention as examples are indeed intertwined: when we debate genre, we necessarily need to debate de-Westernization and also need to reflect our own positions and cultural educations as white academics who cannot speak as cultural insiders (and sometimes are, as in my case, even far removed in geographical terms). The problem the field of Global Indigenous Horror is facing is, to my mind, one that cannot easily be resolved as there is a certain degree of ambiguity involved. What we have in mind when we speak of Horror is a Western genre with Western (literary) historiography and that is deeply embedded in Western culture. To use "Indigenous" as a qualifier for this kind of traditional horror then still puts Western ideas, concepts, and traditions of how Horror has to look and which stock elements need to be present center stage. The Indigenous aspects are mere addenda that are still read in primarily Western terms and understandings. When we demand to find new and more appropriate ways to talk about Indigenous Horror, we need to demand new frames of reference, frames that are grounded in Indigenous methodologies and cultures (as Naomi Simone Borwein does in a number of her texts). These frames, however, still need to respond to Western traditions if we are to still call it horror, as otherwise we would confuse elements of Indigenous onto-epistemologies with what those of us raised in Western cultural traditions read as horror even though it may be read differently, even contrarily, in the various Indigenous traditions, thus renaming, rethinking, and rebranding them.

I therefore think we should talk about Indigenous Horror in terms of a network of intertextualities, anchored in both Western traditions and Indigenous onto-epistemologies. This allows us to come to terms with the inherent ambiguities in Indigenous Horror as, for instance, different understandings of what constitutes reality, fiction, or the speculative. It allows us to read examples of Indigenous Horror within the cultural aesthetics of a Western horror tradition, as well as the legacies of colonial violence in horror terms, and at the same time to acknowledge Indigenous onto-epistemologies. Instead of falling, however, for the fallacy of once again centering a Western tradition (only this time acknowledging how fraught it is), we need to extend our resetting of our frames of references to the narratological level and consider elements of narration (narrator, plot structure, storytelling, etc.) alongside content. All those points I mention here (and more) can be understood as nodes in a network of intertextualities that (literary) examples of Indigenous Horror are connected to—some connections stronger, some weaker—and contemporary Indigenous Horror engages with all of them.

COLLIER-JARVIS A1. Issues and debates surrounding decolonialism, cultural taboos, pan-Indianism/pan-Indigeneity, identity, and "white academics" are and will continue to inform discussions about Indigenous horror and the Gothic. However, a dialectic about genre is particularly potent, as it affects the above-mentioned debates.

Michelle Burnham's article "Is There an Indigenous Gothic?" is one of the foremost pieces addressing the role of Indigenous works in relation to genre. The fact that Burnham's article is posed as a question highlights ongoing debates about inclusion within genre. Burnham notes how Gothic narratives by Indigenous peoples "represent Native American contributions to but also Native American interventions in American Gothic" (2014, 228), which is why they are garnering attention. The disruptive power of these texts, though, is exactly why they should be included within the genre. Lucie Armitt rightly claims that there is "limitless appetite" for the Gothic (2011, 1), and partly, this is due to its propensity to shift. As Maisha Wester and Xavier Aldana Reyes point out in *Twenty-First Century Gothic*, "[t]he Gothic's richness has grown exponentially, and part of the difficulty involved in delimiting it is that the mode has evolved into an artistic palimpsest with tendrils reaching out into virtually every connected genre and subgenre" (2019, 3–4). To suggest that Indigenous-made Gothic narratives are unique, and therefore sit outside the genre, overlooks the disruptive and amorphous power of the Gothic more broadly.

Arguably, the resistance to including Indigenous-authored texts in the genre is less about preserving some kind of "tradition" or authenticity and more so about the need to maintain an Other. Because Indigenous-made Gothic narratives are "overturning the kinds of possessive acts (possession by ghostly spirits, but also possession of material land) established by America's Gothic tradition" (Burnham 2014, 228), the question then becomes, who or what will haunt us. The American Dream (and the Canadian Dream) is partly predicated on "them" wanting what "we" have, and Gothic narratives rely upon the fear of "them" taking it from "us." However, as Burnham points out, Indigenous and non-Indigenous culture "braid together in a hybrid production of textual haunting" (2014, 230), collapsing distinctions between "them" and "us." As such, we would be remiss to exclude such rich contributions to the genres of horror and the Gothic to maintain a hypothetical Other.

While debates about genre in general, and Indigenous contributions to genre more specifically, are important and ongoing, a better question we might ask ourselves is: What does the inclusion of Indigenous voices in horror and the Gothic offer us? What was missing from our understanding of horror and the Gothic by not including Indigenous content, and therefore, what can horror and the Gothic gain from expanding our parameters of genre?

COLLIER-JARVIS (FOLLOW-UP TO Q1). In "Canadian Gothic," Cynthia Sugars addresses the seeming lack of a Gothic canon in Canada, owing its "absence" not to previous assertions that "there are no ghosts" but rather to the idea "that people are too blinkered to see them" (2012, 409). Sugars calls this a "desire for 'settled unsettlement' [that] informs much Canadian writing" (2012, 409). She goes on to note how "it is not the ghosts that haunt, but the fear that they are inadequate to the task" (2012, 409). As such, in Gothic discussions there seems to be a desire for "easy haunting" in the manner that informs European Gothic, owing to its long-chronicled history. Sugars was writing at a time when there was much debate in genre surrounding the inclusion and function of Canadian writing that drew on Gothic elements, and while these debates have never completely subsided, less attention seems to be paid in recent years to whether a particular text may be "Canadian Gothic" and instead focusing on what these texts suggest and unveil about Canadian culture and identity.

We can learn lessons from Canadian Gothic and the battle for its recognition as a subset of the Gothic. According to Sugars, Canadian Gothic "gave Aboriginal authors a means to 'write back' to the colonizing culture by reasserting their own understanding of the Canadian landscape as infused with indigenous spirits" (2012, 410). In this respect, Sugars was already including Indigenous voices in discussions of the Gothic. Indigenous Gothic, by comparison, though, engages with this form of writing back by existing within the context of Canadian Gothic, but also existing separate from it. The challenge then becomes identifying ways in which Indigenous Gothic exists as an inside/outside counterpart of the Canadian Gothic. I propose two such ways of rectifying this seeming bifurcation.

First, owing to the Gothic's resistance to the "newness" of nationhood, Indigenous inclusion in the Gothic provides space for authors and filmmakers to assert how elements that make up the Gothic existed precontact. For example, there are many Inuit stories that take up variations of the Qallupilluk—a figure that arises from the ocean and takes children if they wander too close to the edge of the ice floes. In Inuktitut, the traditional language of some Inuit, there is not a word for "monster," but the Qallupilluk functions similarly to what we would call monsters in other cultures. The term "monster" derives from "monstrum," meaning "that which warns" (Cohen 1996, 4), and tales of the Qallupilluk are told to children to warn them against wandering too close to the breaking ice. This is not to colonize the Qallupilluk within Westernized frameworks of monsters but rather to demonstrate how Western frameworks of monsters share much in common with precontact Indigenous stories and can therefore learn from them. Indigenous Gothic therefore demonstrates that while the term "Gothic" arose as a genre within Europe, it was being taken up by other cultures long before this. Can we therefore expand the Gothic prior to colonization? Second, Indigenous Gothic expands our understanding of how time functions on the land that is commonly called North America, which also goes by the Indigenous name Turtle Island. Indigenous conceptions of time, while varying by community, typically resist chronology, opting for the existence of past, present, and future simultaneously. For example, in Richard Van Camp's short story "On the Wings of This Prayer," the Indigenous narrator sends a message back in time with the help of a dream weaver to warn the dreamer/reader that the negative ecological impact of the Alberta Tar Sands will lead to the rise of zombies if things do not change (2013, 173). Van Camp's story asks us to rethink our concepts of time as well as our relationship to the land—we should be its stewards, not its reapers. Can we therefore expand the Gothic into the future? There is much to learn from including Indigenous voices in discussions of the Gothic, and there is also much to learn from including Indigenous Gothic within discussions of genre. The challenge really becomes unsettling Westernized narrative frameworks of body, time, and place in order to really make space for Indigenous Gothic to do great work. Consequently, perhaps we take up the suggestions put forth by Sugars: we must become unblinkered by making space for Indigenous Gothic to exist and paying attention to it, and we must accept that Indigenous Gothic narratives are, indeed, up to the task of haunting us. However, this ultimately requires us to accept the fact that Indigenous Gothic is not simply "settled unsettlement," at least, not yet.

BORWEIN Q2. What are the potentially beneficial aspects of this new field of research?

SCUDELER A2. Again, Horror is a good way to lure people into Indigenous "issues." Jeff Barnaby's (Mi'kmaq) film *Blood Quantum* is a good way to talk about Canada's Indian Act. A particular favorite novel is Blackfeet author Stephen Graham Jones's *The Only Good Indians* in which four Blackfeet men are stalked by Elk Head Woman after they break protocols by killing too many elk, particularly a pregnant elk. Sure, there is lots of gore in the novel, but it also prompts us to think about what tradition means in the twenty-first century for Indigenous peoples. The characters in the novel know they are breaking protocols but do it anyway, with deadly consequences.

ALTHANS A2. The field of Indigenous Horror expands the field of horror studies in much-needed ways, I think, because it decenters the European point of view on horror studies. Work in this field shows that Indigenous onto-epistemologies as well as narrative traditions must no longer be read as exotic ingredients added to a European genre (or even as unique selling points for literature written by non-Indigenous people), but as a means to reclaim and affirm Indigenous cultural beliefs. Scholarship in Indigenous Horror helps to highlight the ways in which Indigenous cultural expressions, be they literary, filmic, graphic, or entirely different, are not to be studied in anthropology departments but in the respective art departments and in the same ways in which European classics and contemporary cultural expressions are studied.

COLLIER-JARVIS A2. Indigenous horror has the potential to reinvigorate the role of story in history. In *Research through, with and as Storying*, Louise Gwenneth Phillips and Tracey Bunda elucidate that "[f]rom the Aboriginal point of view, story, in all its Aboriginal-language terms, has *always* been. [However, f]rom the white perspective, the word *story* emerged in English in the 1200s, derived from the Latin word *historia*, referring to an account of what had happened" (2018, 5). The authors go on to note that it was not until the 1500s that history and narrative separated, when history became a signifier of truth, and narrative, instead, became a signifier of untruth or fiction (2018, 5). This distinction is a settler one as Indigenous story does not necessarily distinguish between truth and fiction or between history and narrative. Because "history" in its modern-day understanding separated from story around the 1200s and narrative around the 1500s, everything that exists within these two capacities since then has largely stood outside history. This then becomes a large chunk of our history excluded from our "history." The potential of story and its iterations combined with the vital role it plays in many Indigenous communities leaves it poised with the potential to expand our understandings of history over the past eight hundred to nine hundred years. This becomes a kind of reconciliation via restory-ation.

BORWEIN Q3. How do you think a scholar can productively reconcile literary theorizing with ways of knowing in global Indigenous h/Horror?

SCUDELER Q3. I use Indigenous Literary Nationalism (ILN), which advocates using Nation-specific ways of knowing to analyze Indigenous texts. So, I used many Métis sources when writing about the rougarou. ILN is also a way of being humble when writing about a Nation different from your own, that some things are not meant for you but for the community that the author is from. Métis scholar Warren Cariou explains in "On Critical Humility," "I want to put forward a simple definition of humility as an openness to learning. As a mode of listening. A way of showing respect, to the world, to the people speaking, and to the gift of the universe itself" (2020, 6). We must accept that some stories are not for us, that we can understand some of the story but not in the way that someone from that community may understand it. This contradicts the extractive nature of academia. Unfortunately, horror is still seen as just genre fiction, but it needs to be treated with the same respect as all Indigenous literatures and films.

ALTHANS Q3. This is indeed a question I am not sure how to answer satisfactorily. I think what we are faced with here is the very same kind of ambiguity we are faced with when it comes to the subject matter of our research: literary theorizing is very much a product of Western (academic) traditions, whereas Indigenous ways of knowing are dismissed in that tradition. There is much discussion going on in the field of postcolonial studies at the moment, with efforts to decolonize both the syllabus and the approach itself. As becomes clear, however, often this kind of decolonization is still very much colonial in its premises, with nonwhite academics and thinkers still being excluded. And I think it is at this point that we need to start. First of all, Indigenous ways of knowing cannot be incorporated in our research without recourse to Indigenous people themselves. Non-Indigenous scholars not only need to acknowledge the work of Indigenous scholars, but they also necessarily need to use this work as authority on the topic. This is not to mean we should abandon traditional literary theorizing altogether, but rather that we should strive to read the one together with the other. Representations of Indigenous onto-epistemologies in Indigenous Horror at least engage with, if not stand in the tradition of, Western horror, and therefore invite readings informed by literary theory. At the same time, we need to refine the tool kits of our critical approaches to accommodate traditions different from Western standards. One example here is narratology: originally developed with European literary texts in mind, it has come to be applied to a variety of discourses from video games to history and sciences. However, that which allows the narratological tool kit to be used in order to analyze a broad variety of texts and discourses is its claim to universality. As such, narratology so far excludes approaches that do not share its understanding of what constitutes a narrative. Indigenous ways of storytelling, however, might differ considerably from the kind of narrative that narratology claims to be universal, as may the elements of narrative. Acknowledging this allows us as scholars of Indigenous Horror and other Indigenous cultural expressions to change our frames of reference and to critically assess the tools of our methodologies and research. On the one hand, this helps us to better understand and appreciate onto-epistemological as well as structural elements in Indigenous Horror that we were not aware of before, and on the other hand, it also helps to identify and fill in blind spots of literary theories and thus advances scholarship in the different fields.

COLLIER-JARVIS Q3. The first question we can ask ourselves when considering how a scholar can productively reconcile literary theorizing with ways of knowing in global Indigenous h/Horror is whether they are really that different.

According to *The Norton Anthology of Theory and Criticism*, "the complexity of the field of theory and criticism" encompasses an "expansive universe of issues and problems [that] engages ideas not only about literature, language, interpretation, genre, style, meaning, and tradition but also about subjectivity, ethnicity, race, gender, sexuality, class, culture, color, nationality, ideology, institutions, and historical periods" (Leitch 2010, 1). As such, Vincent B. Leitch envisions that "there is no position free of theory" (2010, 1). While this approach is somewhat simplistic on its own, Leitch does raise an important point about the study of literature—it is intimately woven with everything of which theory is designed to address and enhance our understandings. Indigenous ways of knowing are designed to accomplish similar goals, and because Indigenous narratives exist at various intersections in Leitch's survey of literary theory, it can be put into conversation with any and all literary theories that we study today.

For example, within Donna Haraway's ecofeminist studies lies a multi-species approach (sympoiesis) that is so reminiscent of Indigenous land-based approaches, such as the Mi'kmaw concept of *Netukulimk*, that one would think Haraway conceived her theories in conversation with Indigenous peoples. In fact, in *Staying with the Trouble* (2016), Haraway makes mention throughout of Indigenous approaches to nature to better explain her theories. As such, a broader and more inclusive understanding of Indigenous horror arises from placing Haraway's ideas in conversation with *Netukulimk* rather than treating these theories and ways of knowing as each existing in a vacuum.

BORWEIN Q4. Is there one aspect of this research that you feel is particularly important, and why?

SCUDELER Q4. Again, not to see Indigenous horror under the wide umbrella of Indigeneity but to situate it within specific contexts. Yes, you can enjoy the horror, but look for deeper meanings in the text or film. What do I need to know to approach the text with respect?

ALTHANS Q4. I think the most important aspect is to acknowledge Indigenous ways of knowing and methodologies as equal to Western ways and methodologies. Instead of universalizing Western concepts, together with their inherent bias, research needs to incorporate a wide variety of different concepts and to thus decolonize its approaches. This includes not only examining Indigenous ways of knowing but also treating Indigenous scholars as the authorities they are and accepting, for example, oral traditions of knowledge transmission into the canon of research methodologies, as in the case of citing references. To make it a necessary condition to refer to recordings of oral testimonies, transmissions, or knowledge in academia instead of acknowledging oral testimonies in their own right as a proper source is just another one of the ways in which the structures of colonialism are maintained in academia.

COLLIER-JARVIS Q4. Indigenous horror provides Indigenous Nations and individuals with the opportunity to redress trauma and intergenerational trauma. Horror, absolutely, has the potential to trigger; however, it also has the potential to enact positive emotions or outcomes. For example, a 2018 study by Mathias Clasen, Jens Kjeldgaard-Christiansen, and John A. Johnson asserts that horror in general allows individuals to "enter a positive feedback loop by which they attain adaptive mastery through coping with virtual simulated danger," but only if they can "brave the initially aversive response to simulate threats" (2018, 213). Additionally, the viewer's "lingering fear after horror . . . [results in an] elicitation of positive emotions" (Clasen, Kjeldgaard-Christiansen, and Johnson 2018, 215). While not always true, of course, horror in general can have positive outcomes, which can also be true of Indigenous horror.

For example, in a paper I presented at the conference Mass Violence and Its Lasting Impact on Indigenous Peoples: The Case of the Americas and Australia/Pacific Region at the University of Southern California Dornsife Center for Advanced Genocide Research, I reckon with being an intergenerational residential school survivor by lobbying for the power of representation in

Indigenous-made horror, specifically Jeff Barnaby's (Mi'kmaw) residential school film *Rhymes for Young Ghouls* (2013). I argue there is no full first-person account of the residential school experience similar to the double-self that is pervasive in Holocaust literature; Adrienne Kertzer argues that "even the survivor often admits that what she witnessed in the death camps was witnessed by a different self, and only that self understands" (1999, 240). This means that even those who survive (the traumatized selves) are not those who endured the initial experience; therefore, there is no real witness here, even in the residential school memoirs and photographs, so by extension, no real account of the residential school experience. Essentially, all we really have is representation. As such, intergenerational survivors such as Barnaby must draw on the power of representation to understand the trauma he has inherited.

In my chapter in this collection, "Oka-Nada: Historical Contagion and Haunting Back in Jeff Barnaby's *Blood Quantum*," I assert that Jeff Barnaby argues that Indigenous horror "is an Indigenous form of reconciliation" (Leggatt 2019), and that Amy Gore (2018), who pinpoints Indigenous Gothic as "site[s] of subversion," also notes how monsters and supernatural beings in Indigenous novels "contribute to healing" for Indigenous peoples. Reconciliation is an ongoing process rather than an end, so Indigenous Gothic and horror join the ranks of Indigenous cultural forms of resistance. The potential to resist and to reckon with trauma and intergenerational trauma posits Indigenous Horror as a particularly powerful subgenre.

Addendum by Borwein

This epilogue engages scholarly contributors in a more informal discussion than appears in their respective chapters of the construction of Indigenous horror within and as a new field or genre. Responses to interview questions move from exploring horror as an entry point for discourse to proposing actionable methods, such as "Indigenous Literary Nationalism" (ILN) as advocated by Métis scholar June Scudeler, despite the many contentions surrounding ILN as outlined by Kristina Fagan and colleagues (2009), Elvira Pulitano (2003), and Jace Weaver, Craig S. Womack, and Robert Warrior in the volume *American Indian Literary Nationalism* (2006). By reframing epistemological engagements with horror, contributors to this epilogue extend simultaneous actualization of "comparative" conceptual approaches (my contribution and that of Krista Collier-Jarvis). Modern Global Indigenous Horror is the problematic site of hybrid (Indigenous and non-Indigenous as well as intertribal) contemporary productions that are the output of many originary modes, stories, and spaces, and should privilege self-identifying Indigenous writers and their practices. The ultimate goal of this volume is to expound this hybrid site of production, or nexus, catalyze respectful discussions, and offer such an approach (invested with love, humility, respect, and reciprocity) as an empowering tool for Indigenous scholars, writers, and their allies. (For instance, as part of a methodological approach, set contributors to this volume contacted the writers whose work they analyzed, provided preprints, and asked for feedback.) *Global Indigenous Horror* does not seek to portray a genre utilizing purely Indigenous origins. It assumes a hybrid, Indigenous modernity in which Indigenous artistic Horror and dark speculative creations continue to develop an aesthetic/style with roots in both non-Indigenous and Indigenous traditions. A redefinition *process* is necessary, even if definition—lensing, labeling—itself is orthogonal to the endpoint: "defy[ing] genre" as it traditionally exists (Dan Rabarts, Interview B in this volume). Part of that process is conceiving of Indigenous horror and its overlapping apprehensions and visions. Developing a new "tool kit" for Indigenous Horror fiction that resonates with ways of knowing, and theorizing or actualizing, conceptualisms is imperative. Unwriting, whitewashing, or "canceling" the complex hybrid history/histories/pasts/futures/storyings and transcoded discourses and epistemologies is not the answer—unsettle, haunt back, and empower.

GRAND CHALLENGES TO THE RESEARCH COMMUNITY

1. To use Horror as tool for balanced, actionable outcomes in this new field;
2. To expand scholarship on self-identifying practitioners through their own stylistics and actualizations; and
3. To read "Global Indigenous Horror literature" as an overlapping dynamic form, its constituent parts and influences in tandem with ways of knowing, and thus expand scholarship in a respectful manner.

BIBLIOGRAPHY

Armitt, Lucie. 2011. *History of the Gothic: Twentieth Century Gothic*. Cardiff: University of Wales Press.

Burnham, Michelle. 2014. "Is There an Indigenous Gothic?" In *A Companion to American Gothic*, edited by Charles L. Crow, 223–37. Chichester, W. Susx., England: John Wiley and Sons.

Cariou, Warren. 2020. "On Critical Humility." *Studies in American Indian Literatures* 32, nos. 3–4 (Fall–Winter): 1–12.

Clasen, Mathias, Jens Kjeldgaard-Christiansen, and John A. Johnson. 2018. "Horror, Personality, and Threat Simulation: A Survey on the Psychology of Scary Media." *Evolutionary Behavioral Sciences* 14, no. 3 (November): 213–30.

Cohen, Jeffrey Jerome. 1996. "Monster Culture (Seven Theses)." In *Monster Theory: Reading Culture*, edited by Jeffrey Jerome Cohen, 3–25. Minneapolis: University of Minnesota Press.

Cole, Peter. 2006. *Coyote and Raven Go Canoeing: Coming Home to the Village.* Montreal: McGill–Queen's University Press.

Fagan, Kristina, Keavy Martin, Deanna Reder, Daniel Heath Justice, Sam McKegney, and Niigonwedom James Sinclair. 2009. "Canadian Literary Nationalism? Critical Approaches in Canadian Indigenous Contexts: A Collaborative Interlogue." *Canadian Journal of Native Studies* 29, nos. 1–2: 19–44.

Gore, Amy. 2018. "Gothic Silence: S. Alice Callahan's *Wynema*, the Battle of the Little Bighorn, and the Indigenous Unspeakable." *Studies in American Indian Literatures* 30, no. 1 (Spring): 24–49.

Haraway, Donna J. 2016. *Staying with the Trouble: Making Kin in the Chthulucene.* Durham, NC: Duke University Press.

Kertzer, Adrienne. 1999. "'Do You Know What 'Auschwitz' Means?' Children's Literature and the Holocaust." *The Lion and the Unicorn* 23, no. 2: 238–56.

Leggatt, Judith. 2019. "Reconciliation, Resistance, and *Biskaabiiyang*: Re-imagining Canadian Residential Schools in Indigenous Speculative Fictions." In *Canadian Science Fiction, Fantasy, and Horror: Bridging the Solitudes*, edited by Amy J. Ransom and Dominick Grace, 135–49. Cham, Switzerland: Palgrave Macmillan.

Leitch, Vincent B. 2010. "Introduction to Theory and Criticism." In *The Norton Anthology of Theory and Criticism*, 2nd ed., edited by Vincent B. Leitch, 1–33. New York: W. W. Norton.

Peele, Jordan, dir. 2017. *Get Out.* Monkeypaw Productions.

Phillips, Louise Gwenneth, and Tracey Bunda. 2018. *Research through, with and as Storying.* Abingdon, Oxon., England: Routledge.

Pulitano, Elvira. 2003. *Toward a Native American Critical Theory.* Lincoln: University of Nebraska Press.

Robinson, Eden. 2000. *Monkey Beach.* Boston: Houghton Mifflin Harcourt.

Sugars, Cynthia. 2012. "Canadian Gothic." In *A New Companion to the Gothic*, edited by David Punter, 409–27. Hoboken, NJ: Blackwell Publishing.

USC Dornsife Center for Advanced Genocide Research. 2022. "Saving the Child within the Indian: Representing the Residential School Experience." YouTube, November 12. https://youtu.be/wo4OrYQXjbc.

Van Camp, Richard. 2013. "On the Wings of This Prayer." In *Dead North: Canadian Zombie Fiction*, edited by Silvia Moreno-Garcia, 164–73. Holstein, ON: Exile Editions.

Weaver, Jace, Craig S. Womack, and Robert Warrior. 2006. *American Indian Literary Nationalism.* Albuquerque: University of New Mexico Press.

Wester, Maisha and Xavier Aldana Reyes. 2019. "Introduction: The Gothic in the Twenty-First Century." In *Twenty-First-Century Gothic: An Edinburgh Companion*, edited by Maisha Wester and Xavier Aldana Reyes, 1–16. Edinburgh: Edinburgh University Press.

About the Contributors

KATRIN ALTHANS holds an MA in English, German, and media studies from the University of Münster, Germany, as well as a German law degree. She received her PhD in English literature and culture from the University of Bonn, Germany, in 2010 with her book *Darkness Subverted: Aboriginal Gothic in Black Australian Literature and Film*. Her main research areas include law and literature, refugee and forced migration studies, and Australian studies as well as Gothic studies; and she has published widely on a variety of topics covering anglophone literatures from the nineteenth to the twenty-first centuries. Currently, Katrin is a DFG-funded research fellow at the University of Duisburg-Essen, Germany, and working on her second book, *Narratives of Refugees in Law and Literature*.

JAYSON ALTHOFER is an independent scholar based in Toowoomba, Australia, on Country of the Giabal and Jarowair peoples. He works as a curator and research librarian at Toowoomba Regional Art Gallery. His publications include chapters in *The Graveyard in Literature: Liminality and Social Critique*, edited by Aoileann Ní Éigeartaigh (Cambridge Scholars Publishing, 2022), *TEXTile Manifestoes*, edited by Pavel Liška and Robin R. Mudry (Vysoká škola uměleckoprůmyslová v Praze, 2022), and *Microtravel: Confinement, Deceleration, Microspection*, edited by Charles Forsdick, Zoë Kinsley, and Kathryn Walchester (Anthem Press, 2024); and chapters cowritten with Brian Musgrove in *Representing Childhood and Atrocity*, edited by Victoria Nesfield and Philip Smith (State University of New York Press, 2022), and *Gothic Dreams and Nightmares*, edited by Carol Margaret Davison (Manchester University Press, 2024).

NAOMI SIMONE BORWEIN is an academic and a poet. A research associate at Western University in London, Ontario, she teaches at the University of Windsor, which sits on the traditional territory of Three Fires Confederacy of First Nations. Naomi holds a PhD in English literature from the University of Newcastle, Australia, where she studied Aboriginal literature and ways of knowing with Murri scholar Dr. Brooke Collins-Gearing. Naomi's research spans from heterogenous Indigenous literatures, Horror and the Gothic, global anglophone literatures, and historiography to experimental mathematics and its philosophy, and she has published across a broad spectrum of topics. Her research on Indigenous Horror has been reviewed as groundbreaking.

PERSEPHONE BRAHAM is a professor of Spanish and Latin American studies at the University of Delaware. Her research is on monsters and monstrosity in Latin America, and she also writes and teaches about Latin American film, urban space and power, gender and sexuality, and genre fiction. Her book *From Amazons to Zombies* was described by commentator Joseph Pierce as "[a]n accessible and super generative study of how monstrosity—including the cannibal—was a trope used by European colonizers because they were idiots."

KRISTA COLLIER-JARVIS (Mi'kmaw) is a PhD candidate at Dalhousie University and an assistant professor for the Department of English at Mount Saint Vincent University in Halifax, Nova Scotia. Her Social Sciences and Humanities Research Council–funded research applies Indigenous epistemologies to twenty-first-century contagion narratives. In doing so, she draws on the proliferation of zombie narratives to develop a more interconnected multispecies approach that engenders new ways of understanding contagion and climate change. Her other research interests include US and Indigenous Gothic, horror, popular culture, and climate fiction.

SHANE HAWK (enrolled Cheyenne-Arapaho, Hidatsa, and Citizen Potawatomi descent) is a history teacher by day and a horror writer by night. Hawk coedited the international best-selling anthology *Never Whistle at Night* and is the author of *Anoka: A Collection of Indigenous Horror* and other short fiction featured in numerous anthologies. He lives in San Diego with his beautiful wife, Tori. Learn more by visiting shanehawk.com.

JADE JENKINSON recently received her doctorate from the University of Nottingham, UK. Her thesis, which she is currently developing into a monograph, compares Gothic depictions of education within bildungsroman-style novels and films produced in the United States, Australia, and Canada in light of genocidal settler-colonial educational policies toward Indigenous peoples and women's educational experiences in patriarchal institutions. Jade has previously worked in the role of production editor for the *Journal of Languages, Texts, and Society*. She is currently working as a copy editor for Wales University Press's Gothic series and on the British Association for American Studies' Code of Conduct board. She has recently completed a fellowship at the Virginia Museum of History and Culture, where she examined the production of colonial memory in the tourist environment.

JUNE SCUDELER (Métis) is an assistant professor in the Department of Indigenous Studies, cross-appointed with the Department of Gender, Sexuality, and Women's Studies at Simon Fraser University, located on the traditional territories of the xʷməθkʷəy̓əm (Musqueam), Skwxwú7mesh Úxwumixw (Squamish), səlilwəta l (Tsleil-Waututh), and kʷikʷəλəm (Kwikwetlem) Nations. Her research encompasses queer Indigenous studies, literature, film, and art. She is currently delving into Indigenous Horror.

SABRINA ZACHARIAS is a settler scholar and a PhD candidate at Queen's University in Kingston, Ontario. Her research focuses on marginalized identities in Victorian literature and neo-Victorian literature, with an interest in how the Gothic is used in representations of marginalized identities.

INDEX

Aboriginal and Torres Strait Islanders, 130–31, 137n1, 149, 231

Aboriginal art, 206–37. *See also* Watson, Judy

Aboriginal Australian: "Blackfella," 6; constellations, 80; cultures, 80; epistemology, 100n6; Horror, 10–12; land-based knowledge, 17; language, 270; pictogram, 80; silencing/voiding of history, 209; southern lights, 80; textual and visual arts, 21

Aboriginal Australian Dreaming, 10–11, 79, 91, 132, 210, 228; maps, 210; metaphysics, 11; nightmares of the Dreaming, 132; synchronic immersiveness, 228. *See also* Dreaming

Aboriginal bodies, 214, 220, 222

Aboriginal Fantastic, 120n1, 130

Aboriginal Gothic, 135, 209–11, 213–15, 217, 224, 227, 230; denialist toxicity, 231; Djon Mundine, 213; ghostly traces, 215; style, 212

Aboriginal mob, 10, 133, 217, 220

Aboriginal onto-epistemologies, 125, 130, 132, 134, 136

Aboriginal/aboriginal, capitalization, 5

Aboriginality, 214, 224, 228; animism, 132; cartography, 229; constructs, 86; dark aspects of the Dreaming, 132; destructive actions, 207; levels of being, 114; mythology, 132; settler-colonial imaginings of, 214; theoretical, 94–95; totemism, 132; ways of knowing, 112

active reader, 193–95

acts: of resistance, 188, 193; of survivance, 23n5, 187, 202; of witnessing, 196

actualization/actualizing, 5, 7, 8, 13–14, 21, 94, 115, 189, 264–65, 274–75; actualized adaptive theorizing, 95; actualized aesthetics and styles, 22; alternative futures, 189; theory, 13

aesthetic(s): action, 181n11; aesthetics/(not) aesthetics, 23n1; care, 181n11; of excess, 193, 195, 199; Gothic, 14; of horror, 166–67, 171, 178, 181n11; Indigeneity, 111; Kantian and pre-Kantian sensory engagement, 181n11; of seeing, 193, 195, 199

agency, 4, 36, 92, 96, 99n3, 112, 115, 131, 137, 172

Ajean, Elder (character), 33, 43–44, 47n8

alcohol, 46–47, 53, 65

Alexie, Sherman, 5; *Indian Killer*, 174

allegory, 13, 80, 113

Althans, Katrin, 10–11, 21–22, 132, 135, 164, 181n4, 213, 216–17, 226

American Dream, 65, 267

American Indian Literary Nationalism (Weaver, Womack, and Warrior), 23n7, 274

American Indian Movement (AIM), 169, 170, 182n17

ancestors, 76, 83, 108, 210, 215, 217, 223, 262; epistemology, 210; ghosts, 214; knowledges, 163

Andean Horror, 21, 152–55, 156n12; body snatcher/vampirical fat stealer/soul stealer motif, 152; films, 151–52, 154, 156n12; monstrous figures, 152; *pishtaco*, 152; regional horror cinema (*cine de terror andino*), 151–52, 155; violence of colonial history, 152

animism, 117. *See also* Cosmic Horror

Anishinaabe: language, 79; shapeshifters, 33–34; teachings, 36

Anthropocene, 17, 77, 92, 99n5, 100n8, 262, 265; apocalyptic, 17; as eco-racial, 99n5; decolonial rhetoric of, 92; discourses, 265

Anthropocene and the Undead, The (Bacon), 17

antigenre, 108

Antlers (Cooper), 245

Antoine, Dene Elder Jonas, 76, 81; northern lights, 86–87; whistle, 87

Aotearoa, 89, 112, 114, 117; "land of the long white cloud," 89, 112, 117

apocalypse, 6, 94, 111, 119, 186, 190; allusions, 112; biological warfare, 190; chic, 100n8; colonial world, 203; discourse, 6; eco-horror, 95; forced starvation, 190; horror, 8–9, 99n5, 166; light, 110, 119; non-Indigenous Horror, 112; Sci-Fi futurist literature, 112; themes and tropes, 112; vogues, 18; way of knowing, 111; world, 187–88

Apocalypse Now (Coppola), 227

Apocalyptic Futurism, 18, 265

appropriation, 4, 114, 249, 264; fictions, 16; folklore, legends, and symbols, 245; white academics, 264

Araluen, Evelyn, 214–15; *Dropbear*, 214; "The Trope Speaks," 215

Arapaho, 4, 20–21, 76, 108, 241, 244

archive, 131, 149, 219, 223–25, 229; ethnographic, 149; site of bloodshed and genealogy, 223; third, 131

archive of knowledge: Aboriginal, 131; embodied in Country, 131; living snow, 80. *See also* comets of knowledge

artifacts, 108, 134, 207, 209, 222

Ashcroft, James, *Coming Home in the Dark*, 10

Asinnajaq (Isabella Weetaluktuk): cinematic universe, 252, 255, 259, 262; glacial landscape, 114; Indigenous land-water-based epistemologies, 9; innovative reorientations, 9

Asma, Stephen T., 129

assimilation, 68, 70, 132, 163; cultural and spiritual, 43; forced, 50; governmental policies, 164–65, 195

Attridge, Derek, *The Singularity of Literature*, 133

audience, 24, 53, 62, 94, 118, 127–28, 141–42, 147, 151–52, 155, 167, 179, 194, 199, 246, 250, 257, 261

aurora, 79, 81, 86–87, 91, 96–97, 99, 107, 120; constellation of meanings, 83; definition of, 78; fragmented parts, 110; Indigenous interpretation of metaphor, 98, 110; levels of materiality, 83; matrices of knowledge, 81; myth, 97, 110; mythologizing, 86; oral myths, 87; place of ancestral stories, 91; popular culture, 86; popular use of, 84; romanticizing, 86; system, 83; system of thinking and knowing, 91; textualization, 108; translation of, 97, 110; visual arrays and particulate relations, 89

aurora australis: apocalyptic light, 119; Indigeneity, 77; planetary apocalypse, 78, 249

aurora borealis: Dene Elder Jonas Antoine, 76; Ed-Thin, 97; light and the cosmos, 9, 77–78, 86; multisensory immersion/dispersion, 89; northern lights, 76–77, 86, 107; *Three Thousand*, 114. *See also* Asinnajaq (Isabella Weetaluktuk)

Australian(s): Aboriginal blood, 206; colonial horrors, 209; Gothic fiction, 21, 136, 216–17, 227; Indigenous cultures, 176; predatory colony, 208

Ayala, Felipe Guamán Poma de, *Nueva corónica y buen gobierno*, 153

Aymara, 140, 152; *kharisiri*, 152

Aztec horror, 142–45

azteca (Aztec), 144

Baledón, Rafael, *La maldición de La Llorona*, 145

Barclay, Barry: Fourth Cinema, 5, 10, 81; Māori ways of knowing, 5, 81

Barnaby, Jeff, 15, 50–51, 58, 60, 62–69, 164, 243, 269, 274; *Rhymes for Young Ghouls*, 164, 274. See also *Blood Quantum* (Barnaby)

Barthes, Roland, 24n17, 100n9, 175; "neutral" Zero Degree Theory, 24n17

Beaucage, Marjorie (RainbowWarrior), *Rougarou*, 45–47

being, 8–9, 11–13, 37, 41, 69, 77, 80, 85, 87–90, 92, 94–96, 98–100, 113–19, 135, 147, 154, 170, 182n18, 190, 271, 274; and becoming, 9, 85; and co-becoming, 117; Navajo states of being and becoming, 9; states of, 89–90, 92

Belcourt, Billy-Ray: approach to decolonization, 51; haunting, 58

Bello, Lalo Parra, 152–53

B'gwus (Sasquatch), 178

Bhabha, Homi K., 24n17

biculturalism, definition of, 54–55

binary(ies), 4–5, 14, 19, 23n1, 24n12, 35, 47n9, 61, 65–66, 68, 174–75, 176, 181n9; dialectic, 68; Indigenous and non-Indigenous, 5; self/Other, 174

bioluminescence, 97, 110, 119

BIPOC, 23n2

Black, C. F., 130

Black Cranes (Murray and Flynn), 250

Black Marks on the White Page (Ihimaera and Makereti), 7–8, 83

Blackfoot bee, 83–84

Blackfoot/Blackfeet, 13, 17, 21, 76, 83–84, 90, 118, 254, 269

Blak: authors, 130; cosmology, 134; experiences, 125, 137n1; horrors, 133; perspective, 136; realities of Blak scholars, 131; storytelling, 126, 132; term, 137n1; women, 126

Blak Horror, 21, 125–26, 130–36; nature of, 125–37; as shapeshifter, 137

Blak narratology, 11, 21, 125–37; taboo, 137

Blak onto-epistemologies, 125, 134–36; cultural pride and respect, 136; monster of in Gothic terms, 135; monstrous colonialism, 125

Blood Quantum (Barnaby), 15, 50–51, 55, 58–60, 64–66, 243, 269, 274; Charlie, 58, 67, 69; Gisigu, 59, 61–63, 69; immunity, 60; Joseph and Joss, 58, 69; Lysol, 61, 64–65; Mi'kmaw, 58; reconciliation, 274; Red Crow Indian Reservation, 58, 64, 66; as zombie film, 50–71

blood quantum (law), 58, 66–67, 70

bodies: Aboriginal, 220; Aboriginal Gothic, 215; celestial, 111; corruption of, 108–9, 259; First Nations, 214; Indigenous, 50–51, 60, 68, 149, 199; institutional, 179; mathematical, 80; Moloch, 222; monsters as cultural, 35; Ríos Montt and disposal of, 155n7; Settler, 67

Body Horror, 208–9, 245; abstracted, 209

Borwein, Naomi Simone, ix, 8, 10–12, 22, 82, 130–32, 210, 213, 218, 225, 227–30; definition of Indighorror, 132; Dreaming, 132

Botting, Fred, 15, 166, 171, 175, 179, 192–93, 201; barbarity, superstition, and fear, 201; definition of Gothic excess, 175; two strands of ethics, 171

Bradbury, Ray, *Fahrenheit 451*, 115

braiding and weaving, 89; braids, 12, 86, 89, 113, 118, 267

Bram Stoker Award, 118, 250, 254

Bridle, James, *Ways of Being*, 8, 90

"Bringing Them Home" report, 164

Britain, 54–55, 207, 227; invasion and occupation, 207

British Museum, 206–9, 211, 222, 227

Bronfman, Charles R.: Canadianism, 54; CRB Foundation Heritage Project, 52, 54

Brontë, Charlotte, *Jane Eyre*, 182n16

Bronze Age: place-based, 93; star/infinity pool, 93–94

Buñuel, Luis, *Los olvidados*, 155n5

Burnham, Michelle, "Is There an Indigenous Gothic?," 51, 66, 164, 166, 174, 191, 213–14, 226, 267

Bustamante, Jayro, 145, 146, 147, 148, 154, 155; *Ixcanul*, 145–46; *La Llorona*, 146–48, 155

Cabot, John: *Canadian Heritage Minute*, 51–53, 55–56, 61; foundation myth, 51, 59; 1497 voyage, 52, 56; stories of, 51

Campbell, Maria, 34, 36, 38–40, 44, 46, 47; female rougarou, 36; "Josephine Jug of Wine," 39–40, 46; "Rou Garous," 38; *Stories of the Road Allowance People*, 38; storytelling, 47

Canada, 21, 33, 51–58, 64, 67, 70, 84, 94, 163–65, 170, 181n6, 187, 243, 268–69; collective memory and identity, 53; culture and identity, 268; decentering Canadian history, 64; government, 37, 53, 56; identity, 54, 55, 57, 71n5; popular narrative of, 52

Canadian Dream, 65, 267

Canadian Gothic, 51, 191

Canadian Heritage Minute(s), 52–57, 61, 70

Cannibal Holocaust (Deodato), 151

cannibals/cannibalism, 122, 149–50, 152–53, 155n9, 156, 214, 221–22; brain hunters, 154; "Cannibal Law," 150; cannibalistic component of art viewers, 222; colonial, 221; and ethnographers, 155n9; exploitation of the Amazon, 151; figure of, 172, 244; Latin America, 155n9; metaphor for extractivist systems, 153; monsterization, 15; transmutation, 149; Western education and evangelism, 149; zombies, 154

capitalism, 100n8, 171, 208, 210–11

Cardona, René, *La Llorona*, 145

Cariou, Warren, 34–35, 37, 164, 166, 271; "Dances with Rigoureau," 34, 37; "On Critical Humility," 271

Carrol, Noël, 6, 127; art-horror, 127; *The Philosophy of Horror*, 127

Carroll, Lewis, *Alice's Adventures in Wonderland*, 188, 193, 196

Castricano, Jodey, 178, 191, 198, 201; on Eden Robinson's work, 191, 198; "learning to live," 201

Catholicism, 36–39, 146

cautionary tales, 33, 39, 45, 108, 245

celestial phenomena, 80–81, 88–89, 110

Cherokee, 11–12, 21, 118, 180, 188, 197, 209; people, 209; trickster, 197

Chi Kaw Chee (character), 40, 47n6

Chípiy (Ghost) (character), 200–201, 203

Christians/Christianity, 33–34, 36, 37, 40–42, 150, 152, 154, 173, 175–76; cannibalism, 152; crazy tales, 150; strictures, 33, 37

chullachaki, 149–50, 155n8

cine regional, 141, 151–52

cinefantastic horror, 181n13

circle(s), 10, 20, 89, 90–91, 114, 117–18; fanatical Catholic prayer, 146; of hell, 226; Mauna Kea/Loa, 117; Navajo, 89, 90; pictogram, 11; perfect, 114; stone, 91; of tepees, 118; White Australian, 229; yarning, 20

civilization, 38, 42, 61, 116, 150–51, 220, 224–25

civilizing recipes, 219–20. *See also* Lindsay, Norman: *The Magic Pudding*

classifications: genre, 85; genre systems, 6; organic, 24n14; systems of thought, 22

climate change, 90, 111, 245, 262

Coatlicue and Cihuacóatl, 155n2. *See also* legends

co-becoming, 10, 77, 82, 114; and becoming, 98; theory and practice, 82

cod, 52, 55–57, 59–60, 70; consummation of, 55; fishing industry, 56; fishing regulations, 70; moratorium, 56; representation of, 55; zombieverse, 20

Cohen, Jeffrey Jerome: cultural bodies, 35; "Monster Culture (Seven Theses)," 128; *Monster Theory*, 35

Cole, Gina, ix, 5, 12, 21, 78–79, 81, 83, 108, 110, 112, 119; *Black Ice Matter*, 114, 261; *Na Viro*, 78–79, 110, 112–13; whirlpool metaphor, 12, 78, 81, 109–10, 112

Cole, Peter, 3, 7, 10, 83, 100n7; *Coyote and Raven Go Canoeing*, 3, 7, 83; hybrid orality, 7; i/teriture, 7, 10, 84; rebukes, 7; ways of theorizing, 10

collective memory, 53–55

INDEX   287

colonial history, 71, 78, 208

colonial Horror, 134, 202, 209, 229, 262

colonial imagery, 195, 198

colonial power, 4, 6, 97, 165, 167

colonial violence, 134–35, 266

colonialism, 11, 13, 23n1, 39, 63, 78, 128, 134, 149, 153, 155, 167, 173, 187, 192–94, 202–3, 207–8, 215, 221, 249, 262, 273; Anglo-Australian, 11; explorations of colonialism's ongoing reality, 189; specter of victims, 92; structures of, 273

colonization, 6, 33, 39, 41–42, 47, 51, 68, 95, 173, 187, 208, 215, 262, 268, 269; active, 191; colonizer spaces, 42; and colonizers, 35, 37, 38–39, 41–42, 50, 53, 192, 197–98, 212; discourses, 42; and genocide, 257; and hegemonic religion, 249; Portuguese, 140; space, 201; Spanish, 140; stories, 40; ways of thinking, 34

comets of knowledge, 79, 99, 108, 112, 120

comics, 21, 186–203; form, 187, 203n5; Gothic in, 193; gutter spaces, 193–96, 199; and popular culture, 186; as resistance, 203n5; textual and visual aspects, 195

community, 4, 33–34, 36, 39–41, 43–45, 61, 151

conceptualization, 5, 8–9, 24, 107; conceptual framing, 82; conceptualizing, actualizing, and visualizing, 7; conceptualization-actualization framework, 20; conceptualization-actualization-visualization framework, 19; radical, 214

conciliatory, as term, 203n1

Conrad, Joseph, *Heart of Darkness*, 227

constellations, 9, 19, 79–80, 82, 92, 113

contagion, 50 51, 57–58, 60, 62, 64, 98, 109, 274; historical, 50–71, 274; narratives, 98; stories as, 70; theories, 108

Cortés, Hernán, 142–43

Cosmic Horror, 15, 18, 117, 265

cosmology, 13, 85, 91–92, 128, 134; cosmic order, 113; cosmogonic space, 111; cosmological/cosmogonic meaning, 95; mappings, 110, 119; myth, 77

counternarratives, 57, 81, 175

Country, 91, 130–31, 210, 215, 218, 228; interconnectivity, 210; matrilineal, 208. *See also* Aboriginal Australian; Dreaming

Creation, 9, 13, 78, 80, 85, 99, 110, 115, 119; holistic logic of tales, 94; Inuit, 9, 87; Māori framework, 10; myths, 5, 80, 113; narratives, 112; sacred, 5; stories, 17, 80–88, 92, 115, 118

Cree, 4, 15, 21, 33–34, 36, 39, 44, 47n4, 76, 84, 91, 164, 188–89, 199–200; Chípiy (Ghost), 203n6; epistemology, 84; people, 39; shapeshifter stories, 33–34; spirituality, 200; teachings, 36. *See also* Nêhiýaw ceremonial teepee

crows, 175–77

Cruikshank, Julie: *Do Glaciers Listen?*, 95–96, 114; glaciers, 95–96; shapeshifters, 96; Tlingit traditions, 96

cultural amnesia, 173, 262

cultural anxieties, 127, 192

cultural biases, 137, 250

cultural codes, 133, 136

cultural erasure, ix, 150

cultural insiders, 137, 266

cultural lenses, 8, 191

cultural mummification, 214, 225; and Frantz Fanon, 214

cultural outsiders, 128, 151, 169

cure, 44–45, 57, 70, 149. *See also* immunity; rougarou

curse: ancient Indigenous Mexican, 144; *Ghost Bird*, 134; *jarjachas*, 154; La Llorona, 145–46; La Malinche, 143; rougarou, 38, 42

debates, 3, 5–6, 11, 16, 21–22, 82, 265–68; academic, 4; Black versus Blackfella, 6; capitalization, 6; cultural taboos, 267; decolonialism, 267; identity, 267; Indigenized/Indigenizing, 5–6; labels/labeling, 5; pan-Indianism/pan-Indigeneity, 267; popular, 4; syntax, 6; "white academics," 267

288 INDEX

decolonial aesthetics, 4, 6, 22, 24n14

decolonialism, 4, 6, 11, 14–15, 18, 22, 24n14, 51, 60, 85, 92–93, 100n8, 188, 224, 263, 265, 267, 271

Deleuze, Gilles, and Félix Guattari, 77, 99n6

demons, 128, 154, 178, 192

DePeel, Janice, "Attack of the Roogaroos!," 43–45

de-Westernization, 4, 14, 24n14, 264, 265–66

dialogue, 53, 125, 130, 166, 251; dialogic approach, 166; dialogic reading, 130; dialogic relationship, 168

diaspora, 23n3, 77, 87, 98, 100n8, 119–20

Dimaline, Cherie, ix, 20, 33–34, 37, 40–43, 47n1; *Empire of Wild*, 33, 37, 40–43; *The Marrow Thieves*, 47n12; "A New Hunt," 41

Dimock, Wai Chee, 24n14

discourses, 3, 8, 11, 33–34, 42, 98, 52, 56, 77, 83, 108, 110, 119, 271, 275; Anthropocene, 265; apocalyptic, 6; colonizing, 42; critical, 108; futurist, 110, 119; genre, 16; Horror, 77; Indigenous Futurism, 6; minority, 6; national, hyperrealist, and metamythic, 100n8; neocolonial, 6; official, 141; Old World, 33–34; planetary, 6; sustainable, 56; Western, 8

disease, 67, 164, 214, 260, 262

Doolittle, Edward: *being* as site of horror, 9; math/(not)math analogy, 23n1, 80

Dracula (Browning), 144

Dreaming, 10–11, 79, 91, 132, 210, 228; nightmares of the, 132; synchronic immersiveness of, 228; translation, 210. *See also* songlines

Duckert, Lowell, "Maroon," 97. *See also* aurora: myth

Durand-Tullou, Adrienne, 34

dystopian fiction, 100n8, 201–2; horror, 100n8; hyperrealisms, 88

dystopian future, 108, 245

eco-Horror, 94, 97–98, 109, 111, 265; critique, 97; Global, 97; global trends, 108; Indigenized, 94; lens for criticism, 111

ecological collapse, perceived horror, 37, 112–13, 118; ecological horror, 8–9, 15

Eisenstein, Sergei: *Ivan the Terrible*, 182n19; and Mexico, 144; *¡Que viva México!*, 143

El misterio del Kharisiri (Vallejo), 153

Elders, 5, 10, 12, 22, 23n9, 33, 34–36, 38, 44–46, 50, 59, 64, 76, 80–81, 88, 96, 111, 118, 130, 172, 207, 244; Ajean, 33, 43; Albert Marshall, 10; and the community, 244; Gilbert Pelletier, 36; Joe Welsh, 35; Marjorie Beaucage, 45; stories and illustrations, 34–36, 44, 76, 81, 111

Elk Head Woman, 269

Elliott, Alicia, 189

embodying/embodiment, 50, 58–59, 134, 147, 211, 228

English language: colonialism, 187; *story* (word), 270; tool of colonization and genocide, 202; transitive animate constructions, 79

Enlightenment: agenda, 128; post-Enlightenment ideology, 179; rationality, 129, 175; scientific world view of, 129; spiritual, 149

epidemic: historical contagion, 57, 70; illness, 148; MMIWGT2S, 189, 193, 196, 202, 203n4; smallpox, 67

epistemologies, 6, 19, 126; approach, 84; crisis, 128; Indigenous framework, 180; process, 3; space, 88; structures, 8; systems, 9, 78–79, 114; unities, 179

erasure, 54, 192; cultural, 262

Ešenvalds, Ēriks, *River of Light*, 81

Eshaka (character), 258–59

ethics of horror, 166, 168, 171, 179, 181n11

ethnography, 4, 79; accounts of "monstrosity," 87; ethnographic expeditions in Cannibal Horror, 151; ethnographic knowledge production, 149

Etuaptmumk (Two-Eyed Seeing), 10. *See also* Marshall, Elder Albert, Two-Eyed Seeing; Two-Eyed Seeing

Eurocentrism: approaches, 126; literary gaze, ix; pedagogy, 168; terms, 137

Eusebiom, Mélinton, *Qarqacha*, 153

evolution: genre, x; morphological evolution, 60; patterns, 60

excess, 163, 165–67, 175–80, 193; of seeing, 193, 195, 199. *See also* silence

exotic, 7, 84, 107, 134, 207, 223, 270; expectation of human remains, 223; objects, 207

experimentation, 13, 78, 83, 194, 257; comics' sequential art, 194; unsettling settler storytelling practice, 194

exploitation: of resources, 21, 57, 150–51, 210, 214–15, 222; rubber, 150

extinction, 56, 59–60, 149, 172

extraction/extractivist process, 21, 149, 210, 222

Fanon, Frantz, 214, 216

fantastic, definition of, 133

fat stealers and sacred fat, 152–53. See also *lik'ichiri*; *kharisiri*; ñakaq; Niño Ñakaq; *pishtaco*; *sacamanteca*

First Nations: Australia, 211–12, 214, 220–21, 227, 232; blood, 37; colonial museum, 211; Jodey Castricano, 178; oldest culture, 214; psychoanalytic understanding of, 178; Spec Fic, 131; storytelling, 177

Foley, Fiona, *Horror Has a Face*, 227

Folk Horror, 18, 94

folklore, ix, 115, 128, 213; folkloric "figure," 35; Horror, 15, 265; Indigenous nations', 243; Métis, 35; nature of, 249; representation, 111; studies, 141; traditions, 243; werewolf, 35

Fortescue, Michael, 88–89, 92–93

Foucault, Michel, 128

foundation myth, 51, 52–54, 59; and Canadianism, 54; defined, 52

Fourth Cinema: Barry Barclay, 5, 10, 81; Te Ao Māori, 81

Fowler, Henry H.: hogan, 9, 89–91, 111; "Indigenous Ways of Knowing," 89; Navajo circle, 89

frames of reference, 22, 77–79, 126, 129–30, 131, 247, 264, 266, 272; Pasifika, 112

Freud, Sigmund, 35, 58, 172

From Animus to Zombi (Gibson and VanderVeen), 82

Frontier Gothic, 180n4, 214, 221

frontiers: "The Bush Undertaker," 221; fatal, 218; ghastly dimensions, 226; horrors of in museums, 208; poisoning, 219; violence, 220

Frow, John, 24n14, 181n7

Fuller, Lisa, ix, 125, 133–34, 137; *Ghost Bird*, 21, 125–26, 133–34, 136–37

futurism, 18, 112, 109; discourses, 110; futures, 22; subgenres of futurism, 108

Garneau, David, 166–67

Gates, Raymond, 12, 107

Gay'wu Group of Women, 10–11. *See also* Songspirals

gendered violence: rougarou, 41; heteropatriarchal and colonial, 165

genocide, 18, 21, 70, 145–46, 164, 173, 180n1, 181n10, 184, 187, 196–97, 201–2, 203n2, 229, 257; cultural, 187, 194, 202, 203n2; horror of, 145; Indigenous, 18

genre(s), 3, 15, 16, 18, 83, 115, 120, 147, 151, 241, 252, 264–68, 270; aesthetics, 14; analysis, 23n1; Aztec Horror films, 144–45; cross-cultural, 23n1; definition of, 5; elements, 82; genre/(not)genre, 23n1; Horror, ix, 5, 112, 127, 265–66; hybrid, 23n1; Indigenous Horror, 9, 98; nascent, 16; planetarity, 24n14; politics, 6; studies, 24n14; western terms, 24n14

g/Global Indigenous h/Horror, 3, 7, 11, 15, 19, 23, 133, 265–66, 272, 275; cinema, 15; field of, 265–66; literature, 16, 264, 275; literary theorizing, 272; reconciliation, 272; traditions, 133; ways of knowing, 272

ghosts, 58, 148, 172, 174, 182n24, 192, 196, 200, 209–10, 214, 221, 268; citizens, 214; "ghostly" spirits, 9; ghostly stock figure, 201; land, 209; stories, ix

glaciers, 92, 95–96, 98, 114; actualized horror lens, 96; ontological awareness of, 92;

ontology and agency of, 96; transformative states, 92–96

Glissant, Édouard, 126

Global Horror, 14–15, 18–19, 22, 89, 100n9, 265

Global Horror Cinema Today (Towlson), 15

Global South: h/Horror, 15; minority voices, 6; popularized theoretical lens, 14

Goddu, Teresa A., 51, 57

Goingback, Owl, ix, 11–12, 100n8, 110, 118–19, 243; "Animal Sounds," 11–12; "Blood Hunt," 18; *Coyote Rage*, 118; *Crota*, 118; skeleton motif, 11–12; *Tribal Screams*, 118; weaving, 110, 118; weaving metaphor, 12

Gordon, Avery, 58

gore, 151, 208, 212, 270

Gore, Amy Elizabeth, 191

Gothic: autobiographical works, 169; binary, 181n9; catharsis, 169; cross-fertilization, 164; crows and ravens, 182n20; European tradition in Gothic Horror, 125, 128, 131–32, 192; Fantasy, 203n3; flawed label, 164; good and evil, 181n9; Horror, 203n3; Indigenous, 188; literature, 179; metaphysics, 24n12; Science Fiction, 203n3; spaces, 207; sublime, 169, 182n16

Gothic comics: active reader, 193–95; Indigenous, 186–203

Goya, Francisco, 208, 212–13, 225–26

grounded normativity, 165–67, 181n8

Guatemala: civil war, 145–46; filming of *La Llorona*, 147

Guerra, Ciro, 147–49, 151–52, 155, 156n11; *El abrazo de la serpiente*, 147–50, 154

Haraway, Donna, 17, 24n14, 59–60, 66, 69, 97, 100, 272; in conversation with Indigenous peoples, 272; destabilizing binaries, 66; disposable models, 59; ecofeminist studies, 272; Indigenous approaches to nature, 272; multispecies work, 66; sympoiesis, 17, 272

Harper, Stephen, 164

haunted/haunting, ix, 20, 41, 57, 85, 163, 172, 194, 196, 200, 206, 211, 214, 224, 229, 267–68, 269; cultural, 173; definition of, 58; haunted/haunting dynamic, 20, 57; history, 163; lexicon, 85–86; textual, 267

haunt/haunting/haunted back, 18, 50–51, 57, 59, 60, 61, 68–69, 70, 274–75

Hawk, Shane, 4, 8, 11, 21, 76, 85, 107–8, 241; *Anoka*, 110, 115, 119, 244; a-no-ka-tan-han approach, 110, 115, 119; "Behind Colin's Eyes," 4; bioluminescent horror elements, 110, 119; "collapsed stars," 110, 119; Hollywood Indians, 4; lens, 115; star-mapped, 110; "Transfigured," 244

Hawkes, Ernest W., "The Heavenly Regions," 87–88

Hearne, Samuel, 97

Heath, Stephen, 175–76

Heiser, Thomas, *Wolfssegner*, 42

Henderson, Jennifer, 181n5

Henzi, Sarah, 4, 194–95, 198, 203n5

hero(s): El Santo, 145; hero versus villain, 261; hero-worship, 226; "Home from the Wars," 53; Josephine, 40; male hero, 136; monstrosity and heroes, 262; rougarou as heroic figure, 35; stoic and heroic, 65; Tommy Prince, 53

Hestovatohkeoʼo (Two-Face), 244

Highway, Tomson, *Kiss of the Fur Queen*, 164

Hill, Gord, 203n5

hogan, 9, 89–91, 111

Hogan, Linda, 79, 163, 167, 171–74

Hopkinson, Nalo, 108, 263

h/Horror: aesthetics, 5, 7–8, 13, 14–15, 18, 19, 21–22, 93–94, 98–99, 110, 243, 264–65, 272; anticolonial rejection of, 108; approaches, 257; artistic landscape, 246; contemporary hybrid form, 96; counternarratives, 57; diversity of approaches to stories, 109; elements of tales, 96; epistemology of, 19; Eurocentric approaches to Horror and monstrosity,

126 [*see also* monster(s)]; as a form of resistance, 65; Indigenous, 93–94, 99; Indigenous-made, 274; literature, ix, 4, 7, 13–16, 22–23, 24n14, 100n8, 242, 275; metaphors, 77, 91, 116, 264; model, 16, 78; moments of, 110, 114; narratives, 93; and nature, 9, 15, 22, 79, 84, 90, 97, 107, 110–11, 134, 244, 264, 272; newness, 16; oversimplification, 246; patterned places, 257; power of, ix; realism, 8, 15, 16, 22, 108 9, 118, 132; realism paradigm, 22; Sci-Fi or Cli-Fi, 78; sensory genre, 14; Slasher, 118; studies, 16, 125–26, 270; terrain, 254; textual moments of, 98; theory of, 24n13; transmission of, 108; tropes, 6, 23n1, 134 [*see also* stereotypes; tropes: stock]

horror elements, 16, 78, 108, 110, 118–20; dark and horrifying, 132; horror-ethnographic, 15; paradigmatic-theoretic, 108; speculative, 108; structural, 108

Horror Fiction in the Global South (Bhattacharjee and Ghosh), 15

Horror lens: Aboriginal Australian, 10; curtainless window, 118; Global Indigenous, 10; international, 209; Native subjects and subject matter, 108; postcolonial, 126; radical subversion, 8; telescope, 108; terror, 217; unsettled audience/reality, 246

Horror scholarship, 24n14; anglophone critique, 24n11; critical trajectory of, 14

Horror Writers Association (HWA), "Indigenous Heritage in Horror," 12, 16, 118

horrors: colonial invasion, 125; colonial violence, 135; colonization, 232, 258; exploitation, 21; frontier, 208; past, 180; rubber fever, 148; state educational policies toward Indigenous people, 181n5; torture, 171; water wars, 110, 119

Howard, John, 210, 216, 220; absurd, 216; race-based pendulum, 210, 216, 217–18

human/monster/nonhuman: human and nonhuman, 128; human monster, 134; human/monster binary, 66; human/monster dialectic, 65; human-nonhuman dichotomy, 90, 95; imaginary of human/monster binary, 65; Komulainen human/monster binary, 65; monster label, 65

identity, 4, 6, 9, 19, 22, 38, 52–55, 57, 58, 65–67, 85, 107, 115, 116, 119, 144, 258–59, 267–68; curiosity, 221; loss of, 258; oddities, 115

ideology: "apocalyptic chic," 100n8; countering to haunting back, 61; post-Enlightenment, 179; settler and colonial, 55, 57, 186–87, 193, 202, 213; Turtle Island, 51

ill-fated women, myths and history, 143. *See also* La Llorona; La Malinche

imaginary: Canadian, 54; human/monster binary, 65–66; white, 91

immunity, 51, 58, 60, 66–70, 260

imperialism, 149, 208, 214, 221, 255; geographical, 221; imperial project, 129, 133; Western, 149, 155

Indian Act, 67, 269

Indian Residential Schools Settlement Agreement (2005), 180n2

Indians: colonial mindset, 38, 226; Hollywood, 4; noble, 144; vanishing, 42

Indigeneity, 4, 9, 17, 67–68, 77, 81–82, 84, 99n5, 100n8, 111, 119, 152, 176–77, 207, 265, 273; Latin American film, 155n1; registers of, 141, 147; sensationalized/exoticized cliché of, 107; visual clichés of idealized, 144

Indigenization, 187, 192, 193, 196, 200–205; *Alice's Adventures in Wonderland*, 193, 196; Chípiy (Ghost), 200; of the Gothic, 187

Indigenizing, 6, 19, 21, 112, 187, 190, 192–93, 198; act of rewriting settler texts, 193;

cultural production, 19; Gothic comics, 21, 186–203; Gothic-Horror aesthetics, 21; Horror, 6, 19, 193; iconography, 19; mainstream and academia, 19; spectral figures, 198

Indigenocide, 206–7, 211, 215–16, 218–19, 223, 225–26, 229, 233

Indigenous: bodies, 50, 60, 68, 149, 153, 199; communities, ix, 85, 141, 166, 189, 194, 196, 201, 245, 269–70; dark fiction, 21, 76, 243–45, 249; disenfranchisement, 173–74; Educational Gothic, 21, 163–82; epistemologies, 12, 21, 24n14; forced removal of children, 180n1; Futurism, 6, 18, 24n9, 92; knowledges, ix, 21, 51, 80, 82, 84, 114; Mayan conceptual framework, 90–91; metaphysics, 24n14, 108; methodologies, 20, 22, 82, 83, 91, 104, 107, 118, 126, 166, 273; onto-epistemologies, 266, 270, 271; rights, 37, 59, 62–63, 164, 166, 176, 210, 216; sovereignty, 38, 54, 170, 189, 199, 221, 245; speculative fiction, 8, 78, 92, 108, 189; storytellers/storytelling, 5, 8, 10–11, 15, 20, 47, 51, 81, 112, 118, 126, 131–33, 155, 170, 175–77, 182n22, 187, 194, 202, 243, 272

Indigenous cultures: caricatures and simulations of, 107; global and local, 13, 79, 168, 171; as tools, 191

Indigenous Gothic, 51, 57, 165, 180n4, 186–87, 190, 192, 210, 267, 274; comic, 187, 198, 202–3; devices of, 189; narratives, 51; terminology, 192; writing, 174

Indigenous h/Horror, 7, 264; approaches, 24n17; co-becoming of, 82; conceptualizations, 9; definitions, 4, 7, 82–83, 127, 241–77; epistemology, 10, 17; experiential, 83; frameworks, 119; genre, 76; global trends, 6; labels, 82; literary criticism and theory, 120; literature, 4, 13, 22, 82; metaphor, 82; metaphysical, 118; non-Indigenous and Indigenous theorizing, 5, 87; process, 82; and speculative fiction, 260; theorizing, 24n14; ways of theorizing, 9

Indigenous peoples, 40–42, 51, 54, 57, 60, 66, 83, 163, 165, 186, 201, 260, 265, 270; antithesis of savagery, 61; histories of, 53; misrepresented, 53; settler-created depictions of, 186

Indigenous way of knowing, 6, 11–13, 15, 20–21, 23, 42, 44, 77, 91, 97–98, 99n6, 110–11, 264–65, 271, 273, 275; Blackfoot bee, 83–84; experientially, 116; ghedeist, 99n6; heterogeneous global, 10; hogan, 9, 89–91, 111

Indigenous/indigenous, capitalization, 5

intergenerational trauma, 14, 171, 180, 192, 218, 229, 262, 273–74

intertextualities, 132, 266–67

Inuit, 8–9, 20, 50, 56, 87, 89, 92–93, 99n4, 114, 268; aurora myths, 87; cultural universe(s), 89; experimental lens, 114; Inuktitut, 9, 268; local-global theorizing, 92; orientational systems, 89; subdivided regions/spaces/wind/coast/sky, 93; traditional teachings, 50

Isabella (character), 135

i/teriture, 7, 84

iwi (tribe), 109, 118, 251

jarjacha (qarqacha), 153, 154

Jarjacha vs. Pishtaco (Polimeno), 151–54

Johnston, Aviaq, "The Haunted Blizzard," 12

Jones, Darryl, 35–37

Jones, Stephen Graham, ix, 4, 11, 13, 16, 21, 23n8, 51, 78, 100n8, 108–10, 118–19, 242–43, 269; *Chapter Six*, 51; highway horror, 13; Horror lenses, 108; *My Heart Is a Chainsaw*, 100n8, 118–19; *Never Whistle at Night*, 13, 108, 110; *The Only Good Indians*, 118–19, 242, 254, 269; *Zombie Bake-Off*, 51

journey, 3, 7, 20, 21, 77, 83

justice, 137n2, 146, 196–98, 207, 213, 231; failure of, 188

Justice, Daniel Heath, 8, 11, 13, 23n8

Kānaka Maoli, 12, 20–21, 256

Kanehsatà:ke Resistance (Oka Crisis), 170

Karamakate (character), 149–50

kharisiri, 152–53

Kimmerer, Robin Wall, 80; *Braiding Sweetgrass*, 86

kinship, 43, 45, 93, 151, 208

Klein, Dorothee, 130–31

Komulainen, Shaney, *Face to Face*, 64–65

Kovach, Margaret, 12, 21, 82, 84–85, 91, 107

Kristeva, Julia, 132

Kwêskosîw: She Whistles (Cuthand), 76

La Llorona, 21, 141–43, 145–48; horror legends, 142; Indigenous origins of myth, 143; Latin America, 142; Mexican version, 143; postconquest histories, 142; pre-Columbian belief, 141; versions, 143–46, 148

La Malinche, 143, 145, 147, 155n5

la mexicanidad, definition of, 144

labels: bildungsroman, 168; flawed, 164; genre, 22, 85; labeling, 5, 7, 14–15, 22, 52, 82, 85, 117, 131, 164, 264, 275; relabeled, 117

land, 8, 41, 44, 68–69, 77, 92, 107, 175, 210, 229, 262; *Empire of Wild*, 40–42; landback movement, 68, 69; ongoing conflict with Indigenous peoples, 57; reclaiming, 69; sacred, 6

landscape, x, 12–14, 59, 61, 86, 92, 94, 98, 108, 110, 112, 114, 117, 148, 152, 192, 197–99, 202, 218, 226, 246, 256, 268, 297; artistic, 246; Australian, 132, 218; binary, 14; Canadian, 268; glacial, 114; Gothic, 189, 193, 297; haunting, 201; Indigenous, 148; literary, x; narrative, 12–13, 86, 92, 98, 110, 112, 192; of Native America, 226; scars on, 256; urban, 199; zombie-infested, 59

LaPensée, Elizabeth, 47n2, 187, 202; *A Howl*, 47n2

Larocque, Brad, 64–65

Latimore, Jack, 6, 137n1

Latin America, 21, 140–59, 170

Lawn Hill massacre, 211, 220, 226

Lawson, Henry, "The Bush Undertaker," 221

Lederman, Marsha, 40. *See also* missionaries

legends, 8, 11, 13, 36, 44, 55n2, 79, 111–12, 115, 118, 142–43, 145, 147, 244–45

Lemay, Pamphile, 34. *See also* loup garou

lens, genre, 21; Anthropocene, 77, 100n8; eco-Horror criticism, 111; genre hybridization, 15; Global South, 6, 15; Indigenous Horror, 20

lens, global, 100n8, 109; global dominant, 14; Global South, 6, 15; Two-Eyed Seeing, 23n9

lens, Horror, 245; filter of, 96; of terror, 217; "theoretical" lens on Indigenous h/Horror, 13; umbrella term, 19

lens, Indigenous, 89, 192, 196, 200; Hawaiian, 117

lens, ontological: action of, 111; convex, 89; structures, 114; transformative, 82

"lensed": being, 4, 109, 119, 252; cultural appropriation and objectification, 12; filters, 112; as horror trope, 118; lens of Horror, 112

Lessard, Lucien, 63

light and darkness: dichotomy, 249; good versus evil, 248; shadow, 242; visual signifier foreshadowing, 248

Lightning, Georgina, *American Evil*, 164

lik'ichiri, 152

liminal spaces, 35, 38, 134, 254

Lindsay, Norman: death pudding, 219–20; *The Magic Pudding*, 220

linguistics, 5, 8, 12, 89, 148, 195; analysis, 92; groups, 148; modeling, 93; multifurcation of spindle whorls, 12, 89; power structure, 5; *Sixkiller*, 195

live burial, 207, 212, 217, 227

lived horror, 9, 12, 18, 20, 95, 108–10, 112, 119, 262

Locard, Edmond, Exchange Principle, 230–31

logic, 13, 19, 56, 78, 80, 94, 98, 109–10, 214

lore, 8, 11, 34, 142, 150, 152, 244

Los desastres de la Guerra (Goya), 226

Loui, Gregory C., 12, 21, 107–8, 110, 116

loup garou, 33–49. *See also* werewolf

lycanthrope, 37. *See also* werewolf
Lysol (character): *Blood Quantum*, 61, 64, 65; Kiowa Gordon, 61

Macquarie, Lachlan, expedition against "Hostile Tribes," 226–27
Malintzin/Malinalli: Doña Marina, 143; Indigenous women, 155n4; as strategist and linguist, 143. *See also* La Llorona; La Malinche
mana, 12, 99, 109, 116–17, 120, 257–59; "evil," 259; metaphysics model, 108, 116
Māori, 5, 8, 10, 12, 20, 83, 111, 117, 250–51, 253; Creation framework, 10; Fourth Cinema, 5; *iwi*, 109, 118, 251; kaupapa, 83; Māoritanga, 108, 250, 251–52; *matakite*, 109, 253; mythology, 10; Te Po, 111; Te Whanga Lagoon, 117; ways of knowing, 5; Whakapapa, 10, 83, 251
María Candelaria (Fernández), 144
Marshall, Elder Albert, Two-Eyed Seeing, 10, 23n9
Marshall, Joseph M., III, 13
Marx, Karl, 172, 210–11, 221–22
massacre, 145–46, 150, 167, 207–8, 211–15, 220, 225–30, 262; culture, 213; by poisoning, 220
matakite, 109, 253. *See also* Māori
Maya: cosmology, 91; epistemology, 91; languages, 140; victims, 146
McBrien, Justin, 100n8
McCloud, Scott, *Understanding Comics*, 194
Medea, 141, 145
media, ix, 6, 8, 16, 18, 23, 47, 54, 62–63, 65, 81, 92, 94, 96, 100, 109, 127, 140, 144, 170–71, 186, 203, 228, 259; adaptations, 81; auditory and visual storying, 81; Fourth VR, 8; global mass, 18, 96, 100; Indigenous activism, 170; narratives, 23, 169; Oka and Restigouche, 63; pan-Indianist narratives, 65; popular, 8, 16, 92, 109; settler, 203; of transmission, 127; zombie, 259
mestizaje: myths of, 141; politics and cliché, 144

mestizo, 141, 147, 152
metaphor(s): aurora, 19, 20, 77, 79, 82, 86, 88, 109–11, 119; Ceiba/Tree of Life, 91; complex relational, 112; contemporary Indigenous, 88; Creation, 116; disruption of, 99; heterogeneous and hybrid, 108; hybrid, 77, 110, 119; Indigenous, 77, 111; Indigenous alternative to, 79; metaphysical mesh, 108; misarticulated, 88; pendant, 134; re(visioned), 108; rougarou, 41; savagery, 37; transformative, 77, 82
metaphysics, 8, 11–12, 22, 23n1, 24n12, 24n14, 77, 99n6, 108–9, 113, 116, 118, 120n1, 258–59; model, 99n6, 109, 116, 259
Métis: communities, 33, 38; culture, 45; "Métis Rougarou," 266 [*see also* rougarou]; oral tradition, 35; people, 35, 37–39, 41, 47; rights, 37; stories, 20, 33–48; werewolf-like creature, 33; ways of knowing, 34, 38, 43; worldview, 20, 41
mexica/mexika, 144. *See also azteca* (Aztec)
Mexico, 140–44, 155n5
Michif language, 38, 47n4
Mignolo, Walter, 6, 24n9, 24n14
Mi'kmaq, 21, 59, 62–63
Milky Way, 79, 91, 112; Te Ila-Roa, 111–12
Mining the Museum (Wilson), 224
Mirbeau, Octave, *The Torture Garden*, 225–27, 230
mirror: highway horror, 4, 13; iceberg, 9; Two-Eyed Seeing, 20; ways of theorizing, 89, 93, 113, 119–20
Missing and Murdered Indigenous Women, Girls, and Trans and Two-Spirit (MMIWGT2S), 19, 21, 34, 187–88, 192–93, 195–96, 198–200, 202, 203nn4–5
missionaries, 40, 150, 175; missionary expeditions, 207
Mittman, Asa, 127–28
Molina, Cristóbal de, *Account of the Fables and Rites of the Incas*, 152. *See also* evangelism
Monkey Beach (Robinson), 163, 165, 170, 177–78, 181n15, 198, 266; editing process, 170; Haisla copyright, 170

Monster Anthropology, 19, 128–29, 132

monster studies, 125–26, 128, 132

Monster Theory Reader, The (Weinstock), 127

monster(s), 35, 57, 60, 65–66, 94, 116, 126–27, 134, 137, 141, 182n23, 211, 216, 218, 227, 252, 255, 257–58, 268, 274; actual, 133; anthropological discourse, 94; category/categorization of, 127, 129; contemporary, 51; empirical experiences, 128; existence, 127; as fictitious, 127; images of and narratives involving, 127; material, 57; nonexistence, 127; reality of, 132; research, 127; subjects, 127; that haunt, 256. *See also individual monsters*

monstrosity, 10, 19, 38, 65, 87, 126, 128–29, 156n12, 211, 222–23, 231, 262

monstrous femininity, 145

Moore, Christopher, 71n3

Moretti, Franco, 24n14

Morris, Tiffany, *Green Fuse Burning*, 12

Mudrooroo (Colin Johnson), 177, 182n22

museums, 42, 134, 140, 144, 207–8, 211, 217, 220, 222; cataloging, 207; collections, 207, 213, 220; English imperial, 206; ethnographic collections, 223; Gothic spaces, 207; Indigenocide, 207; massacre, 207; system, 21, 206

myth(s), 3, 5, 8, 11, 13, 15, 21–22, 51–57, 59–60, 76–77, 80, 82, 84, 86–88, 93, 96–99, 107–8, 110–13, 115, 118–20, 127, 132, 141, 143, 145, 220; of abundance, 55, 59, 60; of exceptionalism, 55, 59

mythologies, ix, 8, 10, 83, 97, 132, 249, 251

Nahuatl, 140, 142, 144

ñakaq, 152

Nakaq (Huertas), 153

narrative(s): of consumption, 56; fabric, 111; landscapes, 98, 112, 192, 198; space, x; systems, 110; vehicles, 70

narratology, 11, 121, 126, 130–31, 137, 271–72; Aboriginal and Torres Strait Islander, 131; Blak, 11, 21, 126, 130–31, 137; postcolonial, 126; theories of, 126

Native American Gothic, 214, 226, 267. *See also* Indigenous Gothic

Na Viro (G. Cole), 12, 78–79, 81, 109–10, 112–13, 261; braiding and weaving, 12; hologram, 81, 110, 112, 113; Pasifika metaphor, 12, 78; ways of knowing, 12; whirlpool, 12, 78

Navajo, 8, 9, 89, 90, 111; geometry, 9; tradition, 9, 111; way of theorizing Horror, 9. *See also* hogan

Nêhiýaw ceremonial teepee, 91. *See also* Cree

Netukulimk: land-based approaches, 272; Mi'kmaw concept, 17, 272. *See also* Haraway, Donna

Never Whistle at Night (Hawk and Van Alst Jr.), 13, 18, 23n8, 76, 108, 241, 243, 245; ancestors, 108; globe, 245; northern lights, 108; Turtle Island, 108; universal oral myth, 108

Night of the Living Dead (Romero), 154

Nightmare on Elm Street, A (Craven), 65

nightmare(s), 11, 65, 115, 132–33, 181n13, 208, 210, 217, 228

Niño Ñakaq, 152

northern lights, 76–78, 81, 86–88, 92, 107–8, 115; actualization, 80; aurora borealis, 76; bloody colonial history, 86; Dene Elder Jonas Antoine, 76; hypnotic symbol, 115; mapped, 92; media, 76; painted sky, 77; sonic analog, 81; title, 108; whistle, 88

Obama, Barack, 164

Obomsawin, Alanis, *Incident at Restigouche*, 62–63

Ojibwe: constellations, 80, 113; dreamcatcher legend, 115; elders, 80–81

Ojibwe Sky Star Map (Lee, Wilson, Tibbets, and Gawboy), 80–81, 93, 113

Oka Crisis, 51, 63–65, 70–71, 170; *Blood Quantum*, 63; *Face to Face* (photograph), 64; Kanehsatà:ke Resistance, 170; media portrayal, 170

Older than America (Lightning), 181n6. *See also* Lightning, Georgina, *American Evil*

oral memory: ancestor, 84; cultural knowledge systems, 78; extensions of, 78; song lines, 91

oral myth, 76, 87, 107, 110, 119; northern lights, 76–78, 80–81, 86–88, 92, 107–8, 115

oral reality, 85, 111

oral stories, 9, 44, 213; storytelling, 5, 10, 112, 118; tales, 79, 87–88, 120, 245

oral tradition, ix, 24n17, 78, 80, 87, 210, 265; Indigenous knowledge transmission, 273

orality, 7–9, 11, 16, 23, 84, 221

Ortega Matute, Palito, 154; *El demonio de los Andes*, 154; *Incesto en los Andes*, 154; *Jarjacha 3*, 154; *La maldición de los Jarjachas 2*, 149, 154

Other: demonized, contained, and exoticized, 7, 84; mechanisms of, 226–27; othering, 57, 66, 84, 145, 175, 179, 226–27, 267; otherness, 4, 66; ritual barbarity, 145; violent spectacle, 145

Otherwise Worlds (King, Navarro, and Smith), 17

Pasifika Futurisms, 18, 112; anticolonial, 109; holographic whirlpool, 81, 113; three-dimensional, 81, 113; virtual reality simulation, 81; whirlpool, 78

Pasifika/Pākehā, 5; frame of reference, 112; knowledges, 82; metaphor, 12; Pasifikafuturist whirlpool, 78; worldview, 108, 116, 259

Path of Ra novels: drawing on Māoritanga, 250; *matakite*, 253; mental health and crime, 253; monsters, 247. *See also* Rabarts, Dan

patriarchy, 38, 42, 45, 68, 165, 168, 182n16, 262

pedagogy: Eurocentric, 168; land as, 166; Nishnaabeg, 165; pedagogical exchange, 170, 172

Peele, Jordan, 100n8; *Get Out*, 265

Peón, Ramón, *La Llorona*, 142–43

Peru, 141, 146; *cine regional*, 151; civil conflict, 153; *Death in the Andes*, 153

Pettersson, Anders, 24n14

Pinder, Kait, 166

pishtaco, 152–53

Pishtaco (Gamboa), 153

Plains of Promise (Wright): European colonialism, 175; excess and silence, 165; Gothic metaphor, 175; Indigenous Educational Gothic, 163; poinciana, 175; theft of resources, 175

Pocowatchit, Rodrick, *The Dead Can't Dance*, 51

Poe, Edgar Allan, 209, 230; "The Man That Was Used Up," 230; "The Pit and the Pendulum," 210, 213, 215, 217; "The Raven," 182n20

postcolonialism: approaches, 130; counterdiscourse, 132; discourse, 179; ethical disruption, 179; intertextuality, 126, 130, 132; lens, 126, 130; matrix of postcolonial studies, 126; norm, 130; politics, 4; power structures, ix; recentering, 130; reworkings, 132; thinking, 130

posthumanism, 19, 24n12

poverty, 53, 153, 169, 173–74

Powys, Kyle, 100n8

Préfontaine, Darren, 35, 44, 47

Prince, Tommy, 53

Prismatic Ecology (Cohen), 97

Quechua, 140, 152; *pishtaku*, 152

Queensland, 135, 209, 211, 215, 219, 224–25

Quinkins, 99n4

Rabarts, Dan, ix, 12, 21, 78, 107–8, 110, 117, 119; aurora australis, 108, 119; *Blood of the Sun*, 249; *Children of Bane*, 248; dark fantasy settings, 78; darkness, 108; "Floodgate," 252; horror realism, 108; *Hounds of the Underworld*, 247; lenses of urbanization and colonialism, 108; light, 108; Māoritanga, 108; mathematics and Māori horror metaphysics, 23n1;

"Mother's Milk," 117; orientational systems, 117; planetary apocalypse, 78, 108; "Riptide," 247; "The Silence at the Edge of the Sea," 117; supernaturalism, 108
Rabbit (character), 197
Racette, Sherry Farrell, 34–38, 44, 47
racism, 152, 186, 192, 217, 245, 250, 262
Radcliffe, Ann, 166
reality, 116, 126, 129, 177; circular and multidimensional, 91; forms of, 113; postcontact, 11; settler and Indigenous realities, 113; virtual, 8, 81
reappropriation, 5, 23n5
reciprocity, 44, 98, 165
Reder, Deanna, 4, 16
rejection, 77, 84, 89, 100n8, 109
relational order, 5, 10, 13, 23n1, 79, 95; transmaterial, 79
religion, 36, 249, 252; beliefs, 244; monotheistic, 36; polytheistic, 36; practices, 34; sanctuary, 93; structure, 208; supervision, 140
reservations/reserves, 5, 58, 64, 66–67, 69, 71, 97, 215
Residential School Gothic, 164, 174; films, 181n5
residential schools, 42, 163, 164, 174, 169
resistance, 37, 165, 187, 189; destroying zombies as form of, 68; Indigenous peoples, 203n5
respect, 5, 22, 44–45, 83, 85, 96, 131, 136, 177, 195, 232, 244, 251, 265–66
rhetoric: anti-Indigenous, 41; barbaric practices, 150; debates, 4; decolonial, 92; subverting, 42
rhizome theory, 99n6
Ricoeur, Paul, 83, 172, 176
Riel, Louis, 37
Ríos Montt, José Efraín, 146–47, 155n7
Rivera, José Eustasio, *La vorágine*, 148, 151
Roanhorse, Rebecca: Indigenous literature, 167; lived remembrance of massacres, 167; "Postcards from the Apocalypse," 186, 201–2

Robinson, Eden, 163, 167–69, 170–71, 177–78, 181nn14–15, 182n20, 182n23, 191, 198, 265
Robitaille, Guillaume (character), 43
rougarou, 20, 33–37, 41, 43, 46–47; agency, 36, 45; bodily sovereignty, 38; Catholicism, 38; cautionary tale, 39; change (transformation), 36; communal, 45; cure, 44–45; female rougarou, 36; gendered lens, 38; how to defeat, 45; metaphor, 41; Métis culture, 45; old Métis story, 46; patriarchy, 38; regional differences, 35–36; shapeshifting space, 39; syncretic creature, 36
rubber: barons, 148–49; extraction, 148; fever, 148; *La vorágine*, 148, 151; massacres, 150; ravaged jungle, 148
Ruffo, Armand Garnet, "Inside Looking Out," 82
rupture(s), 9, 78, 85, 99n5, 110, 113; of knowledge, 98; moments of, 11

sacamanteca, 152
Sacred Hoop, The (Allen), 82
salmon: fishing, 62–63; harvesting, 94; Salmon Wars, 62; ways of knowing, 95
Sangre y tradición (Inga), 153
Saunders, Mykaela, *This All Come Back Now*, 131–32
savage: antithesis of, 61; colonial mindset, 38; metaphor, 37; peoples, 34, 150; stereotype, 61
Savoy, Eric, 66
scarcity: as horror, 94; of resources, 55, 59
Schoch/Davidson, Angela Elisa, 191–92
science fiction, 6, 50–51, 112–13, 203n3, 246
scopophilia, 167
Scott, Kim: *Benang*, 131; *That Deadman Dance*, 131
settler(s): 3–5, 10, 16, 20, 22, 33, 35–37, 41, 51, 55–56, 58–59, 60–62, 66–69, 113, 116, 165–67, 170, 174–76, 180–81, 190–94, 197–99, 201–4, 207, 209, 213–23, 225–31, 262, 270; binarism, 61, 166; bodies of, 67; consumption, 59;

creator, 190–91; extinction, 59; Gothic, 175; majority, 207; narratives, 10, 188, 192; practice, 51; productions, 181n5; resource positioning, 59; scholars, 4, 33, 35–36, 188; settler-colonial government, 164, 174; settler-colonial nations, 164; settler-colonial project, 165; survivors, 58, 66; traditions, 22; zombies, 60, 66, 69

Seven Sacred Teachings, 200, 203n7

shaman, *nativo*, 152. See also *chullachaki*

shock, 14, 96, 166, 179, 242

Shoemaker, Adam, *Black Words White Page*, 83

silence, 163, 165–72, 174, 179–80

Silko, Leslie Marmon, 209; *Almanac of the Dead*, 211

Simpson, Leanne Betasamosake: "grounded normativity," 165, 181n8; Indigenous continuance, 180; "Nishnaabeg intelligence," 181n8; resurgence as a mechanism, 180

Sixkiller (Francis IV and Alvitre): aesthetic of excess, 195; Alice, 196–97; belief system, 198; comics, 187–88; complex imagery, 194; Creator, 198; excess of seeing, 195; Gothic, 202; Indigenous retelling of *Alice's Adventures in Wonderland*, 188; March Hare, 196; MMIWGT2S crisis, 195–99; monologue, 198; Rabbit, 196–97

Skinner, Laura, 203n1

Slash/Back (Innuksuk): arctic community, 50; film, 15, 50; Indigenous myth, 15

slasher films, 119, 167, 208, 246; theories, 119

Smith, Linda Tuhiwai: *Decolonizing Methodologies*, 4–5, 12, 129–30; epistemic core of colonialism, 129

Solar Storms (Hogan), 79, 163, 165, 170–71; Angel, 163, 171; coming-of-age story, 168; excess and silence, 165; Hannah, 171–72, 174; media, 170

songlines, 91, 131, 228–29. See also Dreaming

Songlines (Neale and Kelly), 131

Songspirals, 10–11

Sontag, Susan, *Regarding the Pain of Others*, 166, 181n12

Soop, Alex, ix; *Midnight Storm Moonless Sky*, 17; *Whistle at Night and They Will Come*, 17, 76

sovereignty, 38, 54, 170, 189, 199, 245; bodily sovereignty of woman, 38; Indigenous, 54

Spanish, 140, 142–44, 146, 149, 152, 155n5

speaking back, 186. *See also* haunting back; writing back

species, 17, 59, 60, 66, 68–71, 93, 272; hierarchies in *Blood Quantum*, 59; interconnected web of relationships, 66; multispecies, 17, 66, 68, 71, 93, 272. *See also* sympoiesis

speculative fiction: Indigenous, 8, 112, 245; Mykaela Saunders, 131; trope, 111

speculative genres: apocalyptic, 112; contemporary, 77; dystopian-utopian fiction, 112; fantasy, 112; futurism, 6; generative, 77; horror, 112; hybrid, 77, 107; postapocalyptic, 112

spirals, 11, 78, 86, 89, 91, 107, 110, 115–16, 118–19. *See also* aurora; Songspirals

spirit(s), 84, 97, 198; of the deceased, 79, 97; malevolent water, 146–47; spirit world, 80, 111, 113; spiritual analog, 149

Steiner, George, *After Babel*: incommensurate with Indigenous knowledge, 82; rebuke of, 85

stereotypes, 4, 11, 22, 53, 77–78, 107, 171, 176, 186; mainstream stereotype, 77; nature, 107; "savage," 61; terra nullius, 61; wild Indian, 13

stock elements: Gothic, 135; tropes, 82, 108, 135, 255

stone circles, 90–91. *See also* circle(s)

stories, 11, 16, 34–35, 38, 44, 85, 95, 108, 110, 126, 130, 194–95, 243, 256; as complex artistic performances, 194–95; creating new, 243

Stories of Our People / Lii zistwayr di la nassyon di Michif (Welsh), 34, 35

story world, 193

storytellers, 12, 46, 51, 118, 194

storytelling, 8, 20, 132, 155, 170, 177, 189, 202, 249; cinema, 155; linear time frame of,

137; modes of, 243; practices, 133, 187; resistance, 189; speculative fiction, 11; survival, 189

strangeness, 179

sublime, 76, 97, 169, 181n11, 182n16, 215, 218, 229

Sugars, Cynthia, 192; "Canadian Gothic," 268

supernatural, 82, 108, 133–34; domain, 84; elements in traditional Métis stories, 35; phenomena, 148

Symbiocene, 17, 99n6

symbiogenesis, 69

sympoiesis, 17, 272

syncretism, 7, 33, 36, 38, 47n4, 141; belief, 141; culture, 38; French and Cree werewolf, 33; influence, 141; popular, 7; rougarou, 36

Taaqtumi (Johnston): "in the dark," 12; Indigenous horror, 17–18; introductions, 16

taboo, 5, 34, 85, 88, 96, 134, 136–37, 265, 267

TallBear, Kim, 93

tangata whenua (people of the land), 253

taxonomy, 78, 83, 129; horror, 95; of meaning, 83; order, 128; schema, 129; systems, 129

Te Po (the unknown), 111. *See also* Māori

terror, 12, 14, 96, 109, 118, 141–42, 151, 154, 166, 168–69, 171, 207, 211–12, 214–15, 217–18, 220, 225–27, 230, 242, 261

themes: apocalyptic, 112; Aztec Horror, 144; Christianity, 34; dark/horrific, 249; eco-racial, 17; Gothic, 192; horror, 23n1

Thompson, Kristin, 175–76

"Those Beneath the Bog" (Condor/Maka Tai Meh), 51

Tolkien, J. R. R., *Lord of the Rings* trilogy, 182n20

tool(s), ix, 3, 11, 84–85, 96, 98, 107, 142, 163, 187, 191, 193–94, 197, 202, 258, 265, 271–72, 275; church, 197; of colonization/colonizer, 187, 197, 203; graveyard, 197; history as, 197; Horror, 107; mental institution, 197; misuse by settler creator, 191; reader's perspective, 193; settler

states, 163; storytelling process, 193; and techniques, 142

Topash-Caldwell, Blaire, 13, 107, 112, 189

Trail of Tears, 164, 209

transient phenomena, 76–77, 79, 86, 89, 91, 93, 96, 98–99, 107–8, 110, 112, 115, 117, 119–20

transmotion, 24n13

trauma, intergenerational: discourse, 14; and Indigenous Horror, 274; transmission of, 171. *See also* intergenerational trauma

trends: contemporary, 17; decolonial Gothic Horror, 18; global, 6; global eco-Horror, 98, 109; Indigenizing eco-Horror, 94; parallel, 16; planetary, 6; popular, 17, 264; theorizing Indigenous, 119. *See also* vogues

tribes: conventions, 243–44; language acquisition, 244; legends and lore, 244; medicinal knowledge, 244; religious beliefs, 244; stories, 245

Trickster, 16, 37, 175–77, 197; Tricksterology, 16

tropes: apocalyptic, 112; Aztec, 144; dystopian, 186; essentialist Indigenous, 78; genres, 51; Gothic, 172, 221; h/Horror, 6, 23n1, 82, 91, 109, 132, 134; hurtful, 245; of nature, 16; shapeshifting, 98, 119; silence and excess, 63, 167; speculative, 111; stock, 108, 255

Troubling Tricksters (Reder and Morra), 16

Trudeau, Pierre, 54

T'sonoqua (monster), 178

Tuck, Eve, 169–70, 198–99; damage-centered research, 169; desire-centered research, 198–99; haunting glossaries, 4, 77, 86; omitted, 170; pathologizing effect, 169

Tuña and Kiolya, 87. *See also* aurora: oral myths

Turtle Island, 17, 52, 55–56, 65, 68–69, 108, 244

21st Century Orc, 116, 256. *See also* Loui, Gregory C.

Two-Eyed Seeing, 10, 14, 20, 23n9, 89, 98; approaches, 20, 98; generalized concept framework, 89; globalizing, 23n9; and

glocal, 14; Haudenosaunee, 89; Māori traditions, 89; Mi'kmaq, 89; Yolngu, 89
two-spirit: and Indigiqueer, 47n9; disrespect of, 47; MMIWGT2S crisis, 21, 34, 47, 187, 199, 201–2

"UenUku and the Mist Maid" (Best), 111
uma, 153
Unaipon, David, *Legendary Tales of the Australian Aborigines*, 79–80
uncanny: behavior of water, 146; as critique, x; definition, 35; existential uncertainty, 35; fear, 35; Freud, 35; and the marvelous, 134; *unheimlich* (unholy), 35
unconscious, theory of, 172. *See also* Freud, Sigmund
universe(s), 9, 23n4, 24n14, 79–80, 85, 89–91, 101, 110–12, 116, 192, 257–59, 271; beyond the universe, 91; block, 90; constituent relational, 80; nonlinear connections, 79; rules, 110–11; universe/otter/earth, 111; us/them, 23n4; western, 24, 111
unsettling, 4–5, 12–13, 20, 119, 167, 175, 187–89, 249; Gothic, 187; of theoretical lenses, 20; ontological certainties, 167, 171
Urueta, Chano, *El signo de la muerte*, 144

Van Camp, Richard, "On the Wings of This Prayer," 51, 269
vanquished race (*la raza vencida*), 143
victimry, 166, 174, 178, 181n10; paradigms, 166, 178; Settler Gothic, 181n10; survivance, 181n10
virtual reality, 8, 30, 81, 99, 113, 120
visual story/storytelling, 9, 15, 81, 186–205
visualizations, 5, 8–9, 14, 19, 22, 78, 81, 93, 114, 119, 149; experimental, 9; framework, 81; of Indigenous peoples, 148
visuals: aesthetics, 120; and auditory elements, 242; clichés of idealized Indigeneity, 144; codex, 99, 120; displays, 80
Vizenor, Gerald, 82, 85, 176–77, 180, 181n4; "aesthetics of survivance," 85; colonial democracies, 176–77; continuance of storytelling, 85; cultural genocide,

203n2; fiction, 85; Frontier Gothic, 180n4; native tricksters, 176–77; philological theories and practices, 85; ravens and crows, 176–77; rebuke, 85; social transformation, 176–77; survivance, 203n2; synthesis and renewal spaces, 203n2; *Treaty Shirts*, 100n8
vogues, 18–19, 22–23, 99, 100n8, 120; Afro-Futurisms, 18; Global Black Horror, 19; and movements, 22; in global Horror, 100n8; popular, 23. *See also* Comic Horror; Folk Horror; Indigenous Futurism; Monster Anthropology; Pasifika Futurisms
vortex, 79, 110, 113. *See also* Rivera, José Eustasio, *La vorágine*

Wald, Priscilla: contagion narratives, 98; microbes, 68
Walkiewicz, Kathryn, 77, 85–86
Warrior, Carol, 35
water-based knowledge, 92–93, 117; *héen*, 92–93
Watson, Judy, 206–31; *burning ghosts*, 209; *a complicated fall*, 209; *experimental beds*, 209; *40 pairs of blackfellows' ears, lawn hill station*, 225, 230; *41 stop-pages—amadou diallo*, 209; *the guardians*, 210; *holes in the land 1–5*, 206, 209, 222, 227–29; *the names of men*, 227; *the names of places*, 221, 228–29; *palm cluster*, 209
Watson, Nicole, *The Boundary*, 136
Watson, Sam, *The Kadaitcha Sung*, 136, 230
ways of knowing, 6, 8–12, 14–15, 18–19, 20–21, 23, 34, 38, 42–43, 44, 77, 80, 83, 84, 88–89, 91–92, 96–97, 99, 100n8, 109, 110, 111, 112, 118–20, 129, 168, 264–65, 270–73, 275; Aboriginal Literature, 83; actualized, 10, 112; apocalypse, 111; directional, 88; eye/lens, 10; horror, 18; Indigenous Horror in practice, 22; motility, 88; Ngāti Porou, 117, 246–53; shifting orientations, 88; theoretical lens, 99; transforms, 77; as ways of theorizing, 19; whirlpool, 112

ways of theorizing, 3, 8–9, 11, 18, 23, 77–78, 81, 86, 89, 94, 96, 100n8, 108, 113–14, 118, 120; actualization, visualization, and conceptualization, 8; embodied, 89; Indigenous, 8–9, 100n8; Indigenous horror aesthetics, 81; Indigenous horror experience, 8; narrative structures/patterns, 81; Navajo Horror, 9; northern lights, 81; structures and patterning, 89; symbolic-conceptual-metaphoric relational, 89

weaving, 12, 24n14, 86, 89, 110, 113, 118; weaving metaphor-methodology, 118

weeping woman, 142–43. *See also* La Llorona

Weinstock, Jeffrey Andrew, *The Monster Theory Reader*, 127–29

Wente, Jesse, 15, 203n1

werewolf, 33–37, 43, 47n2, 128, 211

western classifications: canon, 24n17, 186; categorization system, 5; codifications, 91; dipole, 118; discourse, 8; forms, 14; linguistics, 5; literary canon, 5; nomenclature, 96, 151; semiotic systems, 5; structures, 5

western genre: critique and canon, 98, 119; modern, 86; Spec Fic, 131; systems, 6; terms, 24n14

western theory, 5, 14, 130. *See also* Kristeva, Julia

Whakapapa, 10, 83, 251

whirlpool: actualized ways of theorizing, 112; holographic, 114; Pasifika-specific, 12, 112–13; three-four-n-dimensional, 113; ways of knowing, 12

whistle/whistling, 76, 81, 87–88, 108

White Australia: death-worlding, 223; Indigenocide, 206, 225; Judy Watson, 221; massacre culture, 230; Norman Lindsay, 220; political and cultural unconscious, 206; terror, 211

white space: experimental, 84, 99n2; hybrid orality, 7; sensory impact, 178; theories of alterity, 13; wave icon, 178

White Zombie (Halperin), 50

whiteness, 54, 68

whitewashing: barbarous realities, 230; genre, 275; Indigenous and rural populations, 144; mainstream Mexican films, 144; trauma, 212

Why Indigenous Literatures Matter (Justice), 11

wicked glimpse, 17, 24n15, 76, 108

wihtikow, 33. *See also* cannibals/cannibalism

Will I See? (Robertson, Iskwē, Leslie, and Chomichuk): active reader, 195; alternative third-person perspective, 199; comics, 187–88; Cree, 188; educative narrative, 199; Indigenous audiences, 199; Indigenous culture, 199; Indigenous issues and resistance, 202; May, 188–89, 199–201, 203n6; MMIWGT2S, 199; Rifkind and Fontaine, 199

Wilson, Williams, sky star map, 80–81, 93, 94, 113. See also *Ojibwe Sky Star Map* (Lee, Wilson, Tibbets, and Gawboy)

windigo: Algonquian-speaking cultures, 172; cannibalistic figure, 172; w*nd*go, 244; wétiko/windigo cannibalism, 214; windigo/wendigo/wheetago, 71n2. *See also* cannibals/cannibalism

Wisker, Gina, 6, 190–92, 203, 209, 213

writing back, 17, 57, 132, 175, 268. *See also* haunting back

X-ray style, 80–81, 99, 113, 120; allegory, 113; seeing the unseen, 80; spirit world, 80; un/seen being, 81. See also *Ojibwe Sky Star Map* (Lee, Wilson, Tibbets, and Gawboy); Wilson, Williams, sky star map

yarning circle, 20

zombie, 11, 20, 50, 51, 56–71, 97, 154, 217, 259–60, 269; fish, 20, 59, 60, 62–63; horde, 69; infection, 51; infestation, 60, 69; -like figures, 71n2; media, 259; narrative, 50–71; pathogen, 50, 60,

66; problematic as Indigenous, 71n2; settler, 60, 66, 69; soldier, 64; subgenre, 69; viral plague, 58; viruses, 58; zombieverse, 20, 68

zombie apocalypse, 60, 69; *Blood Quantum*, 60

zombie films: *Blood Quantum*, 50; *Night of the Living Dead*, 154; *White Zombie*, 50

zoonotic virus, 69